razor

wire

women

SUNY SERIES IN WOMEN, CRIME, AND CRIMINOLOGY

Meda Chesney-Lind and Russ Immarigeon, editors

razor wire women

prisoners, activists, scholars, and artists

edited by
JODIE MICHELLE LAWSTON
AND ASHLEY E. LUCAS

Published by
STATE UNIVERSITY OF NEW YORK PRESS
ALBANY

For information, contact
State University of New York Press
www.sunypress.edu

Production and book design, Laurie Searl
Marketing, Michael Campochiaro

Library of Congress Cataloging-in-Publication Data

Razor wire women : prisoners, activists, scholars, and artists / edited by Jodie Michelle Lawston and Ashley E. Lucas.
　　p. cm. — (Suny series in women, crime, and criminology)
　Includes bibliographical references and index.
　ISBN 978-1-4384-3531-2 (hbk. : alk. paper)
　ISBN 978-1-4384-3532-9 (pbk. : alk. paper)
1. Women prisoners. 2. Female offenders. 3. Women—Identity.
4. Prisoners as authors. 5. Prisoners as artists. 6. Arts in prison.
I. Lawston, Jodie Michelle, 1977–   II. Lucas, Ashley E., 1979–
　HV8738.R39 2011
　365'.6082—dc22　　　　　　　　　　　　　　　2010031925

10 9 8 7 6 5 4 3 2 1

For Patricia K. Thorn,
who did not live to see her art honored here.

For the woman we could not find,
may your life on the outside be joyous.

For all razor wire women,
as we strive to find community in one another.

Contents

LIST OF ILLUSTRATIONS, CHARTS, TABLES   xi

3x Denied
ARTIST'S STATEMENT: Dawna (Lessie) Brown   xiv–xv

FOREWORD   xvii
    Kathy Boudin

Ruth Snyder
ARTIST'S STATEMENT: Malaquias Montoya   xx–xxi

ACKNOWLEDGMENTS   xxiii

CHAPTER 1.   From Representations to Resistance:
    How the Razor Wire Binds Us   1
    Jodie Michelle Lawston

Section I.   Girls, Women, and Families

Missing
ARTIST'S STATEMENT: Ricky A. Taylor   20–21

HISTORICAL CONTEXTUALIZATION   23
    Jodie Michelle Lawston

CHAPTER 2.   The Voice of Silence   27
    Je'Anna Redwood

CHAPTER 3.   Doing Time in Detention Home: Gendered
    Punishment Regimes in Youth Jails   31
    Brian Bilsky and Meda Chesney-Lind

CHAPTER 4.   Healer: A Monologue from the
Play *Doin' Time: Through the Visiting Glass*   49
Ashley E. Lucas

CHAPTER 5.   Incarcerated Women: Motherhood on the Margins   51
Barbara Bloom and Marilyn Brown

CHAPTER 6.   Doing Time with Mom: A Nonfiction Essay   67
Shirley Haviland-Nakagawa

CHAPTER 7.   ASFA and the Impact on Imprisoned Migrant
Women and Their Children   75
Martha Escobar

CHAPTER 8.   Carceral State, Cultural Stake: Women behind
American Bars and Beyond   93
Trangdai Glassey-Tranguyen

Section II.   Sexuality, Health, and Abuse

Bound
ARTIST'S STATEMENT: Joanie Estes-Rodgers   102–103

HISTORICAL CONTEXTUALIZATION   105
Jodie Michelle Lawston

CHAPTER 9.   The Prison Mentality   109
Jane Dorotik

CHAPTER 10.   "If I Wasn't Suicidal, That'll Drive You to It":
Women, Jail, and Mental Health   115
Angela Moe

CHAPTER 11.   Patiently Waiting   133
Jen Myers

Caged Innocence
ARTIST'S STATEMENT: Patricia K. Thorn   144–145

CHAPTER 12.   Transgender Women, Sexual Violence, and the
Rule of Law: An Argument in Favor of Restorative
and Transformative Justice   147
Linda Heidenreich

CHAPTER 13.   Prison Rape   165
    Johanna Hudnall

CHAPTER 14.   From Women Prisoners to People in
Women's Prisons: Challenging the Gender Binary in
Antiprison Work   169
    Julia Sudbury

CHAPTER 15.   Giving the Voiceless a Voice   185
    Renita Phifer

Section III.   Education, Writing, and the Arts

Caught up on the Whirlwind
ARTIST'S STATEMENT: Valencia C.   190–191

HISTORICAL CONTEXTUALIZATION   193
    Ashley E. Lucas

Connie Convicta and Vato Emiliano Comics
ARTIST'S STATEMENT: Ana Lucia Gelabert   198–201

CHAPTER 16.   Inside-Out: The Reaches and Limits of
    a Prison Program   203
    Simone Weil Davis

CHAPTER 17.   Desiree   225
    Leslie Levitas

CHAPTER 18.   Restorytive Justice: Theater as a Redressive
    Mechanism for Incarcerated Women   229
    Sara Warner

CHAPTER 19.   On Visual Politics and Poetics:
    Incarcerated Girls and Women Artists   247
    Jillian Hernandez

CHAPTER 20.   Hope in a Box: Sanity Sold Separately   269
    Sisters of Unique Lyrics (SOUL)

CHAPTER 21.   The Life Inside: Incarcerated Women Represent
    Themselves through Journalism   285
    Eleanor Novek

EPILOGUE.   Identifying Marks: What the Razor Wire Hides   301
    Ashley E. Lucas

LIST OF CONTRIBUTORS   305

INDEX   317

Illustrations, Charts, Tables

ILLUSTRATIONS

FIGURE 1   *3x Denied*   G-1, xv
Colored pencil drawing with painting by
Dawna (Lessie) Brown

FIGURE 2   *Ruth Snyder*   G-2, xxi
Painting by Malaquias Montoya

FIGURE 3   *Missing*   G-3, 21
Colored pencil and pastel by Ricky A. Taylor

FIGURE 4   *Visiting*   50
Photo of Ashley Lucas by Billye Lucas

FIGURE 5   *Bound*   G-4, 103
Colored pencil by Joanie Estes-Rodgers

FIGURE 6   *Caged Innocence*   145
Pen and ink drawing by Patricia K. Thorn

FIGURE 7   *Caught up on the Whirlwind*   191
Pen and ink drawing by Valencia C.

FIGURES 8–12 *Connie Convicta and Vato Emiliano*   G-5, 199–201
Comics
Colored pencil drawings by Ana Lucia Gelabert

FIGURE 13   *Gina*   226
Black and white photo by Leslie Levitas

FIGURE 14   *Desiree*   226
Black and white photo by Leslie Levitas

FIGURE 15   *Meredith*   228
Black and white photo by Leslie Levitas

FIGURE 16   *Exhibition View 1*   G-6, 252
Color photo by Rosemarie Chiarlone

FIGURE 17   *Exhibition View 2*   G-7, 255
Color photo by Rosemarie Chiarlone

FIGURE 18   *Panty Series #11*   G-7, 257
Silver gelatin print by Rosemarie Chiarlone

FIGURE 19   *Exhibition View 3*   G-8, 261
Color photo by Crystal Molinary

FIGURE 20   *Subruler of the Element X*   G-9, 262
Color photo by Isabel Moros-Rigau

CHARTS

CHART 3.1   Runaway Arrest and Detention Rates for Girls, 2008   37

CHART 3.2   Detention Home Admissions for Running Away, by Gender, January 1 through March 31, 2008   38

CHART 3.3   Ethnic Distribution, Youth, State of Hawai'i, 2005   39

CHART 3.4   Ethnic Distribution, Detention Home Admissions, January 1 through March 31, 2008   39

CHART 3.5   Length of Work Detail Sanctions by Gender   40

CHART 3.6   Length of Isolation Sanctions by Gender   40

TABLES

TABLE 3.1   Detention Home Admissions by Offense and
            Gender, January 1 through March 31, 2008   37

TABLE 3.2   Incident Report Types by Gender   41

3x Denied

Dawna (Lessie) Brown

ARTIST'S STATEMENT

3x Denied was created when I received my third continuance. My first continuance was for twenty-four months, two more years away from my kids. When I received my third one, I totally shut down. I got my drawing pad, pencils, pastels, and paint, pulled out my foot locker to sit on, and started drawing. Three days later, I came to my room at lunch time, and my drawing pad was open to *3x Denied* on my bed. I sat there staring at it, not believing that I had created something with so much feeling. All my pain and longing was there on paper. The most amazing part to me was the face. I have always had a block when it comes to faces. When *3x Denied* is reversed in Photoshop, there are several faces throughout the drawing. One resembles a child, and one resembles a demon of some sort. Every piece of *3x Denied* represents my longing for home in the hills of Kentucky, my pain of so many years of separation and loss, yet my determination to never give up on regaining my freedom.

Foreword

Kathy Boudin

Women slowly get up from their seats. At least forty in number, standing, turning their bodies at an angle, they stretch their arms up and out; their hands reach toward the light streaming in through the stained glass windows of a chapel. All together they say, "We will never forget. We will remember. We will always remember you"——and one by one, they call out the names of the women they have left behind; those still inside, still scattered throughout five New York State prisons for women. Some of the women have been in prison for thirty years. Some went in at seventeen and are now fifty. Some look at their lives with no possibility of parole: Annie, Buzz, Shana, Milagros, Judy, Dominique, Roz, Deb, Aiesha, Joan, Ita, Rita, Carol, Donna . . . The names come more and more rapidly—as voices fold into each other. Voices crack, holding back tears. Women who were bunkies, a neighbor in the next cell, a woman who braids hair, mothers in a parenting class, a woman who shared walking the circles around the yard, friends, a best friend—still in.

Now outside, these women, no longer wearing their denim green uniforms, instead form a rainbow of colors—of hand-me-down clothes, of clothes from thrift shops or 99-cent stores. Others are spiffy from first pay checks or professional and tailored with the confidence of having been out for a decade. Some have been home for only a month, others for ten years; some served thirty years, and others served four. We have just finished one of our monthly Saturday half-day retreats. We gather because prison doesn't wash off like the sweat after a long work day; it stays on you, stays in you. Coming together is a way to acknowledge that self openly with other women who know about it and who know each other. These women know about what it is to come "home" and to support each other in the search to build a new life.

The number of women in prison has swelled in the past thirty years. The landscape has changed—both inside and outside. Women, particularly African American women, are the fastest growing group entering prison in a society that incarcerates a larger percentage of its population than any other country in the world. And women are part of that larger reality of "mass incarceration," the

"prison nation" a recent *New York Times* editorial referred to. The total separa-
tion between the world of prison and the rest of society is fading. Before the
enormous expansion of prisons, when a person went to prison, society defined
it solely as an individual experience: *she* broke a law; *she* goes to prison. Now so
many people are incarcerated, so many women are in prison, so many children
are separated from their mothers, so many grandmothers are taking care of *their*
children, so many girls are being arrested, that it's not just a woman inside;
it's a whole family, in fact, a whole community that is penetrated and shaped
by prison. The very fact that *Razor Wire Women* is edited by two women with
family members incarcerated is a reflection of the new reach of prisons and of
the new reach of consciousness of prisons.

Although prisons separate, segregate, and isolate those inside from those
outside, the inside and outside can no longer be entirely separated. The very
form of the book *Razor Wire Women*—with its purposeful mixture of writings
by people inside and by people outside, who are connecting through their work
and their writing and their art; scholars from universities, activists in and out,
artists in and out—contributes to and reflects the breaking down of the separa-
tions. The intersection of inside and outside goes beyond that of individuals
in prison and those committed to them. Our society is now shaped by the
economic dependence of entire industries and communities on the economics
of prison—jobs, profits, federal and state budget priorities. The total separation
of inside and out has turned into a dialectic of dependence of our society on
prisons, even as that very dependence also destroys the education system of a
state like California or New York, where more money is now spent on prisons
than higher education—inside and out. Our political process is distorted by
incarcerating so many people and by the laws continuing the punishment on
so many coming home from prison. Some politicians get money for their rural
communities (and for themselves) because the census counts people *inside* prison
who cannot vote as part of the rural communities where the prison is located.
And *outside*, some politicians win elections, as illustrated by the 2000 presidential
election and the results in Florida, because people who are released from prison
are frequently denied the right to vote. The impact on families has always been
understood by the families of those in prison; and still, some communities, in
particular African Americans and Latinos, experience the incarceration realities
far more than others. Prisons remain a key means of social control for the poor
and, in particular, communities of color. But throughout the country, precisely
because of its ubiquity as a form of social control, prison no longer operates in
the invisibility that has so long reinforced its controlling power.

And yet physical and mental segregation continues. Prison is a physical real-
ity—a space behind fences or walls, fragmented and cut off, divided by metal
gates, solid doors, tunnels underground, tree stumps, brittle pieces of bark that
were once attached to the hedges that were cut down so that the surveilling
eye can see better. Grass is enclosed by barbed wire and the razor wire that
catches the sun, letting you know that there is something in and something

out. Some prisons are worse, and some are better, but all prisons are containers of lives contained. In prison you crave space, space to be someone other than a label of "murderer," "bad mother," "drug addict," "baby killer," "terrorist," "victim of abuse," "abuser," "AIDS-ridden," "bitch"—labels from society, labels from one another. What makes it so hard is that those labels often connect to a vulnerable pocket inside the woman. Women are craving space to forge identities that are truer, more complex, and that enable them to move forward instead of being cemented into a hole.

Razor Wire Women helps to create that space by communicating the worlds of women in prison who are complex, neither "victims" nor "demons." It places the individual with agency inside a set of social conditions created precisely to deny such agency.

Finally, *Razor Wire Women* is a book that recognizes the role of art in helping to transcend limits. The painting, the poetry, and the theater permeate the book and allow the reader to connect to the dimensions of lives of women inside that cannot be captured by statistics or journal articles, just as the experience of creation allowed the women to access new ways of thinking and new ways of communicating across the separation. *Razor Wire Women* understands that art is not only about the present but also about the possibility of a different future. As Maxine Green says (2000):

> Artists know about spaces opening in imagination, even as they understand what it means to be situated in the world and to speak (or paint or sing or dance) from the vantage point of their situations. They tell us what happens when they experience new beginning, when they are enabled to see through new perspectives. There is a clearing, a lighting, a reaching beyond what people are convinced they know.

Imagine, as you read *Razor Wire Women*, that these stories might be yours. Imagine, you can make a difference.

KATHY BOUDIN

REFERENCES

Green, M. 2000. "Lived Spaces, Shared Spaces, Public Spaces." In *Construction Sites: Excavating Race, Class, and Gender among Urban Youth,* ed. L. Weis and M. Rine. New York: Teachers College, 293–304.

Ruth Snyder
Malaquias Montoya

ARTIST'S STATEMENT

Just after 11:00 p.m. on January 12, 1928, Ruth Snyder, a housewife convicted of murdering her husband, died in Sing Sing's electric chair. At the very moment of her electrocution, a newspaper photographer with a hidden camera strapped to his leg captured an iconic image of the execution. Snyder's case and the photo of her execution proved to be particularly provocative because of her gender. Ideas of femininity and passive gender roles contrasted sharply with the violence Snyder was purported to have done to her husband and that which was done to her by the electric chair.

While engaged in my research on a series against the death penalty, when I envisioned executions I only pictured men in the electric chair. When I came across a reporter's photo showing a woman's body bound by straps—a feminine hairstyle and the hem of a dress oddly framing the mask and restraints that held Snyder in place—I was shocked. The fuzziness of the photo made it all the more horrible. I added to that feeling by repeating her masked image at the top of the painting. Further, I read that the media attention surrounding the Snyder case sensationalized the idea of female criminality, rather than interrogating the cruelty and ineffectiveness of the death penalty as a means to police our society. My hope is to repurpose the image of Snyder's execution as a reminder of the ugliness and injustice of the death penalty.

This painting is part of a traveling exhibition of my work called *Premeditated: Meditations on Capital Punishment*. I have always been against the death penalty. It is an irrational idea that you kill a person because she or he has killed another. Ruth Snyder was legally murdered by the state, and her execution compounded the injustice of her husband's death rather than moving toward healing and rehabilitation. What concerns me is the following: Why do we kill? What happens to our humanity and to us, as a culture? It is my intention for my art to act as a mirror of reality, to reflect heinous crimes committed in our name, and as a result seek alternatives to the injustices we perpetrate on one another.

Acknowledgments

This book has been in process since 2007, and we are very grateful to the many people who helped to make this work possible. Rebecca Ropers-Huilman and the editorial board and staff at what was then the *National Women's Studies Association Journal* (*NWSAJ*) gave us the impetus and courage to pursue the creation of an edited collection on incarcerated women. The editorial board that we formed as we put together our cluster issue of the *NWSAJ* proved invaluable as we recruited contributors for this volume. Our heartfelt thanks go out to Buzz Alexander, Kristen Bates, Matthew Atherton, Don Braman, Denise DaSilva, Juanita Díaz-Cotto, Soffiyah Elijah, Karlene Faith, Beverly Fletcher, Rena Fraden, Alan Gomez, Linda Heidenreich, Joy James, Paula Johnson, Dreama Moon, Eleanor Novek, Barbara Owen, Dylan Rodríguez, Luana Ross, Nancy Stoller, Julia Sudbury, and Richelle Swan.

Many members of the Prison Creative Arts Project (PCAP) inspired us and linked us to incarcerated poets and visual artists. We find the work that they do to be an inspiration and a place of community to which we could turn during the long journey toward this book's publication. Josmell Pérez and UNC Office of Diversity and Multicultural Affairs stepped in to help us with printing images for this book at a critical moment. Thank you for supporting us and this project without hesitation. Larin McLaughlin, Laurie Searl, and the staff at the State University of New York Press have made this book a reality, and we are thankful for their belief in the value of this collection and its many contributors. The anonymous reviewers of this manuscript provided valuable insight and guidance in structuring *Razor Wire Women*. The color images in this volume would not have been printed without the generous support of a University of North Carolina University Research Council Publication Grant. Phil Christman provided emergency editing services in critical moments of this manuscript's development, and we are grateful for his keen eyes and unflagging encouragement.

Finally, we extend our deepest thanks and appreciation for the many contributors of this book and for those whose work did not make it into the final manuscript. We wish that we could have included even more razor wire women and their supporters.

CHAPTER ONE

From Representations to Resistance: How the Razor Wire Binds Us

Jodie Michelle Lawston

I believe that the more we can have a voice, the more we can reach out to bring understanding to our situation, the more outside people are going to positively respond.   —VONDA WHITE, *formerly incarcerated*

MAINSTREAM REPRESENTATIONS OF SOCIALLY INVISIBLE WOMEN

Prisons, by their very nature, conceal the people who live and work inside them. Those who attempt to gain access to prisons for the purposes of research, activism, family visitation, or even governmental evaluation see and hear little more than what prison officials wish to show to the world. Even those who reside within the prisons walls, and many of those who are employed there, will likely never have a full picture of what takes place day to day in the prison as a whole. Prisoners are often grouped together, packed into tight spaces, and forced to cohabitate with more of their colleagues than the prison was designed to hold, yet they are also isolated from other populations within the prison and can live for years without seeing certain others confined within the same border of fences and razor wire. The systematic obfuscation of knowledge about prisons and prisoners makes it challenging to piece together a realistic depiction of how people experience incarceration.

Perhaps it is this mystery that enshrouds the carceral that fuels the desire for outsiders to create representations of those inside prisons. This statement may be particularly true for incarcerated women, who continue to represent a smaller proportion of the prison population (just 7 percent) and seem to perplex society because they do not fit the traditional mold of what a prisoner is "supposed" to be: male and, in contemporary society, of color. Throughout history, organizations, medical professionals, and the media have rushed to explain what "causes" female criminality and, in so doing, have manufactured representations of women behind bars that are not necessarily congruous with how imprisoned women may frame and understand themselves, their lives, and their experiences with incarceration.

In some ways, society has been preoccupied with representing incarcerated women. In the nineteenth century, women who engaged—or perhaps indulged—in "pleasures of the body" such as drinking in public, having sex outside of marriage, or committing adultery crossed the dividing line between femininity and masculinity and could find themselves serving prison sentences. These women were termed "fallen women" by society and were represented as beyond redemption (Freedman 1981). Gender expectations and a strong double standard meant that men could more freely engage in the same behaviors that led to the social control and punishment of women. It was not until women prison reformers organized to improve prison conditions and establish separate reformatories for "fallen women" that women came to be seen as having potential for rehabilitation (Freedman 1981). This rehabilitation was really a mandate to accept traditional, middle-class gender norms that stressed the maternal role of women in the family; only when a "fallen woman" accepted these values would it be deemed appropriate to release her from prison. Of course, this reform work was focused almost exclusively on white women; incarcerated women of color were overlooked by reformers and remained in separate wings of men's custodial institutions (Rafter 1990). A representation of the "deserving" female prisoner therefore developed, and this image was of a white, young woman who was in desperate need of guidance and reform.

By the midtwentieth century, Hollywood began to represent incarcerated women. Films like *I Want to Live* (1958) and *Caged* (1950) were melodramatic depictions of prison life. *I Want to Live* is based on the story of Barbara Graham, who was executed at thirty-two years of age in California for a murder in which she was allegedly involved with two other men. Nicknamed "Bloody Babs" by the media, the film describes the media frenzy around her case and its representation of Graham as a "bad girl" or "party girl" because she was involved in prostitution, gambling, and drugs. Such representations clearly depict a gender double standard: men can indulge in gambling and drugs, for example, but women who do so, and women who engage in prostitution, have crossed the line between "pure" and "licentious" and are conceptualized, to use Karlene Faith's (1993) term, as "unruly." These representations also remove Graham from the social context of her life and fail to capture the complexity of her time both before and during prison.

On the other hand, the academy award–nominated *Caged* tells the story of a young woman hardened by the prison environment. This film interestingly suggests that healthcare was inadequate in women's prisons in 1950 (a problem that continues today) and shows a well-meaning warden, who champions rehabilitation efforts, in a power struggle with a correctional officer who thinks women inside should be treated like "animals." But it again does little to interrogate the larger social forces that contribute to one's incarceration and fails to capture the complexity of prison life for women behind bars; it also depicts women in prison as desperately needing guidance and charitable help. Moreover, both films overwhelmingly represent white women prisoners; one wonders where all of the incarcerated women of color were.

More contemporary representations of women in prison are obsessed with the idea of incarcerated women as "hardened criminals." The E! Network, for example, currently runs a special entitled, *Women Who Kill,* which chronicles high-profile cases of disproportionately white women who have killed their husbands. This special creates a flat and simplistic picture of the lives of such women, sensationalizes crime and incarceration, and suggests, albeit implicitly, that women behind bars are all crazed killers who are to be feared. Larger processes of racism, classism, and sexism, which contribute to the present-day incarceration of a disproportionate number of women in prison, are not discussed or interrogated, nor is it brought to the viewer's attention that most women in prison are not doing time for violent crimes.

To be sure, sensationalized accounts and portrayals of incarcerated women and their crimes could not be further from the truth. Unlike films, television programs, and even nineteenth-century reformers who turned their attention toward white prisoners, incarcerated women are disproportionately of color and poor: close to 70 percent of these women are black, Latina, First Nation, or Asian (Díaz-Cotto 2006; James 2005; Johnson 2003), and most are poor or working class. A growing percentage of women prisoners are migrant women, overwhelmingly from Mexico.

At least 57 percent of women incarcerated in state prisons report that they have experienced sexual and/or physical violence prior to their confinement; about one-third of imprisoned women report having been raped prior to their incarceration (Lawston 2008; Mauer, Potler, and Wolf 1999). Moreover, incarcerated women are more likely than their male counterparts to be addicted to drugs or to report a drug problem at the time of arrest (Pollock 2002; Owen 1998), more often than not because they are trying to lessen the pain that results from the violence they have suffered. Despite mainstream media portrayals of women in prison as "violent" and "hardened," the majority of incarcerated women do their time for nonviolent drug or property offenses, with drug offenses—largely due to changes in drug laws—being the largest source of growth for the women's prison and jail population (see Lawston 2008; Schlesinger 2008; Reynolds 2008; Díaz-Cotto 2007; Johnson 2003; Mauer, Potler, and Wolf 1999). Additionally, at least two-thirds of incarcerated women are mothers to children under eighteen years of age (Mumola 2000). Although imprisoned women experience incarceration directly, then, their children, families, communities, friends, and other loved ones also suffer from their confinement in myriad and no less painful ways.

A major problem with both current and past mainstream media representations of incarcerated women is that the material presented tells us little about how these women represent themselves, how they conceptualize and process imprisonment and the separation from their communities and families, and how they express dissent and fight for their voices to be heard by those on the outside of prison walls, which as Vonda suggests at the beginning of this chapter is an important goal for many contemporary imprisoned women. Most media representations fail to show the complexity of prisoners' lives, allowing women's crimes and the stigma of criminality to overshadow, and act as a master status to, all other aspects of their identities. These media representations fail to contextualize women's imprisonment within a social system that relies on racism, economic discrimination, and sexism to lock up marginalized groups of women who are our mothers, sisters, wives, partners, and friends. Like all of us, the women that the United States targets for incarceration are infinitely more multifaceted than the simplistic representations that have historically dominated society, and their voices are no less important than any of ours on the outside of prison walls.

CHALLENGING MAINSTREAM REPRESENTATIONS OF INCARCERATED WOMEN: PRISONERS, SCHOLARS, ACTIVISTS, AND ARTISTS

While mass media outlets and traditional reform groups like those found in the nineteenth century attempted (and continue to attempt) to represent women who are confined behind steal doors and razor wire, prisoners, activists, scholars, and artists have nevertheless managed to contribute their varied forms of discourse to the historical record of women's incarceration in the United States. Autobiographical accounts of women's imprisonment in this country date back at least as far as the 1860s, when a number of privileged Southern women were jailed as Confederate spies (Boyd 1865; Robinson 1864). These early accounts are few and far between and describe only the experiences of those literate enough to write their own stories. Although the women's prison reform movement of the nineteenth century is brilliantly documented by several scholars (Freedman 1981; Rafter 1990; Dodge 2006), the literature available suggests that the voices of women in reformatories and custodial institutions were muted by activists who were concerned with reforming women who "stepped out of line." More recent literature, such as Wally Lamb's popular anthologies *Couldn't Keep It To Myself: Testimonies from Our Imprisoned Sisters* (2004) and *I'll Fly Away: Further Testimonies from the Women of York Prison* (2007), as well as numerous scholarly articles, books, and volumes, including but not limited to those edited by Solinger, Johnson, Raimon, Reynolds, and Tapia (2009), Sudbury (2005), Hardon and Hill (1998), Boudin (1998), Girshick (1999), Owen (1998), and Richie (1996) have been more successful at highlighting the voices, knowledge, and testimonies of women in prison.

Activism around women's confinement has also served to contest mainstream understandings of incarceration. Nineteenth-century reformers challenged the idea that criminalized women could not be "rehabilitated" (Freedman 1981) but operated under the assumption that "rehabilitation" is congruous with acceptance of traditional gender expectations. In contrast, more contemporary progressive activism, from the 1970s to today, has not only underscored the importance of women prisoners speaking for themselves, but in some cases has begun to question incarceration in its entirety.

Women activists in the 1970s fell on a continuum: some groups advocated for the reform of prisons (such as through improvement of prison conditions and rehabilitative programs), while others advocated for alternatives to incarceration (such as through the channeling of resources such as education, housing, and jobs in an equitable manner to all communities) (Resources for Community Change 1975). Like many of the men in the radical men's prison movement (Cummins 1994), incarcerated and formerly incarcerated women were an integral and powerful part of this movement, which helped to reframe understandings of imprisonment.

Activists today still fall on a continuum: some organizations primarily strive for prison reform, while others fight for systemic social change and alternatives to incarceration. Many organizations, though, inhabit the liminal space between reform and abolition of prisons; these groups incorporate prisoner support work into their missions while adhering to a vision of a world without prisons. Organizations that fight for prison abolition—such as Critical Resistance—provide public education on the economic, social, and political roots of the U.S. prison regime, its effects on all of our lives, and community alternatives to imprisonment. Incite! focuses specifically on the effects of violence and incarceration on women and also offers suggestions for beginning to move away from a system that relies on violence and punishment to ensure safety. Such organizations are powerful engines for social change that have the potential to radically alter how the United States conceptualizes and approaches "crime."

Art has also been a provocative way to reconceptualize manufactured representations of incarcerated women. Imprisoned women have likely produced creative writing and artwork of some kind throughout U.S. history, but artists' contributions, for the most part, went undocumented until the midtwentieth century. Though it is difficult to document the work of most individual prison artists, a small handful of incarcerated writers, visual artists, musicians, dancers, and theater practitioners have received recognition outside prison walls. Of this select group of published and celebrated prison artists, very few are women, and their work tends to be significantly less well known than the male prisoners working in the same artistic genre.

More organized and larger-scale efforts to promote creative expression in prison began when activist, educational, and artistic organizations made major in-roads into both women's and men's facilities from the 1980s to the present. Performer Rhodessa Jones and her collaborators began creating theater with the women of the San Francisco County Jail in 1989 and subsequently formed the Medea Project, a theater collective of incarcerated and nonincarcerated women. In 1990, Buzz Alexander, an English professor at the University of Michigan, began teaching a theater class in a women's prison and founded the Prison Creative Arts Project, which now facilitates arts workshops in prisons, juvenile detention centers, and urban high schools throughout Michigan. Women on the Rise! a program based out of Miami's Museum of Contemporary Art since 2004, enables professional women artists to collaborate on art projects with girls in the Miami-Dade County Juvenile Detention Center. All three of these organizations are discussed in subsequent chapters of this book.

Arts programs are crucial in that they give participants a creative mode in which to think critically about their lives in relation to the performative and performed power structures of the prison. Incarcerated women's voices and visions, in artistic form, are as essential to struggles for equality and justice as are those of nonincarcerated people, scholars, and activists. The symbols of incarcerated women's fights are embedded in the words and images created by prisoner artists.

Artists from outside prisons also raise awareness and generate dialogue about issues surrounding the carceral by helping unmask the everyday implications of prisons in average citizens' lives.

Particularly unique ways of presenting prisoners' voices and a more complex representation of incarceration can also be found on websites such as *Women in Prison: A Site for Resistance*, run by Beyondmedia Education in Chicago, which includes articles, artwork, poetry, and other creative work by prisoners, scholars, activists, and the families, friends, and children of prisoners. Such work has been critical to challenging archetypical images surrounding incarceration.

REPRESENTATIONS, VOICE, AND RAZOR WIRE WOMEN

It is extremely important to continue contesting monolithic representations of incarcerated women, and in attempting to do so, it is critical that the voices of women who experience incarceration are respected, prioritized, and validated. Returning to Vonda White's statement at the beginning of this chapter, only when imprisoned women speak for themselves—rather than having criminal justice "experts," the media, and medical practitioners speak for them—will it be possible to shatter stereotypical understandings of crime and incarceration.

But it is perhaps equally important to broaden our understanding of *who* is affected by mass imprisonment. Incarcerated women are obviously affected directly in that they are literally locked up, chained and shackled, and subjected to various forms of humiliation by a system whose goal is the systematic subordination and oppression of marginalized groups of people. But families, friends, children, and entire communities are also deeply affected by imprisonment when loved ones are torn away from them. With 2.3 million people incarcerated—two hundred thousand of whom are women, and at least two-thirds of whom are mothers (Talvi 2007)—it should not be difficult to see that the grip of the U.S. carceral system reaches beyond those who are inside of it. Society has produced images of women in prison as out of control, drug addicted, unruly, and sexually promiscuous, and often these stereotypes reach beyond incarcerated women to their families, children, and communities. For example, society assumes that incarcerated women's children are somehow tainted by their mothers' imprisonment or that the communities from which women in prison come are inherently "pathological," "bad," or "groomed" for criminal activity. Moreover, families, children, and communities are hard hit by women's incarceration because women cannot take care of their children, help families monetarily, or contribute to a community's growth.

In this book we extend understandings of the effects of women's incarceration to include not just those who are behind bars, but women outside who are also deeply affected by imprisonment. We employ the concept "razor wire women" to describe those women who experience the criminal justice system in ways that shape their lives profoundly. Razor wire women encounter the criminal justice system in myriad ways; in addition to being prisoners, activists, scholars, and artists, razor wire women are the wives, sisters, caretakers, friends, partners, and extended family members of incarcerated people. Ashley Lucas and I are both the children of prisoners, as is at least one other contributor to this volume. Razor wire women share the common ground of knowing what it feels like for the state to police your body and your family. We live in solidarity with women on both sides of prison walls, understanding intimately how the razor wire binds us.

THE GENESIS OF RAZOR WIRE WOMEN

The challenge of realistically documenting the lives of incarcerated women can best be met by combining many different types of knowledge. *Razor Wire Women* brings together the contributions of prisoners, activists, scholars, and artists because the members of each of these groups possess distinct and vital kinds of information about how women encounter incarceration. This book grew out of a cluster issue of the *National Women's Studies Association Journal* (*NWSAJ*), now titled *Feminist Formations*, which Ashley Lucas and I edited, on the topic of "Women, the Criminal Justice System, and Incarceration: Processes of Power, Silence, and Resistance." When we solicited contributions for that journal issue, we sought out activists, prisoners, and artists, as well as scholars, who are usually the only contributors to academic journals. As activist-scholars ourselves, we felt that the journal could not adequately describe women's incarceration without the voices of those living within the walls and those on the outside who tirelessly advocate for them. Artists on both sides of the razor wire are able to depict the humanity and the emotional life of incarcerated women in ways that scholars and activists cannot. Such an abundance of high quality work was sent to us in response to our call for contributions that we could not use most of it in the limited space of a single journal issue. Even before that issue of *NWSAJ* was published in the summer of 2008, we had decided to put together this collection.

The artwork, scholarly articles, essays, poetry, autobiographical narratives, and drama collected here inform one another through their juxtaposition. The creative work gathered in this volume informs and colors the empirical data found in the scholarly and nonfiction writings throughout *Razor Wire Women*. And the categories of prisoner, activist, scholar, and artist are not mutually exclusive. Many of our contributors fill more than one of these roles and blend the skill sets and the modes of understanding that come from being part of these groups. Other contributors share one specific viewpoint that illuminates a particular aspect of how women experience imprisonment.

The prisoners and former prisoners who offered their writings and artwork for this volume provide us with the most immediate and experiential accounts of their lives, while the activists describe efforts to advocate for prisoners and their families and in some cases, to agitate for alternatives to incarceration. The scholarly writing in these pages presents new research on women in prison and their families, with particular attention paid to some of the most ignored groups within these populations: girls, immigrants, and transgender people. Most edited volumes of scholarly work entrench themselves in one academic discipline or a grouping of related disciplines. *Razor Wire Women* brings together scholarship from the humanities, social sciences, and the arts because we believe that each mode of inquiry used to study women's incarceration offers up distinct and valuable insight. We use the broad interdisciplinary lenses of sociology, feminist criminology, and women's and gender studies to unite seemingly disparate kinds of writing and imagery. Visual artists, dramatists, and creative writers as well as scholars who study the arts have pieces in this collection, which show us how women prisoners use creativity and arts as strategies for resistance, modes of describing their world, attempts at rehabilitation, opportunities for building communities, and ideas for decarceration. This book is a collaborative effort among the editors and contributors to deepen our understanding of how women interact with the criminal justice system and how deeply the policing, prosecution, and incarceration of women affects us all.

CAPTURED IN COLORED PENCIL: A WORD ON
3X DENIED BY LESSIE BROWN

The artist who drew the image used for the cover of this book was a prisoner at the time she made this drawing. When Lessie Brown received word from the parole board that she had been denied for the third time, she retreated to her cell and reached for her sketch pad. Before her incarceration, Lessie had never seen herself as an artist. She was a devoted housewife and mother, and if she drew a picture to amuse her children, they laughed good-naturedly at her terrible likenesses of animals and trees. After she was sentenced to a Michigan state prison, Lessie looked for productive ways to spend her time, and eventually another woman in prison gave her some art supplies and encouraged her to start drawing. Soon Lessie had started a small business from her cell, making cards for women to send home to their families. Her artwork tended to be naturalistic scenes of butterflies, flowers, and the like, because Lessie believed she could not draw human faces. In spite of her record of good behavior and compliance, at her third review the parole board declined to give Lessie the chance to go home to her children. Devastated, Lessie sat on her bunk and began a new drawing without any thought as to what would go in it. She drew feverishly through the night without stopping, and she set down her pad and pencils only when she had to go to her prison job the next morning. She left the drawing on her bed without registering what she had drawn. When Lessie returned to her cell at the end of her shift, the sketch pad lay open on her bunk, with a startling image staring back at her, a drawing she would later title *3x Denied*.

Though the significance of the parole-related studies and campaigns in which scholars and activists engage cannot be underestimated, their writings and speeches convey something very different about what it means for a woman to be denied parole than Lessie Brown's drawing does. The layers of contrasting images in *3x Denied* reveal how incarceration is laden with ideas of freedom, how the machinery of imprisonment works against that which is organic and alive, how people's lives and bodies are impaled on a system that seeks to suppress rather than nourish their humanity. It is our hope that you will read this collection as a series of contrasting yet complementary offerings, as a compilation that enables us to understand women's incarceration through many different types of knowledge.

FRAMING THE DIALOGUE: THE STRUCTURE OF *RAZOR WIRE WOMEN*

This collection has three major sections that reflect important aspects of women's experiences with incarceration and the criminal justice system. All the parts of this book include creative contributions from those who have endured incarceration as well as those who have not, and each section has creative contributions as well as scholarly chapters. Each section begins with artwork by an incarcerated person, which was a deliberate editorial decision: those who have direct experiences with imprisonment have the first word in each section of this book. We privilege this experiential knowledge as a way to ensure that those of us on the outside of prison walls do not mute or overshadow the voices of those who are locked up. In each section we follow the opening artwork with a historical contextualization that connects the chapters of the section to activist, scholarly, or artistic and creative work around women's incarceration.

The first section, "Girls, Women, and Families," provides a rubric for viewing the subjects of this collection as complex human beings who are not solely defined by their relationship to a prison. The contributions in this section interrogate the ways in which the U.S. criminal justice system interrupts familial relationships and life maturation cycles at all stages of development and fails to take into consideration the unique life experiences of the women inside of it.

The opening piece of art, a colored pencil drawing, *Missing*, by Ricky A. Taylor, shows a woman and a boy sitting at a dinner table. Though there are only two of them, the table is set for three. The boy eats his dinner and looks forward, away from the woman. The woman weeps and does not touch her dinner. The empty place setting is closer to the center of the drawing than either of the two figures.

Chapter 2 is written by Je'Anna Redwood, who is currently incarcerated in California. In "The Voice of Silence," Redwood describes the pains of violence and abuse, the effects of silence, and the importance of voicing oneself especially when one occupies a socially marginalized status.

Following Redwood's personal account, chapter 3, "Doing Time in Detention Home: Gendered Punishment Regimes in Youth Jails," written by Brian Bilsky and Meda Chesney-Lind examines conditions in Honolulu's Youth Detention Center, Hale Ho'omalu, and finds that youth are systematically exposed to punitive gender regimes regardless of facility rules to the contrary. Bilsky and Chesney-Lind show that particularly harsh punishment is found in the girls' wing of the facility, where girls are subjected to long hours of isolation, domestic duties, and work detail for minor infractions. The authors point out that these conditions grow out of an institutional mandate for girls' docility and silence. Not too surprisingly, Native Hawaiian girls disproportionately suffer from these gendered punishment regimes.

Chapter 4 is an excerpt from playwright Ashley E. Lucas' play, *Doin' Time: Through the Visiting Glass*, which describes the experiences of prisoners' family members. A little girl describes the difficulties of visiting her father in prison in this monologue entitled "Healer."

In chapter 5, "Incarcerated Women: Motherhood on the Margins," Barbara Bloom and Marilyn Brown turn our attention to the struggles of incarcerated mothers. They explore how motherhood is enacted within the structural context of the prison and how it is problematized by two constraints: forced separation from children and the imperative toward intensive mothering. Bloom and Brown show that imprisoned mothers struggle with their self-image and identity because of separation from children and social expectations that define a good mother as engaging in complete child-centered mothering. They also examine the impact of recent changes in child welfare laws that have had critical consequences for poor mothers, many whom are incarcerated. They argue that women in particular have been affected by the contraction of the welfare state and an increasingly punitive approach to crime.

In chapter 6, "Doing Time with Mom: A Nonfiction Essay," Shirley Haviland-Nakagawa describes the day her sister was sentenced to fourteen years in prison. The narrative focuses on how the family as a whole attempts to navigate the court system and cope with a loved one's incarceration.

In chapter 7, entitled, "ASFA and the Impact on Imprisoned Migrant Women and Their Children," Martha Escobar examines some of the structural obstacles that incarcerated immigrant mothers face in maintaining parental rights. While in prison, immigrant mothers have to deal with the prospective of deportation and the additional burden it places on their parental rights cases. The interaction between these policies shapes relationships between immigrant parents and their children and increases the likelihood of family separation. Escobar considers the stories of two immigrant mothers in prison and uses them to illustrate the ways in which immigration laws and incarceration shape relationships within these families.

In the final chapter of this section, Trangdai Glassey-Tranguyen's nonfiction essay combines autobiographical experiences with an analysis of women's incarceration. Her chapter, "Carceral State, Cultural Stake: Women behind American Bars and Beyond," explores the common experiences of women enduring blatant sexual violence, legal inequality, and economic exploitation in the United States and other parts of the world. She argues that incarcerated women are subjected to injustice and violence regardless of their geopolitical positioning. Ultimately she asks how we can be cognizant of these types of injustice so that the rights and safety of women can be ensured.

Section 2 of *Razor Wire Women*, "Sexuality, Health, and Abuse," explores the ways in which prisons intervene in the physical and mental health of incarcerated women. The neglect and abuse of incarcerated women runs rampant throughout U.S. prisons, and the contributors in this section provide testimonials of their own experiences, descriptions of what they have discovered is happening to others, and analyses of the histories of abusive practices against women in prison.

The opening piece of art in section 2, *Bound,* is a drawing that shows a kneeling woman with her head hanging down bound by ankle chains to prison bars. The scene surrounding the main figure in prisoner Joanie Estes-Rodgers' drawing depicts the crumbling edifices of a loan office, a church, and a home. A husband and a crying toddler both reach out to the bound woman. A bottle of alcohol sits on the ground in front of her, and a bottle of prescription medicine peeks out of the pocket of her jeans. Phone bills, a bag of groceries, and a broken truck are all impaled on the prison bars around her. In or out of prison, the figure in the drawing is bound by her addictions, obligations, and debts.

In chapter 9, "The Prison Mentality," Jane Dorotik focuses on the institutionalization of prisoners' minds. Dorotik, who is currently incarcerated in California, describes the scarcity of resources to which prisoners have access and explains how these living conditions encourage prisoners to believe that people have to dominate one another in order to survive. This chapter specifically engages with the ways in which the prison system exercises power over women.

In chapter 10, " 'If I Wasn't Suicidal, That'll Drive You to It': Women, Jail, and Mental Health," Angie Moe focuses on the mental health–related needs of women in short-term confinement. Findings are based on a sample of thirty women who voluntarily participated in semistructured life history interviews while confined in an urban southwestern detention center. The women were asked to talk about their lives prior to and during incarceration from their own perspectives, or standpoint, resulting in rich and descriptive narratives, which included discussions of mental health problems that had been only marginally addressed, if at all, during confinement. Moe argues that detained/jailed women are a neglected population of inmates who are in dire need of mental health care programming. Often entering the system in a state of crisis and emotional turmoil, failing to address the immediate psychological and psychiatric needs of these inmates will only hinder their adaptation to confinement, ability to understand and assist in their own criminal cases, and progress in future treatment, should it become available.

In chapter 11, formerly incarcerated Jen Myers' poem "Patiently Waiting" describes the utterly deficient health care that incarcerated women receive and the terror of knowing that you are more likely to be left to suffer—and even to die—if you develop a serious health problem in prison.

After Myers' chapter, a pencil drawing by former Michigan prisoner Patricia K. Thorn—entitled *Caged Innocence*—depicts a young woman in a prison cell. She sits at a table, arms crossed and head down. Her head and arms rest on an open book with the words "Caged Innocence" on the pages.

Chapter 12, "Transgender Women, Sexual Violence, and the Rule of Law: An Argument in Favor of Restorative and Transformative Justice," is written by Linda Heidenreich. This chapter maps the relationship between gendered violence in the U.S. penal system and the gendered rule of law that structures the larger U.S. society and the "gendered models of citizenship" that flow from it. It places the lives of transgender women at the center of its analysis and asks the questions, "How is it that such intense violence is tolerated when it is directed against transgender women?" and, "If such violence is not tolerable, what remedies are available?" Ultimately it argues that the policing of gender is central to U.S. society and hence intensified in its penal system, which functions as a heterotopia. Thus, the safety of transsexual women is dependent upon a radical transformation of the penal system and the larger gendered society with which it shares a dialogical relationship. Restorative justice provides us all with some concrete steps toward making those changes.

Current Nevada prisoner Johanna Hudnall survived a prison rape. She eventually became a member of the advisory board for Stop Prisoner Rape, a national organization that works to end sexual violence against all people in any form of detention. Chapter 13, "Prison Rape" is an autobiographical essay that chronicles her journey through abuse and into activism.

In Chapter 14, "From Women Prisoners to People in Women's Prisons: Challenging the Gender Binary in Antiprison Work," Julia Sudbury explores the ways in which transgender and gender nonconforming prisoners and activists complicate existing understandings of what constitutes progressive scholarly and activist work around "women in prison." As Sudbury argues, prisoners who do not identify as women who are held in women's prisons and women held in men's prisons are overlooked by feminist (anti)prison researchers, but increasingly are claiming a space in antiprison activism.

Turning again to violence in prisons, Renita Phifer, a current New York prisoner, writes about instances of sexual and physical abuse involving guards and incarcerated women. Chapter 15 is her nonfiction essay, "Giving the Voiceless a Voice," which exposes the power dynamics that enable the exploitation of incarcerated women.

Section 3 of *Razor Wire Women*, "Education, Writing, and the Arts," explores the ways in which women in prison, educators, artists, and activists are creating spaces inside prisons where intellectual growth and creativity can flourish, despite the confining nature of their surroundings. Many of these pieces argue that education and the arts are rehabilitative in nature and that prison arts can be used to educate and inform the public as well. In tandem, the pieces of the collection coalesce to affirm the human dignity of all women, to protest the abuse of already confined and vulnerable people, and to advocate for further opportunities for intellectual growth and artistic expression for prisoners.

Section 3 opens with artwork by Valencia C., entitled *Caught up on the Whirlwind*. Valencia C. is currently incarcerated in California. This piece is rich, drawing our attention, for example, to hands in handcuffs, a mother reaching for her child through prison bars, a sleeping Lady Justice, and a dove weighed down by shackles. Several prisoners stand inside a prison, one in a wheelchair, while the Statue of Liberty—the sign of "freedom" and "democracy," towers above.

Ana Lucia Gelabert, who is currently incarcerated in Texas, draws a series of comics about a married couple who go to prison. Printed here are two episodes of the *Connie Convicta and Vato Emiliano* comics, which are a combination of captivating drawings and compelling facts in story form about the prison system's impact on the Texas economy.

Simone Weil Davis used the model of the Inside-Out Prison Exchange Program to develop a course in English and creative writing, bringing together incarcerated and recently released women with female students in western Massachusetts's Five College system. Chapter 16, "Inside-Out: The Reaches and Limits of a Prison Program," describes the class Davis taught, and questions the idea that when women reveal themselves through writing, their story must necessarily follow the conventions of either the confession or recovery narrative. Even when the writing is therapeutic, when women sit in a circle and write these, tales of the individual are not all that are told. The practice of writing itself tells a story, about community building and social change.

In chapter 17 former prisoner Leslie Levitas's short story, "Desiree," depicts the life of a troubled woman inside the San Francisco County Jail. Paired with her creative writing are several photographs taken by Levitas of women on the street in San Francisco. Her work that appears in this collection is part of a photography and oral history project entitled "Tell Me about Your Life," which was supported, in part, by an Individual Artists Program grant from the Peninsula Community Foundation.

In chapter 18, "Restorytive Justice: Theater as a Redressive Mechanism for Incarcerated Women," theater scholar Sara Warner analyzes one remarkable theater company's efforts to use performance and storytelling to move society toward restorytive justice. Rhodessa Jones' the Medea Project Theater for Incarcerated Women is an internationally renowned community arts organization that has been working with inmates at San Francisco County Jail for almost twenty years. This article explores the Medea Project's performance praxis, what Warner calls "restorytive justice." Rooted in testimony and witnessing, Jones' praxis of restorytive justice provides incarcerated women with the unique opportunity to explore their positions as both agents and objects of crime. The women's stories are transformed into full-length theatrical productions that are staged by the inmate/authors for the public (the only group in the entire country to do this) at one of the Bay Area's premiere theaters. Warner argues that restorytive justice enables these women to break through the narrative prison house of legal discourse and facilitates the healing of individuals and communities.

Chapter 19, "On Visual Politics and Poetics: Incarcerated Girls and Women Artists," by Jillian Hernandez, presents an academic analysis of the artwork created in an arts and incarceration program she cofacilitated for girls. This chapter draws on girls' studies literature to contextualize artists' interactions with students and offers pedagogical strategies for youth practitioners working in detention centers. The aim of the *MOD 11* exhibit is to share the experiences of the girls and women involved in order to demonstrate how feminist artistic practice and community coalition building can promote critical consciousness in and social justice for court-involved girls and generate further dialogue among the realms of art, activism, and girls' studies.

The Sisters of Unique Lyrics (SOUL) is a poetry workshop that meets weekly at Scott Correctional Facility, a maximum-security women's prison in Plymouth, Michigan. SOUL was established as a poetry workshop in 2004 through the Prison Creative Arts Project (PCAP), an organization housed in the English Language and Literature Department of the University of Michigan, Ann Arbor. PCAP's mission is to strengthen the community through creative expression. Since it began, more than thirty women have participated, and it is one of the longest running poetry workshops offered by PCAP. At the time the poems in this book were written, SOUL was comprised of eight women, including the two facilitators who provide a loose structure for the workshop but who are fully active participants in the poetic process. Chapter 20, "Hope in a Box: Sanity Sold Separately," is a collection of poetry from one twenty-week cycle of SOUL's workshop meetings. The members of SOUL invite readers to view these poems that make up the chapter as not simply a body of poetry but as a representation of their own discovery into the depths of the lives of women and prison.

Writing is a strategy that lets women resist the social death of incarceration and define the terms that shape their experiences. The form of prison writing described in chapter 21, "The Life Inside: Incarcerated Women Represent Themselves through Journalism," by Eleanor Novek, falls under the broad category of prison journalism and complements Ana Lucia Gelabert's comics. This article, which closes section 3 of *Razor Wire Women*, offers an interpretive media ethnography of the ways incarcerated women represent themselves in journalistic writing. It is based on interpretive analysis of inmates' writings from fifty issues of a prison newspaper published between 2001 and 2008. The incarcerated women journalists Novek describes challenge society's definitions of themselves as deviants with oppositional meanings that are rich in lived experience and self-expression. Perhaps more important, these writers defy the dehumanization that has been imposed on them by corrections institutions and value themselves as people with unique personalities, talents, and insights.

MOVING PAST THE RAZOR WIRE

It is our sincere hope that the multiple knowledges included in *Razor Wire Women* inspire people to think outside of the box when it comes to addressing issues around criminal justice. The incarceration of 2.3 million people does nothing to address the structural issues—such as racism, economic discrimination, sexism, and poverty—that are the root cause of crime and imprisonment. We are committed to a future world where prisons are not relied upon for social control and punishment, where social and economic resources are used for education, healthcare, jobs, housing, and community building rather than the destruction of entire groups of people. We envision a world where dignity and respect are fostered for all human beings and where alternatives to incarceration, such as transformative and restorative justice, dominate. Although this book focuses on women in prison, we also maintain that solidarity must be forged with men in prison—particularly black and Latino men, who make up a disproportionate number of prisoners—gender nonconforming prisoners, and immigrant prisoners and detainees, in the movement for alternatives to incarceration. Such solidarities are critical to a more just, sustainable, and healthy world.

REFERENCES

Boudin. Kathy. 1998. "Lessons from a Mother's Program in Prison: A Psychosocial Approach Supports Women and Their Children." In *Breaking the Rules: Women in Prison and Feminist Therapy,* ed. J. Harden and M. Hill, 103–26. New York: Harrington Park.

Boyd, Belle. 1865. *Belle Boyd in Camp and Prison.* New York: Blelock.

Cromwell, John, dir. 1950. *Caged.* Warner Brothers.

Cummins, Eric. 1994. *The Rise and Fall of California's Radical Prison Movement.* Palo Alto, CA: Stanford University Press.

Díaz-Cotto, Juanita. 2006. *Chicana Lives and Criminal Justice: Voices from El Barrio.* Texas: University of Texas Press.

Dodge, L. Mara. 2006. Whores *and Thieves of the Worst Kind: A Study of Women, Crime, and Prisons, 1835–2000.* DeKalb: Northern Illinois University Press.

Faith, Karlene. 1993. *Unruly Women: The Politics of Confinement and Resistance.* Vancouver: Press Gang.

Freedman, Estelle B. 1981. *Their Sister's Keepers: Women's Prison Reform in America, 1830–1930.* Ann Arbor: University of Michigan Press.

Girshick, Lori. 1999. *No Safe Haven: Stories of Women in Prison.* Boston: Northeastern University Press.

Harden, J., and M. Hill, eds. 1998. *Breaking the Rules: Women in Prison and Feminist Therapy.* New York: Harrington Park.

James, Joy. 2005. *The New Abolitionists: (Neo) Slave Narratives and Contemporary Prison Writings.* Albany: State University of New York Press.

Johnson, Paula C. 2003. *Inner Lives: Voices of African American Women in Prison.* New York and London: New York University Press.

Lamb, Wally, and the Women of York Correctional Institution. 2004. *Couldn't Keep It to Myself: Testimonies from Our Imprisoned Sisters.* New York: ReganBooks.

———. 2007. *I'll Fly Away: Further Testimonies from the Women of York Prison.* New York: HarperCollins.

Lawston, Jodie Michelle. 2008. "Women, the Criminal Justice System, and Incarceration: Processes of Power, Silence, and Resistance." *National Women's Studies Association Journal* 20, no. 2: 1–18.

Mauer, Marc, Cathy Potler, and Richard Wolf. 1999. "Gender and Justice: Women, Drugs and Sentencing Policy." Washington, DC: Sentencing Project.

Mumola, Christopher J. 2000. *Incarcerated Parents and Their Children.* Washington, DC: Bureau of Justice Statistics.

Owen, Barbara. 1998. *In The Mix: Struggle and Survival in a Women's Prison.* Albany: State University of New York Press.

Pollock, Joycelyn. 2002. *Women, Prison, and Crime.* 2nd ed. New York: Wadsworth.

Prison Creative Arts Project. 2009. http://www.lsa.umich.edu/english/pcap/. Retrieved on January 30, 2009.

Rafter, Nicole H. 1990. *Partial Justice: Women, Prisons, and Social Control.* New Brunswick, NJ: Transaction.

Resources for Community Change. 1975. "Women behind Bars: An Organizing Tool." Barnard Center for Research on Women. http://www.barnard.edu/bcrw/archive/prison.htm. Retrieved on January 15, 2009.

Reynolds, Marylee. 2008. "The War on Drugs, Prison Building, and Globalization: Catalysts for the Global Incarceration of Women." *National Women's Studies Association Journal* 20, no. 2: 72–95.

Richie, Beth. 1996. *Compelled to Crime: The Gender Entrapment of Battered Black Women.* New York: Routledge.

Robinson, F. W. 1864. *Memoirs of Jane Cameron, Female Convict.* London: Hurst and Blackett.

Schlesinger, Traci. 2008. "Equality at the Price of Justice." *National Women's Studies Association Journal* 20, no. 2: 27–47.

Solinger, Rickie, Paula C. Johnson, Martha Raimon, Tina Reynolds, and Ruby Tapia. 2009. *Interrupted Life: Experiences of Incarcerated Women in the United States.* Berkeley: University of California Press.

Sudbury, Julia, ed. 2005. *Global Lockdown: Race, Gender, and the Prison Industrial Complex.* New York and London: Routledge.

Talvi, Silja. 2007. *Women behind Bars: The Crisis of Women in the U.S. Prison System.* California: Seal.

Wise, Robert, dir. 1958. *I Want to Live.* Figaro.

Women and Prison: A Site for Resistance. 2009. http://womenandprison.org/. Retrieved on January 30, 2009.

section I

Girls, Women, and Families

Missing

Ricky A. Taylor

Missing was created with colored pencil and pastels. Its creation was conjured up from my mind to express a dysfunctional family when an element of the family is missing. It expresses—from a man's point of view—the sorrow, suffering, and pain that women go through when the man or father is missing from the family structure.

Not only does the picture of the family (man, woman, and child) seem to be missing a value, but the equity of the quality of life is missing. The woman is pushed into the roles (usually against her choosing) of man and woman, caretaker and provider, of tenderness and strength for the family.

The woman misses out of the life she had chosen or envisioned when she made the choice to lie with a man and produce another life. Her life is then altered. Future choices are directed by the choices of the man; whether he left her for another, fell on hard times, cannot cope with his life, or landed in prison, his choices caused one thing or another—thing after thing that goes MISSING.

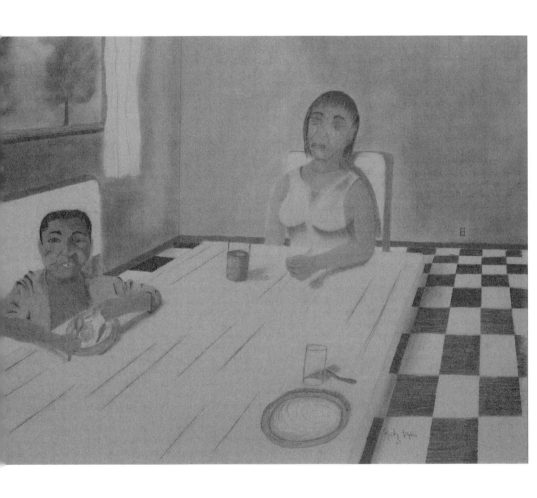

Historical Contextualization

Jodie Michelle Lawston

Although men have disproportionately experienced incarceration, prisons have nonetheless profoundly shaped and influenced the lives of girls, women, and families over the course of United States history. Much has been written, in particular, about girls and young women who were imprisoned during the midnineteenth century (Freedman 1981; Chesney-Lind 1989; Rafter 1990; Dodge 2006). The "crimes" of women were typically crimes against chastity (Freedman 1981), and girls' crimes were typically termed "immorality" and "waywardness" (Chesney-Lind 1989); girls were subject to gynecological exams to determine if they had engaged in sex. Both women and girls, then, were subject to a policing of their sexuality and their bodies. Women in particular were termed "fallen," and those who were unfortunate enough to receive this label were originally housed in separate wings of men's institutions. This often resulted in overcrowding, harsh treatment, and sexual abuse at the hands of male guards—conditions that continue in juvenile detention centers, prisons, and jails across the nation.

Although a growing movement of male reformers worked to "rehabilitate" criminalized men, they ignored the social problems associated with the imprisonment of women. Strong societal expectations and norms conceptualized women and girls as pure, innocent, docile creatures who had more to lose if they crossed, questioned, or resisted traditional gender boundaries. The "fallen woman" was framed by society as more degenerate than a criminalized male, and beyond help. With this mindset, male reformers refused to address the conditions of women's imprisonment and did little to nothing to alleviate the sexual violence that imprisoned women experienced.

According to Estelle Freedman (1981), the tables began to turn between 1840 and 1900. During these years, a movement of white, middle-class, educated, mostly Quaker women located in the Northeast and Indiana organized to ameliorate the conditions of women's incarceration. These women were particularly shocked by the environment in which "fallen women" were forced to live and worked to establish separate female institutions (Freedman 1981). As Freedman (1981) shows, these reformers followed the influence of Elizabeth Fry in England; they made the case that "fallen women" could be rehabilitated and sought to redefine the origins of women's and girls' crime as resulting from circumstances outside of their control, such as family issues, abuse, poverty, and even men, who were blamed for negatively influencing women.

Women's prison reform during this time period emphasized three principles: separate women's prisons, feminine care, and control over women's prisons by female staff (Freedman 1981, 46). These principles were the driving forces behind the creation of reformatories in Indiana, Massachusetts, and New York. Reformers argued that if under the care of female staff, the fallen woman would be reformed for domestic duties, learn to refrain from masculine activities such as alcohol consumption and use of profanities, and be taught to read and write (Freedman 1981; Pollock 2002). Interestingly, reformers stressed the importance of family and women's roles in the family. Although literature on this time period does not enumerate the effects of incarceration on the families and children of women prisoners, reformatories sometimes included nurseries where women could hold, and interact with, babies. The belief was that such activity would bring out women's domestic and maternal instincts, would prepare them for their future family life, and would rehabilitate them from their unruliness (Faith 1993). Of course, we are not privy to the voices of imprisoned women themselves during this time, so we have little knowledge of how they felt about these processes and how they conceptualized themselves, their experiences in reformatories, and their own lives.

Because there were only a handful of new reformatories, space was limited. More typical than not, those who were white and young and those who had committed misdemeanors were eligible to serve their time in a women's reformatory (Freedman 1981; Pollock 2002). The vast majority of women were forced to remain in custodial institutions; these women were overwhelmingly of color (especially black) and were confined to wings or separate buildings on the grounds of men's prisons (Pollock 2002). Prison reformers of the nineteenth century, then, did not take into consideration structural racism and economic discrimination, two forces that continue to serve as critical determining factors for *which groups of women and girls* get sent to prison, jail, or detention centers, and *which families suffer from the separation and pains of imprisonment*.

Although the effects of incarceration on girls, women, and families continued to be a serious issue from the nineteenth century onward, it did not gain significant attention again until the 1970s, when prison activists—from those who were reformist to those who were abolitionist—once again organized to draw attention to conditions in women's prisons. As section 2 of this book explains in the opening historical contextualization, women activists—both incarcerated and nonincarcerated—organized to improve healthcare in prisons, draw attention to institutional violence against imprisoned women, and suggest alternatives to incarceration. But it was not until after the rates of imprisonment skyrocketed in the 1980s that more attention was paid to incarcerated women and girls and, more recently, to the effects of imprisonment on families.

According to Mauer, Potler, and Wolf (1999), between 1980 and 1997, the women's prison population increased by 573 percent, in contrast to a 294 percent increase in the rate of incarceration for men. These rates have continued to climb, with women now constituting 7 percent of the prison population. Silja Talvi's work shows that more than 200,000 women are confined in U.S. prisons and jails, in addition to 94,000 women on parole and 958,000 women on probation. As is becoming common knowledge, close to 70 percent of these women are black, Latina, Native American and Asian American (Díaz-Cotto 2006; James 2005; Johnson 2003); most are also poor and working class. Concurrently with this "prison boom," the conditions in women's prisons have increasingly made headlines in newspapers across the nation, highlighting inadequate healthcare; physical, sexual, and psychological violence at the hands of correctional officers; prison overcrowding; and harsh sentencing laws such as Three Strikes, mandatory minimums, and sentencing enhancements, which are largely responsible for the significant increase in women's incarceration. Girls, too, have been affected: girls' commitments to juvenile facilities increased by 88 percent between 1991 and 2003, while boys' commitments increased by only 23 percent (Snyder and Sickmund 2006). Both scholars and activists increasingly concern themselves with the experiences of women and girls in prison and, importantly, the effects of incarceration on families and communities. Unlike organizational work that occurred around incarceration in the nineteenth century, at the center of contemporary analyses, activist work, and artistic work are the voices of imprisoned girls, women, and their families, who increasingly represent themselves and their own experiences and refuse the silencing effects of prison.

The following section of this book makes a significant contribution to the historical and contemporary literature on the effects of incarceration on girls, women, and families. The contributors to this section provide important insights into what it means to be an incarcerated woman or to be imprisoned as a young girl, offer vivid descriptions of the emotional pain that results from imprisonment and separation from families, and present analytical frames with which to understand the challenges of mothering from the inside. Taken together, these chapters urge us to consider the unique experiences of women and girls in prison and the families they leave behind and push us to rethink the U.S. reliance on incarceration as a means of social control.

REFERENCES

Chesney-Lind, Meda. 1989. "Girls' Crime and Women's Place: Toward a Feminist Model of Female Delinquency." *Crime and Delinquency* 35 (1): 5–29.

Diaz-Cotto, Juanita. 2006. *Chicana Lives and Criminal Justice: Voices from El Barrio.* Texas: University of Texas Press.

Dodge, L. Mara. 2006. *Whores and Thieves of the Worst Kind: A Study of Women, Crime, and Prisons, 1835–2000.* DeKalb: Northern Illinois University Press.

Faith, Karlene. 1993. *Unruly Women: The Politics of Confinement and Resistance.* Vancouver: Press Gang.

Freedman, Estelle B. 1981. *Their Sister's Keepers: Women's Prison Reform in America, 1830–1930.* Ann Arbor: University of Michigan Press.

James, Joy. 2005. *The New Abolitionists: (Neo) Slave Narratives and Contemporary Prison Writings.* Albany: State University of New York Press.

Johnson, Paula C. 2003. *Inner Lives: Voices of African American Women in Prison.* New York and London: New York University Press.

Mauer, Marc, Cathy Potler, and Richard Wolf. 1999. "Gender and Justice: Women, Drugs and Sentencing Policy." Washington, DC: Sentencing Project.

Pollock, Joycelyn. 2002. *Women, Prison, and Crime.* Wadsworth: Thomas Learning.

Rafter, Nicole H. 1990. *Partial Justice: Women, Prisons, and Social Control.* New Brunswick, NJ: Transaction.

Snyder, H. N., and M. Sickmund. 2006. *Juvenile Offenders and Victims: 2006 National Report* (NCJ 178257). Washington, DC: U.S. Department of Justice, Office of Justice Programs, Office of Juvenile Justice and Delinquency Prevention.

Talvi, Silja. 2007. *Women behind Bars: The Crisis of Women in the U.S. Prison System.* California: Seal.

CHAPTER TWO

The Voice of Silence

Je'Anna Redwood

In the darkness she remains, defiled and restrained. The pitch black surrounds her like a thick fog, while she waits for the ringing in her ears to stop. Her mind plays tricks on her as he swirls ghastly visions of the tyrant stalking toward her, introducing her to a new kind of pain. Silence is all she hears as she hugs her legs, trembling, alone, feeling the hot salty tears sting as they trickle down into the open gashes on her face. Her heart beats in time with the ticking of the clock outside the door. Dizzy from the recent tirade of erratic and explosive assaults, she tries to breathe. But even now, death seems a more welcome friend.

Questions dig their way to the surface, like a mole in search of food. Answers are what she needs, and nothing seems to make sense. *Why* is the only thing that keeps reverberating in her mind, while the haunting sound of his malicious laughter echoes back at her, taunting her, jeering at her to the point of exhaustion. The metallic taste of blood fills her mouth as she runs an engorged and lacerated tongue across her jagged and missing teeth. Searing pain of simply moving her tongue forces her to abort the inquisition abruptly, and she gags on the vile thought of how she must look. "Not so pretty now," the voice taunts her. She can only hang her head in silent agreement as the truth of his venomous words pound deep within her. Defeated.

As she struggles against the waves of nausea and fear, something else is trying to rise to the surface. Slowly, a new emotion creeps beneath the bile that is forming in her throat. Clawing its way, while seizing her heart, anger tries to break free. She gulps it down because she is afraid of what it will bring. She tries to scream, but that too is lost within the grip of fear. Alas, she is left gasping the thick, black, putrid air that burns her lungs.

Hope is diminished in an instant while she becomes invisible, fading into the nothingness of the closet she is locked in. The restraints are unyielding, and the gag on her mouth is a cruel form of torture. Its presence prevents her from spitting out the tooth fragments, bile, and blood, and she is forced into the humiliation of swallowing it.

Quickly, anger gives way to panic as it slams against her like a freight train. *How will she get out of this hell,* her mind screams. Will someone find her in time? Will she die alone in her closet of misery and shame? Fear spreads its tentacles and grips her heart, squeezing it and squelching the life out of her until the burning pain causes her to pass out.

Jerking awake, what seems like only moments later, she hears the sound of voices. Too muffled to make out words or distinguish who is talking, she struggles against the darkness to catch something familiar. Suddenly, the door bursts open, light chasing the darkness, momentarily blinding her. Startled, she cringes and cowers in the corner while trying not to cry out in protest. A hand reaches for her, and she jerks and scoots away, trying to shield herself as she anticipates the blows that are never delivered.

A soft voice filters through the chaos in her mind, "It's going to be alright. We won't hurt you." She looks up to meet the soft and genuine blue eyes of her hero. Shaking violently, she tries to wrap voice around reason, and finally succumbs to another hero's strong arms lifting her out of her dungeon.

Carefully the gag is removed, and the gasps that escape their lips confirm her own suspicions. *No one will want me now,* she thinks. She wanted to cry, but couldn't muster the strength that it took. The medic tenderly attended to the wounds on her tiny face and chest, as the restraints were cut away from her wrists and ankles. Her small hand clutches the strong hand of her blue-eyed hero, and as he lifts her onto his lap, she remembers the sound of his voice as she drifts into darkness.

While this is a personally true story, the glimmer of hope is the same for all of us survivors—the Voice of Silence really can be heard!

The sound of a voice can be melodic harmony that sings life or the chaotic, degrading screeching that holds you hostage of a fate worse than death . . . silence. Words of degradation seep into your soul like a toxic poison that causes a slow, malicious death. While the effects are subtle, they can be long lived.

Silence isn't golden. It polarizes you into a perpetual state of fear while it emasculates your strength and resolve down to its desired goal: death, death of the senses, spirit, emotions, and feelings. Silence renders you to the monster that rages against you. Combating the effects of silence is like trying to catch smoke. So how can we break free of the impending and life-threatening grip it holds us in? How do we shed the filthy skin of shame and guilt? How do we erase the vivid images that dance in our minds like mocking marionettes?

STAND! Ball your fists in protest! Cry those bitter tears, and scream with all of your might: "I DON'T DESERVE TO BE TREATED LIKE THIS!" Who will take a stand with me against the diabolical tyrant of gagging restraint?

Who will allow the healing to begin? The scars run deep inside us, and they need tending to. But how?

For me, after a while of sitting in the midst of the wreckage of my past, I began to gaze upon something that was oblivious to me before. Scattered about were others, like me, who were broken, battered, or considered the "walking wounded." Sure, we still had all of our appendages intact. There were no outward signs, save for the scowl that guarded our tender hearts or perhaps the sad look in the eyes of those less fortunate to effectively ward off the would be offender.

Yes, we're all here. From the weak and desperate, begging to be loved, to the proud and dying, yearning for a hand to hold. One by one, I search the faces for that "Been there, done that" tell tale sign. But we are proud, even in our pain. It took a good many years to finally figure out I was looking in the wrong place. I needed to look inside of the people, and the only way to identify with them was to identify me first. Who am I? The one society has labeled "murderer?" No, that's what I did. The question nags at the shores of my mind, as possible answers swirl around like an undercurrent beneath this hard exterior.

Slowly, I rise from the place that I sit in, brushing off the debris. I try desperately to rub off the odious stains of guilt and shame that cling to me like a second skin. With head hung low and downcast eyes, I gingerly navigate my way through the mess. I try avoid the hidden landmines of hopelessness, worthlessness, and perpetual failure, narrowly escaping the carnage they bring.

I look down and begin to pick up what I think is salvageable—a burned piece of truth, a shredded piece of tenderness, a charred particle of trust that is fused into a melted piece of love, a crumpled, soggy piece of courage, and a piece of strength so worn that it is almost unrecognizable.

One by one, I put them in my pockets for safe keeping. The ashes plume up with each step I take and are a reminder of life that once was. Somehow, in the destruction of it all, I find an invisible calm, and for the moment, I know I'll be alright.

And I stand, my heart screaming in anguished silence, my fists balled tightly at my sides. Through the streaming tears, my heart beats wildly and I cry again.

Stand! Yes, rise. For in numbers there is strength that no one can tear down. Take my hand; let's walk side by side to march against the enemy that has tried to silence us. Let your voice be heard!

CHAPTER THREE

Doing Time in Detention Home:
Gendered Punishment Regimes in Youth Jails

Brian Bilsky and Meda Chesney-Lind

Girls now account for nearly one-third (29.1 percent) of juvenile arrests (FBI 2007). This is a remarkable shift from decades earlier when girls accounted for only about one in five juvenile arrests (Chesney-Lind and Shelden 2003). Moreover, girls are increasingly being arrested for crimes of violence, not necessarily because they have become more violent, but because their disputes (often with family members) are likely to be labeled as simple assaults rather than traditional status offenses (Chesney-Lind and Irwin 2007).

The relabeling and "upcriming" of girls' delinquency has also had a dramatic and negative effect on girls' detention trends, undoing decades of "de-institutionalization" efforts. Between 1991 and 2003, girls' detentions rose by 98 percent compared to a 29 percent increase seen in boys' detentions. And despite the hype about violent girls, it was relatively minor offenses that actually kept girls in detention. Thirty-nine percent of all girls in detention in the United States in 2003 were being held for either a status offense or a "technical violation" of the conditions of their probation, compared to only 25 percent of the boys (Snyder and Sickmund 2006). Girls being detained for "violent" offenses were far more likely than boys to be held on "other person" offenses such as simple assault (as opposed to more serious, part 1 violent offenses such aggravated assault, robbery, and murder). Over half (51.8 percent) of the girls but less than one-third of the boys in detention (31.2 percent) were held for these minor forms of violence (Snyder and Sickmund 2006, 210).

Research on detained youth in St. Louis suggests even more directly that girls were more likely than boys to be detained in nonserious cases. The researchers examined the detention decisions involved in serious (violent felonies) and nonserious cases (status offenses and misdemeanors) and found that even after controlling for factors such as criminal history, girls were nearly twice as likely as their male counterparts to receive detention in nonserious cases (McGuire 2002). A study of youth detained in Cook County added some other important information and perspective to these findings. Researchers found that while both boys' and girls' detention rates were about the same (41 percent), the reasons for the detention differed. Specifically, girls were being detained "as a result of their family situations" (often either "domestic violence" or "parents refusing to take the girl home"), while boys were being detained because of the "seriousness of the offense" (Sherman 2005, 34).

As increasing numbers of girls are being arrested and detained (often for very minor offenses), attention must again turn to the conditions of confinement in youth detention centers. In truth, concerns about the purpose of youthful confinement, as well as periodic scandals regarding the abuse of youth held in these settings, emerged from the very beginning of the juvenile justice system. These debates also dominated juvenile justice in the last century (see Chesney-Lind and Shelden 2003), and as this chapter will document, remain a concern in the twenty-first century.

BRIEF HISTORY OF JUVENILE INCARCERATION IN THE UNITED STATES

The first juvenile reform facility in the United States was the New York House of Refuge, officially opening January 1, 1825. A product of the American elite's reaction to a rising tide of immigration, the New York House of Refuge, among others that were quickly established in Boston (1826), Philadelphia (1828), and Baltimore (1830), helped to ultimately shape our understanding of both delinquency and the core official response to youthful misbehavior, resulting in the juvenile custodial institution (Bremner 1970, 1: 678–82). The bill that established the New York House of Refuge included the first statutory definition of "juvenile delinquency" and contained vague descriptions of those subject to official intervention and commitment to the New York House of Refuge. Being "homeless," coming from an "unfit" home, and lacking a "good home and family" were examples (Hawes 1971, 33). Important here is the fact that children committed to the House of Refuge (and others to follow) never committed an actual crime; they were deemed "incorrigible" or "beyond control." Most were living under conditions that those in authority deemed "unwholesome" or likely to lead to delinquency and criminality. The goals of the founders of the refuge movement were to identify potential delinquents, isolate them, and then "reform" them.

Predictably, only one of the seventy-three wards admitted to the New York House of Refuge in the first year had been convicted of a serious crime: grand larceny. Nine were for petty larceny, "and the remaining sixty-three (88 percent) were in the House for vagrancy, stealing, and absconding from the Almshouse"

(Fox 1970, 1192). After a century of growth, three relocations, different managers and techniques, and public dissatisfaction, the Refuge finally closed. In 1901 there were charges of a "chamber of horrors" and a "barbaric prison colony," while an external investigation made "charges of brutality" (Pickett 1969, 271). Efforts at reform backfired, and critics charged that rather than preventing crime, the youth placed in these facilities "invariably later entered either the City Penitentiary on Blackwell's Island or the New York State Prison" (Pickett 1969, 181).

Significantly, the earliest court challenge to the refuge movement involved a young girl. Filed in 1838, *Ex Parte Crouse* arose from a petition of habeas corpus filed by the father of a minor, Mary Ann Crouse. Without her father's knowledge, Crouse had been committed to the Philadelphia House of Refuge by her mother on the grounds that she was "incorrigible." Her father argued that the incarceration was illegal because she had not been given a jury trial. The justices of the Supreme Court of Pennsylvania rejected the appeal, saying that the Bill of Rights did not apply to juveniles.

The ruling assumed that the Philadelphia House of Refuge (and presumably all other houses of refuge) had a beneficial effect on its residents. It "is not a prison, but a school," and because of this, not subject to procedural constraints (Sutton 1992, 11). Further, the aims of such an institution were to reform the youngsters within them "by training . . . [them] to industry; by imbuing their minds with the principles of morality and religion; by furnishing them with means to earn a living; and above all, by separating them from the corrupting influences of improper associates" (Pisciotta 1982, 411).

What evidence did the justices consult to support their conclusion that the House of Refuge was not a prison but a school? Sadly, only testimony by those who managed the institution had been solicited. However, a more objective review of the treatment of youths housed in these places might have led the justices to a very different conclusion. For instance, Pisciotta (1982) found that there was an enormous amount of abuse within these institutions. They were run according to a strict military regimen in which corporal punishment (girls in one institution were "ducked" under water and boys were hung by their thumbs), solitary confinement, and a "silent system" were part of the routine. Work training was practically nonexistent, and outside companies contracted for cheap inmate labor. Religious instruction was often little more than Protestant indoctrination (many of the youngsters were Catholic). Education, in the conventional meaning of the word, was almost nonexistent.

Reporting on the dynamics in total institutions, Goffman (1961) examined social life in mental hospitals and prisons and their "initial effects of *institutionalization* on the social relationships individuals possessed before becoming inmates" (Goffman 1961, xiv). Goffman found that total institutions serve to preserve predictable and regular behavior of both wards and their guards, a ritual function of "institutionalizing" both classes so they know their social role and function. Decades later, Foucault (1995) would trace the genealogy of the modern Western prison, and like Goffman's concept of institutionalization, found the prison cannot help but create delinquents, new knowledge about delinquents, and more rationale for surveillance. "The carceral system combines in a single figure discourse and architectures, . . . *programmes for correcting delinquents and mechanisms that reinforce delinquency*" (Foucault 1995, 255).

Concern about the appropriateness of institutionalization of noncriminal youth was at the heart of the Juvenile Justice and Delinquency Prevention Act of 1974, which provided federal grant money to states that would comply with four core requirements: (1) The *deinstitutionalization of status offenders*; (2) The separation of juvenile and adult offenders; (3) The removal of juveniles from adult jails; (4) The *reduction of disproportionate minority contact*. As this chapter will document, issues around race and gender, as well as the purposes of detention, continue to haunt the juvenile justice system. This is particularly the case since juvenile and family court judges seem extremely reluctant to give up the ability to incarcerate noncriminal youth. Over the decades, judges and other personnel in the juvenile justice system have devised legal maneuvers (like their effort in 1980 modifying the JD Act to allow for the imprisonment of youth who violated "valid court orders") to subvert the original intent of the JD Act (Arthur 2008). As a result, the number of petitioned status offense cases more than doubled from 1985 to 2004 (Puzzanchera 2007, 2). By 2001, status offenders and youth held on technical probation violations still made up roughly one-third of all youth in secure detention (Austin, Johnson, and Weitzer 2005). And as noted earlier, more recently, there has been the tendency to relabel girls' (and some boys') arguments with their parents, as well as their minor fights in schools, as "assaults," similarly permitting youth detention (Chesney-Lind 2004).

A focus on the conditions of confinement in the nation's detention centers is again appropriate, particularly since as this section has noted, the numbers of girls, and to a lesser extent boys, in these facilities is rising steeply.

HAWAI'I'S DETENTION CENTER

Like many youth facilities around the country, Honolulu's Youth Detention Center, Hale Ho'omalu, has been a source of controversy for decades (Altonn 1979). The facility is actually part of the Family Court, First Circuit, but it is the only detention facility in the state so it actually houses youth from all four counties. In recent years, Family Court has sought the assistance of outside agencies (including the National Juvenile Detention Association (NJDA)) to assess the facility, the most recent of which was quite critical for the drop in resident perceptions of safety, failure to stop resident-on-resident assaults, and abusive behavior by staff (mostly among boys) (Rousch 2007). In response, the court sought to involve the facility in the Annie E. Casey Foundation's Juvenile Detention Alternatives Initiative (JDAI). After initial political resistance and mixed success, JDAI has spread across the country with roughly one hundred sites operating in twenty-four states and the District of Columbia (Annie E.

Casey Foundation 1997). According to the Casey Foundation, the core objectives of JDAI are to:

1. Eliminate the inappropriate or unnecessary use of secure detention;
2. Minimize rearrest and failure-to-appear rates pending adjudication;
3. Ensure appropriate conditions of confinement in secure facilities;
4. Redirect public finances to sustain successful reforms; and
5. Reduce racial and ethnic disparities.

JDAI has since been recognized for its success in sharply reducing detaining the numbers of youth awaiting detention hearings, reducing youth detention facility populations (which in turn improves the safety of those who are confined), and significantly reducing the number of youth sentenced to youth correctional facilities and other residential programs. A small number of sites have even begun to have success in reducing racial and ethnic disparities in sentencing rates. JDAI is considered by many to be the national standard for juvenile detention, the critical first stage of the juvenile justice system (Mendel 2009).

Hawai'i became an official JDAI site in 2008, and the JDAI self-assessment is the first stage of the detention reform program. The data for this study were collected during this assessment process, specifically in the area of "training and supervision of employees," "restraints, isolation, due process, and grievances," and "safety."[1] Other assessment teams focused on: "classification system and intake," "health care," "access issues," "programming," and "education." We also had access to the reports of these subcommittees, which were aggregated to direct the corrective action plan following assessment.

METHODOLOGY

As part of the JDAI assessment, we systematically reviewed all 32 grievances filed between June 6, 2007, and January 31, 2009 (the total number of grievances made available to the JDAI team). The grievances were coded to note gender and age of grievant, date of grievance, substance of grievance, and outcome of grievance. We reviewed and coded a random sample of incident reports. The incident reports were collected by month in thick binders. We selected six seven-day periods in each of the months submitted to our committee for review; each weekly period was selected in a different portion of the month reviewed so as to vary the time of month reviewed (August 2008 to January 2009). This resulted in a sample of 204 incidents involving 255 youth. We coded incidents by date, type of incident or grievance, number of youth involved, gender of the youth(s) involved, age when available, types of sanctions when applicable, and finally we recorded all pertinent details of the incidents.[2]

As per JDAI guidelines we also reviewed a large number of documents, including but not limited to policies and procedures and any posted materials around training and supervision, restraints, disciplinary due process, room confinement, isolation, grievance policy, and safety; audits, inspections, or accreditation reports of inspections; discipline/due process reports for individual youth pertaining to incidents of use of physical force, restraints, or isolation; orientation materials given to youth; living unit logbooks with respect to misbehavior and discipline or punishment imposed; room check sheets for youth in room confinement or other mechanism for documenting room checks; incident reports, grievances, workers' compensation claims, child abuse reports, and citizen complaints for a period of at least six months; statistical compilations on violence, use of force, restraints and isolation for a period of at least six months; medical records indicating injuries to youth and staff. Facility staff were also available to clarify these materials, and based on this review, we have also included information from one interview with an adult male-to-female transgender person who was previously detained at DH (which will be part of a larger study of youth experiences of the facility).[3]

FINDINGS

Hawai'i's detention facility (hereafter DH) is a deteriorated structure built in 1944 that is located in downtown Honolulu. It is due to be replaced by a new facility located on the west side of the island of Oahu, where Honolulu is located. DH is still housing a large number of youth charged with running away, despite decades of both national and local efforts at the "deinsitutionalization" of youth charged with these offenses. Admission records for second quarter 2008 show a full 34 percent of youth were admitted for running away from home. While juvenile arrests in the state decreased by over 16 percent from 1998 to 2007, runaway arrests increased 6.7 percent (Department of the Attorney General 2008).

Besides runaway offenders, the use of "criminal contempt of court" is a common way of relabeling a status offense to a criminal act. Also, it is likely that "abuse of family member" involves youths and parents in tussles, which result in the youth's arrest (Buzawa and Hirschel 2010). Table 3.1 shows how these three mostly noncriminal behaviors represent the majority (52 percent) of admissions to DH. A variety of charges such as truancy, curfew, incorrigibility, and other traditional status offenses make up most of the "other" category and only increase the number of noncriminal offenders crowding the detention home.

Admission data reveal patterns of detention that were both gendered and racialized, consistent with national trends. Boys had higher rates of admission for assaults and theft and a much more diverse list of other offenses that resulted in their detention. Girls meanwhile had a much higher rate of detention for noncriminal activity, notably runaway.[4] Over half of the girls (56 percent) at DH were admitted for running away, while only 20 percent of the boys were held for this offense (see table 3.1). This means that although girls made up just 37 percent of all DH admissions, they made up fully 61 percent of runaway admissions (See chart 3.2). Girls are also detained for running away at a higher

TABLE 3.1. Detention Home Admissions by Offense and Gender, January 1 through March 31, 2008.

OFFENSE/CHARGE	FEMALES	PERCENT FEMALES	MALES	PERCENT MALES	PERCENT AT DH
RUNAWAY	54	56%	35	20%	33%
CRIMINAL CONTEMPT OF COURT	10	10%	12	7%	8%
ABUSE OF FAMILY MEMBER	7	7%	23	13%	11%
ASSAULT	3	3%	13	7%	6%
THEFT/ROBBERY	5	5%	14	8%	7%
OTHER	6	6%	33	19%	14%
NO CHARGE LISTED	11	11%	45	26%	21%
TOTAL	96		175		

Source: Statistics Pertaining to Juvenile Admissions to Hale Ho'omalu

rate than their rate of arrest for the same offense (47% compared to 56%, See Chart 3.1) (Fuatagavi and Perrone 2009, 109).

Second, only 7 percent of youth detained were Caucasian, whereas 18 percent of youth in Hawai'i are white (See charts 3.3 and 3.4). And while a wide diversity of nonwhite youth can be seen in the DH population, over half (52 percent) of detained youth were Hawaiian or part Hawaiian, far greater than the 30 percent of the state of Hawai'i's youth they represent. (See charts 3.3

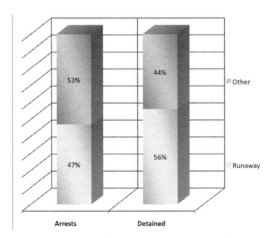

CHART 3.1. Runaway Arrests and Detention Rates for Girls, 2008
Crime in Hawai'i 2008, Attorney General & Statistics Pertaining to Admissions to Hale Ho'omalu

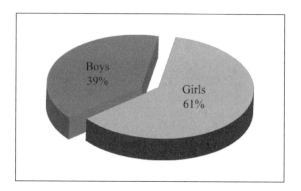

CHART 3.2. Detention Home Admissions by Gender, State of Hawai'i, 2008
Source: Statistics Pertaining to Admissions to Hale Ho'omalu

and 3.4) (Amimito and Kamimura 2009; Hawai'i Department of Health, Office
of Health Status Monitoring 2005). Moreover, the gender disparity was greater
among the girls than the boys; 58 percent of girls and 49 percent of boys were
Hawaiian or part Hawaiian.

A review of the DH classification system and intake processes found that
while intake and classification related policies do exist, actual practices vary by
staff, day, and shift. The team reported that police need clarity as to which
youth should be brought to DH, since youth who do not meet DH criteria for
detention are routinely admitted on weekends to hold until their hearings the
next business day. And a lack of alternative options for youth with severe mental
health issues, alcohol or drug-intoxicated youth, or youth with disabilities poses
a real problem (Matsuoka and Hawai'i JDAI Subcommittee 2009).

Particularly troubling are the number of youth in detention for more than
ten straight days and some for more than thirty days. Admission records showed
a full 27 percent of youth stayed at DH for more than ten days—5 percent more
than thirty days. Percentages were nearly identical for boys and girls, though we
already know girls were admitted at much higher rates for noncriminal behavior
(Amimito and Kamimura 2009). Therefore, girls are spending lengthy periods
in detention for less serious offenses than their male counterparts.

A systematic review of incident reports and grievances supplies an impor-
tant perspective on the conditions of confinement of these youth. Virtually all
the incident reports were written by staff and signed off by supervisors, usually
the facility administrator, for the purpose of punishing the youth or youths
involved in the incident. "Work detail" and "isolation" are routinely given as
punishment with the occasional "wall" sit for boys or "red chair" for girls. Work
detail consists of menial "make work" chores such as taking out garbage, wiping
down surfaces, sweeping the floor, cleaning the kitchen, and the like (we did
find that the girls clean the kitchen every morning regardless of their behavior or

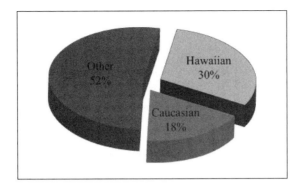

CHART 3.3. Ethnic Distribution, Youth, State of Hawai'i, 2005, 31
Source: Hawai'i State Department of Health

track record). Our team's review also found that "isolation" at DH is routinely conflated with "room confinement." The "wall" and "red chair" are where boys or girls are told to sit still and quiet, forbidden to communicate with anyone in the room or surrounding area. There is also no communication allowed during work detail or isolation. There are only certain hours during the day that count toward isolation or when work detail can be done, so eight hours of either can take two to three days to complete.

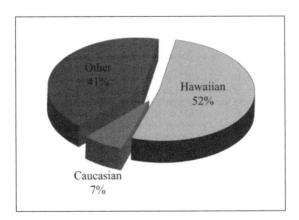

CHART 3.4. Ethnic Distribution, Detention Home Admissions, January 1 through March 2008
Source: Statistics Pertaining to Admissions to Hale Ho'omalu

Eight hours of work detail is by far the most common punishment followed by the same for isolation (See charts 3.5 and 3.6). Eight hours of work detail are given to boys for talking when they are supposed to be quiet, "shadow boxing" while playing basketball, or very often for looking out their dorm windows

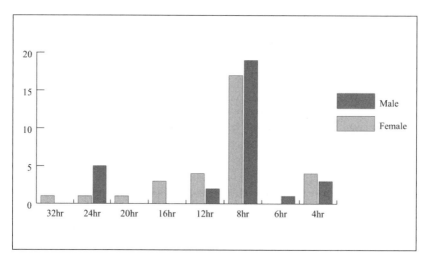

CHART 3.5. Length of Work Detail Sanctions by Gender

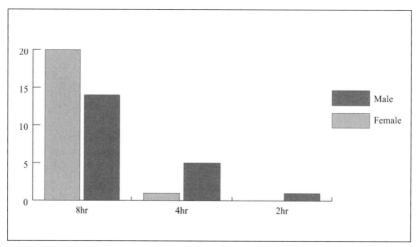

CHART 3.6. Length of Isolation Sanctions by Gender

during isolation (which is apparently prohibited). Boys are punished with work detail and isolation as a result of roughhousing, tough talk to each other or to staff, and fighting. Of the twenty-two aggressive behavior incidents (nine fights, five horseplay, and seven threats to staff or other wards), only three involved girls (one horseplay and two threats to other wards; see table 3.2).

Girls at DH, because of limited space, lack any recreational physical activity to break up their day and often spend long periods on "mats" on the floor with no books or reading material. Perhaps as a consequence, while girls only made up 37 percent of admissions reviewed, they were the subject of 60.61 percent of those involved in written "incidents" in our sample (See table 3.2). Girls accumulated eight hours of work detail for things such as "wetting their hair in the bathroom after a warning not to," for talking when they were supposed to remain quiet, for writing their names and boyfriends' names on walls, and most often for arguing with staff over rules and conditions. They also made many more requests for medical attention than did boys (75 percent of requests for medical attention came from girls).

One girl was given four hours of work detail for putting something in her ear, "just to keep my ear piercing open." Two female wards were given eight hours of work detail and required to write essays on obeying staff after saying "goodbye" and "good luck" to another ward leaving for the dentist, after both wards were repeatedly warned to remain quiet. Another female was given sixteen hours of work detail after admitting she carved her name in the wall. The incident reports are filled with such examples, and there is little evidence of any

TABLE 3.2. Incident Report Types by Gender

	TOTAL IDENTIFIABLE*	FEMALE	PERCENT	MALE	PERCENT
TOTAL INCIDENTS:	198	120	60.61%	78	39.39%
SUICIDAL	9	7	77.78%	2	22.22%
SELF-MUTILATION	4	4	100.00%	0	0.00%
ARGUE WITH STAFF	24	18	75.00%	6	25.00%
TALKING/MAKING NOISE	19	11	57.89%	8	42.11%
MEDICAL/SICK	34	25	73.53%	9	26.47%
FIGHTING/ASSAULT	9	1	11.11%	8	88.89%
THREATS/ARGUMENTS	12	4	33.33%	8	66.67%
HORSEPLAY	8	1	12.50%	7	87.50%
TEASING	2	0	0.00%	2	100.00%

*Incidents where a male(s) or female(s) was involved and sanctions were identifiable

graduated punishment scheme or opportunities for positive reinforcement for good behavior (despite the institution reporting the existence of such a system).

One girl was given eight hours of isolation when during admission, she was found to have four cigarettes in the menstrual pad she was wearing after having told staff she had nothing. Staff called the police for a possible "contraband" charge, though they were told it is not contraband when found during admission. This incident is representative of a punitive philosophy that was much in evidence in the review of the incident reports. Police were routinely called to the facility so as to add charges (frequently "criminal property damage" for etching on the facilities' walls), despite the obviously deteriorated and poorly maintained nature of the facility's exterior and interior surfaces.

Another major trend at DH was that youth were punished for not following DH rules accompanying their existing punishments. Punishment battles ensued with youth collecting even more penalties for noncompliance. These were common on both sides though again, particularly acute for the girls.

One girl was given four hours of isolation for refusing her present work detail and awaiting reassignment. Another girl was given eight hours of isolation in addition to her already accumulated twenty-nine hours of work detail after complaining that she'd never be able to work them off. And yet another female, already in isolation, was given eight additional hours of isolation *and* sixteen hours of work detail for the second marking of her name on a partition wall.

These findings are reminiscent of a study of disciplinary practices for men and women in Texas prisons that found that not only were women far more likely to receive citations than men, but they were reprimanded for different offenses (and mostly trivial at that) and received harsher punishments. The "violation of posted rules" were the most common citation for women and included such offenses as "excessive artwork ('too many family photographs on display'), failing to eat all the food on their plates, and for talking while waiting in the pill line." Contraband citations included an extra bra or pillowcase and even a correctly borrowed comb or hat (McClellan 1994).

Also prevalent at DH on the girls' side were suicide threats and attempts and self-mutilation. Of the fourteen suicidal or self-mutilation incidents only two were from boys. One boy, who after receiving twenty-four hours of work detail and eight hours of isolation for fighting, admitted he was repeatedly picked on for being white and for his big ears. He went on to claim he felt suicidal. The other boy, prior to walking into a courtroom for sentencing, said he wanted to kill himself.

The girls meanwhile had multiple instances of actual self-mutilation and possible suicide attempts. One girl was found bleeding and scratched up. She had cut herself with a small piece of glass because she missed her boyfriend. Another female detainee was found in isolation having repeatedly tried to harm herself. She had tried to choke herself with her socks, her t-shirt, and finally a torn strip of cloth from her sheet. Her neck, legs, and arms were all red when they found her. Another girl threatened to kill herself after the court refused her permission to see her forty-four-year-old boyfriend. The threat was serious as a staff member noted that the girl had a history of hurting herself and cutting her arms.

There were far fewer grievances to review, just thirty-two extending over an eighteen-month period. This suggests the grievance policy is under-used. Perhaps one reason youth rarely access the grievance system is the fact that very few of these were decided in the youth's favor. Only two grievances filed by youth (6.3 percent) were sustained, while in three other cases, the outcomes were unclear. For example, the administrator "denied" the complaint but then went on to request that staff change their behavior. This means that 84.4 percent of the time, youth grievances were denied.

Grievances ranged from the trivial to the serious. There is a lot of dissatisfaction by youth with seemingly arbitrary and unreasonable levels of punishment over trivial matters. Also prevalent were complaints of staff mistreatment, two of which were sustained. Girls complained of being "hit with thrown shoes by staff," of staff throwing "a piece of toilet paper" at a girl in isolation, and once, after repeated pleas for access to the bathroom, a girl being called an "ugly child." One boy felt threatened after learning that an uncle said to others he would beat up the ward if he found him on the outside, while another complained that after being told to "fucking go to my fucking room" and heading there, he turned to see the same uncle "making a masturbating gesture," telling the ward to "go jerk off."

Documents reviewed by our team also suggested more sinister problems, notably staff-on-youth violence, staff use of profanity and racial slurs, threats to wards and their families, youth being slammed into walls when taken to isolation, and violence at the "back lockers" (Rousch 2007; Nelsen and Griffs 2004). An interview with a male-to-female transgender adult previously detained at DH as a minor confirmed one alarming instance of staff violence. While being held on the boys' side (arrested for running away and incarcerated for over a year) she witnessed a staff member attack and beat up another transgender youth in her cell because of that youth's gender identity and sexual orientation. She said male guards "always intimidate mahus or gay people."[5] Our committee review of incident reports and grievances found another male-to-female transgender youth reporting sexual harassment for her sexual identity by both youth *and* staff. Although a memo went out to staff from the facility administrator to stop the harassment, the youth in question was never informed that anything had been done. Instead she continued to use self time-outs to isolate herself from the community. Gendered disparities in confinement appear to be more severe for transgendered or queer youth, a pattern also seen at the Hawai'i Youth Correctional Center (ACLU Hawai'i 2006).

Our review of the other teams' assessments reveals a lack of programming, both educational and activities based, at DH. While the education team found well-intentioned teachers and youth interviewed spoke highly of them, they also noted an absence of gender responsive and culturally informed programming (Matsuoka and Hawai'i JDAI Subcommittee 2009).

Hawai'i Board of Education (HBOE) policy 4160 requires a six-hour school day; no less than thirty hours distributed over a five-day week (360 minutes per day). DH requires youth to attend a mere 135 minutes, or about one-third of the HBOE standard, each day, though students who choose physical education in the morning may actually attend only ninety minutes of instruction in core academic subjects throughout the day. Afternoon instruction was, at the time of the assessment, optional, and many youth opted out. Additionally, the Individuals with Disabilities Education Act (IDEA) Part B mandates educational services and supports in accordance with each student's Individual Education Plan (IEP). The low required classroom time at DH makes it nearly impossible to meet the federal mandates of IDEA (Matsuoka and Hawai'i JDAI Subcommittee 2009).

Aside from only 135 mandatory minutes of school each day, DH suffers from a lack of activities programming as well. The team that reviewed programming at the facility found youth spending far too much time simply sitting in boredom, often in silence. The teams found this especially acute on the girls' side where there were virtually no recreational opportunities for large muscle exercise or access to the outdoors. The boys meanwhile have an open courtyard with a basketball court. Girls have access to the boys' basketball court/courtyard only on certain days, staff levels permitting, and complain of boredom and jealousy over the boys' physical activity. Moreover, after breakfast, while the boys attend a silent reading program, girls must clean the dishes and the kitchen where breakfast was prepared. Recall that, at DH, kitchen cleaning later in the day is used as punishment through work detail, but here considered routine morning duties for the girls.

The team that reviewed classification and intake systems found intake form questions poorly written and insufficient to gain vital details from youth necessary for accurate diagnoses. And due to the lack of detention alternatives, youth with serious mental health issues, as well as alcohol and drug-intoxicated youth, were frequently wrongfully admitted. These problems were particularly acute on the weekends. Therefore, potentially misdiagnosed youth and youth in need of services other than confinement (and quite often with conditions and symptoms that confinement will only exacerbate), find themselves trying to navigate this terrain and expected to remain obedient.

To illustrate how dangerous and counterproductive incarceration of misdiagnosed youth can be, consider this study from 2000 of girls held in detention in Philadelphia: The Female Detention Project found that 81 percent of girls studied reported being subject to some sort of trauma, that is, sexual or physical abuse, witnessing violence and abandonment. Despite the fact that "many of the girls reported symptoms that are characteristic of Post-Traumatic Stress Disorder," the girls were diagnosed with "Oppositional Defiant Disorder." Although ODD is "characterized by a persistent pattern of negativistic, hostile, disobedient and defiant—but not violent—behavior," most girls were incarcerated for assaults, often school related. Due to the misdiagnoses, these girls were missing out on specific treatments that could address their PTSD (Ambrose, Simpkins, and Levick 2000).

CONCLUSION

This study reveals a youth detention system that still houses large numbers of youth who have been arrested for status offenses, notably runaways, despite decades of efforts both nationally and locally to prevent this occurrence. Girls are clearly over-represented among the youth held for this offense. Native Hawaiian youth are dramatically overrepresented among those detained at the state's only youth jail again despite decades of focus on "disproportionate minority confinement."

In the facility, it is clear that youth in detention in Hawai'i are systematically exposed to punitive gender regimes despite official facility policies to the contrary. Harsh punishment over mostly trivial matters is particularly acute on the girls' "side" where facility structure and practices insist on domestic duties and hours of boredom sitting on the floor often with no access to reading material. Girls are frequently subjected to long hours of isolation and work detail for extremely minor infractions, often growing out of these institutional requirements for silence and inactivity. Girls are also exhibiting clear evidence of depression and PTSD with suicide threats and attempts and self-mutilation. For boys, horseplay, obscenity, violence, and threats of violence from other boys dominate their detention experience.

From the lack of curriculum resources and failing classroom technology to noncompliance with different state and federal statutes, this facility clearly makes only a token effort to educate the youths it houses. Simply put, the facility is not designed or staffed to deliver the many educational needs and challenges of youth in confinement, many of which are required by law.

Combine the lack of programming, a lack of educational services, poor intake screening and practices, and limited mental health services, and one has some sense of why the poorly trained staff resort to almost medieval forms of punishment to control youth. Formally written policies and procedures are woefully lacking, and training is spotty, unattended, and instead mostly "on the job." Taken together and inside the purely custodial design of the facility, youth have little to respond to or focus on except their boredom, their plight, each other, and staff.

Ultimately, all these children suffer from the failure of adults to deliver what the juvenile justice system promised youth roughly two centuries ago when it began locking them up. Youth are crowded in institutions that have virtually no meaningful educational or programming and mental health services. Bored and subjected to elaborate and gendered punishment regimes, they are sanctioned when they fail to comply with often arbitrary staff demands and then often further penalized when they protest their harsh punishments.

JJDPA, most recently authorized in 2002, requires that states develop plans for providing "needed gender-specific services for the prevention and treatment of juvenile delinquency" and denotes a category of funding for "programs that focus on the needs of young girls at risk of delinquency or status offenses" (Sharp and Simon 2004). And one of JJDPA's original core requirements in 1974 and in each reauthorization since has been the reduction of disproportionate minority representation. Despite these initiatives, in Hawai'i, large numbers of Native Hawaiian girls face double disadvantage when it comes to detention. They are doing time in abusive institutions while the system that holds them employs glowing rhetoric to justify their jailing. Whether it is focus on "schools" aiming to "reform" the youth through training from centuries past or today's focus on "protection" of girls from the dangers of the streets, the results of carceral impulse within juvenile justice are distressingly similar: large numbers of youth, particularly girls from marginalized communities, are forced to spend time in arbitrary, harsh, and abusive juvenile jails.

NOTES

1. Our team was made up of Meda Chesney-Lind, PhD, professor of women's studies; Attorney Martha T. Torney, executive director of Hawai'i's Department of Human Services Office of Youth Services; Attorney Laurie A. Temple of ACLU Hawai'i; and Brian Bilsky, a graduate student of political science and women's studies at the University of Hawai'i at Manoa.

2. This research design sought and received IRB approval from the University of Hawai'i Committee on Human Subjects by Meda Chesney-Lind, who gathered the data.

3. Brian Bilsky sought and received IRB approval from the University of Hawai'i Committee on Human Subjects for interviews of adults previously detained at DH. Also requested but not delivered, as they are confidential, were personnel files. Video recordings of incidents of use of physical force, restraints, or isolation were also unavailable. We were told that cameras do not pick up much because of their limited placement in this very old facility and that what footage does exist is barely decipherable due to very old and broken cameras.

4. Hawai'i juvenile court judges would be quick to point out that they are able to detain a youth who ran either from home or placement because the youth had an underlying criminal offense somewhere in his or her record. This device, like a "violation of a valid court order," which the courts in Hawai'i also use, is a common technique to permit the incarceration of youth who are arrested for status offenses.

5. *Mahu* is the Hawaiian word for homosexual or transgendered person.

REFERENCES

ACLU Hawai'i. 2006. "Hawai'i Youth Correctional Facility to Pay over Half a Million Dollars for 'Relentless Campaign of Harassment' of Gay and Transgender Youth: Settlement Reached in ACLU Federal Lawsuit on Youths' Behalf." June 15. http://www.acluhawaii.org/index.php?id=234.

Altonn, H. 1979. "Child Detention Facility Need Studied." *Honolulu Star-Bulletin*, November 5.

Ambrose, A. M., S. Simpkins, and M. Levick. 2000. "The Prevention Researcher: The Female Detention Project: The Typical Girl in Detention in Philadelphia." http://www.tpronline.org/article.cfm/The_Female_Detention_Project__The_Typical_Girl_in_Detention_in_Philadelphia.

Amimito, Garrett, and Janis Kamimura. 2009. "Statistics Pertaining to Juvenile Admissions to Hale Ho'omalu." March 20.

Annie E. Casey Foundation. 1997. Juvenile Detention Alternatives Initiative. *The Annie E. Casey Foundation.* http://www.aecf.org/MajorInitiatives/JuvenileDetentionAlternativesInitiative.aspx.

Arthur, Pat. 2008. "The Incarceration of Status Offenders under the Valid Court Order Exception to the Juvenile Justice and Delinquency Prevention Act." June 18. www.youthlaw.org/.../ncyl/.../Homeless_Youth_Presentation_2_.pdf.

Austin, James, Kelly D. Johnson, and R. Weitzer. 2005. "Alternatives to Secure Detention and Confinement of Juvenile Offenders." U.S. Department of Justice, Office of the Juvenile Justice and Delinquency Prevention, September.

Bremner, R. H. 1970. *Children and Youth in America: A Documentary History.* Vol. 1. 3 vols. Cambridge: Harvard University Press.

Buzawa, Eve, and David Hirschel. 2010. "Criminalizing Assault: Do Age and Gender Matter?" In *Fighting for Girls*, ed. Meda Chesney-Lind and Nikki Jones. Albany: State University of New York Press.

Chesney-Lind, Meda. August 2004. "Girls and Violence: Is the Gender Gap Closing?" *National Electronic Network on Violence against Women.* http://www.vawnet.org/DomesticViolence/Research/VAWnetDocs/ARGirlsViolence.php

———, and Katherine Irwin. 2007. *Beyond Bad Girls: Gender, Violence, and Hype.* 1st ed. Routledge.

———, and Randall G. Shelden. 2003. *Girls, Delinquency, and Juvenile Justice.* 3rd ed. Wadsworth.

Department of the Attorney General. December 2008. Juvenile Justice Information System Newsletter. Department of the Attorney General, Hawai'i,

F.B.I. 2007. *Crime in the United States 2006.* Washington, DC: U.S. Government Printing Office: Federal Bureau of Investigation. http://www.fbi.gov/ucr/cius2006/index.html.

Foucault, Michel. 1995. *Discipline and Punish: The Birth of the Prison.* Vintage Books.

Fox, Sanford J. 1970. "Juvenile Justice Reform: An Historical Perspective." *Stanford Law Review* 22 (6): 1187–1239.

Fuatagavi, Lydia Seumanu, and Paul Perrone. August. 2009. *Crime in Hawaii 2008* (Annual)—Attorney General. http://hawaii.gov/ag/cpja/main/rs/Folder.2005–12–05.2910/copy_of_cih2007/.

Goffman, Erving. 1961. *Asylums: Essays on the Social Situation of Mental Patients and Other Inmates.* New York: Anchor Books.

Hawai'i Department of Health, Office of Health Status Monitoring. September 2, 2005. Hawai'i State Department of Health. http://hawaii.gov/health/statistics/hhs/hhs_04/index.html.

Hawes, Joseph M. 1971. *Children in Urban Society Juvenile Delin.* Oxford: Oxford University Press.

Matsuoka, Judge Carol T., and Hawaii JDAI Subcommittee. August 24, 2009. *Hale Ho'omalu: A Self-Assessment of the Conditions of Confinement.*

McClellan, Dorothy Spektorov. 1994. "Disparity in the Discipline of Male and Female Inmates in Texas Prisons." *Women and Criminal Justice* 5 (2): 71–97.

McGuire, Dyan M. 2002. "Interactive Effects of Race, Sex, and Offense Severity on Detention Processing Decisions." *Journal for Juvenile Justice and Detention Services* 17 (2): 59–78.

Mendel, Richard A. 2009. "Two Decades of JDAI: From Demonstration Project to National Standard." http://www.aecf.org/KnowledgeCenter/Publications. aspx?pubguid={245B4489-CC0E-41DA-8D0F-A2A51017487D}.

Nelsen, Anne, and Nelson Griffs. January 30, 2004. "A Conditions of Confinement Assessment of the Hale Ho'omalu Detention Facility: Report Findings." NJDA.

Pickett, Robert S. 1969. *House of Refuge Origins of Juvenile Reform in New York State 1815–1857.* Syracuse: Syracuse University Press.

Pisciotta, Alexander W. 1982. "Saving the Children: The Promise and Practice of Parens Patriae, 1838–98." *Crime and Delinquency* 28 (3): 410–25.

Puzzanchera, Charles. January 16, 2007. "Trends in Juvenile Justice System's Response to Status Offending: OJJDP Briefing Paper." National Center for Juvenile Justice.

Rousch, David W. October 30, 2007. "Hale Ho'omalu Juvenile Detention Facility Conditions of Confinement Review: Report of Findings." Center for Research and Professional Development.

Sharp, Christy, and Jessica Simon. 2004. *Girls in the Juvenile Justice System.* Washington, D.C.: Child Welfare Leauge of America.

Sherman, Francine T. 2005. "Detention Reform and Girls: Challenges and Solutions." *Annie E. Casey Foundation.* Pathways to Juvenile Detention Reform.

Snyder, H. N., and M. Sickmund. March 2006. *Juvenile Offenders and Victims: 2006 National Report.* Washington, D.C.: U.S. Department of Justice, Office of Justice Programs, Office of Juvenile Justice and Delinquency Prevention, Sutton, John R. 1992. *Stubborn Children: Controlling Delinquency in the United States, 1640–1981.* 1st ed. Berkeley: University of California Press.

CHAPTER FOUR

Healer: A Monologue from the Play
Doin' Time: Through the Visiting Glass

Ashley E. Lucas

She called for a layin' on of hands. My hands. A healing. Momma always said I had healing hands. I can cure the sick and heal the wounded. I can suck the aching from your skull or slow down your heart when it beats too fast. That's what I do for Momma a lot. Her heart gets to beating fast, and she just says, "Child, come here. I need a layin' on of hands." And I go to her, and I put my hands on her chest, right under where those knobbly little bones make two little lumps before your neck starts. Right there. Right there it's just solid bone. I listen to her heart beating pitter patter pitter patter way too fast. "Breathe, Momma," I tell her, and that solid bone place moves up and down real slow until her heart figures it out and slows down to more like what her breathing's doing. Then she puts her hands up to God. That's how she thanks God, and then she thanks me by kissing me up on top of my head.

Healing doesn't just work on Momma. I can do it on just about anybody, so long as I can lay hands on 'em. I got feelings about who needs healing. I get this aching feeling in my heart and this empty feeling in my gut, like I'm a column of air, like there's this big space inside me that even an ocean couldn't fill. I don't feel better until I've got my healing done. I've had this particular feeling goin' on five years, since they took my daddy. Most times I know who needs healing, and I just take off down the road until I come to whoever needs me. I know right where my daddy is over yonder, and I see him 'bout once a month. I just can't do my healing because I can't lay hands on him. I go in the visiting room and sit down with Momma and look at him needing the biggest healing I ever done. I put my hands up on the glass, and he does, too. But I just get real cold. There's nothing colder than that glass in the visiting room and

that plastic phone on your cheek, and I start to think there must be something wrong with me because that cold visiting room is the place I love the most in all the world. It's the place I'm always trying to get back to. I think it's that hurtin' part of Daddy callin' to me, callin' me back all the time so that I don't want to be anywhere else. I suppose I'll just have to keep goin' back 'til they let him come home so I can heal 'im, but who's gonna come when I need a layin' on of hands?

CHAPTER FIVE

Incarcerated Women:
Motherhood on the Margins

Barbara Bloom and Marilyn Brown

INTRODUCTION

In this chapter, we investigate how motherhood is enacted within a specific structural context: that of the prison. In the context of imprisonment, a woman's status as mother is "troubled" by two constraints. One is the obvious constraint posed by confinement and forced separation from her children. The other constraint is the way in which unorthodox motherhood (McMahon 1995) is called into question by both ideology and law. The cultural imperative of intensive mothering—in which motherhood is child-centered and exclusive of self-centered pursuits (Hays 1996)—is fundamentally challenged by the incarcerated mother (Sharp and Marcus-Mendoza 2001). Since both law and social policy are grounded in the ideology of intensive mothering within the nuclear, heterosexual family (Arendell 2000; Fineman 1995), the parenting woman who is a prisoner departs utterly from the "culturally privileged model" (McMahon 1995, 29) of motherhood. This departure, and social reactions to it, reminds us that although motherhood occupies an ideologically venerated position in society, the experiences of individual mothers are often devalued (Luker 2000).

Several decades of feminist scholarship have pursued the issue of motherhood in both objective and subjective senses. Motherhood has been examined as a focus of gendered regulation as well as an enactment of social identity. On the one hand, motherhood has been identified as a key component of women's inferior status under patriarchy (Roberts 1995). On the other hand, motherhood has been examined as an account of female gender and social adulthood (McMahon 1995). The diversity of women's experiences in childbearing and childrearing is also reflected in an ever-increasing literature. Rather than a universalizing perspective on what motherhood is (or should be), recent feminist work draws attention to the multiple meanings of "kinscripts" (Stack and Burton 1994, 33) and the various standpoints within which motherhood is conceptualized and realized (Arendell 2000). Motherhood is socially constructed in diverse ways as both a source of identity and a target of gendered social control. Moreover, both identity and control come into sharper focus in the unique context of mothering in prison (Ferraro and Moe 2003).

This chapter suggests that women carry their gendered identities as mothers into prison with them, regardless of their previous behaviors. Knowing that they have already fallen short in terms of cultural expectations of motherhood, they face a huge problem in terms of self-image and identity. Their attempts to rescue their identities as mothers may lead them to be even more vulnerable to regulation by correctional authorities. Thus, the problems that incarcerated mothers face are both subjective and objective in nature. And their difficulties have been made objectively worse by the increased legal penalties occasioned by contemporary sentencing policies and adoption law.

We argue that women have been in the cross hairs of the contraction of the welfare state and the increasingly more punitive approach to crime. The former has often meant a deepening of female poverty, especially among women of color (Burnham 2001). A more punitive approach to crime, drug-related crime in particular, has driven up the numbers of incarcerated women, the majority of whom are mothers. Indeed, studies show that incarcerated mothers, while at high risk for poverty and intimate violence, are incarcerated mainly for drug-related crimes (Greene, Haney, and Hurtado 2000). So profound an effect have harsher sentencing policies had on African American women, the war on drugs has been described as a war against black women (Bush-Baskette 1998). Thus, the fact that so many mothers are incarcerated is predominantly due to social policies that have often resulted in unacknowledged consequences.

Some of these consequences have been the subject of scholarly investigation, and we examine a number of them in this chapter. But our investigation has a second focus as well. Namely, we explore the impact of recent changes in child welfare laws that have had enormous consequences for poor mothers, growing numbers of whom are incarcerated. Given the contemporary articulation of corrections and child welfare systems in the lives of poor women, an examination of both systems best describes the plight of imprisoned mothers.

In the following section, we review studies of incarcerated mothers, including the ways in which women manage their families from prison. We then examine the impact of changes in child welfare law on this population, followed by a consideration of the growing extension of state control of poor mothers who are subject to involvement in both child welfare and correctional systems.

STUDIES OF INCARCERATED MOTHERS

A large majority of women in jails and state and federal prisons are mothers. Most are under thirty-five years of age, economically disadvantaged, undereducated, and disproportionately members of minority groups (Jensen and DuDeck-Biondo 2005; Mumola 2000). Approximately 64 percent of mothers confined in state prison and 84 percent of women in federal prison lived with their children prior to their incarceration, compared with 44 percent and 55 percent of fathers (Mumola 2000). Maternal incarceration is, of course, not new in the American experiment with the prison. Women's reformatories dating back to the nineteenth century not only incarcerated parenting women, but their chief means of regulating female inmates was reinforcing the identities of mother and spouse (Bosworth 1996; Carlen 1983; Hannah-Moffat 2001; Rafter 1990). However, with the dramatic increases in the incarceration of women, the issue takes on a scope not seen in the past. The rate of growth in the numbers of women serving sentences of at least one year has outpaced that of men for several decades, growing at a rate of nearly 757 percent between 1977 and 2004, compared to 388 percent for men. The average annual growth rates for women exceeded those for men in most of those years, showing a steady gap in the rate of growth of women for each of the years from 1992 to 2004 (Frost, Greene, and Pranis 2006).

While there is an expansive literature on parenting women in prison, a great deal of this consists of small-scale studies with fewer studies that are larger in scope (Glick and Neto 1977; McGowan and Blumenthal 1978). Emerging themes in this literature include the scope of maternal incarceration; the undermining of maternal identity and consequent distress related to separation from children; symbolic threats to gendered identity posed by incarceration; the connection between the feminization of poverty and imprisonment; the overlapping effects of criminalization and racial disparity on women; management of the maternal role and relations with children's caregivers; and the impact of child welfare regulation upon incarcerated mothers.

The first theme in the maternal incarceration literature is descriptive and comparative in nature. Despite concerns that women's improved occupational status would lead to changes in the seriousness and scope of their offenses, women are still incarcerated largely for traditional reasons. Women are less likely than men to be incarcerated for a violent offense (35 percent versus 53 percent) and more likely than men to have served time for a drug or property crime (59 percent versus 40 percent) (Greenfeld and Snell 1999). Parenting female inmates are even less likely than their male counterparts to have been convicted of a violent offense (26 percent versus 45.4 percent); they are much more likely to be serving time for drug and property crimes than incarcerated fathers (Mumola 2000). The feminization of poverty, women's offending, and their intersection with race are themes in many studies of incarcerated mothers (Ruiz 2002; Enos 2001, 1998). Studies of incarcerated women in general indicate that they have below average levels of education and employment experience (Bloom, Chesney-Lind, and Owen 1994). Mothers report low levels of employment prior to their incarceration, with fewer than half reporting being employed in the year prior to prison (Mumola 2000). In fact, most female offenders are young women of color with dependent children, poorly educated, and with few marketable skills (Ruiz 2002).

The next theme to emerge in studies of incarcerated mothers concerns the constraints upon motherhood posed by incarceration. Many studies (Baunach 1988; Galbraith 1998; LeFlore and Holston 1989; Owen 1998; Giallombardo 1966) point to the role that women's separation from children plays in the "pains of imprisonment." When studies of prison populations focused almost exclusively on men, the loss of freedom and autonomy was the focal concern of this research (Sykes 1958). For inmate mothers, the loss of children and the nullification of any claims to the status of "good mother" were identified in many studies as one of the defining ways that men's and women's incarceration experiences differed (Jensen and DuDeck-Biondo 2005). A related literature describes the incarceration of pregnant women. According to a report by the Bureau of Justice Statistics, 4 percent of state and 3 percent of federal female inmates said they were pregnant at the time of their incarceration (Maruschak 2008). Reproductive health services in most women's facilities are inadequate, and pregnancy outcomes are often poor. However, there is no consensus about whether this is due to women's poor health profiles prior to prison, the conditions of incarceration, or both (Martin et al. 1997; Siefert and Pimlott 2001). Not only are women who give birth while incarcerated soon separated from their infants, but they may in fact be subject to traumatizing conditions during labor and delivery such as placement in shackles or other restraints (Amnesty International 2000).

Another dimension of the literature focuses on motherhood as gendered identity—one threatened symbolically due to the sociocultural impact of criminalization upon women. Criminal women are subjected to a heightened stigmatization for violating both the criminal code and gendered expectations about women's behavior (Schur 1983). Incarcerated mothers are considered even more blameworthy—in the eyes of others as well as their own. Geiger and Fischer (2005) compared identity negotiation among male and female offenders and their justifications for offending. Within the normative perspective of street life and its context, a range of deviant identities could be embraced or, at least, justified by both men and women. However, all attempts at justification failed when women were confronted with the label of "failed mother." Several studies analyze the discourse of incarcerated mothers, especially themes in the emergent construction of motherhood. The constraints of prison on the practice of motherhood, in conjunction with women's troubled childbearing experiences in the past, make it all the more likely that women attempt to maintain whatever aspects of this self-image they can. Thus, they may attempt to describe their intentions and behaviors in ways that are more consistent with cultural expectations associated with being a good mother (Jensen and DuDeck-Biondo 2005; Forsyth 2003). This may have the result of making women even more vulnerable to regulation while in prison. Correctional authorities may well exploit the incarcerated mother's attempts to salvage her identity by ordering her to attend parenting classes or by withholding visitation for disciplinary reasons (Brown 2003). Constructing the subjective aspects of motherhood while in prison has resulted in important sociological insights into the construction of gendered identity. However, women also deal with the objective and practical aspects of motherhood while incarcerated. This they do primarily by proxy, through engaging with their families at a distance, as described in the following section.

MANAGING MOTHERHOOD IN PRISON

The barriers posed by prisons to the enactment of motherhood are substantial. Literature suggests that maintaining bonds with children during a woman's incarceration poses a far more complicated set of problems than for men. There is no legal basis per se for correctional systems to interfere with visitation or other forms of communication. Most jurisdictions acknowledge the constitutional rights of parents to have access to their children, although not all incarcerated parents may be aware of their rights or have recourse to legal assistance (Lewis 2004). However, barriers to the enjoyment of these rights exist that are sometimes related to the organization of the prison system itself and sometimes reside in the structure of gendered roles.

Women's prisons have historically been few in number and often distant from their families, posing a hardship for visitation by family members, caregivers, and children. Travel distances and associated costs are the main reasons for low visitation rates (GAO 1999). In 1997, more than half of incarcerated mothers reported having had no visits with their children during their time in prison. This same study reported that most mothers kept in touch by weekly phone calls (27 percent) or by letters (35.6 percent) (Mumola 2000). Although most women prisoners are classified as minimum-security inmates, the majority is held in medium or maximum-security facilities because their small numbers in each state do not justify the expense of building more women's prisons. The conditions of maximum security may affect the development of parent-child programming and impact the experience of visiting children at these prisons.

The primary reason cited by Bloom and Steinhart (1993) for infrequent visitation or nonvisitation by children of mothers in their study was the distance between the child's residence and the correctional facility, as noted elsewhere. Over 60 percent of the children lived more than one hundred miles from the mother's place of incarceration. Women's prisons are often located in rural areas far from urban centers where the family members generally reside, and they are often inaccessible by public transportation. Incarcerated women are usually placed farther from their homes than their male counterparts because there are fewer prisons for women in most states.

Some differences in the frequency of visits were noted by Bloom and Steinhart between children who lived with their mothers prior to arrest and those who did not. Children who lived with their mothers prior to arrest were nearly twice as likely to visit their mothers in jail or prison (54 percent) as children who did not (28 percent). Even so, mothers and children living together prior to arrest had an overall no-visit rate of 46 percent. Letters were the mothers' main form of contact with their families, followed by telephone calls, as noted above. However, the rates of these institutional phone calls (which must be made collect) are exorbitant and represent a substantial burden to caregivers.

The lack of contact between children and their incarcerated mothers appears to worsen over time for mothers but not fathers. Koban (1983) found that the women prisoners in her study experienced a significant disadvantage compared to male prisoners in attempting to maintain consistent contact with their children and the caregivers of these children—a factor that was associated with problems during reunification with their children. Koban reported that while more mothers than fathers received at least one visit from their children during incarceration, the frequency of parent-child visits decreased after one year for mothers, while it remained stable for fathers. The general situation for maternal visits may have worsened with the increase in women's incarceration. Only 8 percent of the women surveyed in the original "Why Punish the Children?" study had no visits from their children (McGowan and Blumenthal 1978). However, the 1993 reprise of that study by Bloom and Steinhart found that 54 percent of the children never visited their incarcerated mothers, a percentage that remains unchanged in state prisons (see Mumola 2000).

The Bureau of Prisons attempts to place all federal inmates in facilities within five hundred miles of their release residences, but due to their small numbers, women incarcerated in one of the fifteen federal facilities housing females are more likely than men to be at some distance from family (GAO 1999). The emergent trend of transferring inmates to prisons in other states in an effort to make more bed space available has compounded these difficulties. For approximately a decade, the State of Hawai'i has transferred male and female inmates to correctional facilities on the mainland, foreclosing for most the possibility of visitation. Just under a dozen states have similar practices, adding to the problems associated with distance (Brown 2006).

Finally, some mothers do not want their children to visit them in prison. They may feel shame or embarrassment related to their children's awareness of their criminal involvement; indeed, some choose not to tell their children that they are in prison. The extent of powerlessness experienced by some mothers who are separated from their children is so severe that they sever their emotional ties to their children out of sheer self-preservation (Bloom and Steinhart 1993). When children do visit their mothers in prison, contact may be quite limited. For example, some prisons offer minimal visiting opportunities or have stringent rules regarding legal guardianship, which make it difficult for the children's caregivers to bring them to see their mothers. In recognition of the general "unfriendliness" of prison to families, some correctional institutions have opened children's centers, also known as family preservation centers. At least ten states permit children to visit overnight with their mothers (Kauffman 2001).

CHILD CUSTODY AND CAREGIVERS

The effects of institutional, cultural, and systemic dynamics that subordinate women are clearly revealed when gendered roles meet the reality of women's incarceration. The roles associated with contemporary childrearing make themselves felt in the dynamics of maternal incarceration and patterns of child custody. Fathers (90 percent in state prisons) were far more likely to report that the child was in the care of its other parent compared to mothers (28 percent in state prisons). Moreover, children of state inmate mothers were far more likely to go into the foster care system compared to the children of fathers (1.8 percent versus 9.6 percent) (Mumola 2000). While the children of incarcerated fathers for the most part remain in the custody of their mother during his entire incarceration, only about a quarter of children of incarcerated women remain with the same caregiver (Koban 1983). In the more recent study by Mumola (cited above), the child's grandparent was the most likely caregiver (53 percent) along with other relatives (26 percent) when a mother is incarcerated. Therefore, a mother's incarceration means that she is dependent upon relative caregivers to be allies in the maintenance of a mother's ties to her children.

Relative caregivers (whether foster care or kin) vary in their ability to support the incarcerated woman's relationship with her children. Reluctance on the part of a caregiver to allow visitation was cited by Bloom and Steinhart (1993) as a reason for lack of mother-child contact. Caregivers are sometimes angry with the mother for her prolonged periods of substance abuse, criminal activity, or repeated incarcerations and may believe that it is detrimental for the child to have contact with her. Some foster parents are reluctant to assist children in maintaining contact with their imprisoned mothers due to concern about the mother's "fitness" as a parent or fear of losing their own relationship with the children (Bloom and Steinhart 1993).

Caregivers to the children of incarcerated women share their economic and other problems since they often occupy similar social positions. While most children are placed with relatives, these family members are often already caring for their own families under difficult circumstances. In poor, urban African American communities ravaged by epidemics of crack-cocaine and HIV/AIDS, the prevalence of grandmothers caring for grandchildren has been dealt another blow by the incarceration of their daughters (Ruiz 2002). Even grandparents who were not economically disadvantaged acquire children of their incarcerated children at a time of declining health and income. Indeed, surrogacy itself may result in declining health for these caregivers (Minkler, Roe, and Robertson Beckley 1994).

Recent studies building on the above (particularly those examining racial and ethnic differences in child living situations) have presented more complex analyses of issues concerning incarcerated mothers and their children. Sandra Enos (2001) explores how mothers "manage" motherhood from prison, examining how they go to great lengths to preserve their roles and identities as mothers. She demonstrates how racial and cultural factors exert an influence both before and during incarceration, shaping how women enact motherhood from prison. According to Enos, for African American women, pathways to prison did not exclude family networks and sometimes were contingent upon family ties. Both African American and Hispanic women were more likely to have preserved family ties despite their legal troubles and were more often able to count on family help with children than imprisoned white women.

INCARCERATED MOTHERS AND THE CHILD WELFARE SYSTEM

When mothers are unable to place children with relatives or friends, the child welfare agency having jurisdiction will place them in foster care. Children of incarcerated parents make up a growing percentage of all children in foster care, with some estimates ranging from 20 to 30 percent (Johnson and Waldfogel 2002; Ehrensaft et al. 2003). It is generally estimated that between 7 percent and 13 percent of the children of incarcerated mothers are in foster care with nonrelatives (Bloom and Steinhart 1993; McGowan and Blumenthal 1978; Mumola 2000). While correctional systems were never designed with family concerns at the forefront, child welfare systems likewise do not articulate easily with prisons. Nor was the incompatibility of these two systems much questioned until recent dramatic increases in the rate of women's incarceration.

Managing motherhood from prison is fraught with difficulties, particularly when children are placed for care within the child welfare system. Shapiro, Vogelstein, and Light (2001) report both attitudinal and practical barriers exist among caseworkers who are reluctant to bring children to a correctional facility. Some believe that prison visits have a negative impact on children. In any case, long distances (as reported in this study of New York State) all too often make visitation impractical. Of course, the importance of visitation and the maintenance of the parental bond cannot be overstated with respect to children in care—if mothers are to avoid the termination of their parental rights while in prison (Hayward and DePanfilis 2007).

Various authorities (Barry, Ginchild, and Lee 1995; Henriques 1982) have found that contact between caseworkers and mothers is strained and infrequent and that mothers are uninformed about their legal status and responsibilities. Beckerman (1994) drew attention to this in a study that found that the prerequisite conditions deemed necessary for a mother's involvement in permanency planning—including frequent interaction and collaboration between caseworker and parents of children in foster care—are not present among imprisoned women. Over the past decade, this issue has become all the more problematic under current federal law that emphasizes permanency planning, often at the expense of reunification. We turn next to a consideration of the impact of this law.

THE IMPACT OF ASFA

The Adoption and Safe Families Act (ASFA), passed in 1997, altered the landscape of permanency planning for children in foster care, accelerating the time frame within which family reunification must take place. Under the revised legislation, agencies are required to move to permanency planning, including termination of parental rights, in cases where children have been in foster care for fifteen of the previous twenty-two months. Unable to participate as required in normal family reunification service plans (such as parent education, counseling, drug treatment, and job training) incarcerated mothers are at high risk of having their parental rights terminated. Imprisoned women are too frequently unable to involve themselves in case planning and their children's lives as directed by the child welfare agency. They may not be apprised of hearings or have a chance to attend hearings they are advised about in advance. Communications with the child's caseworker may be difficult or impossible for the mother to manage (Halperin and Harris 2004).

Some of the collateral consequences of mass incarceration and its effects on families have spread to other public agencies—the child welfare system is a primary example. The relationship between agencies of child welfare and correctional institutions is a new arena of exploration—one where individual child welfare caseworkers and their departments are confronted with the realities of an unfamiliar prison system. Prisons traditionally are closed institutions that present obstacles to communications with the outside world. When an incarcerated mother's children are placed in foster care, the normal procedures associated with case management and planning are subverted to the discipline and regulations of the prison bureaucracy. Mothers who attempt to maintain their parental rights from prison, as well as their children's case managers, are often both operating in uncharted territory.

Beckerman (1998) noted that until the numbers of incarcerated women reached substantial proportions, the number of such children in foster care was small and workers had little experience dealing with these cases. There is very little institutional experience or formal intra-systems policy incorporated into caseworker practice. It is unclear to what extent a mother can fulfill the terms of the case plan from prison, since she has little control over whether or when she might receive the required job training, mental health, or substance abuse treatment mandated by her service plan. Since a permanency plan must be in place twelve months after the child goes into foster care, this timeline, combined with the difficulties in coordinating case planning with an incarcerated mother, make termination of parental rights all the more likely (Halperin and Harris 2004).

The Child Welfare League of America's (CWLA) 1998 survey of 38 state child welfare agencies underlined the fracture between the agencies and the corrections systems that have custody of parents. States had little information on numbers of children in the system whose parents had histories of being in custody. Among the very few states that could estimate the number of children in care who had incarcerated parents, various estimates (1.6 percent to 29.5 percent) were offered. This scanty data provided little in the way of demographics, type of program children were enrolled in (child protective services, independent living, adoption services), or length of stay—all crucial variables. Only a handful of states gather information about parental incarceration routinely upon intake and assessment, although other states indicated at the time of the survey that plans were in place to begin collecting such data. Finally, the CWLA study found that policies of states regarding this issue varied a great deal—with only six states having specific policies involving incarcerated parents, although twenty-seven states had policies that encouraged the involvement of incarcerated parents in permanency planning. These findings amplify the idea that there is, as Halperin and Harris (2004) suggest, a "policy vacuum" regarding these children and their mothers whom the state has in custody. While a handful of states have some proactive approaches in place, in most jurisdictions practices are doubtlessly arbitrary and uninformed by any specific policies based on sound institutional knowledge of the problem.

In response to this issue, the Child Welfare League of America has published a handbook for child welfare personnel covering topics pertinent to both child welfare and correctional systems (Wright and Seymour 2000). Admittedly, during the twelve-month period when permanency service plans are implemented, caseworkers may have difficulty in determining whether the incarcerated parent will be able to provide a reasonably safe and stable home. The CWLA manual advises caseworkers to examine issues such as the mother's interest in visitation, the quality of these visits, alternative forms of communication when visits are not possible, and involvement with the child's life. Additionally, as with any parent subject to these procedures, incarcerated mothers need to comply with treatment programs that are part of the service plan and to be involved in hearings. Since reintegration services for inmates leaving prison for the community are inadequate, caseworkers may be confused by the question of whether a woman can set up a stable home after prison. In view of the fact that many women are subject to prison sentences beyond twenty-two months and that inmates have little control over their lives, it is clear that even with the efforts of conscientious caseworkers, inmate mothers are at high risk for the termination of their parental rights.

Termination of parental rights, now even more common since the passage of ASFA, is having a disturbing impact on incarcerated mothers. As onerous as it may be for mothers living in the community to comply with ASFA requirements, the short deadline means even more severe hardship for incarcerated mothers who serve an average of eighteen months. The Adoption and Safe Families Act's strict time limits for permanency hearings and initiating petitions to terminate parental rights undermines families with an incarcerated parent and children in foster care. A recent study suggests ASFA provisions have had significant effects on incarcerated parents, based on the "significant overall increase" between 1997 and 2002 in the number of cases in which parental rights have been terminated (Lee, Genty, and Laver 2005).

Although child welfare agencies and correctional systems are unwilling bureaucratic partners in the enterprise of assisting families, the incarcerated mothers we have been discussing so far often find themselves caught up by both systems. The same factors that place women at risk for offending and prison, namely poverty, substance abuse, mental illness, and marginality, mirror those that put women under the scrutiny of child welfare systems. In the following section, we examine a seldom-explored area: the overlap of these two systems of control in women's lives.

OVERLAPPING SYSTEMS, OVERLAPPING CONTROLS

The state's control has been extended in scope through the expanded use of incarceration and categorically through an increasingly punitive child welfare system (Brown 2003). Prison systems and child welfare systems converge in the lives of poor women to create an ever-expanding correctional population. Just as child welfare policies have criminalized and undermined the families of African Americans and other women of color (Roberts 2002), prison systems are being filled with many of the same families. These developments are both forms of what Renny Golden refers to as "traumatic state intervention" (2005, 3) into the lives of poor women and their children. There is an emergent feminist literature on the gendered nature of welfare and correctional interventions (see Haney 2004), but few studies have examined specifically the intersection of these interventions in women's lives (Brown and Bloom 2009).

The politics that have transformed systems of welfare and punishment nationally have created an environment in which increasing numbers of women have been drawn under state control. Parenting women are not only imprisoned but frequently find themselves under the control of child welfare agencies. This process of dual criminalization—of women as offenders and as subjects of child welfare investigations—has had a particularly deleterious impact on minority women (Roberts 2002). While mass imprisonment has caught up increasing numbers of poor women, especially women of color in jails and prisons, harsher child welfare regulations threaten to sever forever the ties of mothers to their children. Given the structure of poverty, race, and gender in the United States, the child welfare regime of control is likewise racialized. Women who are involved in both of these systems find themselves subjected to alternating forms of coercive control by welfare and correctional institutions. As Haney (2004) argues, state systems such as corrections and welfare in general are gendered regimes, where women make up the majority of one (welfare) and the smaller portion of the other (prison). Haney's analysis of welfare (now reconfigured as Temporary Aid to Needy Families), we suggest, applies equally well to the child welfare system.

The evidence for these overlapping state controls is circumstantial at present because the movement of women through child welfare systems and criminal justice control has not been studied. George and colleagues (2000) documented the movement of children between income maintenance programs and foster care, finding that a majority of children in foster care were from state welfare rolls. We know very little about the degree to which parental incarceration is part of this picture. While child maltreatment is clearly not confined to disadvantaged families, the rolls of child protective agencies across the country are filled with the poor and ethnic minorities (Jones 1997). Institutionalized racism, not unlike that which has filled correctional institutions, has populated the child welfare system with children of color (see Roberts 2002). Parents who become involved in the criminal justice system often have risk factors for a range of issues affecting their abilities to parent (Johnston 2006). Although we know that the population of imprisoned mothers has a large interface with those whose children are in foster care, more needs to be known about the sequencing of the involvement in systems of corrections versus child welfare.

Parenting women who become incarcerated resemble those who become caught up in the child welfare system in terms of demographics such as poverty and race. As well, they share similar biographical narratives in terms of violence at the hands of intimates, substance abuse, trauma, and economic marginalization. Women who are imprisoned are (or often have been) subject to child welfare involvement, although we have few studies of the extent to which this is true. Brown and Bloom (2009) found that among the group of 203 parenting women on parole in Hawai'i in 2001, nearly 24 percent had records of child welfare agency investigation at the time of their sentencing. Nearly 16 percent of these women had their parental rights terminated for at least one child. The impact of the termination of parental rights on outcomes for women involved in the criminal justice system needs also to be documented.

CONCLUSION

This chapter has reviewed a burgeoning literature on incarcerated mothers. It is common for women whose pathways to prison often include exposure to violence, alienation from education and employment, mental illness, and substance abuse to also lose control over the conditions of their reproductive lives. This may be manifested by early pregnancy, lone motherhood, economic dependence, and involvement in systems of social welfare control, including child welfare. The final assault on their parenting situation comes when they are incarcerated and lose most of their remaining control over their lives and those of their children. Once incarcerated, those who attempt to manage motherhood from a prison cell have to adapt not only to the prison regime but to the condition of mothering from a distance as well (Owen 1998).

The extent to which women are successful in this enterprise often depends upon their position in a network of kin and caregivers who are able and willing to help. As we have seen, the management of motherhood from prison and the availability of assistance are highly correlated with race and class. The racial disparities in both prison populations and the populations of children in foster care point to the heavier risk that women of color, overall, face in having their children placed and, subsequently, losing their parental rights.

We have examined the overlapping systems of women's incarceration and exposure to child welfare control, noting that the risk factors along the pathways women journey to prison are very similar to those that place them at risk for child welfare system involvement. Unknown numbers of women have been subject to child welfare investigation prior to or coinciding with becoming involved in the criminal justice system. But we have raised more questions than answers. The causal dynamics that precipitate the overlap between the two populations have not been examined. For instance, does involvement in the child welfare system lead to greater detection of criminal behavior? Or do variables such as poverty, mental illness, domestic violence, and substance abuse amount to the conditioning factors leading to both outcomes? The exploration of child welfare services as a gendered disciplinary system should be coupled with studies of women's criminalization. We recommend more qualitative studies to examine how child welfare agents work (or fail to work) with correctional facilities. As well, we call for more prospective studies of women's pathways to offending with particular emphasis on the role that contact with child welfare agencies may play in their criminalization.

Finally, in view of the fact that the majority of incarcerated women are at low risk for committing serious crimes, we call for an extensive decarceration of women's correctional facilities and an expansion of women-centered programming in the community. In particular, substance abuse treatment that accommodates women with children should be greatly expanded. The social costs of incarcerating parents, and mothers in particular, are only now being calculated, showing substantial harm to the incarcerated woman, her family, and the community. While much of the cost for mass incarceration is borne by society, substantial costs are incurred by the inmate's family and the inmate herself in terms of lost quality of life, reduced employment prospects, and shifts in child care (Lengyel 2006). Therefore, we suggest that the task ahead may reside in humanizing the problem of incarcerated women and their children while continuing to document the extensive collateral effects of mass imprisonment.

REFERENCES

Amnesty International. 2000. "Pregnant and Imprisoned in the United States." *Birth* 27 (4): 266–71.

Arendell, Terry. 2000. "Conceiving and Investigating Motherhood: The Decade's Scholarship." *Journal of Marriage and the Family* 62: 1192–1207.

Barry, Ellen, River Ginchild, and Doreen Lee. 1995. "Legal Issues for Prisoners with Children." In *Children of Incarcerated Parents*, ed. K. Gabel and D. Johnston. New York: Lexington Books.

Baunach, Phyllis Jo. 1988. *Mothers in Prison.* New Brunswick, NJ: Transactions.

Beckerman, Adela. 1998. "Charting a Course: Meeting the Challenge of Permanency Planning for Children with Incarcerated Mothers." *Child Welfare* 77 (5): 513.

Bloom, Barbara, and David Steinhart. 1993. *Why Punish the Children?* San Francisco: National Council on Crime and Delinquency.

Bloom, Barbara, Meda Chesney-Lind, and Barbara Owen. 1994. "Women in California Prisons: Hidden Victims of the War on Drugs." San Francisco: Center on Juvenile and Criminal Justice.

Bosworth, Mary. 1996. "Resistance and Compliance in Women's Prisons: Towards a Critique of Legitimacy." *Critical Criminology* 7 (2): 5–19.

Brown, Marilyn. 2006. "Gender, Ethnicity, and Offending over the Life Course: Women's Pathways to Prison in the Aloha State." *Critical Criminology* 14 (2): 137–58.

———. 2003. "Motherhood on the Margins: Rehabilitation and Subjectivity among Female Parolees in Hawai'i." University of Hawai'i at Manoa, Dissertation, Sociology, Honolulu.

Brown, Marilyn, and Barbara Bloom. 2009. "Colonialism and Carceral Motherhood: Native Hawaiian Families under Corrections and Child Welfare Control." *Feminist Criminology* 4 (2): 151–69.

Burnham, Linda. 2001. "Welfare Reform, Family Hardship, and Women of Color." *The Annals of the American Academy of Political and Social Science* 577 (1): 38–48.

Bush-Baskette, Stephanie R. 1998. "The War on Drugs as a War against Black Women." In *Crime Control and Women,* ed. S. L. Miller. Thousand Oaks, CA: Sage.

Carlen, Pat. 1983. *Women's Imprisonment: A Study in Social Control.* Boston: Routledge and Kegan Paul.

Ehrensaft, M., A. Khashu, T. Ross, and M. Wamsley. 2003. "Patterns of Criminal Conviction and Incarceration among Mothers of Children in Foster Care in New York City." New York: Vera Institute of Justice.

Enos, Sandra. 1998. "Managing Motherhood in Prison: The Impact of Race and Ethnicity on Child Placements." *Women and Therapy* 20 (4): 57–72.

———. 2001. Mothering from the Inside: Parenting in a Women's Prison. Albany: State University of New York Press.

Ferraro, Kathleen, and Angela M. Moe. 2003. "Mothering, Crime, and Incarceration." *Journal of Contemporary Ethnography* 32 (1): 9–40.

Fineman, Martha Albertson. 1995. *The Neutered Mother, the Sexual Family, and Other Twentieth Century Tragedies.* New York: Routledge.

Forsyth, Craig J. 2003. "Pondering the Discourse of Prison Mamas: A Research Note." *Deviant Behavior* 24:269–80.

Frost, Natasha, Judith Greene, and Kevin Pranis. 2006. "The Punitiveness Report-HARD HIT: The Growth in Imprisonment of Women, 1977–2004." Institute on Women and Criminal Justice. Women's Prison Association. http://www.wpaonline.org/institute/hardhit/index.htm. Retrieved Jan. 10, 2010.

Galbraith, Susan. 1998. *And So I Began to Listen to Their Stories: Working with Women in the Criminal Justice System.* Delmar: Policy Research.

GAO. 1999. "Women in Prison: Issues and Challenges Confronting U.S. Correctional Systems." Washington, DC: United States General Accounting Office.

Geiger, Brenda, and Michael Fischer. 2005. "Naming Oneself Criminal: Gender Difference in Offenders' Identity Negotiation." *International Journal of Offender Therapy and Comparative Criminology* 49 (2): 194–209.

Giallombardo, R. 1966. *Society of Women: A Study of a Women's Prison.* New York: Wiley.

Glick, R. M., and V. V. Neto. 1977. "National Study of Women's Correctional Programs." Washington, DC: National Institute of Law Enforcement and Criminal Justice.

Goerge, R. M., B. J. Lee, M. Reidy, B. Needell, A. Brookhart, D. Duncan, and L. Usher. *Dynamics of Children's Movement among the AFDC, Medicaid, and Foster Care Programs Prior to Welfare Reform: 1995–1996.* http://www.aspe.hhs.gov/hsp/movement00/report.htm#im3 (retrieved Dec. 29, 2006).

Greene, Susan, Craig Haney, and Aida Hurtado. 2000. "Cycles of Pain: Risk Factors in the Lives of Incarcerated Mothers and Their Children." *Prison Journal* 80 (1): 3–23.

Greenfeld, Lawrence A., and Tracy L. Snell. 1999. "Special Report: Women Offenders." Washington, DC: Bureau of Justice Statistics, U.S. Department of Justice.

Halperin, Ronnie, and Jennifer L. Harris. 2004. "Parental Rights of Incarcerated Mothers with Children in Foster Care: A Policy Vacuum." *Feminist Studies* 30 (2): 339–52.

Haney, Lynne. 2004. "Introduction: Gender, Welfare, and States of Punishment." *Social Politics* 11 (3): 333–62.

Hannah-Moffat, Kelly. 2001. *Punishment in Disguise: Penal Governance and Federal Imprisonment of Women in Canada.* Toronto: University of Toronto Press.

Hays, Sharon. 1996. *The Cultural Contradictions of Motherhood.* New Haven: Yale University Press.

Hayward, Anna, and Diane DePanfilis. 2007. "Foster Children with an Incarcerated Parent: Predictors of Reunification." *Children and Youth Services* 29 (10): 1320–34.

Henriques, Zelma W. 1982. *Imprisoned Mothers and Their Children.* Washington, DC: University Press of America.

Jensen, Vickie, and Jill DuDeck-Biondo. 2005. "Mothers in Jail: Gender, Social Control, and the Construction of Parenthood behind Bars." *Ethnographies of Law and Social Control* 6: 121–42.

Johnson, Elizabeth I., and Jane Waldfogel. 2002. "Parental Incarceration: Recent Trends and Implications for Child Welfare." *Social Service Review* 76 (10): 460–79.

Johnston, Denise. 2006. "The Wrong Road: Efforts to Understand the Effects of Parental Crime and Incarceration." *Criminology and Public Policy* 5 (4):703–20.

Jones, Loring P. 1997. "Social Class, Ethnicity, and Child Welfare." *Journal of Multicultural Social Work* 3 (4): 123–38.

Kauffman, Kelsey. 2001. "Mothers in Prison." *Corrections Today* 63 (1): 62–65.

Koban, L. A. 1983. "Parents in Prison: A Comparative Analysis of the Effects of Incarceration on the Families of Men and Women." *Research in Law, Deviance, and Social Control* 5:171–83.

Lee, Arlene F., Phillip M. Genty, and Mimi Laver. 2005. "The Impact of the Adoption and Safe Families Act on Children of Incarcerated Parents." Child Welfare League of America.

LeFlore, Larry, and Mary Ann Holston. 1989. "Perceived Importance of Parenting Behaviors as Reported by Inmate Mothers: An Exploratory Study." *Journal of Offender Counseling, Services, and Rehabilitation* 14 (1): 5–30.

Lengyel, Thomas E. 2006. "Spreading the Pain: The Social Cost of Incarcerating Parents." New York: Healing the Divide.

Lewis, Pamela. 2004. "Behind the Glass Wall: Barriers That Incarcerated Parents Face Regarding the Care, Custody, and Control of Their Children." *Journal of the American Academy of Matrimonial Lawyers* 19:97–115.

Luker, Kristin. 2000. Afterword. In *Ideologies and Technologies of Motherhood: Race, Class, Sexuality, Nationalism*, ed. F. W. Twine and H. Ragone. New York: Routledge.

Martin, Sandra L., Kim Haesook, Lawrence L. Kupper, Robert E. Meyer, and Melissa Hays. 1997. "Is Incarceration during Pregnancy Associated with Infant Birthweight?" *American Journal of Public Health* 87 (9): 1526–31.

Maruschak, Laura M. 2008. "Medical Problems of Prisoners." Washington, DC: Bureau of Justice Statistics, Department of Justice.

McGowan, Brenda G., and Karen L. Blumenthal. 1978. *Why Punish the Children?* Hackensack, NJ: National Council on Crime and Delinquency.

McMahon, Martha. 1995. *Engendering Motherhood: Identity and Self-Transformation in Women's Lives.* New York: Guilford.

Minkler, Meredith, Kathleen M. Roe, and Relda J. Robertson Beckley. 1994. "Raising Grandchildren from Crack Cocaine Households: Effects on Family and Friendship Ties of African American Women." *American Journal of Orthopsychiatry* 64 (1):20–29.

Mumola, Christopher J. 2000. "Incarcerated Parents and Their Children." Washington, DC: Bureau of Justice Statistics, U.S. Department of Justice.

Owen, Barbara. 1998. *In the Mix: Struggle and Survival in a Women's Prison.* Albany: State University of New York Press.

Rafter, Nicole Hahn. 1990. *Partial Justice: Women, Prisons, and Social Control.* New Brunswick: Transaction.

Roberts, Dorothy. 2002. *Shattered Bonds: The Color of Child Welfare.* New York: Basic/Civitas.

Roberts, Dorothy E. 1995. "Motherhood and Crime." *Social Text* 42:99–123.

Ruiz, Dorothy S. 2002. "The Increase in Incarcerations among Women and Its Impact on the Grandmother Caregiver: Some Racial Considerations." *Journal of Sociology and Social Welfare* 29 (3): 179–97.

Schur, Edwin W. 1983. *Labeling Women Deviant: Gender, Stigma, and Social Control.* Philadelphia: Temple University Press.

Shapiro, Lauren, Lynn Vogelstein, and Jennifer Light. 2001. "Family Ties: Representing Formerly Incarcerated Women with Children in Family Court." *Clearinghouse Review* 35:243–52.

Sharp, Susan F., and Susan T. Marcus-Mendoza. 2001. "It's a Family Affair: Incarcerated Women and Their Families." *Women and Criminal Justice* 12 (4): 21–49.

Siefert, Kristine, and Sheryl Pimlott. 2001. "Improving Pregnancy Outcome during Imprisonment: A Model Residential Care Program." *Social Work* 46 (2): 125–34.

Stack, Carol B., and Linda M. Burton. 1994. "Kinscripts: Reflections on Family, Generation, and Culture." In *Mothering: Ideology, Experience, Agency*, ed. E. N. Glenn, G. Chang, and L. R. Forcey. New York: Routledge.

Sykes, G. 1958. *A Society of Captives.* Princeton, NJ: Princeton University Press.

Wright, L. E., and C. B. Seymour. 2000. "Working with Children and Families Separated by Incarceration: A Handbook for Child Welfare Agencies." Washington, DC: CWLA.

CHAPTER SIX

Doing Time with Mom: A Nonfiction Essay

Shirley Haviland-Nakagawa

I can still remember when my sister was the little girl who pinched her thumb and forefinger together and held them up high for a cup of tea. With her blue-eyed doll cradled in the elbow of her arm, she was for one moment in time a young mother and my neighbor visiting me. I cuddled my own peach-faced baby doll and invited her into my house through the invisible doors as we mimicked grownups. Mama's canned foods stacked on a crate in the patio became my kitchen cupboards, but I only offered the taste-less, odorless, imaginary cup of tea—and she sipped it so sophisticatedly. Her long brown hair fell all around her soft pale face and shoulders. With no color in her cheeks, it made her predominately brown eyes illuminate.

The tea parties were a smash, but when Rocky found us he sent Natalie screaming out through the back yard gate. "Run," she screamed, "It's the monster!"

Rocky barked and chased us all the way to the school yard, a block and a half up Bell Harbor Avenue. Past the monkey bars was the fireman pole, and we climbed the steel stairway to the top of the castle where the monster could not get us. We screamed for help as Rocky yipped and wagged his tail. Sliding down the cold steel pole, we ran for our lives back to our house where Rocky could be heard behind us in chase. Bursting through the front door exhausted we fell upon the living room carpet while our monster licked our faces and waved his tail with victory. I still feel a sense of disbelief when I think of her in prison now. In reality, she just could not out run all the monsters in her life.

Behind prison walls at the California Institution for Women (CIW), my sister has remained pale, and her features have become a bit more washed out. Her eyebrows have faded to an almost unnoticeable shadow, giving her large almond eyes a deep-set appearance. The most colorful things about her appearance now are the tattoos she has donned since she turned a rebellious fourteen. The large red rose centered on her right hand, surrounded with leaves of two shades of green, is not just an emblem of beauty, but an deliberate coverup of an ugly memory: the name *MIKE* lies beneath. On her back is a professional tat of a sword with a ribbon that once read, "Sworn to fun—Loyal to None," until another bad memory, Rick G., came along. He had a flower inked on the letter, "N." Now it reads, "Sworn to fun-Loyal to *One*." Clever bastard. It is *him* that I'd like to blame for her incarceration in the California state prison, but he did not have anything to do with this charge. Not this time.

At seventeen Natalie met Rick G., a carpenter by trade. He wore his thick wavy brown hair in a ponytail that came just past his shoulders. His hazel eyes shone brightly and were surrounded with thick brown eyelashes. The rest of his features were hidden under his full ZZ Top-style beard. He sported a black Harley Davidson t-shirt with large brown wings outlined in orange, and I realized what they had in common besides the multitude of tats up and down his arms.

Just as I had suspected, his stereotypical bad boy image was indeed a warning. He was trouble, and when they married for better or worse, it was for the worse. They racked up serious felonies that I will not list here, to protect the innocent and the not so innocent. She had just turned eighteen when she went to CIW for the first time. There were no "three strikes" laws back then, 1979 to 1980. The charges were serious, and she did her time. However, with her felony charges in 2002, the new three strikes law reached back to the old 1979 charges as the prosecution's tool to use the past felonies as strikes to convict her. With so many years passed came many changes and maturity in Natalie—changes that the law refuses to see.

In 2002, anyone who knew Natalie saw the transformation as she became a functional citizen as well as a loving mother. She attended church, and moving in and out of jails and prison was now years behind her as she settled into a somewhat domestic lifestyle. Still far from perfect, my little tea partner had become a medium-built woman in tight jeans and spaghetti straps, quick to tell anyone where to go at any time and more interested in coffee than tea. We bore a strong resemblance and duped people on the phone with our voices so much alike, but our similarities ended there. We argued a lot about our differences, but we were sisters and counted on love to bond us like super glue.

I lived in Fresno and took an hour drive to find her under a car on most Saturday afternoons, lathered in motor oil and reeking of gasoline. On any other day of the week, however, she would be been found with her hair feathered back wearing plum red lip-gloss that shimmered her perfectly shaped lips that matched her satin midrift halter. As if she had discovered her colorless beauty, she never wore rouge to blush her cheeks. We greeted each other with a hug, and I detected the faint hint of the White Diamonds perfume that I bought her for her April birthday in place of a real diamond—her birthstone—but usually her perfume collection consisted of incense oils that reminded me of the scented candle section in a Hallmark store.

Excitedly she told me she had been accepted into the program Habitat for Humanity. As the community of volunteers began to build her house, Natalie and her children—Kevin, thirteen, and Angel, fifteen—helped hammer and frame the new home that they would never know.

Kevin was the living image of his deceased father; his bright yellow curls popped out from under his baseball cap that he wore to shade his translucent skin from the sun. His blue eyes lit up from under the bill of the cap, and although he was handsome, his coloring did not match that of his mother or sister, Angel. Angel was Natalie's mini-me and now closely resembled the rebellious teen I once knew, although I never saw Angel hold a doll; she was more the stuffed animal type. Her brown, animated fawnlike eyes frightened me as I wondered how much she could be like her mother. For now, the young girl hung her whole weight on my arm and pulled me like a tug boat to her room when I came to visit. I would get another tour of her domain as if it were the first time. Indeed, this time the smell of crayons and play dough was replaced with the aroma of vanilla musk and the perfume Exclamation! On top of her dresser was a makeup gallery, and her walls displayed magazine cut-outs and posters of Britney Spears.

Video movies were a traditional way to end a long visit before heading back to Fresno. We watched *Erin Brockovich* as Natalie snuggled on the floor with her children like a mother cat with her kittens. She seemed more like a tiger to me, but watching her at this moment from the couch, she was tender as a kitten finger stroking their hair. If I had known then what I know now, I would have lain down there on that floor and joined them. At least I told her that I loved her as I always did before I entered my car to leave.

Weeks later, before Mother's Day, my cell phone rang, and I received what I thought was a prank call. A young voice said, "My name is Adriane, and you need to come get Angel and Kevin because Natalie's in jail."

"Funny!" I hung up on the pranksters.

My caller ID showed the area code (209), and I couldn't believe Natalie's kids would play a joke on me like that. It was out of character. The phone rang again, and I saw the same area code. Before I could lecture the person on the other end, I was interrupted.

"My name is Adriane, I'm twenty-seven, and my little brother is Angel's boyfriend. This is not a prank call!"

The only muscle in my body that moved now was my heart, and I was sure that had stopped. My caller remained silent long enough for my mind to fast forward a file of the minor charges that could possibly have caught up with Natalie, like that six-foot round swimming pool in her backyard that she had stolen from Wal-Mart. Adrian's voice brought me back as she gave me a brief of the previous night's events.

She explained that the night before, Natalie had a few drinks at the annual Mayday Fair in Los Banos. Natalie's medication, Paxil, included a warning to avoid alcohol. She believed that the warning meant that the medication would just intensify the alcohol, so she drank. It would become the last thing she remembered. According to Kevin, his mom was "really messed up." He saw one of Angel's friends whisper something into Natalie's ear, which got Nat mad at Angel. Intoxicated, she started throwing things around towards the van. Although she did not aim at him, one of the objects hit Kevin in the mouth and bruised the inside of his bottom lip. When the cops came they took Natalie to jail, and one of the charges against her was a felony assault on a minor.

Natalie remained in jail for more than a year fighting her felony charges; the new three strikes law now demanded a twenty-five-years to life sentence. If it were not for the three strikes law, these charges would usually demand rehabilitation and parenting classes.

As her trial date drew near, Kevin and I drove to Merced County to deliver to her attorney a newly purchased dress, black low-heeled shoes, and makeup. I walked into Marty Garza's office, and Kevin waited for me in the car. Garza was out to lunch. When he returned, I met him in the parking lot, where Kevin witnessed a conversation that escalated to yelling.

"There's not gonna be a trial!" said Garza loudly. "It's a sentencing! She doing twenty-five to life!" He turned and walked toward his office, and I followed.

"But twenty-five to life is not fair for a black-out!" I said as if pleading to a judge. "I'm sure you drank and had black-outs when you were a law student in your college years," I gambled.

Garza's tone became more ominous as he spun around and answered, "Yeah! But I didn't go around beating people up!"

There was silence in the parking lot as it sank in that Natalie was in serious trouble. Slowly my eyes moved toward my car where Kevin sat staring silently at the man who was supposed to defend his mother. Garza turned to look, and for the first time he noticed there was someone there.

Later in the car Kevin told me, "I knew my mom was screwed right then." He slowly shook his head and pulled his hair away from his eyes as he continued, "He was supposed to defend my mom, but he sounded like a prosecutor!"

Kevin and I drove to Los Banos to find and tell Natalie's circle what had happened. Friends and family quickly wrote letters to the judge to wave a red flag and update the judge with her record with good reports of her character.

Later at home, I waited for the collect call from the county jail, but when Natalie finally called, it was too late. When I told her about the dress and preparations for trial, she realized that her own attorney had betrayed her.

"My Gawd, Shirley! He told me my family didn't want to go through a trial!"

"He's a fuckn' liar, man!" I raised my voice and became pumped. "You should'a heard him when we dropped off the dress! And Kev, heard it all too!"

"Shirley, he slammed a fourteen-year deal and told me that's the best offer I'm gonna get, and I signed it!"

"Fourteen years! That's a deal?"

"Shirley, call the State Bar for me and have the forms sent here fast. I'll find out what to do in here; you make calls out there."

"Your friends . . . everyone's writing letters to the Judge," I assured her. "I'll fax them so that for sure the judge will get them immediately."

I couldn't resist calling Garza as soon as we hung up. I let him know that I knew the dirty deed he had done. His secretary insisted he wasn't there whenever I called after that, and I deliberately became a pest. Even when I blocked my number, only an answering machine would pick up my calls.

Weeks later, three carloads of Natalie's friends and family went to court and took the last two rows on the right of the surprisingly small Merced County courtroom. There were many cases to be heard that day, according to the filled seats that surrounded us. Natalie did not terminate Garza due to the prosecution's threat to recommend twenty-five years to life again if she started over with a new lawyer. That made fourteen years sound good. Garza was caught in the hallway and looked surprised when he saw us. When questioned, he denied any knowledge of the letters. She was already judged and sentenced, and we all knew it. This sentencing was just a formality, and we, her supporters, were ready to proceed in prayer.

Separating our seats from the judge's platform was a three-foot wooden divider. It was just a visual of division in the room separating us from what resembled a wooden, polished throne where the judge would sit. The large round seal of Merced County hung on the wall behind the judge's seat. When the judge sat down it hung above his head, giving an illusion of a self-proclaimed halo. To the right, four rows of empty seats lined vertically to face the judge. The courtroom hushed as a back door opened and chains jingled on the ankles of the prisoners now taking those empty seats. More chains wrapped around their waists and secured their wrists. They did not speak as their eyes scanned the courtroom for relatives and supporters. Some smiled in recognition when they spotted a loved one; others didn't bother to look. Sitting closest to the back door was Natalie. Her eyes bounced from one face to the other in our group, as she gave us her best but nervous smile.

When her case was called, we were granted permission to speak before the judge. Each person spoke of the qualities that Natalie had acquired over the years.

"One bad night should not reflect her transformation," urged Marilee, one of the pillars of Los Banos. She was a school nurse, owned one of the gas stations off highway 152, had a seat in city counsel, and was an elder of the church Natalie went to. The tall woman with gray hair pinned neatly on top of her head told the judge how Natalie had taken an interest in canning and baking and about the hours they spent together in her kitchen as Natalie eagerly became her pupil. She spoke for a time about church and family activities and concluded, "She never had a mother to teach her these things, and I kind'a became her mother figure." "Thank you," said the Judge with an unchanged face.

He then looked at the rest of us until the next person stood up. Each person urged him to recognize the maturity process that had taken place as eighteen-year-old Natalie had become a mature mother and that Natalie's criminal record was decades old. Natalie's friend, Teri, gave an account of the camping trips

Natalie took her kids on without their deceased father, how she taught her son to fish and took them to church, worked the night shift, and fixed cars on the side. Teri testified that she never saw Natalie discipline her children with any excessive roughness. She pleaded for the members of the court to send Natalie to a program if they believed she had a drinking problem or to send her to parenting classes if the court found her to be an unfit parent but to have mercy because of her fourteen years. The judge looked bored.

When it was my turn, I found within me a dim glow of hope for justice. Just for reassurance, I asked the judge if he had received the letters I faxed to him, but he said, "No." I spoke faster explaining how I had faxed the letters to make very sure he received them on her behalf. He again denied ever seeing any letters for this case. I verbally gave my version of the contents of my letter. When I was finished, he just looked at me, and I took my seat.

Kevin then took his turn to speak before the judge. He wore a white, crisp button-down shirt that he tucked into his black, creased pants. The cuffs were buttoned at his wrists, giving the sleeves a slight balloon effect.

Without his usual baseball cap, the lights above were caught in the waves of his bright yellow hair. When he began to speak, only the howls and cries of his soul filled the courtroom. I quickly went to him as he became crestfallen and held him in my right arm, speaking on his behalf.

I pled to the judge to recognize how much these children's lives would be devastated without their mother, who never had a complaint or a child protective services case brought against her. Looking at Kevin and back at the judge, I reminded him that Kevin (still choking and sobbing) would be twenty-four upon her release, with time served. The judge looked as if he wanted me to get to the point.

I looked at my sister helplessly and out of ammunition. She was now crying too, but it was for her son. Her arms could not hold him even if her chains dropped to the floor—the chains that were linked to at least thirty other prisoners, both men and woman. Rows of jumpsuits and t-shirts made them all look alike except for their hair and features. I saw through the jumpsuits as their hardened faces softened with compassion as Kevin sobbed, but the judge remained unmoved. I gave one last look of astonishment at the judge, knowing I could not crack his icy glare, which reminded me of the glaze that rolls over a lizard's eyes when it sleeps yet appears to be awake.

The judge sentenced Natalie to fourteen years then staggered many in the courtroom by signing a restraining order, which said that Natalie's children could not visit her until they reached the age of eighteen. He referred to them as victims! Shock jolted the family, and I heard Natalie's friend Teri cry. The others went out the door quickly to catch Garza outside. We could hear the people that surrounded us murmuring on Natalie's behalf. Outside, the tall slim nurse cornered Garza in private in the parking lot. Her stern, square jaw line was firm as her eyebrows bundled tightly together, and although her voice was inaudible, I was sure she gave him a good tongue-lashing.

Kevin seemed confused about the restraining order. He didn't feel the necessity to be protected from his mother and complained, "They aren't protecting us!" He protested, "They don't know anything about us . . . Ya know . . . they never did any kind of follow up or asked us what happened. I have visited my mom every Wednesday since she's been in jail—for over a year! It's just another way to *hurt her!* It's not to protect *us.*"

I agreed with Kevin.

Throughout the years, Kevin could not visit his mother, but he wrote her frequently. Angel picked family friends to foster her in Los Banos, but they coveted her and eventually would not accept collect calls from Natalie. When Angel ran away from them, she stayed with high school friends. Kevin stayed with friends and family until he was sent to a foster home due to the slow process of the county's red tape. Kevin's uncle, Rick Blackketter, was jumping through hoops, fingerprinting, and playing phone tag with the foster care social worker. Before the process was complete, Kevin ran away from his foster home in Atwater, California, a town unfamiliar to him, and returned to Los Banos to be near his sister and friends.

Habitat for Humanity completed the house, and it was now occupied by another family. The community and family members became a coop to keep these "now fugitive runaways" from the system at their own risk. It was difficult for the kids to remain in contact with their mother under these conditions. This was the sentence of the innocent as Kevin and Angel awaited their eighteenth birthdays—two of the millions of children who are doing time with mom.

When Kevin turned eighteen in 2007, he and his long-time girlfriend, Courtney, went to CIW for the first time to visit his mom. When they returned home, they brought back photos of the visit. I eagerly reached for the photos, but my excitement quickly faded. How small my sister had become. The photograph became a yardstick that measured time. Kevin had grown taller over the years, and he now dwarfed his mother. I retained an image of a mother who embraced a son who reached *her shoulders,* but now Kevin towered over his mother. His arms looked large around her as her head now reached *his shoulder,* as if they were trading places.

Kevin and Angel grieved for their mother throughout the years. When Natalie filed a writ of habeas corpus, she was denied. She appealed on the grounds that it is against the Constitution for a lawyer to hold animosity against his own client, as Garza had demonstrated. Another violation was that her lawyer had lied to her to persuade her not to go to trial. In addition, we learned much later that judges do not receive faxed letters; the judge in her trial did not receive the letters sent on Natalie's behalf, as he had stated. Rather, letters must be sealed and sent through the mail for legal reasons. If the judge's secretary, or Garza, had cared enough to inform us of the legalities, perhaps the family and community would have been heard and would have made a difference. Perhaps not. Perhaps in reality, life is not always fair, and neither are hearings, and one must wonder if hearings have anything to do with being heard.

POSTSCRIPT

In 2008 Kevin and Courtney were married. Both tried to join the army, but Courtney failed her physical. She was six weeks pregnant, so they returned to Fresno. Natalie became a grandmother in March 2009. She was not permitted visitation until she went through a lengthy process of red tape, even though the court restricted only her children's visitation as minors. Natalie's visitation privileges to visit with minors were finally reinstated, and she will hold her grandson for the first time after January 2010. Angel, now twenty-four and single with no children, is a proud auntie and live-in babysitter for her nephew, Kalvin.

CHAPTER SEVEN

ASFA and the Impact on Imprisoned Migrant Women and Their Children

Martha Escobar

In the summer of 2004 I interned with Justice Now, a prison abolitionist organization located in Oakland, California. The organization works with women in prison to address some of their immediate concerns while remaining committed and working toward the vision of creating a world without prisons. I worked with four Mexican migrant women imprisoned in Central California Women's Facility, in Chowchilla, California. This group of women faced termination of their parental rights, which means that their children would be "released" for adoption. In addition, they were all going to be deported at the end of their sentences. In this chapter I use two of these stories, Lupe's and Laura's, as case studies to explore the impact of the Adoption and Safe Families Act of 1997 (ASFA) on the relationships of imprisoned migrant mothers with their children. The analysis exposes how women's noncitizen status shaped their mothering from within prison. Rather than marking their experiences as exceptional—rather than considering the citizen/noncitizen divide as the factor that enables the separation and violability of these families—the analysis is grounded in literature that addresses the racialized impact of ASFA imprisonment on mother-child relationships. I mark the temporary and permanent family separations that occur in these case studies as continuances of racialized child welfare practices that work against the integrity of nonwhite families. Rather than reify problematic conceptualizations of the heteronormative family, by characterizing the imprisonment of migrant women and the separation of their children from their families as forms of captivity structured through federal legislations, I attempt to destabilize the state's ability to intervene in the most intimate spaces of women's lives.

ROADMAP

The chapter begins with a discussion of ASFA and a review of the literature on its role in separating families with imprisoned mothers, and I pay close attention to the ways that ideas about race inform these practices. In addition to illustrating that ASFA increases the likelihood of family separation between imprisoned mothers and their children, it also underscores its racialized impact and highlights that families of color disproportionately face family separation. This is followed by a discussion of ASFA in relation to U.S. immigration and welfare laws enacted in 1996: the Illegal Immigration Reform and Immigrant Responsibility Act (IIRIRA), the Antiterrorism and Effective Death Penalty Act (The Antiterrorist Act), and the Personal Responsibility and Work Opportunity Act (the Welfare Reform Act). The discussion provides the context within which to examine the family separation that Lupe, Laura, and their families encountered; it also underscores how these policies criminalized migrant motherhood and structured a situation in which migrant parents in prison face deportation and possible permanent separation from their children. The core of the chapter concentrates on providing an examination of the case studies and illustrating the additional barriers that noncitizen mothers face in maintaining their parental rights from within the confines of prison. In addition to providing a summary of findings, the essay concludes with a discussion of how migrant women's imprisonment crystallizes their construction as *bad mothers* through the discourse of personal responsibility, which ideologically validates the disintegration of their families. I also direct our attention to several questions that children's placements generate with regards to the socioracial formation of the United States.

CONTEXTUALIZING MIGRANT MOTHERING FROM PRISON

Prisons are important sites where the regulation and control of migrant women's mothering takes place (Bortner 2002).[1] Family separation is an intrinsic aspect of women's imprisonment (Enos 2001; Raeder 2003; Golden 2005; Gabel and Johnston 1995). Legal theorist Myrna S. Raeder (2003) examines family separation caused by imprisonment and underscores the disregard the state demonstrates toward parents in prison. She cites Brand in the 1990 case *U.S. v. Brand*, who argued that family separation is an inevitable aspect of imprisonment: "[S]uch a situation is not extraordinary. A sole custodial parent is not a rarity in today's society, and imprisoning such a parent will by definition separate the parent from the children. It is apparent that in many cases the other parent may be unable or unwilling to care for the children, and that the children will have to live with relatives, friends, or even in foster homes" (181).

Raeder continues and cites Brand's conclusion, in which he states that the defendant's "situation, though unfortunate, is simply not out of the ordinary" (181). Brand's comments attest to the ways that family separation is naturalized under the current logic of imprisonment. Observing a similar trend of government intervention in families of imprisoned mothers, Clarice Feinman notes that many states have enacted laws that enable the state to declare an incarcerated mother unfit and have reserved the right to take custody as a way to remove children from such influences (1994, 60).

While the separation of imprisoned parents and their children has a long history in the United States (Beckerman 1994; Enos 1998), this was exacerbated with the enactment of the Adoption and Safe Families Act (ASFA) (Genty 2008; Day 2005; Smith and Young 2003). ASFA amended the Adoption Assistance and Child Welfare Act of 1980 (U.S. Children's Bureau November 1997). Its objective was to promote safety and permanence for children in the foster care system. It was originally intended to address the needs of children in foster care who are alleged or determined to be *abused* and/or *neglected*. One of the changes ASFA implemented was a *permanency* hearing within twelve months of children's placement in foster care. Prior to this act the hearing took place eighteen months after placement and was termed a "dispositional" hearing.[2] The hearing must include a permanency plan for the child, whether this is family reunification, parental rights termination, placing the child with relatives, or long-term foster care placement. The twelve-month period for the permanency hearing begins "(i) the date of the first judicial finding that the child has been subjected to child abuse or neglect; *or* (ii) the date that is 60 days after the date on which the child is removed from the home."[3] This means that children in foster care do not necessarily have to be neglected or abused, but rather the simple fact of being placed in foster care is a basis for processing children for adoption. In addition, the policy established that for parents with children who remain in foster care for fifteen of the previous twenty-two months, termination of their parental rights must be initiated unless there are demanding circumstances and the welfare agency finds that it is not in the best interest of the children to have their parental rights terminate.[4] The act expedited timelines for determining the permanent plan for the children, whether this is returning them to their parents, adoptive homes, or other permanent arrangements.

The discourse employed throughout ASFA is the promotion of the health and safety of children in foster care; it constantly marks the child's safety as the paramount concern. The problem is not the focus on children's safety but rather how safety is defined. Part of what is encompassed under the child's health and safety is the idea of stability. For imprisoned parents "stability" takes on a different meaning given their confinement. Barbara Bloom notes that child welfare laws allow "termination of parental rights if the parent has failed to maintain an adequate relationship with a child who is in foster care. Imprisonment, by its very nature, poses serious obstacles to the maintenance of the mother-child relationships" (2003, 66). While enacted to protect *abused* and/or *neglected* children, in its implementation ASFA results in punishment for imprisoned parents with children in the foster care system since the majority of people in prison have sentences that exceed fifteen months.[5] In other words, parents in prison are losing their parental rights solely because they are imprisoned, which in addition to negatively affecting imprisoned mothers (Enos 2001; Renny 2005; Day 2005), also has negative consequences for their children (Bloom and Steinhart 1993; Lee, Genty, and Laver 2005; Simmons 2000; Gabel and Johnston 1995; Sharp and Eriksen 2003; Renny 2005).

It is important to consider the racialized impact of ASFA on families with imprisoned parents since women of color make up the majority in prisons (USBJS 2007; Silliman and Bhattacharjee 2002). Children of color are overrepresented in foster care (Roberts 2002), and this number is increasingly composed of children of incarcerated parents (Johnson and Waldfogel 2002). Scholars have documented the disproportionate impact of ASFA on black families (White 2006; Greenaway 2003; McRoy 2005; Roberts 2002). This scholarship shows that ASFA unevenly impacts black families and contributes to their disintegration. Christina White marks this disintegration as federally mandated, meaning that ASFA, as federal legislation, is intimately implicated in structuring the experiences of separation that occurs within black families. Antoinette Greenaway (2003) goes one step further and shows that ASFA has a significant role in the disintegration of families of imprisoned black mothers given the strict requirements and time limits imposed by this legislation. I discuss the situation of black families with mothers in prison to situate the experiences of imprisoned migrant women and their families within a larger history that demonstrates the central role of race in the state's intervention in women's lives. The discussion highlights the centrality of the state's intervention in ensuring the violability of women of color and their families. In the following section I place ASFA in conversation with other federal legislation, and the examination reinforces the argument that federal legislation unevenly shapes family separation.

THE STRUCTURING POWER OF FEDERAL LEGISLATION

In the case of migrant mothers in prison, the effect of ASFA on their families needs to be read in relation to federal policies enacted in 1996 that changed immigration control. These include the Illegal Immigration Reform and Immigrant Responsibility Act (IIRIRA), the Antiterrorism and Effective Death Penalty Act (The Antiterrorist Act), and the Personal Responsibility and Work Opportunity Act (the Welfare Reform Act). Together, these policies increased the number of crime deportations, criminalized migrant motherhood, and increased separation of families with imprisoned parents. I provide a discussion of their impact on the gendered criminalization of migrants and conclude the section by discussing how these policies intersect with ASFA to structure the situation of imprisoned migrant mothers and their families.

In the last decade the number of migrants in U.S. prisons has expanded considerably, particularly Mexican migrants. On February 18, 2009, the Pew Research Center published "A Rising Share: Hispanics and Federal Crime," a study that shows that changes in enforcement of immigration laws have resulted in making Latinos the largest ethnic group in the federal prison system (Lopez

2009). Criminalizing practices are highlighted through the following example. In 1995 the percentage of Mexican citizens in U.S. federal prisons was 9.8 percent (Bureau of Prisons 1995), and in 2007 they comprised 17.1 percent (Bureau of Prisons 2007). Rather than migrants' increased engagement in criminalized acts, this growth reflects changes in legislation that redefined the meaning of crime and penalized migrants. During the decade of the 1990s we witnessed the passing of punitive legislation that fused migration to state dependency and criminality. Two of the most significant include IIRIRA and the Welfare Reform Act. IIRIRA was presumably enacted to target "criminal aliens." In partnership with the antiterrorist act passed during the same year, IIRIRA increased the number of deportable migrants (Welch 2002; Morawetz 2000; Dole 2006). Combined, these two legislations amended and added new offenses to the definition of *aggravated felony* and made this new definition apply retroactively. In addition, the changes implemented in 1996 created a "criminal alien identification system," intended to locate migrants with prior convictions who were now made deportable. These policies facilitated the deportation of imprisoned migrants, regardless of their legal status. To underscore their significance, let me provide some numbers. In 1998 47,945 people were deported for criminal status (Office of Immigration Statistics 2005). That number increased to 94,505 by 2008 (Office of Immigration Statistics 2008), a 50 percent increase within ten years.

In addition to expanding the number of deportable migrants, it also included restrictions for migrants' access to state resources. IIRIRA contains a section titled "Restrictions on Benefits for Aliens." The following is a summary of this section provided by the Immigration and Naturalization Services (INS): "Title V contains amendments to the welfare bill, the Social Security Act, and the INA which are directed at limiting aliens' access to public benefits. Proof of citizenship is required to receive public benefits and verification of immigration status is required for Social Security and higher-educational assistance. A transition period (until April 1, 1997) is established for aliens who are currently receiving food stamps" (U.S. INS 1997). What is significant for our purpose is to emphasize the punitive nature of these policies that criminalize and expand the number of migrants that can be deported and the way that the logic of IIRIRA conflates migration with state dependency and criminality.

The same year that IIRIRA passed, the Welfare Reform Act was enacted. Incorporating many of the restrictions that California's Proposition 187 attempted to implement, the Welfare Reform Act targeted migrants' use of public resources. It restricted access to Medicaid, food stamps, cash assistance for poor families, and assistance for the disabled and elderly migrants. In addition to limiting migrants' access to these benefits, it targeted people convicted for felony drug offenses by banning them for life from certain resources, including the Food Stamp program. Again, what I stress is that similar to IIRIRA, the logic of the Welfare Reform Act merged migration, crime, and state dependency. In discussing these anti-immigrant policies, activist scholar Syd Lindsley argues that the criminalization and attacks that migrants undergo, especially Mexican migrant women, at the most basic level has little to do with the costs that this group has on the state and the nation. Rather, these policies "reflect assumptions about the value of immigrant mothers in U.S. society," and their passing is "an attempt to regulate and control immigrant women's mothering" (2002, 185).

I provide this reading of migrant criminalization through federal policies to contextualize the impact of ASFA on migrant families. Concerns over women's reproduction, highlighted in the criminalization of migrants via charges of state dependency, increasingly made women targets of the state, including imprisonment.[6] As in the general population, migrant women tend to be the primary caregivers for their children prior to imprisonment. Imprisoned migrants' imminent deportation intersects with the time restrictions imposed by ASFA and the class bias of child welfare policies. Together, these policies structure imprisoned migrant mothers' ability to maintain their families' whole. In their cases, their noncitizen status shapes the decisions that are made over their children's futures, and, as the following case studies demonstrate, ideas over children's "safety" and "stability" are differentially marked by their mothers' and families' noncitizenship status.

MOTHERING FROM THE INSIDE AS A "NONCITIZEN"

As discussed, losing custody of their children to the state is not unusual for mothers in prison. ASFA increased the likelihood of parental rights termination for parents in prison. Child welfare policies, especially with regards to home placement, impose regulations that are extremely difficult to adhere to. These regulations promote an understanding of children's *welfare* in economic terms, which limits imprisoned parents', friends', and families' ability to obtain custody of their children. For example, specific home arrangements and the ability to *provide* for the children are two of the requirements to have children placed with a family. These requirements make it extremely difficult for poor and migrant families to become children's caretakers. In some cases, parents in prison can request to have their children placed with relatives or friends in their country of origin, but the same standards have to be met as in the United States.

In addition, U.S. immigration status generates further constraints in securing placement of children. This is especially the case if the individuals attempting to obtain custody are undocumented. First, the involvement in child placement cases requires direct interaction with state authorities, which serves to deter some undocumented individuals from attempting to obtain custody. Second, in some cases, even when undocumented individuals want to care for the children, they are denied because, according to the court, their undocumented status presents a form of instability for the children since undocumented individuals permanently run the risk of deportation. The following case studies illustrate how class and noncitizenship status inform the placement of children of imprisoned migrant mothers.

LUPE

Lupe Martin arrived at the Central California Women's Facility in July 2003. At the time of her arrest she was the primary caretaker of her six children and was the one seeking legal aid for her parental rights case, placing most parental responsibility on her. Her sentence was going to be completed in October 2004. Lupe's imprisonment resulted from giving a friend a ride. When they were stopped by police for a traffic infraction, her friend was caught with drugs, and both were arrested. Lupe was given a three-year sentence. Her husband, Salvador, was in prison at the time of her arrest, and her children were placed in foster care.[7] To avoid having her children placed in foster care Lupe had to provide "adequate" guardians, which included the placement home having enough rooms for the children and everyone in the home being fingerprinted.[8] Lupe and her husband requested that their children be placed with Alberto, Salvador's brother, and his wife, Lucia. Lupe and Salvador signed forms giving power of attorney and temporary guardianship of the children over to them. However, Alberto and Lucia were found inadequate to care for the children,[9] which I discuss further below.

Lupe requested that if the children could not be placed with Alberto and Lucia, they be placed with Roberto and Berenice, family friends. Lupe and her children had lived with this couple prior to her arrest, and the children knew them as their aunt and uncle.[10] The couple offered to care for the children until Lupe was released from prison. During our phone conversations and letter exchange, Lupe asked me to help this couple obtain custody of the children. Lupe wrote: "Can you talk with them and orient them on how they can do it so that the children can be placed with them while I get out? On September 20 at 8:30 I have an appeal for my children, and I have to have who they are going with, but I in no way want my children to be placed for adoption or have them send them to my mother to Mexico. She has also asked for them. I want to be sure that I am not going to lose my children."[11] As had happened with Alberto and Lucia, Roberto and Berenice were told that due to their "inadequate" living arrangements, which was premised on them having a small home, the children could not be placed with them. Due to their financial situation Lupe's friends could not afford to move and were denied the custody of the children, although they continuously attempted to negotiate with the children's social worker.[12] Throughout Lupe's imprisonment, the couple maintained contact with the children and were able to obtain regular visits with them.

Lupe's lawyer filed a complaint in which they argued that the court had erred in removing the children and not placing them with relatives. The complaint was met with a response by the Health and Human Services Agency[13] in which they defended their position and stated, "The agency investigator believed the children could not be placed with Alberto and Lucia because they lived in a two-bedroom apartment with one other adult and three children and did not meet the criteria for foster care licensing regulations. Further, Alberto had not obtained the necessary supplies to take care of six more children, refused to be fingerprinted, and was an undocumented illegal alien."[14] The court cited that the situation would have resulted in three adults and nine children living in a two-bedroom apartment. This was perceived as a threat to the well-being and safety of the children, particularly since some of the children have serious health issues. In short, the children were not placed with their uncle and aunt because they were defined as poor. The court also cited the fact that Alberto and his wife are undocumented and thus subject to deportation at any time, which made the children vulnerable. The court used these factors to argue that the parents had not made suitable arrangements for the care of their children during their incarceration.

Besides trying to have the agency place the children with these two couples, Lupe also submitted names of relatives in Mexico who could care for them. In the complaint Lupe's lawyer submitted, he argued that Lupe and Salvador had provided the names of relatives in Mexico who could care for her children. The agency responded:

> The parents also assert the court erred in taking jurisdiction over the children because they made other arrangements for the children to live with relatives in Mexico. However, two of the persons they identified were unwilling to take the children. Another was unwilling to be fingerprinted. Home evaluations were in process, but had not been completed, for other persons identified by the parents. In any event, there is no evidence the parents had spoken to the relatives about taking the children, any of these relatives had agreed to take the children while the parents were incarcerated, or that the parents had executed letters of temporary guardianship for these relatives. Consequently, there is no evidence the parents had made alternative arrangements with other relatives to care for the children.[15]

Lupe's imprisonment limited her communication with her family in Mexico, complicating her situation. However, Lupe and her mother wanted the children sent to Mexico. The children's grandparents' home was evaluated by the Mexican social services agency and was found inadequate for placement. The U.S. Health and Human Services Agency called upon the Mexican social services to carry out the job of the U.S. agency, which was to evaluate homes for placement. This process of a U.S. agency calling upon the Mexican agency to carry out its job blurs the national lines of distinction between agencies, and it is indicative of the role that they have in society—crossing national boundaries and making judgments over "adequate" parents on both sides of the border. This process erases the particular historical development of each individual country informed by issues of class and race and places equal requirements on everyone on both sides of the border. In other words, a standard shaped by white middle-class ideals is established, and people in both the United States and Mexico are expected to meet these measures. While the intent of the process can be to conduct a thorough investigation and a genuine attempt to place the children with family members, the standards themselves limit people's ability to care for children of imprisoned migrants since they are difficult to comply with.

Rather than considering the structural inequalities produced through noncitizen status and middle-class requirements imposed by child welfare policies, the court cited Lupe's inability to provide "fit" guardians as the reason for not placing the children with the couples Lupe suggested. Therefore, the implementation of these policies results in limiting the ability to place children with relatives, especially if they are poor and/or undocumented. The removal of Lupe's children was rationalized as her fault. Her inability to make "suitable arrangements" for her children was cited as the cause for the children's foster care placement. In an attempt to establish that the court did not commit any error in deciding to not place the children with Alberto and Lucia, it resorts to prior cases, *In re Aaron S., In re Monica C.,* and *In re Athena P.,* and it argues that these cases "support the proposition that the arrangements made by the parent must be suitable or adequate." The purpose of dependency law is to "ensure the safety and well-being of children" (3002). To do this, "the Agency must be able to challenge and the court must be able to review whether childcare arrangements made by incarcerated parents after Agency intervention are suitable." The agency goes on to claim that

> if the Agency presents substantial evidence that the arrangements made by the parents after Agency intervention are not suitable or adequate and will not protect the children from a substantial risk of harm, true findings under section 300, subdivision (g) must be upheld . . . Here, the Agency demonstrated by a preponderance of the evidence that the arrangements with Alberto and Lucia were not suitable.[16] The arrangements made by the parents would result in three adults and nine children living in a two-bedroom apartment. Such overcrowding would not protect the well-being or safety of the children, particularly those children with significant health issues.[17]

The requirements that prevented Alberto and Lucia from having the children placed with them are mostly based on issues of class and their overall lack of resources. The criteria prevented Lupe and Salvador from placing their children with family members indicating that the parents made "unsuitable" and "inadequate" arrangements for their children.

According to Lupe, her lawyer strongly advocated for her parental rights case and remained in contact with her consistently.[18] Lupe believed that her children were not taken from her because of the support she had from her lawyer, who contested the decisions of the state pertaining to her children. Lupe was told by her lawyer that as soon as she was deported she should contact him, so he could begin the process of family reunification, and the children would be sent to her in Mexico, which is what eventually occurred.[19] However, this is not always the case, as the following story demonstrates.

LAURA

As in Lupe's case, for Laura, class and her noncitizen status dramatically shaped her children's placement. Laura had three children from her first marriage: Jose, twenty-one, Cristian, thirteen, and Jennifer, six. Her two youngest children were U.S. citizens. Laura left her husband and then met Javier, who was her partner at the time of her arrest and with whom she had a two-year-old baby girl, Alondra. In March 2003, Laura, Javier, their three youngest children, and a friend moved from Colorado to California. The friend joined them on the trip to help with the driving but was planning on returning to Colorado within a week. The family and their friend rented a motel room while they searched for an apartment. During the stay at the motel room Laura found a suitcase with drugs that belonged to their friend who was leaving that day. Her friend was not around, so she put the suitcase away so that her children would not find it. Laura had left the motel room, and when she returned, she found her friend being arrested. When asked about the drugs, she was told that her friend had already confessed and that she should cooperate. Laura gave the police the suitcase, but in an attempt to save her friend said that the drugs belonged to another person who was not there. The police in turn arrested Laura and set her friend free. The children were placed in the custody of child protective services until Javier arrived. Javier had left to pick up the key to their newly rented apartment and returned to find that Laura had been arrested and the children were gone. There was a police officer waiting for Javier, who was arrested also but released as soon as he was determined drug-free. He was given the number to the children's social worker. Because it was late Friday, Javier was told by the social worker to call on Monday. In the meantime the children would be in their care. The following Monday happened to be the Cesar Chavez holiday, which meant some state offices were closed, including Child Protective Services. When Javier was finally able to get a hold of the social worker on Tuesday, he was informed that the children had been placed in state care because the seventy-two-hour limit to claim them had passed and now he had to go through the court system to claim the children.[20]

Javier attempted to obtain custody of the children. In Laura's account of her story she described the many complications she and Javier faced. She wrote that when they went to court for the children to be placed with Javier, the judge told him that he had to obtain a two-bedroom apartment and beds for the children. The following is her written account:

> Javier did everything they asked him to do. In another court hearing they told him to look for someone to provide child-care for the children and he looked for someone from Child Development Resources. He

presented the business card of the person that was going to care for the children and they told him that no, to look for a family to take the children. A couple from church . . . offered themselves to take care of the children. They asked them to fill out an application. They did everything they were asked to do. Jessica (the children's social worker) went to their home and I asked her how everything was and she said that it was fine and that she was just waiting on whatever the court said. Jose Cortez and Victoria Cortez were waiting to hear from the court but they never called them. Then in the next court hearing they gave the little girl, Nereida Castro, and they went to look at Javier's apartment and told him that it was fine and that that week he would be given custody of Carlos and Kimberly. They told Javier to look for another job so he could sustain them well. Then he obtained another job. He would go in at 9:00 a.m. and would get out at 3:30 p.m. Then he would go into the next job at 4:30 p.m. and would get out at 10:00 p.m. and didn't have time to visit the children, but he would call them on the phone whenever he had a chance. Then in the next court they told Javier that he didn't visit the children. That his visits were irregular. Then in October 2003 I spoke to Jessica and she told me that they had given Javier the papers to fill out again and she asked me if I still wanted the children placed with Javier once I was transferred to prison and I said yes. Before coming to prison I wrote a letter to Jessica in which I told her that I wanted the children placed with Javier because I told her everything that they were asking from him and I wanted them to help him out economically so that he only had to work one job so that he could spend more time with the children. I came to prison thinking that the children were going to be placed with him. When I would speak with Javier he would tell me that Bisbin, our lawyer, would always give him hopes that the children were going to be placed with him. In a court hearing in October of 2003 they told me that I was going to have a hearing on April 22, 2004, at which I wasn't present. In those days I received a paper in which they had changed my court hearing to April 8th, 2004, where they were going to terminate my rights as mother.[21]

Laura's written account of the barriers presented to them is indicative of imprisoned parents' experiences. First Javier was required to have a home where the boy would have his own room and the two girls had their own room. He rented a large enough home in order to qualify to have the children placed with him. However, in the meantime he rented part of it to a family with the understanding that they would leave when Javier was granted legal guardianship of the children. The fact that there were people living in the children's rooms was used as basis to deny him custody, even though the social worker was informed that this was a temporary arrangement. Laura's nephew, Ramiro, offered to care for the children. However, he was undocumented and lived with his aunt who was also undocumented and who refused to be fingerprinted because she feared deportation, and thus the children were not placed with him. Unfortunately, the fact that Javier is not the biological father of Cristian and Jennifer, the obstacles created by placement requirements, and Ramiro's undocumented status and living arrangements prevented both of them from obtaining legal custody of the children.

As soon as the fifteen-month time limit stipulated by ASFA was met, Laura's parental rights were terminated. The judge said that she did not see any "inconvenience"[22] for the children to be placed for adoption and they were adopted by what Laura and Javier called "los gringos rancheros," meaning the white ranchers. Laura asked Maria Valle, the children's social worker, why the children were being adopted, and Maria responded, "Ellos tienen modo," meaning that the couple had the "means" to adopt and care for the children.[23] Maria's comment is indicative of how ideas of parenthood are tied to class and the parents who are able to provide for the children materially are privileged. Javier, who had limited resources, was unable to provide economically in the same way that the "gringos rancheros" could. The children's first social worker told Laura at one point that she and Javier did not have the resources to buy the children clothes, highlighting the way in which Laura and Javier were marked as unfit to care for the children based on their economic situation. During one of our visits, Laura told me that she worried about the children because she did not know what kind of people they had been placed with. At one point she said, "I don't know the people who they are with. I don't know if they use drugs, alcohol, if they have anger problems. I don't know how they do those things without knowing the persons."[24] Laura's concerns over her children are about their safety and the treatment they will receive from their adoptive parents. She could not fathom how the children could be placed with this couple and questioned me on the criteria in selecting them over Javier, who had been part of their life for over three years. Laura's children were adopted, and she was deported.

CONCLUSION

Lupe's and Laura's case studies reveal some of the obstacles presented to imprisoned Mexican migrant mothers in maintaining their parental rights. The time constraints that ASFA places to terminate parental rights combined with the class-informed requirements for placement resulted in temporary and permanent separation of their children from their families. In many instances, the language of ASFA as holding the child's health and safety paramount and having the best interest of the child in mind erases the violent process of removing children from their families. In the case of imprisoned mothers, taking their children takes place mainly because of the time limits implemented by ASFA and because of the obstacles presented to poor families, and not necessarily through documentation that the children were abused or neglected. Taking their children is rationalized through the language of stability, a family ethic that is allegedly broken by imprisoned mothers since their imprisonment is considered the cause for the children's instability and initial placement in foster care. The implementation of these policies overrides the consideration of factors such as structural criminalization of poor communities of color and the impact that strict placement standards have on poor and undocumented families.

The role of legislations in organizing the process of family separation is obscured by placing fault on the women themselves. Being labeled "criminal" automatically marks them as *bad mothers,* and therefore taking their child(ren) is rationalized as actions performed in the best interest of the child(ren). In turn, taking their children ideologically authenticates the identity of *bad mothers* attached to women in prison. Women are valued based on notions of motherhood, and constructing them as *bad mothers* naturalizes any consequences that are assumed to occur because of their *choices.* In the case of imprisoned Mexican migrant mothers, loss of their children furthers their identity as undesirable and provides additional rationale for deportation. Law professor Clarice Feinman makes the point that imprisoned women are denied a relationship with their children based on "being declared unfit mothers by state law or a general attitude that female offenders should be punished for not fulfilling their role in womanhood" (1994, 57). In addition to the denial of a relationship with their children, punishment for violating gender roles for Mexican migrant women comes through deportation.

More than providing answers, these stories generate new questions on the issue of U.S. nation-state formation and the many ideas that inform this development. Policies such as IIRIRA, the Antiterrorism Act, and the Welfare Reform Act speak to the ways that migrants are imagined through ideas of criminality and dependency, often joining the two. However, in these cases where state agencies have to decide over the children of migrants and whether they are placed in the United States or in their parents' home country, we have to question how these decisions are made. What ideologies inform who stays and who leaves? What difference does the parents' and the children's legal status make? What does it mean that as a society we define children's well-being in economic terms that privilege white middle-class standards of living? Furthermore, what do these stories tell us about national sovereignty when a U.S. agency, Health and Human Services, assigns a Mexican agency, social services, to conduct home evaluations based on U.S. measures? The experiences of migrant mothers in prison are sites where these questions emerge and that direct our attention toward the continued presence of the state in people's lives. In a time when we continuously find ourselves asking what the role of the state is in light of increasing globality, these stories speak back. In these cases, prisons serve as sites where decisions about national membership are negotiated, and by extension the social formation of the nation-state. Lupe's and Laura's experiences, rather than simply exposing state policies as strategies for exclusion, reveal dialectical processes that generate multiple forms of (non)belongings for imprisoned parents and their children that need to be further examined.

NOTES

1. While both men and women face parental rights' termination, in the majority of cases women are the primary caretakers, so I concentrate on the situation of mothers in prison.

2. Title III. Sec. 302(2).

3. Title I Sec. 103(b)(3)(i) and (ii).

4. Title I Sec.103 (a)(2)(E).

5. In 2005, for example, the average prison sentence was 47.7 months, and the average time served was 24.8 months. *California Department of Corrections Fourth Quarter 2005 Facts and Figures.*

6. The War on Drugs has been central to the imprisonment of migrant women not just in the United States but globally (Díaz-Cotto, 2007).

7. Lupe's written account, August 13, 2004.

8. Under Title I Sec.106., ASFA established that in order to place children, criminal records checks are required.

9. Interview with Lupe, August 13, 2004, Chowchilla, California.

10. Her own account, August 13, 2004, and phone interview, August 19, 2004.

11. Lupe's own account, August 13, 2004.

12. Phone interview with Alberto, August 10, 2004.

13. From here on referred to as the "agency," which is the term the report employs.

14. Court of Appeal, Fourth Appelate District, Division One, State of California, January 24, 2005.

15. Court of Appeal, Fourth Appelate District, Division One, State of California, January 24, 2005.

16. The agency spends a significant portion of its brief asserting that the residence was not suitable because it did not meet the criteria for licensing of a foster care home. In this case, we need not address whether a home must meet those criteria to be considered suitable arrangements under section 300, subdivision (g).

17. Kimberly had open heart surgery in 2002 and was taking three medications to prevent infection. Santiago and Gilberto had asthma and had to use inhalers.

18. Interview with Lupe, July 30, 2004, Chowchilla, California.

19. Ibid.

20. Laura's story is compiled from her July 30, 2004, written account, interview with Laura on the same day, and phone interviews with Javier on August 2, 2004, and August 12, 2004.

21. Laura's written account of her story, July 30, 2004.

22. Interview with Laura on August 13, 2004, Chowchilla, California.

23. Interview, July 30, 2004, Chowchilla, California.

24. Interview with Laura, July 23, 2004, Chowchilla, California.

REFERENCES

Beckerman, Adela. 1994. "Mothers in Prison: Meeting the Prerequisite Conditions for Permanency Planning." *Social Work* 39: 9–14.

Bhattacharjee, Anannya, and Jael Silliman. 2002. *Policing the National Body: Race, Gender, and Criminalization.* Cambridge: South End.

Bloom, Barbara, and David Steinhart. 1993. *Why Punish the Children? A Reappraisal of the Children of Incarcerated Mothers in America.* San Francisco: National Council on Crime and Delinquency.

Bloom, Barbara E. 2003. *Gendered Justice: Women in the Criminal Justice System.* Durham: Carolina Academic.

Bohrman, Rebecca, and Naomi Murakawa. 2006. "Remaking Big Government: Immigration and Crime Control in the United States." In *Global Lockdown: Race, Gender, and the Prison-Industrial Complex*, ed. Julia Sudbury, 109–26. New York: Routledge.

Bortner, Margaret A. 2002. "Controlled and Excluded: Reproduction and Motherhood among Poor and Imprisoned Women." In *Women at the Margins: Neglect, Punishment, and Resistance,* ed. Josefina Figueira-McDonough and Mary C. Sarri, 255–70. New York: Hawthorn.

Day, Sally. 2005. "Mothers in Prison: How the Adoption and Safe Families Act of 1997 Threatens Parental Rights." In *Wisconsin Journal of Law, Gender and Society* 20(2).

Díaz-Cotto,, Juanita. 2007. "Latina Imprisonment and the War on Drugs." In *Race, Gender, and Punishment*, ed. Mary Bosworth and Jeanne Flavin, 184–99. Piscataway, NJ: Rutgers University.

Dole, Robert J. January 2006. "Anti-Terrorism and Effective Death Act of 1996." Washington DC: U.S. Senate and Congress.

Enos, Sandra. 2001. *Mothering from the Inside: Parenting in a Women's Prison.* New York: New York.

———. 1998. "Managing Motherhood in Prison: The Impact of Race and Ethnicity on Child Placements. *Women and Therapy* 20 (4): 57–73.

Feinman, Clarice. 1994. *Women in the Criminal Justice System.* Westport: Praeger.

Gabel, Katherine, and Denise Johnston. 1995. *Children of Incarcerated Parents.* New York: Lexington Books.

Genty, Philip M. 2008. "The Inflexibility of the Adoption and Safe Families Act and Its Unintended Impact upon the Children of Incarcerated Parents and Their Families." In *Child Welfare* 360.

Golden, Renny. 2005. *War on the Family: Mothers in Prison and the Children They Leave Behind.* New York: Routledge.

Greenaway, Antoinette. 2003. "When Neutral Policies Aren't So Neutral: Increasing Incarceration Rates and the Effect of the Adoption and Safe Families Act of 1997 on the Parental Rights of African-American Women." In *National Black Law Journal* 247.

Johnson, Elizabeth I. and Jane Waldfogel. September 2002. "Parental Incarceration: Recent Trends and Implications for Child Welfare." In *Social Service Review.*

Lee, Arlene F., Philip M. Genty, and Mimi Laver. 2005. "The Impact of the Adoption and Safe Families Act on Children of Incarcerated Parents." Washington DC: Child Welfare League of America; Washington.

Lindsley, Syd. 2002. "The Gendered Assault on Immigrants." In *Race, Gender, and Criminalization*, ed. Jael Silliman and Anannya Bhattacharjee. Cambridge: South End.

Lopez, Mark Huga. February, 2009. "A Rising Share: Hispanics and Federal Crime." Pew Hispanic Center, http://pewhispanic.org/reports/report.php?ReportID=104.

Luibheid, Eithne. 2002. *Entry Denied: Controlling Sexuality at the Border.* Minneapolis and London: University of Minnesota Press.

McRoy, Roth. 2005. "Expedited Permanency: Implications for African-American Children and Families." In *Virginia Journal of Social Policy and the Law* 475–89.

Morawetz, Nancy. 2000. "Understanding the Impact of the 1996 Deportation Laws and the Limited Scope of Proposed Reforms." *Harvard Law Review* 13(8).

Office of Immigration Statistics. 2005. *Yearbook of Immigration Statistics.* Washington DC: U.S. Department of Homeland Security.

———. 2008. *Yearbook of Immigration Statistics.* Washington DC: U.S. Department of Homeland Security.

Office of Research. 2004. *Third Quarter Facts and Figures.* Sacramento: California Department of Corrections.

Raeder, Myrna S. 2003. "Gendered Implications of Sentencing and Correctional Practices: A Legal Perspective." *Gendered Justice: Women in the Criminal Justice System*, ed. Barbara E. Bloom, 173–207. Durham: Carolina Academic.

Roberts, Dorothy E. 2002. *Shattered Bonds: The Color of Child Welfare.* New York: Basic Books.

Sharp, Susan F., and M. Elaine Eriksen. 2003. "Imprisoned Mothers and Their Children." In *Women in Prison: Gender and Social Control*, ed. Barbara H. Zaitzow and Jim Thomas. Boulder: Lynn Rienner.

Simmons, Charlene Wear. 2000. "Children of Incarcerated Parents." California Research Bureau.

Smith, Carrie Jefferson, and Diane S. Young. 2003. "The Multiple Impacts TANF, ASFA, and Mandatory Drug Sentencing for Families Affected by Maternal Incarceration." In *Children and Youth Services Review* (25) 7: 535–52.

Smith, Gail T. 2006. "The Adoption and Safe Families Act of 1997: Its Impact on Prisoner Mothers and Their Children." In *Women, Girls and Criminal Justice.* Kingston, NJ: Civic Research Institute.

U.S. Bureau of Justice Statistics. "Corrections Statistics." Washington, DC: Department of Justice. February, 2007.

U.S. Children's Bureau. November, 1997. "Adoption and Safe Families Act of 1997 Public Law 105–89, 105th Congress." Washington, DC: Department of Health and Human Services.

U.S. Department of Justice. 1995. *State of the Bureau.* Washington, DC: Federal Bureau of Prisons.

———. 2007. *State of the Bureau.* Washington, DC: Federal Bureau of Prisons.

U.S. Immigration and Naturalization Services. March 1997. "Illegal Immigration Reform and Immigrant Responsibility Act of September 30, 1996." Washington DC: Department of Justice.

Welch, Michael. 2002. *Detained: Immigration Laws and the Expanding I.N.S. Jail Complex.* Philadelphia: Temple University Press.

White, Christina. 2006. "Federally Mandated Destruction of the Black Family: The Adoption and Safe Families Act." In *New Jersey of Law and Social Policy* 303.

CHAPTER EIGHT

Carceral State, Cultural Stake:
Women behind American Bars and Beyond

Trangdai Glassey-Tranguyen

CONTEXTS AND POSITIONALITY

This entry reflects parts of my work toward peace and justice in the broader sense of these two terms. While U.S.-focused in content, the chapter has benefited from my lived experiences and research in Vietnam, the United States, and various parts of Europe over the last three decades. It is important to point out this transnational orientation because the United States, as is true for the rest of the world, has become increasingly globalized with a complex transnational history dating back to the pilgrim and enslavement periods. Hence a U.S.-situated topic does necessitate a mindfulness of various racial groups with differing backgrounds, even when its analytics remains American-oriented.

I deem, as several scholars and activists would concur, that incarceration is a highly contestable and sensitive issue. More often than not, I find myself wedged in the negotiation with different orientations and perspectives, more particularly so in an ethnic community context. In the end, though, my goal is to seek out the voices of and advocate for the stakes of the imprisoned with a critical assessment of both the legal system and the social environment in which the incarcerated reside. Such a position is an ongoing struggle between the prisoners' rights and the society's attitudes or values toward imprisonment.

It is arguable that there are limitations in any efforts to work toward justice for the imprisoned for very obvious reasons. Here, I would like to take a close look at the social and cultural stakes of Vietnamese American women in spite of and alongside all the inherent constraints that I discuss in the next sections. For now, I will locate myself in this work and by so doing, hope to be transparent about my views and goals. As true for my activist scholarship at large, this entry is inspired and informed by my activist endeavors in both the ethnic and academic communities. I elect to highlight a few experiences that will make clear my stance and directions.

I have worked as a community activist in the Vietnamese Orange County community, particularly in Little Saigon, since 1994. My involvement has encompassed areas such as education, cultural development, ethnic language retention, literature, ethnic-language media, faith-based and spiritual ministries, youth leadership, immigration, social justice, political equity, and community empowerment. Given this wide-ranged and long-term commitment, I have witnessed how advocacy for the imprisoned has never gained major attention from the community, nor has it become an issue of import. The prison ministries carried out by the Catholic Church, while a much-needed stewardship, have mostly entailed personal visits and spiritual support and remained shy of advocacy or effecting change on a systemic scale.

The direct involvements I have had in prison advocacy and exposure include a host of activities. First, there was my internship as a NAFEO-SAMHSA intern with the Department of Health and Human Services in Washington, D.C., in summer 2001 (NAFEO National Association for Equal Opportunity in Higher Education; SAMHSA Substance Abuse and Mental Health Services Administration). During my six years in student leadership at CSU Fullerton from 1998 through 2004, I was involved in discussions about and considerations of assistance for immigrant Vietnamese women without language accommodations and legal access in U.S. prisons. Though I will not be able to discuss the specificities of these cases due to confidentiality, I will convey the needs and challenges these Vietnamese immigrant women face behind American bars.

In particular, I gained insights from stories about personal, spiritual, or cultural needs that Vietnamese immigrant women had in prisons via conversations with Dr. Son Kim Vo and fellow CSUF students. I continued my community involvement during my studies at Stanford University from 2005 through 2007, particularly as a member of the board of directors for San Jose–based Vietnamese Second Chance Family, whose objective is to provide housing and job-search assistance to former inmates in their efforts to rebuild their lives. Postprison persons continue to face resentment from the ethnic community, in spite of the fact that they have already served their terms and sought to lead a new life.

Given all the aforementioned contexts and trajectories, my discussion here is grounded in racial equality and justice scholarship. I place my analytics in discussion with works by activist scholars such as Ruthie Wilson Gilmore, Paul Gilroy, Robin Kelley, and Mae Ngai, to mention only some. Last but not least, this entry is written with a perspectival approach, which I think is appropriate for two distinct reasons. First, the discourses of most incarcerated women are not available in the "official" or metanarrative records of the U.S. law enforcement system. Second, their voices are often relegated to the back if at all present, unacknowledged, and excluded. In such a context, their perspectives and personal experiences are what we need to closely engage with and take stake in to combat the lack of a formal (written) depository of information about them. This perspectival approach is in the spirit of Renato Resaldo's perspectival history as analyzed in his work on the Ilongots in the Philippines (Rosaldo 1980), a group of people without written language and believed to be without a history. Yet Resaldo insists that they have their own history according to the stories and perspectives that survive across the generations.

A FEW HOURS MOVING BEHIND BARS

It was a fine summer day in 2001 when the NAFEO fellows at the Department of Health and Human Services in Washington, D.C., gathered to visit a prison in Montgomery County. In the parking lot, we split up into different groups assigned to different sections of the jail. My group was to meet with female inmates who were undergoing "correctional training" from substance abuse.

It was a very real feeling when we were led through the front door and admitted through the iron gate, operated remotely. The guard let us through more automated gates, which locked immediately behind us. The ceiling was low and the walkway narrow. Suffocating was an understatement. Even without the handcuffs or a prison uniform, I felt imprisoned. It was a stark contrast to the space I experienced a few minutes before under the blue open sky. The ceiling caved down, and albeit my average height, I felt as if bent physically and mentally.

We walked through corridors and the men's jail before reaching the women's section. It was my first time having physically been inside a jail, since my previous visits at California prisons took place in the visiting areas and not in the inmates' living quarters. The female inmates' cells surrounded the common area that we were led into. Some inmates were already out and sitting at the table, and others were coming.

Not all inmates were willing to talk. They did not seem to care whether we were there or not. I read on their faces the hopelessness and anguish of being incarcerated. But one young lady, aged thirty, was particularly sincere and open. Mother to a seven-year-old daughter, she told us how she wished with all her heart that during her ghetto childhood, someone had told her that substance abuse and drug addiction would terminate all of her dreams. No one was there for her, just free cigarettes and enticing alcohol. A kid knew no difference. No one told her then. Who will tell her daughter now if she is locked up and absent?

She recounted how, upon seeing her daughter pick up the cigarette butts she threw out, she was determined to quit, but the addiction she had known since her primary years was hard to shake off. Here, twenty some years later, she was still affected profoundly by the environmental racism in which she grew up. As a person of color, she had lived in spatially discriminated-against neighborhoods where role models were absent and disadvantages abundant.

And the cycle goes on. From her addiction and destroyed dreams, she saw how her daughter was running similar risks, and she wanted to change that for the child. But what tools did she have to pull her child away from such traps, especially while mothering from behind bars? I was so taken by her story that I was unaware of how I had forgotten about the physical constraint of the place. Not until the guard announced that visiting time was over did I regain consciousness of the jail reality. We moved on to another section before departing.

The sky outside was unbelievably welcoming, the fresh air precious, the green leaves a boon. The physicality of imprisonment became very real to me at that point, although I was experiencing from the vintage point of a visitor and for a very brief window of time. Those "impossible subjects," to borrow Mae Ngai's term, though not legal aliens, were placed on a racial map of difference and dictated into a surveillance territoriality by the U.S. government (Ngai 2004).

CARCERAL WOMANHOOD:
A VIETNAMESE AMERICAN PERSPECTIVE

Advocacy for the imprisoned—or even the formerly incarcerated—has never been an easy path. Condemnation of alleged crimes committed precedes other more tolerant and constructive attitudes from the society at large. This condemnation is heightened among certain groups, especially some minority enclaves. Therefore, it is almost impossible to advocate for the incarcerated as one of the major community issues in some populations. Furthermore, given the sensitivity and confidentiality of information about those imprisoned, it is quite challenging to obtain appropriate data to articulate a compelling argument.

Another cultural factor that hinders the efforts to help female inmates comes from the stereotype that Vietnamese prisoners behind American bars are mostly male. Given the lack of information on imprisonment, there has been no formal research conducted on incarcerated Vietnamese American women. Moreover, from the perspective of the ethnic community, a supposedly criminal woman is morally false and socially unworthy. They become ostracized subjects without a community, and with their language barrier and lack of legal access, they *become highly visible in the U.S. criminal system but doubly invisible in their social milieu.*

In some ethnic communities, the work for justice and equality for the imprisoned can be neglected as a result of imprisonment being taboo in itself. Immigrant communities trying to establish themselves as a success case or a model-citizen entity can sidestep the prison issues in order to make a statement about their aspiration and strive toward American liberal ideals. In efforts to attain a positive image, an immigrant community usually chooses to distance itself from the less desirable members in a process of selective exclusion.

When the Vietnamese Information Center, a now-defunct nongovernment organization based in Little Saigon, hosted a series of lectures pertaining to community issues in the early 2000s, the attendance was exponentially low when the topic was on gangs and prison. Community participation was very high when the topics pertained to education or cultural identity. In the last three and a half decades, there have been several talk shows in the Vietnamese-language media dedicated to assorted subjects, but none deals exclusively with the discourses of the incarcerated.

Therefore, activists committed to serve and advocate for the rights of those behind bars need to be both self-determined and to continue to forge community connections to work toward justice and equality for the incarcerated. Given this backdrop, I will now discuss considerations for cultural and language needs among Vietnamese American women serving time behind bars. Since the image of a prisoner has been stereotypically one of male villain for the Vietnamese, the image of a woman behind bars augments the resentment toward her and her alleged crime. This attitude can preclude considerations for the possibility of her innocence or for needed support from her end.

Let me first call attention to the fact that there are arrests that, due to language barrier, take place falsely, but the civilians in question are not able to articulate their rights and innocence or have the means to procure legal advice. Some immigrant women, given their socioeconomic status, have little knowledge of the American laws and therefore do not know their rights or how to protect themselves in cases of false arrests.

Cultural differences also play a role in how the criminal justice system can act unjustly toward women of color. Certain cultural practices among minority groups in the United States remain unknown to the law enforcement personnel, resulting in misunderstanding or misinterpretation of behavior when an issue arises in the presence of the police. In such cases, law enforcement inherently imposes the dominant cultural paradigm on the involved individuals.

During her tenure at CSU Fullerton, Dr. Son Kim Vo at one point worked with a Caucasian law intern who was interested in the case of a Vietnamese American woman behind bars without access to legal assistance or language accommodations. Moreover, her case was not reviewed in a timely manner, and she continued to stay behind bars, waiting for a trial. She went mad from being separated from her young child and from not knowing how the child was doing.

Moreover, many immigrant women are extremely vulnerable because of their legal status in this country. If incarceration equals the termination of humanhood and dreams for the thirty-year-old mother I met in the Montgomery County Jail, going behind bars means the exclusion from American polity for many immigrants who have not yet acquired U.S. citizenship. In early 2008, as a member of the first class of Helen Zia Fellows for Social Change and as part of my ongoing commitment to justice work, I engaged in community and student advocacy against the Memorandum of Understanding (MOU) signed clandestinely between the American and Vietnamese governments.

Formalized in January 22, 2008, the MOU would allow for the repatriation of Vietnamese immigrants who had entered the United States on or after July 12, 1995, and had subsequently been ordered removed from the United States. Several politicians and activists openly objected to this agreement because of its violation of human rights, civil rights, and immigration rights. But the ethnic community's responses have varied. In Seattle, the Vietnamese American community had made it a concern for the leadership to help the "deportable" Vietnamese immigrants. Yet, in other places, the reactions from community were not in support of those affected by the MOU. A young Vietnamese American in a youth organization in San Diego expressed his view:

> This is NOT a new issue: let's look deeper into the issue before we start fanning the flames. The LAW is clear that if you are convicted of a crime, you lose your immigration status. Although this may not be "fair," it is the law. Criminals (especially those who are in "limbo" with immigration) need to remember this as a deterrent before committing their crimes. There should not be leniency just because they have been here for 1 year or 10 years.
>
> I have to side with the United States Government on this issue. Their take on this is that they want to have law-abiding immigrants living here/naturalized. If an individual chose to break the law, then they choose (*sic*) their own path and the government has the right to punish them. I have heard of some cases where these people are living here illegally, so if the local authorities work with the federal authorities this makes our streets safer, and like someone else had said, this is an answer to 9/11.

In like manner, advocacy for those affected by the MOU was precluded in the model-citizen attitudes in community groups in Little Saigon, Orange County. Many groups shied away or ignored the matter all together. Like the young man quoted above *had* stated, the whole attitude toward being law-abiding immigrants runs deep in certain segments of the community, rendering those "in limbo with immigration" a deserving destiny of deportation should they commit misdemeanors or other crimes. However, where in this picture can we account for criminal profiling, police brutality, and targeted immigration raids?

TOWARD A CULTURALLY APPROPRIATE POLICY: INCARCERATED LIVES BEYOND THE CELL

Violence against women, especially those incarcerated, is an onerous issue for women across borders and racial backgrounds. Sexism and racism, among other forms of discrimination, remain prominent in American society today. Women being put behind bars, nonetheless, are faced with greater vulnerability and discrimination. Their needs are neglected, their rights taken away, and their legal belonging denied. Having encountered incarcerated women in various contexts, I argue that their safety is rarely whole given the blatant sexual violence, legal inequality, and economic exploitation—the threads that run through the experiences of women behind American bars albeit the shrouded nature of these processes. I ask how we can be cognizant of the subterfuges in criminal injustice so that the rights and safety of women can be ensured. As I attempt to portray here, incarceration can take place outside of conventional forms of confinement via environmental racism and legal stratification against immigrants. What defines a women's freedom? What responsibilities do societies have when it comes to women's equality? If the legal system fails, which it has in several cases, how can we mobilize and optimize the human conscience to take the right and just actions?

In the variegated systems under which the explored cases demonstrated, incarcerated women are subjected to injustice and violence regardless of their geopolitical positioning. From the open-ended history of enslavement with its long arms reaching today's realities, to contemporary practices of criminal profiling, the cases of incarcerated women beg the questions of inalienable rights, women's rights, and human rights. What lessons can we glean from the cases in point? How can we keep such violence and violations from recurring to women in other parts of the world? What redress should be in place for these women?

As Ruthie Gilmore puts it, the "fatal couplings of power and difference" (Gilmore 2002) work to create a particular place to incarcerate certain bodies in accord with gender, class, and scale. In the case of Vietnamese immigrant women, their place in the U.S. prison is forged by a particular political geography of race that is both disabling and unjust. While this group can benefit from advocacy and assistance from their own ethnic community, their stake has relevance to the U.S. mainstream and other ethnic populations as well. The work to be done, then, need not be confined to the response of the Vietnamese American activists and collectives, though it best starts there.

REFERENCES

Gilmore, Ruth Wilson. 2002. *The Professional Geographer.* 54(1): 15–24.

Ngai, Mae. 1994. *Impossible Subjects.* Princeton: Princeton University Press.

Rosaldo, Renato. 1980. *Ilongot Headinghunting 1883–1974.* Stanford: Stanford University Press.

section II

Sexuality, Health, and Abuse

Bound

Joanie Estes-Rodgers

I drew the picture *Bound* while serving time because I let life and the things I was bound to in life lead me to self-destruct. I had always treasured life with my sons and husband (my soul mate and best friend), and I would not go back and change anything in my life with the exception of my personal flaws. I sat down one day to figure out who I was and what happened to me to make me go numb and self-destruct. We are all bound to things in life, as parents and as spouses. Sometimes it feels like an overloaded amount, but if you're not feeling that pressure, then you must not be living a full life. I believe you cannot allow the things in life that are bad to control your path but use them as your drive to overcome.

Historical Contextualization

Jodie Michelle Lawston

Throughout history and in the present, activists have been and are engaged in on-the-ground work to address imprisoned women's rights in terms of sexuality, health, and abuse. As previously explained in the historical contextualization of section 1, women prison reformers of the nineteenth century were propelled into action when they learned of and witnessed the conditions of overcrowding and sexual violence to which incarcerated women were subject. These reformers organized not only to "reform fallen women" but to ameliorate harsh prison conditions, particularly for young white women.

Interestingly, by 1900 there was a significant shift in prison reform work. Organizers at the turn of the century—Progressive-era female prison reformers—began to deconstruct women's traditional roles in the family and economy and to argue that women prisoners would benefit from training that prepared them for the "male world" of labor so that they could financially support themselves (Freedman 1981, 123). These reformers challenged traditional gender stereotypes by training incarcerated women in nontraditional work such as carpentry, bookbinding, painting, and cobbling (Freedman 1981). While there was some progress in the ways in which gender was conceptualized, the means by which race and class intersected to determine *which groups of women* were imprisoned were not yet discussed or examined by prison reformers, at least not according to the literature available on this movement (Freedman 1981; Rafter 1990).

Not surprisingly, twentieth-century reformers encountered resistance to change. After WWI more women were imprisoned due to the Harrison Act (1914), which outlawed narcotics, and the Volstead Act (1919), which implemented prohibition (Freedman 1981). Freedman (1981, 47) also notes that after 1917, there was a resurgence of antiprostitution activity that "unleashed deeply held fears of the harlot as a threat to society." Because of the increase in the incarceration of women who worked as prostitutes or used drugs and alcohol, the women's prison population shifted from one that was largely young and included first-time offenders, to one that included older women who often had medical problems (Freedman 1981). Reformatories also became more racially mixed as black women migrated north. These changes combined so that the women who were imprisoned in reformatories were framed as the most "dangerous" class of women—perhaps not merely because of changes in the crimes represented in these institutions also but because of racist stereotypes about women of color—not the most hopeful cases. As a result of shifts in laws and ideological discourse, the influence of women who worked to reform prison conditions declined (Freedman 1981).

Although it is likely that women's efforts for prison reform continued well into the twentieth century, there is no literature available, to our knowledge, of this work. Women's prisons did not garner significant public attention again until the 1970s, at the tail end of the radical men's prison movement (Cummins 1994). While male prisoners and the conditions of their confinement received a considerable amount of attention in the 1960s and 1970s, women in prison and corresponding issues of sexuality, health, and abuse received virtually no attention from activists in the radical men's prison movement (Faith 1996). Angela Davis's writings from the early 1970s drew attention to her case of wrongful imprisonment and the struggles of male and female political prisoners, but the campaign surrounding her detention and subsequent acquittal was one of the few successful efforts to draw attention to women in prison during this period. Incarcerated women's smaller numbers (they constituted only about 4 percent of the prison population in the 1970s) and relative silence in comparison to men in prison, combined with the focus on male prisoners of the radical men's prison movement, rendered women in prison invisible in both the movement and social and political discourse on incarceration (Faith 1996).

As a result, groups—many of them feminist-oriented, grassroots, and comprised of both women of color and white women—emerged to address the ignored struggles of imprisoned women and the conditions of their confinement, which mirrored the injustices that incarcerated women have historically faced: guard abuse, poor healthcare, fewer educational and vocational facilities in comparison men's institutions, and training in stereotypical female occupations. These organizations exposed harsh and unjust prison conditions and gendered violence within prison walls but fell on a political continuum: some focused on prison reform and the provision of resources to incarcerated women, and others focused on prison abolition. Unlike reformists in the nineteenth and early twentieth centuries, most of the organizations working around women in prison in the 1970s took race into consideration as an imperative organizing principle of society and a crucial variable that determines which groups of women are targeted for incarceration (Resources for Community Change 1975).

The argument for prison abolition emerged from the revolutionary spirit of the 1960s and 1970s, which problematized the often taken-for-granted American notions of democracy, capitalism, freedom, and law-and-order. This spirit provided the basis for a powerful and compelling sociopolitical critique of prisons, which was present not only among activists but also among academics, prisoners, and former prisoners. While political prisoners in the radical men's prison movement called for a complete restructuring of American society (Cummins 1994), formerly incarcerated women called for alternatives to incarceration and prison abolition. They critiqued the carceral system and wrestled with how to best approach crime while working toward a world without prisons (Resources for Community Change 1975).

Like most cycles of activism, the reformist and abolitionist groups that mobilized around women in prison in the 1970s disbanded at different times, with the next cycle of women's prison activism emerging in response to the prison boom of the 1980s and 1990s. The campaigns for prison expansion in the latter part of the twentieth century, as previously discussed in the historical contextualization of section 1, disproportionately targeted poor women and women of color. As these populations of women were targeted for policing, arrest, prosecution, and incarceration, activists mobilized—both in and outside of prisons—to contest incarceration and prison expansion, sentencing laws, substandard prison conditions, inadequate healthcare, sexual violence, and overcrowding, likewise, the scholarship on women's incarceration began to grow, and has continued to grow, substantially in recent decades, picking up steam in the 1980s and 1990s and expanding even more rapidly since the turn of the millennium. A similar trend has taken place in the scholarship on the families of the incarcerated, and this literature focuses primarily on women and children.

Contemporary activists and scholars are both reformist and revolutionary in their goals. Reformist groups fight to improve prison conditions for women; to stop sexual, psychological, and physical violence against prisoners; and to improve prison healthcare. Radical activists, in turn, continue in the revolutionary fervor of the 1960s and 1970s and fight to abolish the prison system and establish alternatives to incarceration that ensure safe and secure communities. Importantly, they increasingly expose issues of violence against gender nonconforming people in prison.

The following section of this book makes a significant contribution to the work that activists have done to expose issues of health, abuse, and, increasingly, sexuality in women's prisons. The contributors to this section examine violence—defining the term broadly to include psychological abuse, lack of mental and physical healthcare, and sexual assault by correctional staff—within women's prisons. Unique to this book, contributors to this section—specifically Linda Heidenreich and Julia Sudbury—urge us to examine the relationship between gender violence and the United States carceral regime by turning our attention to the cases of transsexual, gender nonconforming, and transgender people in prison. These two contributors nudge us to move past gender binaries in scholarship and activism and, additionally, highlight the importance of alternatives to incarceration. All of the writings and art in this section contribute to both scholarship and the growing antiprison movement, expose the violence of prison life, and push us all to rethink, challenge, and move past the gender binary upon which we draw in writing about and engaging in antiprison work.

REFERENCES

Cummins, Eric. 1996. "The Politics of Confinement and Resistance: The Imprisonment of Women." In *Criminal Injustice: Confronting the Prison Crisis*, ed. Elihu Rosenblatt, 165–83. Boston: South End.

———. 1994. *The Rise and Fall of California's Radical Prison Movement*. Palo Alto, CA: Stanford University Press.

Freedman, Estelle B. 1981. *Their Sister's Keepers: Women's Prison Reform in America, 1830–1930*. Ann Arbor: University of Michigan Press.

Resources for Community Change. 1975. "Women behind Bars: An Organizing Tool." Barnard Center for Research on Women. http://www.barnard.edu/bcrw/archive/prison.htm (retrieved on January 22, 2010).

CHAPTER NINE

The Prison Mentality

Jane Dorotik

There exists a prison mentality, a way of thinking, that is hard to understand or even describe unless you have experienced it firsthand. Unfortunately I have experienced it firsthand—and continue to experience it—and I believe the prison mentality is *the* most devastating aspect of being incarcerated, worse than restricted freedom, worse than being separated from family and friends, worse then being prevented from leading a normal, healthy life.

There is an attitude, a mindset, a culture of dominance that is so pervasive and so totally devastating that it is truly astonishing to observe. This culture of domination is all encompassing, not just specific to the guards or the managerial staff; it seems to infect and become a way of being and thinking for all prisoners, all who come in contact with it.

I know a version or degree of this mentality, a basic hierarchy of importance, exists in almost every bureaucracy. However, it is so exaggerated and explicit in here, so dramatically amplified, that it is one of those hit-you-in-the-face, blow-your-hair-back kinds of experiences.

I am ashamed to admit that prison is something I thought little about before being sent here. And what little thinking I did, I generally assumed everyone in prison pretty much deserved their fate. After all, they had violated others or thwarted society's norms.

I couldn't have been more blind. Society does need to think about this. What creates it? What allows it to flourish in this setting? What are the outcomes or consequences when one person or one segment of society dominates another? What are the consequences for all of society or for our future evolution?

Dominance is a theme here, a culturally accepted way of being. But then, in the much broader picture, dominance is also a theme for the United States' relationship with the rest of the world's countries, with our "land of the free" consuming 65 percent of the entire world's resources. The United States also constitutes 5 percent of the world's population and yet incarcerates 25 percent of the world's incarcerated populations.

The prison mentality is one of scarcity and dominance. It is at the extreme far right of the spectrum of scarcity versus abundance. It is driven by an underlying and overriding premise that one group *must* dominate another in order to achieve order and ensure survival.

The United States has incarcerated 2.2 million people. The Prison Industrial Complex is big business, and its investors are on Wall Street. Many, many companies benefit from cheap prison labor. The Justice Department puts the annual cost of the U.S. prison and jail system at close to $100 billion. We spend 50 percent more incarcerating 1.3 million nonviolent offenders than the entire $16+ billion the federal government currently spends on welfare programs to serve 8.5 million underprivileged people.

How did we get here? What does this say about our values and priorities as a society? And what fuels this race to incarcerate? Where does this thinking come from that says *punish*? Punish someone, anyone, so "justice" can be served, and the victim can have "closure."

Nowhere is it more acutely demonstrated than here in California's prisons. Approximately 173,000 people are locked away in spaces designed to hold fewer than 100,000. The overcrowding and constitutional violations are so severe that medical and mental health care have been placed in federal receivership. California is currently battling a federal court order to reduce the prison population by some 40,000 prisoners.

As Dr. Corey Weinstein so eloquently put it, "California incarcerates everyone [it] can, not everyone who needs it."

And that really is the crux of the dynamic: "Lock 'em up, throw away the key" thinking. Prosecutors proudly report their 95 percent conviction rates. Lawmakers are able to claim their "tough on crime" credentials by enacting more and more draconian drug laws.

These practices feed the flame of the prison mentality and reinforce the domination model. In a publication from the Justice Policy Institute dubbed "The Punishing Decade," the following statistic is reported. Almost seven hundred thousand prisoners were added to institutions in the 1990s. This is almost thirty times as many as the average numbers added in each of the previous five decades.

So that is the larger picture. But what of the more personal picture behind these walls?

You can see this culture of abuse and dominance played out in many ways: prisoner to prisoner, guard to prisoner, guard to guard, and systemic reactions to prisoners trying desperately to maintain their individuality and their sanity.

When I first came to prison almost six years ago, I was hit head on with a typical systemic response to housing prisoners. When a woman enters the prison and is assigned a housing unit, it is basically a next-available-bunk kind of assigning. "Eight women live in 248 square feet in a space designed to house four, and with huge disparities in age, race, temperament, and cultural background, daily living is very challenging, to say the least." On paper the system has a method of providing for "courtesy" bed moves. But in practice the courtesy moves never happen. Women beat each other up or refuse to lock in (which ends up being a quick ticket to administration segregation), to avoid being beaten up, before a bed move is allowed. The prison administration is well aware of the level of violence within the cells. They use it to demonstrate and perpetuate the dominance—corrections officers (COs) will tell you, "Regulate your cell-mate," or, "Handle your business," and everyone knows what they really mean: "Beat Her Up." Simple requests, like grouping the few nonsmokers in the same cell so that they don't have to choke on everyone else's secondhand smoke, are disregarded, laughed at, or worse, treated with overt hostility, because to even consider such a request would be an admission of a smoking problem in the cells—in violation of state laws. The prison system would never want to admit that.

When I first arrived in prison at the Central California Women's Facility (CCWF) and made such a request (even providing the sergeant with a list of eight nonsmoking women willing to move to have a smoke-free room), I was told, "That's a good way to get yourself beat up." It seemed like a simple request, but I learned the hard way that the system does not tolerate those who illuminate their internal problems. After numerous requests through every avenue I could think of—all of which were ignored—I took my request for a nonsmoking cell to my classification committee hearing (a formal hearing held early in every prisoner's incarceration to assess custody status, prison job assignment, vocational needs, etc).

Now prisoners are emphatically discouraged from speaking at these "formal" proceedings. They are spoken about as if they were not present; they are talked over if they attempt to speak; and they are treated as a commodity.

So I was definitely out of line for speaking up. The captain in the classification hearing first said, "All cells are nonsmoking cells." This captain did finally admit that smoking in the cells was a problem and agreed to move me. But instead of honoring my request and moving all the named nonsmokers together into one cell, the captain moved me into a cell with the biggest known drug dealer in the prison. So now I had to contend with not only secondhand smoke but also drugs hidden in the room (and most prison drug dealers are savvy enough to not hide their drugs in their own bed area in the cell). After weeks and weeks of strife and fear I was finally able to get moved out of that cell and slowly created a nonsmoking cell through my own efforts.

Another example of a systemwide culture of domination is the new sexual misconduct policy. This policy is presumably instituted to prevent/reduce indecent exposure. A prisoner can now be written up for displaying a body part. And how can the prisoner avoid displaying a body part when the window to the cells, including the bathroom door and the shower door, are all wide open to provide maximum visibility (for "security" reasons)? Women try to protect one another by standing in front of the toilet cubicle or the shower when the jingle of keys announces a correctional officer walking down the cell block. Prison rape is a far more common and destructive problem behind prison walls than indecent exposure, and it is seldom reported because of the retaliation.

All of this is designed to demoralize—intended to humiliate—to make very, very sure that we understand we are prisoners, at the bottom of the ladder, that we've got "nothing coming."

This dominating culture replicates the concept of stepping all over others to get to the top, to get your needs met. Even individuals who try to care for each other, as many women do, end up tacitly agreeing to the hierarchy of domination just to survive, just to avoid being different (which is not tolerated in here).

So the guards get right into it and readily adopt the culture. Guards often make prisoners wait to get through locked doors (and lest we forget, this is prison with many, many locked doors), sometimes causing the prisoner to be written up for being late to work. Guards talk to and about prisoners as if they weren't there. "Hey Joe, do you want me to let these scumbags in?" Or, "Ladies, stop passing gas in front of 506 and keep moving. You are attracting flies." Or the constantly repeated adage, "How do you know when an inmate is lying? 'Cause her lips are moving." All of these—and many more—are repeated loudly and frequently. This behavior is designed to humiliate, to demonstrate dominance, to make very certain that we are reminded that *we* are the prisoners (translated: garbage, worthless, a scourge on society), and they are the COs (translated: in charge, crime-fighting machines), as if we could possibly be confused. A common admonition repeated by guards and prisoners alike is, "Be careful what you ask for." In other words, if you challenge something (like a CO's abusive behavior), be prepared to receive a lot of retaliation directly and indirectly, individually and collectively, against you, your cell mates, and your unit. Your room will be searched, your mail will come up missing, and any requests or notification of visits will be delayed, will be ignored, or will be denied. Or there will be other methods of retaliation. It becomes unbearable—and that is the point. You are firmly and emphatically put in your place.

So I could regale you with story after actual story of how life unfolds behind prison walls, how mismanaged, bureaucratic, and hostile this culture is, how nothing, literally nothing, is given to kindness or consideration. But really the greater point, the larger perspective, is how did we (society) allow this to happen? How did we *all* allow this prison culture to flourish and grow? How is it that the very same hatred-driven gang violence that society works so hard to eradicate has not been just *allowed* but actually *encouraged* and supported in here? We have rogue COs creating a "green wall of silence" to hush up the abusers. How did we get here? Are we so full of fear and hatred and judgment that we can't see the forest for the trees? Are we not breeding a culture of hatred and violence far more destructive than any foreign terrorist group could ever be? Look at the atrocities in Abu-Ghraib. It is not just a coincidence that many of the leaders sent to set up the Abu Ghraib prison honed their abusive techniques in American prisons.

It all boils down to trust and our perception of our world. If we see the world as distrustful, unbearable, and hostile, we will enter into all relationships with this overarching belief system, which will then become a self-fulfilling prophecy. Trust is at the core of everything.

We must believe, and show through our actions, that we acknowledge that all people can make valuable contributions to mutual growth and development.

One very poignant example of women trying to assist one another, but being met with resistance, occurred early in my incarceration days. Women quickly learned that I was a registered nurse and would come and ask me questions about the healthcare they were (or in most cases were not) receiving. They also learned I was a mental health professional and would often ask me to advocate on behalf of a mentally ill woman (California prisons house more mentally ill women than mental hospitals do).

One day Shirley brought a mentally ill woman over to me. The woman was twitching her leg, mumbling incoherently, and hearing voices. The woman told me she couldn't get the voices out of her head, and she was afraid of what they might tell her to do. She was thinking of cutting into her head to stop the voices.

I walked her over to the health clinic and explained the urgency to the staff. They responded, "We won't see her without a pass."

I walked her into her unit (going "out of bounds" myself), to alert her housing staff to the urgency. They said, "Go away, you are out of bounds and could be disciplined. We know how to handle her."

The next day I saw the woman walking around the yard mumbling and twitching. Half of her head was shaved and she had lacerations all through her scalp. She had obviously attempted to quiet the voices, to no one's great alarm.

When the acts of others, whether careless or with malicious intent, cause suffering and grief, we are much more likely to achieve genuine healing, reconciliation, and forgiveness if the persons involved are acknowledged as possessing at least some potential for goodness or an elementary level of humanity. We *must* believe that human beings are innately inclined toward goodness, toward becoming life affirming, constructive, responsible, and trustworthy. Human beings are not born violent; we become violent through what is learned and experienced by the culture that surrounds us, by the belief system than envelopes us.

All of society benefits from individuals who have learned to nurture themselves and each other to support healthy growth and social evolution.

This prison mentality is simply a microcosm of the United States, albeit an exaggerated and very brutal microcosm.

As Diane Eisler has said so much more clearly than I, "Will future generations be living in a nation where fear and hostility are fanned for political reasons, a nation of glaring contrasts, of poverty vs. wealth, homelessness, heartlessness and hopelessness? Will they see in mass media and much of reality, a culture that is violent, pulverized, and cynical?"

Certainly that is what this prison system is breeding. And 95 percent of those incarcerated are released back into society, 650,000 annually, carrying back with them an infected view of society.

I don't have immediate answers to all these questions, but I do know that subject is something we must think about. Our society, our attitudes are simply a reflection of our current thinking. "As a man thinks so he is."

Couldn't we begin thinking a little differently? What of these women? The twin prisons of Central California Women's Facility and Valley State Prison for Women house more than eight thousand women (the world's largest concentrations of incarcerated women in a few square miles outside of Fresno, California). Whose mothers are there? Whose daughters, sisters, and friends are they? Wouldn't they and the community be better served if they participated in community service—planting in community gardens, cleaning inner-city graffiti, assisting with Habitat for Humanity? I can think of hundreds of examples of community volunteerism, anything and everything that reminds us in clear and compelling ways that this world is all of ours, and the future is what we, all of us together, make of it.

CHAPTER TEN

"If I Wasn't Suicidal, That'll Drive You to It:" Women, Jail, and Mental Health

Angela Moe

CONCEPTUAL BACKGROUND

Crime policy over the last few decades has been characterized by conservative ideologies supportive of formalization, harshness, and rigidity. Commonly known under the rubric *get tough,* such ideologies have resulted in more people being criminalized, for fewer and less severe offenses, without regard to their individual circumstances. Additionally, an equality discourse has become commonplace in the justice system, calling for equal treatment of women and girls, as compared to men and boys. This has resulted in what Meda Chesney-Lind has termed "equality with a vengeance" and has had devastating consequences (1997, 152). This is especially true given that the criminological circumstances and treatment needs of female offenders have historically been neglected by mainstream research, policy makers, and criminal justice practitioners. While progress has been made by feminist criminologists in recent decades (see Belknap 2007 for a review), full recognition of the gendered nature of criminality and criminalization has been thwarted in large part because of calls for gendered equality.

In the absence of widely understood explanations of female offending, women and girls in the justice system are assumed to have committed their crimes for the same reasons and under similar contexts as men and boys. Presumably then, their treatment, both as defendants in the crime processing system and as convicted offenders in the correctional system, ought to be comparable. However, females are much more likely than males to commit nonviolent offenses (e.g., drugs, prostitution, running away, theft, property crimes), which under close scrutiny appear disproportionately to occur out of duress, coercion, or perceived necessity

(Arnold 1990; Federal Bureau of Investigation [FBI] 2007; Chesney-Lind 1997; Chesney-Lind and Shelden 1998; Lake 1993; Moe 2004, 2006; Sargent, Marcus-Mendoza, and Yu 1993). Indeed, women and girls are much more likely to be abused, both physically and sexually, by family members and male partners than vice versa (Tjaden and Thoennes 2000). Consequently, crimes committed within the context of victimization are much more common (Comack 2006; Daly 1992; Gilfus 1992; Moe 2004; Pollock 2002; Richie 1996).

Just as the gendered contexts of criminalization are misunderstood, so are treatment needs. Gender-specific programming has become a topic of funding and research only in recent years, and much remains to be learned and implemented in this regard (Bloom, Owen, and Covington 2003; Chesney-Lind and Shelden 1998). What has been widely understood within feminist criminology is that the programming and services of greatest need by female offenders often relate to the contexts of their criminalization, such that psychological-mental health assessment and treatment, health care, parenting assistance/advocacy, domestic violence counseling, education, substance abuse treatment, housing, and employment assistance top the list of needs (American Correctional Association [ACA] 1990; Shaw 1992; Veysey 1998).

While a fair amount of cross-disciplinary research has documented criminalized women's health-related experiences, much of it has focused on the prison setting. Jails and detention centers, which are intended to provide short-term confinement (typically less than one year), have remained a neglected site for academic inquiry. This is unfortunate given that more women actually pass through jail and detention centers than through prisons (Greenfeld and Snell 1999). It is important to also note that some do not merely pass through these facilities but instead spend years awaiting trial and sentencing, transfer to overcrowded prisons, or through repeated incarcerations for petty offenses and probation violations. Nonetheless, only a handful of studies have examined the health care needs and services for women in jails and detention centers (ACA 1990; Baxter 1991; Beltrami, et al. 1997; El-Bassel, et al. 1995; Ferraro and Moe 2003; Greenfeld and Snell 1999; Moe and Ferraro 2003). Even fewer have focused on mental health specifically (ACA 1990; Moe and Ferraro 2003; Teplin, Abram, and McClelland 1997; Veysey 1998).

However, women in jails and detention centers do indeed have distinct needs, particularly with reference to mental and physical health care. Because so many lack health insurance or fear accessing subsidized health coverage due to intimate partner victimization, drug addiction, or other criminal activity, they are likely to enter the system with immediate medical needs. Thus the goal of this chapter is to contribute to the research by focusing on the mental health–related needs of women in short-term confinement. Findings are based on a sample of thirty women who voluntarily participated in semistructured, life history interviews while confined in an urban detention center. The women were asked to talk about their lives prior to and during incarceration, which resulted in rich and descriptive narratives that included discussions of mental health problems that had been only marginally addressed, if at all, during their confinement.

THE FEMINIZATION OF CRIMINALIZATION

While women currently make up just 7.5 percent of the U.S. prison population and 13 percent of the jail population (Bureau of Justice Statistics [BJS] 2007), these percentages are up from 6 percent in the prison population (BJS 1992) and 9 percent in the jail population (BJS 2007) in 1990. Indeed, the incarceration of women has increased six-fold over the past two decades (Chesney-Lind and Pasko 2004). This is due in no small part to the substantial increase of female arrests during this time period. According to Uniform Crime Reports for the last two decades, female arrests rose 28 percent between 1986 and 2006 (1,535,932 in 1986 to 1,967,748 in 2006), while male arrests decreased by 17 percent (7,334,777 in 1986 to 6,273,496 in 2006) (FBI 1996, 2007).

Much of this increase is related to the War on Drugs, from which women have suffered disproportionately. From 1993 to 2001, arrests of women for drug abuse violations rose 22 percent, compared to 16 percent for men (FBI 2003). And while drug-related offenses accounted for one-third of the increase of men in prison between 1986 and 1995, they accounted for one-half of the increase of women in prison (Mauer, Potler, and Wolf 1999). Drug-related crimes, along with stricter sentencing mandates, account for the largest increases in the burgeoning imprisonment rates for women (Covington 1998). Hence, the War on Drugs has been equated to a war on women (Chesney-Lind 1997).

The increased criminalization of women has disproportionately affected those at the social, economic, and political margins, with the majority being un- or undereducated, poor, mothers of color (African American, Hispanic, and native American) with high rates of mental and physical illness (Bush-Baskette 2000; Davis 1998; Kaplan and Sasser 1996). Women's heightened involvement in the system has been further aided by greater formality and less discretion throughout the crime processing system—at charging/prosecution, sentencing, and postsentencing (probation and parole) (Belknap 2007; Chesney-Lind and Pasko 2004; Leonard 2002). Now more than ever, women are facing harsher sentences and increased correctional security, alongside scarce and often misguided psychological, physical, educational, and vocational services (Davis 1998).

INCARCERATED WOMEN'S HEALTH

From cross-disciplinary research on criminalized women's health-related needs and experiences, we know that incarcerated women have myriad health problems (Barry 2001; Ingram-Fogel 1991; Maeve 1999) and that they suffer higher rates of serious and chronic physical and mental illness than the general population (Birecree et al. 1994; Maeve and Vaughn 2001; Teplin, Abram, and McClelland

1996). In fact, 60 percent of incarcerated women report at least one significant medical problem (Young 1998). Additionally, incarcerated women experience higher rates of drug/alcohol addiction (Birecree et al. 1994; Chesney-Lind, Harris, and deGroot 1998; Regier et al. 1990). A majority of them have also been victimized, primarily within their intimate relationships, which can wreak havoc on one's mental and physical health (American Correctional Association [ACA] 1990; Browne, Miller, and Maguin 1999; Gilfus 1992; Harlow 1998; 1999; Moe 2004; Richie 1996). Because so many women live in poverty with little or no health insurance prior to their incarceration, most enter the criminal justice system with some sort of medical need that has not been adequately treated (Barry 2001). Along with the gendered and classed nature of incarcerated women's health needs, there is also a racial dimension to service attainment. Women of color are less likely to use available medical services and to perceive their treatment by medical personnel as less favorable than do white women (Young 1999).

Unfortunately, jails and detention centers have remained a neglected site for research. A common approach is to either assume the experiences of imprisoned women mirror those of jailed women, or to simply call for further research on women in jail (see as examples Barry 2001; Leh 1999; Macher and Goosby 2000; Resnik and Shaw 1981; Sigurdson 2000). However, women in shorter-term confinement have distinct needs from those who are in longer-term confinement. Of foremost concern is that women often enter the system with immediate and untreated injuries, conditions, and diseases (Ingram-Fogel 1991; Maeve and Vaughn 2001; Moe and Ferraro 2003; Staton, Leukefeld, and Logan 2001; Young 1998). Mental illness, intermittent homelessness, hunger, victimization, and addiction only exacerbate their circumstances (Shaw 1992; Versey 1998). Indeed, the immediacy of physical health–related concerns regarding HIV infection and prevention have been studied with regard to jailed/detained women (Baxter 1991; El-Bassel et al. 1995), along with higher than average rates of syphilis (Beltrami et al. 1997) and discriminatory access to health care (Shaw, Browne, and Meyer 1981). A lack of gynecological and obstetrical services, including pre- and postnatal care, have also been documented (ACA 1990; Ferraro and Moe 2003; Greenfeld and Snell 1999), as have lagging services, despite great demand, for mental health programming (ACA 1990; Moe and Ferraro 2003; Teplin, Abram, and McClelland 1997; Veysey 1998).

Beyond these studies, some of which are quite dated, a shortage of research exists specifically on health care, and more specifically, for the purposes of this study, on mental health care. This is unfortunate since approximately 70 to 80 percent of jailed women have at least one diagnosable psychiatric disorder (Teplin, Abram, and McClelland 1996), and only 20 to 24 percent of them receive mental health care while detained (Harlow 1998; Teplin, Abram, and McClelland 1997). Because jails and detention centers are intended for short-term confinement, and thus experience high turnover, most neither develop serious programs nor receive the external scrutiny for their lack of services. However, studies suggest that jails are becoming primary health care providers for the mentally ill, indigent, and homeless (Ditton 1999; Fuller 1995; Sigurdson 2000). As such, it is critical that research highlight the specific mental and physical health-related needs of recently incarcerated women.

RESEARCH PROCESS, SAMPLE DEMOGRAPHICS, AND METHODOLOGY

The data on which this analysis is based were derived from thirty qualitative, in-depth, and semistructured life history interviews with women confined within an urban detention center. The women were recruited for participation in this study through the cooperative efforts of administrators and staff within this detention center, who announced the research and obtained a list of sixty-five interested volunteers (out of a total of two hundred inmates) in advance of the interviews. I, along with my research collaborator, Kathleen Ferraro, conducted the interviews over a series of weekends. We interviewed whoever was available from the list within private rooms of the facility. Upon each woman's consent and in accordance with our university's human subjects review board, the interviews were audio-taped and later transcribed. They lasted between thirty minutes and three and a half hours. The interviewees were given remuneration of between ten and twenty dollars (dependent upon grant resources and facility regulations) on their accounts and were offered the opportunity to select their own pseudonyms for confidentiality purposes (most did choose their pseudonyms).

The women ranged from twenty-one to fifty years of age, with an average age of thirty-four years. Fifteen (50 percent) of them identified as white, seven (23 percent) as black, three (10 percent) as Latina, two (7 percent) as American Indian, and three (10 percent) as biracial. This distribution was comparable to the proportions of women in each racial/ethnic group in the jail at the time (53 percent white, 13 percent black, 24 percent Latina, 9 percent American Indian) as well as with national jail data (Davis 1998; Greenfeld and Snell 1999; Richie 2001). Almost all of the women had low or no incomes prior to incarceration. Nine (30 percent) had obtained less than a high school education, four (13 percent) had either completed high school or obtained a GED, sixteen (53 percent) had completed some college or obtained a college degree, and one (3 percent) had attended graduate school. Twenty-seven (90 percent) were mothers. Drug offenses, property crimes, and prostitution were the most common types of crimes reported. Twenty-five (83 percent) of the women had already been convicted and sentenced and were either serving their sentences or being detained on probation violations. Three (12 percent) were awaiting sentencing, and two (7 percent) were awaiting trial. The length of time in which each woman had been incarcerated varied greatly. Some had been in the detention facility for less than one week, while others had been there over a year. It is also worth noting that few were being detained for the first time, which is suggestive of the way in which jails have become a revolving door for the most marginalized people (Greenberg and Rosenheck 2008; Kushel, Hahn, Evans, Bangsberg, and Moss 2005).

Because the interviews were semistructured, the women were encouraged to talk about whatever experiences and concerns they had with regard to their criminalization and confinement. The initial goal of the interviews was to examine the ways in which the women made sense of their lives and the circumstances surrounding their criminalization. However, because the interviews were conducted in an open and flexible way in terms of content and flow, several additional themes emerged. Health care was quite salient among these, as nineteen (63 percent) of the women discussed it without being prompted. A strong subtheme within health care was mental health needs and services, addressed by eleven (37 percent) of the women. Given the frequency of unprompted discussion of mental health, all transcripts were inductively analyzed for the purposes of this chapter. This allowed for a more nuanced and grounded analysis of the women's narratives, including those that did not make specific mention of mental health but perhaps alluded to it in other ways. Thus all thirty interviews were included in this analysis.

Charmaz' constructionist grounded theory guided the analysis, with its adherence to methodological flexibility and emphasis on the views, values, beliefs, feelings, assumptions, and ideologies of a study's participants (2006). As such, this research supplements the developing body of literature on the vantage, or standpoint, of jailed women, who are arguably in the best positions to elucidate the impact of correctional policy and practice. Such epistemological position-ing is consistent with the feminist standpoint tradition, which holds that the experiences and voices of women who participate in research, particularly those of marginalized status (historically, politically, socially, legally, economically, etcetera) ought to be privileged over other, more hegemonic discourses (Harding 1987; Hartsock 1985; Smith 1989; Romero and Stewart 1999). Indeed it may be argued that such marginalized groups are better positioned than members of socially dominant groups to describe the ways in which the world is organized according to the oppressions they experience (Hartsock 1987; Hill Collins, 1989). Such an approach has become a prominent means of examining women and crime (see Arnold 1990; Gilfus 1992; Richie 1996).

While not generalizable in the traditional sense, these data provided a deeply rich, detailed, descriptive, and diverse set of narratives that would not have been possible through alternative means (Kvale 1996; Lofland, Snow, Anderson and Lofland 2006). Since so little substantive research exists on jailed women's experiences, relying on smaller samples that allow for a more exploratory and nuanced understanding of women's experiences and needs is appropriate. With such an approach it is possible to contribute toward theoretical generation and transferability by informing conceptual undercurrents of future research in the area (Esterberg 2002; Guba 1981; Johnson 1997; Kvale 1996).

FINDINGS

Aching to be Heard: Acknowledgment of Need

As noted earlier, discussions of health care during the interviews arose spontaneously as the women were asked to describe their experiences leading up to their criminalization. Without prompting, several quite vividly told of the need for mental health services during confinement, either for themselves or for other inmates. Angel's explanation was illustrative:

> A lot of times the things that motivate you to do wrong have nothing to do with your understanding, your values of right and wrong. It's deeper than that. There's so many deeper issues. I see so many girls in here that don't need to be. They need to be intensively in some sort of therapy. They've been so severely abused that their personality is just splintered . . . [T]hey don't even know who they are. They're just, they're not in touch with who they are. They're just shells of people. They need to be put back together before they can begin to be expected to understand any kind of responsibility or consequences.

From the way in which Angel described the inmates, as well as how several expressed their own emotional-psychological state, it was clear that many of the women felt depressed, lonely, frustrated, and scared. As Sherrie commented, "Yeah, I've got to get some of this stuff out. You know, you people are the first people I've talked to . . . I've told nobody any of this, you know, and it's hard." Sherrie went on to express a sense of urgency in terms of dealing with her emotional state:

> And even right now it's just the bare surface, you know? If I start talking, I'm going to be like Humpty Dumpty. I'm going to fall and you ain't going to find all of those pieces. That's what I'm afraid of, that I'll lose it completely mentally, you know? It's going to take a lot . . . It's like a self-destruct mode and it's like, I'm hurting myself more than anything . . . [I]t's easier to hide the pain than to deal with it. It's going to take a lot of hard work for me to get through this.

This excerpt illustrates the mental state many of the women were in, as well as the very real and immediate needs they had in not only acknowledging their feelings and concerns, but having some professional assistance in working through them. Without appropriate support, women like Sherrie could lapse into deeper depression, which can become very dangerous within a confinement setting where despair and hopelessness run rampant.

Ambiguity and Benign Neglect: Serious Mental Illness

Such sentiments may also be illustrative of a more serious mental illness [SMI]. In fact, Sherrie briefly mentioned that she had been diagnosed with multiple personalities. However, in explaining how she received the diagnosis, she indicated that her mother-in-law had financially influenced a court-ordered psychiatric evaluator to diagnose her in order to win the upper hand during a child custody battle. She did not acknowledge or elaborate on any mental illness beyond this, so it was not clear whether she did indeed have a SMI or not. Given that the only source of data available for this research were the women's interview narratives, it was not possible to crosscheck Sherrie's claims or to validate whether or not she had a clear sense of what had happened with her child custody case. However, the sense of desperation, confusion and injustice within voices like Sherrie's is telling in and of itself—certainly they longed for an explanation, understanding, and support.

Only two other women acknowledged a diagnosed mental illness. Similar to Sherrie, Twila said that she had been found "mentally unstable" when child protective services terminated her parental rights. While she did not elaborate further, she did state that she was on medication. The other woman, Orca, elaborated quite a bit more: "I need to be on meds. I've been in denial of that. Maybe I've been self-medicating with cocaine because it made me feel good. I'm manic-depressive. I need head meds to keep me from being too down or too manic. When I'm manic, I'm just like, 'Don't piss me off you son of a bitch.' It's the depression and the downs that scare the shit out of me." While Orca was clear about her mental condition and medication needs, she did not report having seen a psychologist or psychiatrist while in the detention center. There was also no indication that she was on any medication at the time of the interview. Given that an estimated 70 to 80 percent of female jail inmates suffer from at least one lifetime psychiatric disorder (Teplin, Abram, and McClelland 1996), it is reasonable to assume that more women were interviewed who were either not aware of or chose not to share the specifics of their psychiatric conditions. Indeed, more women did appear to be distraught, depressed, and disoriented in ways that may have indicated a serious mental disorder; however, unless they identified such conditions, no such presumptions were made. Regardless, what was clear was that greater attention toward the mental health needs of women detainees, like Sherrie, Twila, and Orca, was sorely needed.

One Size Fits All: The Institutional Response

Within the detention facility, mental health services were addressed through one employee (a female counselor) and one means (group counseling). Aside from Christian-based religious services and substance abuse groups, there were no other rehabilitative programs. The women seemed to do what they could with these limited services, often attending anything that would offer a distraction from the monotonous daily routine. Many seemed anxious for any type of support or expressive outlet. As Gillian noted, "I just go to all the churches. I go to AA (Alcoholics Anonymous), CA (Cocaine Anonymous), and counseling. That's all they offer here."

Despite the scarcity of mental health services, the group-based counseling did include a range of supportive and self-awareness components, aimed at addressing many of the issues the women faced within their lives, including domestic violence. As Patrice commented, "I go because I know that the relationship that I had been in for the last five years wasn't good for me." Other specific issues were addressed as well. According to Crystal, "It's counseling for drugs, for violence, anything." The relative comprehensiveness of the support group may have been unique since according to the National Institute of Justice (Harlow 1998) and other research (Teplin, Abram, and McClelland 1997), only 20 to 24 percent of incarcerated women receive any form of mental health assistance in jail. However, the support group was based on volunteer involvement, so not all of the women made use of it. While many did, others refused to attend if they did not recognize a direct link between what was covered in the sessions and their own circumstances. Indeed, there was a feeling among the inmates that the facility administrators believed that all could be served within this single program. Lonna, who went to the group meetings because she "figured counseling would help," described the program as being overly comprehensive and generalized, to the point that she felt an assumption was being made that all of the women had the same types of problems. This was not the case, as she commented, "Nobody has problems like I have. I have just totally different problems." Lonna identified her abusive husband as the primary cause of her "problems," as she had been incarcerated for welfare fraud after her husband drained the family's resources.

Accessibility versus Discretion: Medication and Assessment

The group-based therapy was not adequate for those with more serious forms of depression and other mental illnesses. Certainly a woman suffering from depression and anxiety requires distinct and separate care from one suffering from bipolar disorder. While group and individual counseling may be adequate for some, intense and long-term psychotherapy and medication may be necessary for others. With regard to medication, the ability of the women to obtain the requisite medication for their conditions was unclear. As mentioned earlier, Twila, who admitted to mental illness, indicated that she was on medication while at the detention center. However, Orca, who also admitted to mental illness, did not. Brina offered her observations on the matter, which suggested that bureaucratic and discretionary issues underscored access to medication:

> People have these medications in their purse. They come in here and they're telling the guards, "Hey, I need my medication. I'm supposed

to take my medication." They give them the runaround. They have to call the doctor, and they have to get it okayed even though you have the prescription in your purse. The pills have your name on them. It doesn't matter. The guards don't okay them until the doctor says so . . . For people with multiple personalities or other psychological problems, they won't give them their medicine, sometimes for the entire time they're in here. That's dangerous. They're in general population. There is this one woman who has serious mental problems and can flip out really bad.

So while many prior studies (conducted mostly in prison settings) have found that psychotropic drugs are the means of choice for dealing with female inmates (e.g., Morash, Haarr, and Rucker 1994; Ross 1998), this may not be the case within short-term confinement settings. There was no indication of any regular psychiatric screening practices; at least none of the women described going through such screenings. This seemed to be handled on a case-by-case basis, depending upon what women were able to document regarding their mental health upon admission to the facility. Such a practice would be consistent with findings from the American Correctional Association, which estimated that 30 percent of women's jails do not provide any type of psychiatric care (1990).

Making the Best of It: Group Therapy

So with regard to what mental health programming was available, the women best served through the group-based counseling were those who did not have a serious mental illness. Instead they reported feelings of emotional crisis, loss, and anxiety about the future. Several were also recovering from past victimization and/or struggling with drug or alcohol addiction. Given the generalized nature of this one program, however, it is doubtful that even these concerns were addressed sufficiently for any individual. Nonetheless, the women were quite appreciative of the social support and feeling of camaraderie offered through the group. They were particularly fond of watching and discussing videos, which they believed helped them to think through their own lives and circumstances within a supportive environment. As Brina described:

> They showed that movie about Tina Turner's life and the violence, *What's Love Got to Do With It.* Tomorrow, we're going to watch the second half of the movie [*Losing*] *Isaiah*, which hits home for me because of losing my baby. I didn't necessarily put her in a trash can but the consequences are still the same. I think it is a good movie to show. It brings hope to the women in here who have maybe not put their children in a garbage can but have lost them to circumstances. It gives you hope that you can straighten yourself out. You can get everything rearranged and on the right track.

Indeed, several commented on how helpful they found this group therapy to be and that they had not been given an opportunity to participate in anything like it prior to their confinement. Even Lonna, who did not always see counseling applicable to herself, remarked, "While I'm here, I'm not going to make it a waste of time. I'm going to do what I can to get ahead." Of particular note are the positive feelings the women expressed about the counselor who led the group. As Twila commented, "The one we've got here, she's a very caring person. She tries to understand our feelings and stuff. It's kind of hard for her, but she's doing good. A lot of people don't care." It appeared that the group, according to the women's perspectives, could easily change and not be as useful if another counselor headed it.

Desperation versus Debilitation: Self-Harm and Suicide Watch

On a much less positive note, for the women with more serious mental health needs, it seemed that the only way immediate attention toward their mental state was garnered was through a threat to commit suicide. However, "suicide watch," which was aimed at preventing an inmate from hurting herself, did little to address the reasons behind her threats or attempts to do so. In fact, what was described would in all likelihood exacerbate the situation for inmates:

> When I came here it was the second time I thought about suicide. Oh wow, after four days I was ready to just, "That's it, I'm hanging it up, I'm punching out." Then I heard about their suicide watch. "Nope, nope, I'm happier than a pig in shit." [Q: What's their suicide watch?] They chain you naked to a . . . [long pause as she begins to cry]. Let's put it this way, I did it once, and I won't tell anybody in here that I'm sad again. I won't cry in front of nobody because then they start watching you. Then they take you and put you in a holding cell that's smaller than this [motioning to an approximately six-by-eight-foot attorney-client meeting room where the interview was being held]. There's a bunk in there, and they chain you to it. They take away your clothes and your blanket, everything (crying harder). You have nothing. You can't even get over to the toilet. If you have to go to the bathroom, you do it right there. I was on suicide watch for forty-eight hours. If I wasn't suicidal, that'll drive you to it.

Despite such drastic efforts to prevent women from hurting themselves, some still successfully found ways to do so. Interestingly, the inmates who described such incidents were adamant that the majority of suicide victims had not come to the facility with visible psychiatric problems but rather digressed mentally through the course of their stay. As Anne explained: "Three months ago a girl committed suicide in here . . . she hung herself with a sheet. She didn't come in here psycho or schizo. She didn't need to be put in the mental ward. She wasn't on any medication. She must have just been really depressed about it all . . . I think she got sentenced to prison for like two years or something. She took a sheet and went to the shower and hung herself from the stall." Anne's sentiments, that untreated ailments contributed to incidents of self-injury such as mutilation and suicide, have been confirmed in many previous studies (Haywood et al. 2000; Pollock-Byrne 1990; Shaw 1992; Sigurdson 2000). Prior research suggests that because scarce treatment resources are typically given to those with clear and visible mental illness, those with moderate or less recognizable mental disorders are less likely to receive services (Steadman, Holohean, and Dovoskin 1991; Teplin, Abram, and McClelland 1997). However, my findings suggest neglectful treatment regardless. Whether due to a sudden onslaught of depression and an inability to cope or an aggravated SMI that went unrecognized, greater screening and preventative efforts aimed at mental health were clearly needed. Unfortunately, in this facility and others, few initial or routine assessments of women's health-related needs occur. Intermittent screenings seem dependent upon the observations of individual inmates made by various correctional and medical staff (Gorsuch 1998; U.S. General Accounting Office (GAO) 1999; Veysey 1998).

Taking Matters into Their Own Hands: Self- and Mutual Help

Almost as if in recognition that any one of them could suffer such despair, the women had taken upon themselves to try to help each other. As Boo explained: "You have to laugh at least once or twice a day in here to get by, you know, so we clown a lot. We make each other laugh and stuff. Otherwise we'd be sitting in our rooms, and we'd go crazy. That's why a lot of people do the things they do. I've seen a couple people hang themselves in here. I've seen people go crazy." Thankfully, the counselor who ran the group therapy sessions recognized the need for such peer support, institutionalizing the idea by allowing some of the women to create and facilitate group sessions themselves: "I've done a lot since I've been here. I taught a class . . . [T]he counselor here is really, really good, and she lets us do what we want to do in the group. So now since I've taught the class, a couple of the other girls are putting together exercises and they're going to also get up and teach the class. It's a lot of fun, because you need to have something to do in here, and there's not enough programs here" (Angel). Again, the activities and level of involvement within the group counseling sessions were appreciated by the women for the most part. Given the range of their needs and the scarcity of resources available to the sole counselor available within the facility, such efforts are certainly admirable. It was unquestionably helpful and empowering for the women to have a forum through which to help themselves and each other, as such opportunities probably did not exist elsewhere in their lives. While notable and positive, it is also quite unfortunate and intolerable that these women had to be arrested and face criminal records in order to receive it.

CONCLUSION

The purpose of this chapter was to present the narratives of jailed women with regard to mental health and mental health care. The qualitative and open nature of the interviews in this study allowed for the sample of detained women to talk openly in ways that framed the carceral experience from their own perspectives. From their standpoints, mental health care needs were varied and widespread throughout the detention facility. However, institutional responses to such needs were minimal and geared mostly toward those who needed social support through group-based counseling.

On the whole, the women who made use of the group counseling did not admit to being mentally ill. Although some of them certainly may have been and simply chose not to disclose their situation or were not aware of it, what they instead described were crisis-filled lives involving such things as violence, abuse, drug addiction, homelessness, and loss of children. In this way, they seemed well suited to the group-based counseling available in the detention center and indeed could benefit from greater and more intensive services in this regard. Those who admitted to suffering from mental illness seemed neglected, if not abused, in the most severe of circumstances. While only a handful of these women were interviewed, there appeared to be no programming specifically geared toward their needs. According to the women, no formal assessments were made regarding mental health upon admittance to the facility or during their stay. This occurred regardless of the interviewees' sentiments that the poor mental and psychological health of inmates was easy to observe, particularly as it digressed with time served. Medication even seemed to be difficult to arrange. It is clear from the women's descriptions that they are a neglected demographic in terms of this pivotal aspect of health and well-being.

Jails and detention centers are unique environments, as compared to prisons, with their continuous turnover and diversity of inmates. This distinctiveness provides an excellent opportunity for addressing the immediate needs of women with varying levels of involvement in the criminal justice system. Within this setting, intake screenings, classification based on programming needs, and appropriately aimed mental health services are all possible. To assume that these women cannot benefit from mental health programming, or that it is unfeasible to provide any level of mental health care within a short-term confinement setting, is not only a social injustice but also a logistical, pragmatic, and financial mistake. No interests are served by allowing jailed women to deteriorate in mental health. They become risks to themselves, their criminal cases, other inmates, correctional staff, and any family members, including children, waiting for them on the outside.

However, in placing this study within a larger social, economic, and political context, these findings are not surprising. In many ways, the women's sentiments mirrored the culture, and environment marginalized women encounter within the United States. Indeed, there appears to be little concern for providing health care for poor women in general (Smith and Dailard 1994). As poverty rates increase for single women and their children, welfare and health care subsidies continue to be eroded (Mink 1999; Roth 2006), and mental health services have virtually disappeared for the un- or underinsured (Sigurdson 2000). Until due attention is given to the larger social structures and politics that maintain the marginalization of women at greatest risk for criminalization, little long-term progress will be made with those who end up on the inside of the system.

REFERENCES

American Correctional Association. 1990. *The Female Offender: What Does the Future Hold?* Washington, DC: St. Mary's.

Arnold, Regina. 1990. "Processes of Victimization and Criminalization of Black Women." *Social Justice* 17:153–66.

Barry, Ellen M. 2001. "Bad Medicine: Health Care Inadequacies in Women's Prisons." *Criminal Justice* 16 (1): 38–43.

Baxter, Sandra. 1991. "AIDS Education in the Jail Setting." *Crime and Delinquency* 37 (1): 48–63.

Belknap, Joanne. 2007. *The Invisible Woman: Gender, Crime and Justice*. 3rd ed. Belmont, CA: Wadsworth.

Beltrami, John F., Deborah A. Cohen, Joseph T. Hamrick, and Thomas A. Farley. 1997. "Rapid Screening and Treatment for Sexually Transmitted Diseases in Arrestees: A Feasible Control Measure." *American Journal of Public Health* 87 (9): 1423–26.

Birecree, Elizabeth A., Joseph D. Bloom, Mary D. Leverette, and Mary Williams. 1994. "Diagnostic Efforts Regarding Women in Oregon's Prison System: A Preliminary Report." *International Journal of Offender Therapy and Comparative Criminology* 38 (3): 217–30.

Bloom, Barbara, Barbara Owen, and Stephanie Covington. 2003. "Gender-Responsive Strategies: Research, Practice, and Guiding Principles for Women Offenders." Washington, DC: U.S. Department of Justice, National Institute of Corrections.

Browne, Angela, Brenda Miller, and Eugene Maguin. 1999. "Prevalence and Severity of Lifetime Physical and Sexual Victimization among Incarcerated Women." *International Journal of Law and Psychiatry* 22 (3–4): 301–22.

Bureau of Justice Statistics. 2007. "Prison and Jail Inmates at Midyear, 2006." Washington, DC: U.S. Department of Justice, Office of Justice Programs.

———. 1992. "Census of State and Federal Correctional Facilities 1990 (NCJ 137003)." Washington, DC: U.S. Department of Justice, Office of Justice Programs.

Bush-Baskette, Stephanie R. 2000. "The War on Drugs and the Incarceration of Mothers." *Journal of Drug Issues* 30 (4): 919–28.

Charmaz, Kathy. 2006. *Constructing Grounded Theory*. London: Sage.

Chesney-Lind, Meda. 1997. *The Female Offender: Girls, Women, and Crime*. Thousand Oaks, CA: Sage.

————, and Lisa Pasko. 2004. *The Female Offender: Girls, Women and Crime.* 2nd ed. Thousand Oaks, CA: Sage.

————, Mary Kay Harris, and Gabrielle deGroot. 1998. "Female Offenders." *Corrections Today* 60 (7): 66–144.

————, and Randall G. Shelden. 1998. *Girls, Delinquency, and Juvenile Justice.* 2nd ed. Pacific Grove, CA: Brooks/Cole.

Collins, Patricia Hill. 1989. "The Social Construction of Black Feminist Thought." *Signs* 14: 745–73.

Comack, Elizabeth. 2006. "Coping, Resisting, and Surviving: Connecting Women's Law Violations to Their Histories of Abuse." In *In Her Own Words: Women Offenders' Views on Crime and Victimization,* ed. Leanne Fiftal Alarid and Paul Cromwell, 33–43. Los Angeles: Roxbury.

Covington, Stephanie S. 1998. "Women in Prison: Approaches in the Treatment of Our Most Invisible Population." In *Breaking the Rules: Women in Prison and Feminist Therapy,* ed. Stephanie Covington, 141–55. Binghamton, NY: Haworth.

Daly, Kathleen. 1992. "Women's Pathways to Felony Court: Feminist Theories of Lawbreaking and Problems of Representation." *Review of Law and Women's Studies* 2:11–52.

Davis, Angela Y. 1998. "Public Imprisonment and Private Violence: Reflections on the Hidden Punishment of Women." *Criminal and Civil Confinement* 24:339–51.

Ditton, Paula M. 1999. *Mental Health and Treatment of Inmates and Probationers.* Bureau of Justice Statistics Special Report (NCJ 74463). Washington, DC: U.S. Department of Justice Office of Justice Programs.

El-Bassel, Nabila, Andre Ivanoff, Robert F. Schilling, L. Gilbert, D. Borne, and D. R. Chen. 1995. "Preventing HIV/AIDS in Drug-Abusing Incarcerated Women through Skills Building and Social Support Enhancement: Preliminary Outcomes." *Social Work Research* 9 (3): 131–41.

Esterberg, Kristin G. 2002. *Qualitative Methods in Social Research.* Boston: McGraw-Hill. Federal Bureau of Investigation. 2007. Uniform Crime Reports: Crime in the United States, 2006. Washington, DC: Department of Justice, U.S. Government Printing Office.

Federal Bureau of Investigation. 2003. *Age-Specific Arrest Rates and Race-Specific Arrest Rates for Selected Offenses, 1993–2001.* Washington, DC: Department of Justice.

————. 1996. *Uniform Crime Reports: Crime in the United States, 1995.* Washington, DC: Department of Justice, U.S. Government Printing Office.

Ferraro, Kathleen J., and Angela M. Moe. 2003. "Mothering, Crime and Incarceration." *Journal of Contemporary Ethnography* 32 (1): 9–40.

Fuller, Torrey E. 1995. "Editorial: Jails and Prisons: America's New Mental Hospitals." *American Journal of Public Health* 85 (12): 1611–13.

Gilfus, Mary E. 1992. "From Victims to Survivors to Offenders: Women's Routes of Entry and Immersion into Street Crime. *Women and Criminal Justice* 4:63–90.

Gorsuch, Nikki. 1998. "Unmet Need among Disturbed Female Offenders." *Journal of Forensic Psychiatry* 9:556–70.

Greenberg, Greg A., and Robert A. Rosenheck. 2008. "Jail Incarceration, Homelessness, and Mental Health: A National Study." *Psychiatric Services* 59:170–77.

Greenfeld, Lawrence A., and Tracy L. Snell. 1999. *Bureau of Justice Statistics Special Report: Women Offenders* (NCJ 175688). Washington, DC: U.S. Department of Justice.

Guba, Egon. 1981. "Criteria for Assessing the Trustworthiness of Naturalistic Inquiries. *Education, Communication, and Technology* 29 (2): 75–91.

Harding, Sandra. 1987. "Is There a Feminist Method?" In *Feminism and Methodology: Social Science Issues,* ed. Sandra Harding, 1–14. Bloomington, IN: Indiana University.

Harlow, Caroline Wolf. 1999. *Prior Abuse Reported by Inmates and Probationers: Selected Findings* (NCJ 172879). Washington, DC: Bureau of Justice Statistics.

———. 1998. *Profile of Jail Inmates, 1996* (NCJ 164620). Washington, DC: Bureau of Justice Statistics.

Hartsock, Nancy C. M. 1987. "The Feminist Standpoint: Developing a Ground for a Specifically Feminist Historical Materialism." In *Feminism and Methodology: Social Science Issues,* ed. Sandra Harding, 157–80. Milton Keynes, Great Britain: Open University Press.

———. 1985. *Money, Sex, and Power: Towards a Feminist Historical Materialism.* Boston: Northeastern University Press.

Haywood, Thomas W., Howard M. Kravitz, Laurie B. Goldman, and Anderson Freeman. 2000. "Characteristics of Women in Jail and Treatment Orientations: A Review." *Behavior Modification* 24 (3): 307–24.

Ingram-Fogel, Catherine. 1991. "Health Problems and Needs of Incarcerated Women." *Journal of Prison and Jail Health* 10 (1): 43–57.

Johnson, Joy L. 1997. "Generalizability in Qualitative Research." In *Completing a Qualitative Project: Details and Dialogue,* ed. Janice M. Morse, 191–208. Thousand Oaks, CA: Sage.

Kaplan, Mark S., and J. E. Sasser. 1996. "Women behind Bars: Trends and Policy Issues." *Journal of Sociology and Social Welfare* 23 (4): 43–56.

Kushel, Margot B., Judith A. Hahn, Jennifer L. Evans, David P. Bangsberg, and Andrew R. Moss. 2005. Revolving Doors: Imprisonment Among the Homeless and Marginally Housed Population." *American Journal of Public Health,* 95 (10): 1747–52.

Kvale, Steinar. 1996. *InterViews: An Introduction to Qualitative Research Interviewing.* Thousand Oaks, CA: Sage.

Lake, Elise S. 1993. "An Exploration of the Violent Victim Experiences of Female Offenders." *Violence and Victims* 8 (1): 41–51.

Leh, Sandra K. 1999. "HIV Infection in U.S. Correctional Systems: Its Effects on the Community. *Journal of Community Health Nursing* 16 (1): 53–63.

Leonard, Elizabeth Dermody. 2002. *Convicted Survivors: The Imprisonment of Battered Women Who Kill.* New York: State University of New York Press.

Lofland, John, David A. Snow, Leon Anderson, and Lyn H. Lofland. 2006. *Analyzing Social Settings: A Guide to Qualitative Observation and Analysis.* 4th ed. Belmont, CA: Wadsworth.

Macher, Abe M., and Eric P. Goosby. 2000. "Issues in Correctional HIV Care: The Pregnant Inmate and Prevention of Perinatal HIV Transmission." *American Jails* 14 (3): 46–47.

Maeve, M. Katherine. 1999. "Adjudicated Health: Incarcerated Women and the Social Construction of Health." *Crime, Law and Social Change* 31 (1): 49–71.

———, and Michael S. Vaughn. 2001. "Nursing with Prisoners: The Practice of Caring, Forensic Nursing, or Penal Harm Nursing?" *Advances in Nursing Science* 24:47–64.

Mauer, Marc, Cathy Potler, and Richard Wolf. 1999. *Gender and Justice: Women, Drugs, and Sentencing Policy.* Washington, DC: Sentencing Project.

Mink, Gwendolyn, ed. 1999. *Whose Welfare?* Ithaca, NY: Cornell University Press.

Moe, Angela M. 2004. "Blurring the Boundaries: Women's Criminality in the Context of Abuse." *Women's Studies Quarterly* 32 (3–4): 116–38.

———. 2006. "Women, Drugs and Crime." *Criminal Justice Studies: A Critical Journal of Crime, Law, and Society* 19 (4): 337–52.

———, and Kathleen J. Ferraro. 2003. "Malign Neglect or Benign Respect: Women's Health Care in a Carceral Setting." *Women and Criminal Justice* 14 (4): 53–80.

Morash, Merry, Robin N. Haarr, and Lila Rucker. 1994. "A Comparison of Programming for Women and Men in U.S. Prisons in the 1980s." *Crime and Delinquency* 40 (2): 197–221.

Pollock, Joycelyn M. 2002. *Women, Prison and Crime.* 2nd ed. Belmont, CA: Wadsworth.

Pollock-Byrne, Joycelyn M. 1990. *Women, Prison, and Crime.* Belmont, CA: Wadsworth.

Regier, Darrel A., Michael E. Farmer, Donald S. Rae, B. Z. Locke, S. J. Keith, U. Judd, and F. K. Goodwin. 1990. "Co-morbidity of Mental Disorders with Alcohol and Other Drug Abuse: Results from an Epidemiologic Catchment Area [ECA] Study." *Journal of the American Medical Association* 264 (19): 2511–18.

Resnik, Judith, and Nancy Shaw. 1981. "Prisoners of Their Sex: Health Problems of Incarcerated Women." *Prison Law Monitor* 3 (3, 4): 57, 68, 83, 89, 104, 115.

Richie, Beth E. 2001. "Challenges Incarcerated Women Face as They Return to Their Communities: Findings from Life History Interviews." *Crime and Delinquency* 47 (3): 368–89.

———. 1996. Compelled to Crime: The Gender Entrapment of Battered Black Women. New York: Routledge.

Romero, Mary, and Abigail J. Stewart, eds. 1999. *Women's Untold Stories: Breaking Silence, Talking Back, Voicing Complexity.* New York: Routledge.

Roth, Campbell. 2006. "House and Senate Play Grinch with Budget, Tax Cuts." *National Organization for Women (NOW) National Times* 38 (1): 1, 10.

Ross, Luana. 1998. *Inventing the Savage: The Social Construction of Native American Criminality.* Austin: University of Texas Press.

Sargent, Elizabeth, Susan Marcus-Mendoza, and Yu Chong Ho. 1993. "Abuse and the Woman Prisoner: A Forgotten Population." In *Women Prisoners: A Forgotten Population,* ed. Beverly R. Fletcher, Lynda Dixon Shaver, and Dreama G. Moon, 55–64. Westport, CT: Praeger.

Shaw, Margaret. 1992. "Issues of Power and Control: Women in Prison and Their Defenders." *British Journal of Criminology* 32 (4): 438–52.

———, Nancy Stoller, Irene Browne, and Peter Meyer. 1981. "Sexism and Medical Care in a Jail Setting." *Women and Health* 6 (1–2): 5–25.

Sigurdson, Chris. 2000. "The Mad, the Bad, and the Abandoned: The Mentally Ill in Prisons and Jails." *Corrections Today* 62 (7): 70–78.

Smith, Brenda V., and Cynthia Dailard. 1994. "Female Prisoners and AIDS: On the Margins of Public Health and Social Justice." *AIDS and Public Policy Journal* 9 (2): 78–85.

Smith, Dorothy E. 1989. "Sociological Theory: Methods of Writing Patriarchy." In *Feminism and Sociological Theory,* ed. Ruth A. Wallace, 34–64. Newbury Park, CA: Sage.

Staton, Michele, Carl G. Leukefeld, and T. K. Logan. 2001. "Health Services Utilization and Victimization among Incarcerated Female Substance Users." *Substance Use and Misuse* 36 (6–7): 701–16.

Steadman, Henry J., Edward J. Holohean Jr., and Joel Dovoskin. 1991. "Estimating Mental Health Needs and Service Utilization among Prison Inmates." *Bulletin of the American Academy of Psychiatry and the Law* 10 (3): 297–307.

Teplin, Linda A., Karen M. Abram, and Gary M. McClelland. 1997. "Mentally Disordered Women in Jail: Who Receives Services?" *American Journal of Public Health* 87 (4): 604–09.

———. 1996. "Prevalence of Psychiatric Disorders among Incarcerated Women." *Archives of General Psychiatry* 53:505–12.

Tjaden, Patricia, and Nancy Thoennes. (2000). *Extent, Nature and Consequences of Intimate Partner Violence: Findings from the National Violence against Women Survey* (NCJ 181867). Washington, DC: National Institute of Justice.

U.S. General Accounting Office. 1999. *Women in Prison: Issues and Challenges Confronting U.S. Correctional Systems.* Washington, DC: Author.

Veysey, Bonita M. 1998. "Specific Needs of Women Diagnosed with Mental Illnesses in U.S. Jails." In *Women's Mental Health Services: A Public Health Perspective,* ed. Bruce Lubotsky Levin, Andrea K. Blanch, and Ann Jennings, 368–89. Thousand Oaks, CA: Sage.

Young, Diane S. 1999. "Ethnicity and Health Service Use in a Women's Prison." *Journal of Multicultural Social Work* 7 (3–4): 69–93.

———. 1998. "Health Status and Service Use among Incarcerated Women. *Family and Community Health* 21 (3): 16–31.

CHAPTER ELEVEN

Patiently Waiting

Jen Myers

Patiently.   Patiently waiting.

this is all we ever do.
are supposed to do.   What else?

where else?
At home mother. You with your babies.

they ain't that nice to us here.
here, dear in this prison home.

Yesterday, someone died in her cube.
oh.
now, what are they going to do?
women are upset.
now, protest!   This woman sick for a long time officer.
what she doing in her cube?
why she die sir?
no, the CPR didn't work this time officer
                    (as six inmates and friends looked on)

What the hell is going on?

                    Today. Yes, this morning. An ambulance came
                    and took another one away. Three hours later I

was in my cube. Patiently waiting for my shoes
to dry.

my new clean shoes
you/tennis shoes/you.
my one pair of two shoes
only, tennis shoes.

(Big announcement over the speaker outside)

"The upper compound is closed"
"The lower compound is closed"

what is going on now, I think.   i sit.
              i sit patiently in my cube.
              (not wanting drama)

don't disturb me.
you inmate.
you officer.
you.
no one say my name.
I am having privacy time.
My time. Me time.
It's all about me sometimes.
And this is my five minutes.

no sanity in here, and the girls are looking out their cube windows now.
                 and talking loud.

I am ear hustling, and now distracted.
    my private thoughts, swept up, collected.
another one is going out, they say.
carried out, swept out.
now not in my head, but in an ambulance bed.

The officers are standing around outside of the medical building now.

the unit manager
the medical supervisor
the safety supervisor.

what now, is going on?

i want to know now sir.
tell me.

we are guessing now, and the girls are pressed against the glass windows
looking out.

RED-LIGHT

        flashing.   bright.   red.

                    and the ambulance is here.

another down.
and 1298 to go.
we are dropping like flies,
and boy, oh boy
you should hear the rumors fly.

the anger. the blame. the BOP sucks.
they caused this.

                  this is their fault.
(i want out)

boy, oh boy!
and we need therapy for our drug use?
why don't you slap us on the wrist and call it a day?
how are we supposed to function in this disarray?
           three down now, sir.
           and only in two days!

      1. Dead on arrival.
      2. Heart attack.
      3. Lung problem (so they say).

And now, here's the drum roll . . .
           "Please give it up for the winner!"

    "THE COMPOUND IS CLOSED"   You win, you do sir.

Number four wins the prize.
      It's a beautiful heart attack again!   (surprise)
But you can't say she was original about it.

There she goes, in the bright red lit ambulance machine on auto drive.
let's give these women something else to blame them—
the BOP
Yet, is it lack of health care?
scattegories, categories.
um,
what game are we playing?

                                   what is going on sir?

Four, now in two days,
Three today.
And how does the ambulance driver feel about this sir?

                   Is he going through McDonalds, just for a
                   McMuffin break before coming back again to
                   this compound for his next victim?

                                        (I mean passenger.)

Dead or alive, we'll take em.
         They don't need target practice, these officers here.
         They don't need guns, dear.
                   We're getting shot down by poor medical care in here, sir.
please take care,
watch your step,
you are now entering the 'prison zone'
step down, please.
cause you are goin down,
down the rabbit hole adventure game,
And it's called the BOP.

              The officers like to play Russian Roulette with our
         tombstones.
              Oh, I mean, they target practice on our death beds.
         (as we die in our heads).
oh, two days ago, after the first woman died in the wee hours of the morning.
I was still in my cube, preparing for my innocent day, another prison stay, when
I heard the rumor wafting to my ears, from across the silent hall.
                                        (ear-hustling again).
"someone died."   i mean, what?

         "someone died" . . . the words moving closer to my ears, my heart.

    now a whisper . . . "someone died"

some.   one.   died.

The compound closed, and we were locked
in. Two whistles blew. Means, stay where you
are, you, inmates, you. Yes sir! Officer, you in
the blue and gray, with the clinking of keys,
walking my way. Hide it, and stop what you
are doin! Don't want to get in trouble now,
do you? No, shot in my room. No incident
report. No way. I want to go home, nothing
worth this way to play.

wait.   wait.   read.
read the *New York Times*.   read the *New Yorker*.   write a letter.

reorganize my locker.   eat a cinnamon toasty (no milk).

why are we locked in?
we all agreed we really didn't know.
when do we ever.
only pretend we do.
as we sit and watch *Prison Break* on T.V.
and live prison break every day.
women in prison,
watching shows about people in prison.
do you know this is what women in prison do?

let's really limit it to prison.
if the 'theme' prison does not exist,
then the product cannot be watched,   consumed,   or read.

prison in my head.
prison in my eyes.
prison in my mouth.
prison, prison, prison sir. No, not prism. (that's rainbows, dear).

P   R   I   S   O   N   (we come in plane loads, dear).

Now, LOUD VOICE . . .

"Up front ladies.   Everyone up front. We are having a town hall meeting"

"Now."

we are called in
we are locked in
we are having a
                meeting
        up front.   and we cram up front.

who's here,
what supervisor dear, to
call this meeting.
clues begin forming mental
rumors in our heads of early release.
are we getting immediate release?
                really?

we are called up front.

"okay, ladies, as you know there has been a death in this prison family,
        and earlier today, this here woman, Sarah, she died."
"We are holding this meeting, because we care so much about your well
        being, and we wanted to know if anyone has any questions, you can
        ask them now if you do."

"we know some of you may be upset"   (oh, really?)
"upset by the news."   (yes, well, i guess she did die
in her
cube).

(I wasn't upset, but I am now. I am thinking).

I am thinking of a question in my mind.   (nothing of any sense pops
                                                 up for some reason).

            Everyone is quiet.

every.   one.   is.
        quiet.

they ask again.

"No one has any questions?"   (okay, please ask, they are thinking because
                                 they feel so guilty right now).

quiet.
calm.
looking around.

one   small voice: "How did she die?"   (why did she die?)
now, good question.   i think to myself.
what else is there really to ask?
and actually, they really don't want us to ask this question.
or any other question, they are following protocol duty.
so the record can state:

(logged in)

>   "September 25, 2006: Inmate dies today in her cube. Officer responds
>   in urgent manner to emergency call. Attempted CPR for 20 minutes.
>   Ambulance called. later, compound closed. Held town-hall meeting in
>   all Ranges. Informed inmates officially of death of fellow inmate, and
>   friend to some. Name: Rogers. Inmate #45678-190. Held open discussion.
>   Grief therapy offered."

so, okay, sir. "How did she die"

good questions.   um.   yes?   um.

"I'm sorry, but we cannot disclose confidential medical information."

End of that one.

Are there any more questions?   good.   I mean, no?

okay, well, there you have it.
Folks, you can all go back to your cubes.
(No, I want to go home.)
                              why are we here?
                              why do we question?
                              why you teasin us with
                              all of your messing around, you fools?

today, after the second ambulance was called they closed the compound down
at 9:30 am. As I said. As you now know.
it did not reopen until about 10:45 am.

yes, just in time for lunch!   boy, sir, I am NOT hungry!

           chow time.
           lunch time.
           meeting friends time.

I met my close friend Ericka for lunch, and we walked down together, in
peace.
Grateful it was not each other's death we were silent for.

we were greeted with a treat.
      lunch consists of:
           grilled cheese sandwich (x2)
           corn niblets (optional)
           cheese on wheat cracker packets
           bag of plain potato chips (x1)
           heated cinnamon roll
           potato soup

wow. what a meal. and boy, will those girls who said they were not coming down
the hill for lunch be disappointed now.   be upset.   cause we had cinnamon rolls.

oh boy, sir.   what's the special occasion,
too many expiration dates.
more protocol, and the delivery truck's comin.
freezer, overstocked?
or,
trying to keep up quiet on this one.   too many deaths sir?

(feed em and keep em happy).

Ericka and I sit in silence, trying to digest our weird food combination and
the recent deaths we've been witness to:
      (1)   death.   heart attack   Range A-2
      (2)   no death yet.   heart attack   Range A-3
      (3)   no death yet.   heart attack   Range A-1
      (4)   no death yet.   lung problem   Range A-2

      thank god it's not on my side of the compound.   the B side.

what side?
the prison side?
the medical side.

the GOD side.
who made you chief, sir?

> i sit quietly with my best friend by my side.
> in front of me. i silently finish my grilled
> cheese sandwich (x2), and my cinnamon
> roll. i eat half of my bag of chips.

Ericka wants to take her crackers out, but I see they are searching us
at the back door.
so, i tell her to leave it.

"Leave it," I say to her.
she does.

> and we walk to the door after i throw my silverware into the metal
> shiny CDRshute. i watch it slide down, easier than the food down
> my throat a few minutes

ago.
we walk to the door.

> towards the door, and i slide by the inspections going on in front
> of me. i walk casually out the double back doors leading to
> my nonfreedom.

the medical supervisor is searching up front.
the medical supervisor is searching up front.
(can you write this 100 times on the chalkboard, please, sir).

the medical supervisor is searching up front, after he had
> one death, 2 heart attacks, and one lung problem.
problem.
problem, is there a problem here, dear?

> yes, sir. you are searching up for chips and crackers,
> and there is a death sitting on your left shoulder.
> i can see it.
> It's right THERE.
>> right HERE, sir.
> can't you feel it?
>> do you feel?
> are you in on it?

>> tag, you're it.   death says.

be cautious.
be clear.
be conscious
unconscious.

not in here.   they choose none of the above.

in my head, i mark off all three.
it's answer C, "All of the above."

how are we supposed to feel? As if this is normal?
where are the psychologists?
where are the people who are human here?

why is everyone acting as if this is okay?

    and why am i still able to feel my heart beating quickly inside
        of my chest, and my throat is closing up, and I think I may have an
  anxiety attack, and my friend who lives in the cube next to me looks
        a little ill, and maybe she is next, and her money didn't come
      in, and she's almost out of email minutes, and needs to talk to her
      attorney before next week about her rule 35 so she can get out of here
      before July, and
    she has no money on her phone, and she'll have to call collect,
but the compound is closed
again, and she needs to call NOW,
      because they are shutting down our
ability to purchase more
      email minutes
          at 3:00 pm today,
            till Sunday.
                And I am sorry, sir
                  but this is
                      way
too intense
for me.

There is just too much going on, I say.

        and i think my head may explode.
        i mean just pop right off my little
        shoulders and explode into a
        million pieces, all over the place,
        and i mean right now sir. right here

in this peaceful little book sanctuary.
my head will be spewed all over the
typewriter and on the laminate square floor.
what am i to do sir?

the lump in my stomach won't go away.

and i have to teach class, sir,
and tonight we will sit on our mats,
and suck our navel to our spine,
and I will be a big girl, and teach Pilates anyways.
head, or no head.
i guess i don't need one.

prison or no prison.
they'll punish us anyways.
come on, just slap our wrists, and tell us now
it will be okay.

death, or no death.
we are all prisoners.

anyways.   sit tight.   pray.

Caged Innocence

Patricia K. Thorn

ARTIST'S STATEMENT

Sadly, Patricia K. Thorn passed away during the writing of this book. She had been released from prison shortly before her death. Her mother, Sherry Thorn, granted permission for the printing of "Caged Innocence."

CHAPTER TWELVE

Transgender Women, Sexual Violence, and the Rule of Law: An Argument in Favor of Restorative and Transformative Justice

Linda Heidenreich

The horrors experienced by many young inmates, particularly those who, like the petitioner, are convicted of nonviolent offenses, border on the unimaginable. Prison rape not only threatens the lives of those who fall prey to their aggressors, but is potentially devastating to the human spirit.

—Justice Blackmun,
Concurring Opinion, *Farmer v. Brennan*

[R]ather than try to imagine one single alternative to the existing system of incarceration, we might envision an array of alternatives that will require radical transformations of many aspects of our society. Alternatives that fail to address racism, male dominance, homophobia, class bias, and other structures of domination will not, in the final analysis, lead to decarceration and will not advance the goal of abolition.

—Davis, *Are Prisons Obsolete?*

This chapter is located at the intersection of research and experience, rooted in my experiences as a volunteer in a detention ministry program and a sister and auntie to incarcerated persons and my academic research at a university in the Pacific Northwest. It is preliminary, taking my own firm belief in restorative justice as a base for understanding the violence in our current penal system and from there beginning to map the status of transsexual women in the United States correctional system. Other scholars are producing more in-depth studies on the subject (Saffin 2008; Rosenblum 2000;

Rose 2001); this chapter seeks to provide a structural and historical mapping of a problem and to suggest remedies.[1] Of particular interest to the author is the importance of remedies and how of all of us, womanists, feminists, mujeristas, and/or humanists, can work to implement remedies today and each day that we breathe and walk and eat as free or unfree people in the United States.

One path out of the violent system our society has built is restorative justice. Moving from the understanding that the retributive system we now possess inflicts harm as it seeks revenge or retribution, restorative justice instead seeks wholeness (Magnani and Wray 2006; Wachtel and McCold 2001). It does this by focusing on relationships, community, and wholeness and also by focusing on harm and creating a community where people are free from harm. In the words of legal scholar and restorative justice advocate John Braithwaite, "[B]ecause crime hurts, justice should heal" (Braithwaite 2003, 402). Important to this chapter, where systematic violence is addressed, restorative justice allows us to examine relationships between systems—critique our understanding of crime, as well as systems such as gender. If our society is not whole, what are the causes of its brokenness? Could our gender system be part of the problem?

Transgender women are among the most vulnerable populations of incarcerated persons in the United States today (Rosenblum 2000; National Center for Lesbian Rights 2006). Often placed in men's facilities, they are subjected to sexual harassment and assault; they have little recourse for challenging such violence (Rosenblum 2000; Talvi 2007, 12). This fact alone should be enough to drive us to action, to demand justice for incarcerated transgender women. Yet when we slow down to ask why it is that transgender women are so vulnerable in today's penal system, it becomes apparent that the answer to this question and the possible solutions to the problem affect all of us. Transgender women are vulnerable in U.S. society and in its penal system in particular, because we live under a rule of law that is gendered. Until we challenge and transform this gendered system, transgender women and especially such women from poor and working-class backgrounds will continue to be the target of police and civilian hostility (DeCrow 1975, 237; Talvi 2007, xiv).[2]

This chapter argues that the gendered violence of the U.S. penal system is dialogically related to a gendered rule of law that structures the larger U.S. society and the "gendered models of citizenship" that flow from it (Spade 2006, 218). It places the lives of transgender women at the center of its analysis and asks the question: How is it that such intense violence is tolerated when it is directed against transgender women? and if such violence is not tolerable, what remedies are available? Ultimately, it argues that the policing of gender is central to U.S. society and hence intensified in its penal system, which functions as a heterotopia—an institution which, as Michel Foucault and Rosaura Sánchez have demonstrated, is both constructed by and constructs the larger society (1986; 1995, 50). A gender-racial policing of society is produced by our correctional institutions, which exist as hypergendered and hyperraced and classed spaces. The larger society reflects these same values at the same time that correctional institutions produce and exploit bodies to fuel the larger social structure. Thus people who are sent to U.S. correctional institutions emerge transformed, both by the violence of incarceration and by the stigma that is attached to exconvicts. Having undergone the violence of incarceration, former inmates are also marked by the larger society, as exconvicts for life (Magnani and Wray 2006, 36; Talvi 2007, 27).

Thus gender is central to the construction of our social system and its policing. In relation, as argued by Kendall Thomas, it functions as a contract. In U.S. society, a person is accepted and protected by fellow citizens and the state if they maintain their gender contract; if they violate it, they lose their rights to be protected as members of the society. Thomas goes so far as to argue that those of us who violate gender contracts are no longer viewed as human or worthy of human rights in U.S. society (2006, 316). If we are ever to succeed in protecting the lives and dignity of all women, then we must advocate for radical alternatives to the current prison system, alternatives that challenge the gender-racial institutions that continue to structure our country both within prison walls and without.

INCARCERATION AND THE PRODUCTION OF U.S. GENDER

Initially, correctional institutions were designed for male inmates. For the most part, women who violated the law and/or social customs were disciplined by their husbands. Until the midnineteenth century, women in many states in the United States were legally beaten by their husbands; in 1824 the courts went so far as to invoke the "rule of thumb."

> I believe it was in a case before Mr. Justice Raymond, where the same doctrine was recognized, with proper limitations and restrictions well suited to the condition and feelings of those who might think proper to use a whip or rattan, no bigger than my thumb, in order to enforce the salutary restraints of domestic discipline.
> —*Bradley v. State*, Miss. 1824

> Because a husband was civilly and criminally liable for the actions of his wife, he also held the right to discipline her.
> —Truss, "The Subjection of Women"

Prisons were gendered institutions from their very inception (Rafter 1985, xx; Davis 2003, 60; Baumler 2008, 42).[3] They were built to discipline and punish men because they were independent people, capable of redemption. In the world of public and private spheres from which the prison system emerged, women were dependents. If they were incarcerated, it was because they were fallen and, thus, beyond redemption. Such women were constructed as "monsters of depravity" and thus could be incarcerated in men's facilities, with male guards and so on (Rafter 1985, 49). Women inmates were not worthy of protection.

And how did women lose the right to physical and mental well-being? By violating gender roles. Silja Talvi reminds us that throughout early U.S. history dominant attitudes about incarcerated women "had everything to do with the idea that women who defied their gendered roles" were depraved women (2007, 12). Women who engaged in prostitution or public drunkenness or who were caught in extramarital affairs were punished harshly because their gender-deviant behavior challenged the very foundations of U.S. society (Rafter 1985, 49; Baumler 2008, 46).

When, in the midnineteenth century, the reformatory movement swept the country, it sought to redeem young men by instilling a sense of "manliness" in them and to redeem women by teaching them feminine traits (Rafter 1985, xxii). Thus women who were sentenced to reformatories were taught to sew and knit, to cook and wait on tables. That such institutions were not just gendered but also gender-racial institutions becomes clear when noting racialized sentencing patterns for women sent to such institutions: white working-class women were sent to reformatories; black poor and working-class women were sent to traditional penitentiaries or, in the South, sentenced to the deadly lease system (Rafter 1985, 37). In the nineteenth century, as in the twentieth and twenty-first, poor and working-class people were overrepresented in all institutions (Rafter 1985, 89; Talvi 2007, xv; Magnani and Wray 2006, 35; Goldberg 2000, 205).[4]

This gendered ideology of the penal system is critical to understanding the status of incarcerated women today at two levels. First, it establishes a long tradition of devaluing people who do not conform to dominant gender roles. Second, it demonstrates that the prison system's treatment of transgender women follows the pattern of our larger society, where women who violate gender roles are deemed worthy of violence.

POLICING GENDER

The United States is a country governed and structured by rule of law, where the customs and culture are codified, and those codes are enforced through a recognized police force. In the United States as well, laws are rooted in Protestant religious beliefs. According to Magnani and Wray, from "colonial times, crime was tied up with definitions of sin. Today, the fact that crime is thought to be strictly a legal concept obscures the extent to which our criminal law continues to be rooted in moralistic biases about unacceptable individual behavior" (8). From the time Euro-Americans arrived on the continent, gender representation was considered a moral and a legal issue (Valdez 1995, 6; 2005, 1443).

Evidence of the policing of gender in everyday life can be seen in the earliest histories of Euro-Americans in North America. In the seventeenth century, for example, British colonists were expected to wear gendered clothing that matched their genital identity—adults with penises wore shirts and breeches; adults with vaginas wore gowns and aprons.[5] Such alignment of gender and sex was seen as a moral and criminal issue. People who transgressed gendered dress codes found themselves in court, as did Thomas, also known as Thomasine Hall (Little 2001, 243; Vaughan 1978, 146).

Thomas/ine was brought before the Virginia court because s/he sometimes dressed as a man, sometimes as a woman. People from Hall's community were brought in to testify to his/her gender, providing mixed results: some people claimed to know Hall as a man, some as a woman. The courts ordered several examinations of Hall's genitals, but to no avail. Ultimately, the court ordered that Hall wear breeches and an apron—to signify his/her indeterminate genitalia (Little 2001, 244; Vaughan 1978, 148). For the first European colonists to this continent, consistency between one's genitals and one's gender identity was heavily policed—by courts and neighbors. Sex-gender consistency was important to the rule of law—to the larger order of things.

The centrality of sex and gender to the rule of law continued postindependence and was codified unevenly across the United States so that U.S. history is replete with cases of sex and gender policing. In 1904, in New York, a person by the name of Becker was sentenced to six months in jail for wearing women's clothing. In Becker's case, it was a woman who turned him in to the authorities, thus demonstrating that men and women both reinforce the gendered rule of law; institutions such as the police alone cannot be blamed for policing gender. Other cases from the early twentieth century include Randolph Milburn, a music teacher in Washington, Ohio, who in 1906 was arrested for wearing women's dresses.[6] And in 1907, John Becht of New York was arrested for wearing women's clothing and "masquerading as a woman." The charge filed against him was "endangering public morality" (Hirschfield 1991, 276).

A central function of police in theUnited States, then, has been to police gender. This policing has been accomplished through the law and also through violence. Recent scholarship has demonstrated how violence, throughout U.S. history has played a critical role in maintaining dominant social structures. Those who cross and/or transgress gender roles may be "refus[ed] civil and human recognition" (Juang 2006, 150).

TRANSSEXUAL WOMEN FIGHTING PRISON VIOLENCE

Transsexual women are placed within a violent system where sexual violence has, for many years, been accepted as part of the police system. The normalizing of this violence can be seen throughout the prison system itself and throughout popular culture. Ironically, today, many people are being held on charges for nonviolent crimes such as drug possession, prostitution, forgery, and credit card fraud (Talvi 2007, 33; Magnani and Wray 2006, 9). Transsexual women seem to fit this pattern; while some women are charged with violent crimes, many are incarcerated for nonviolent, sometimes "victimless," crimes (Baus, Hunt, and Williams 2006). This section of this chapter will examine the cases of two incarcerated transgender women and their struggles for justice within a violent system.

In June 1994, the Supreme Court of the United States handed down a decision in the case of *Dee Farmer v. Edward Brennan*. Dee Farmer was a young transsexual inmate who was raped during her incarceration at the United States Penitentiary in Terre Haute, Indiana; Edward Brennan was the warden at that institution. While the vulnerability of transgender and transsexual inmates in male penitentiaries is common knowledge both within and without correctional institutions (Magnani and Wray 2006, 115; Rosenblum 2000; Rose 2001, 506), Brennan had failed to take any actions to protect Farmer from such violence.

By the time she was eighteen years old, Dee Farmer had already rejected the gender identity imposed on her by the dominant society. She took estrogen, had breast implants, and had even undergone surgery to have her testacies removed. The surgery was "black market," and it failed. It was after this, when she was eighteen and woman-identified, that she was arrested for credit-card fraud. She was prosecuted to the full extent of the law and sentenced on federal criminal charges (*Farmer v. Brennan*).

Once incarcerated, Dee Farmer was diagnosed, by a physician working for the Bureau of Prisons, as transsexual, but she was not allowed to continue hormone therapy, most probably because of the Bureau's policy of continuing hormone therapy only for prisoners with documented histories of hormone therapy, at the levels prescribed by their physicians before incarceration and at the discretion of a prison medical practitioner (Rosenblum 2000, 501; National Center for Lesbian Rights 2006; Federal Bureau of Prisons 2005). Because the majority of prison inmates come from low-income families, and thus do not have regular access to health care, no such prescriptions exist for many transsexual inmates.[7] So Farmer took hormones smuggled into the prison system through illegal means, wore her uniform off-shoulder, and continued to live and identify as female.

Often, the institutions where Farmer was incarcerated held her in segregation—at times as punishment for prison infractions, but often for her protection. As will be discussed below, segregation is considered by many, including Human Rights Watch and the United Nations, a violation of human rights. Following four years of incarceration, much of it in isolation, in March of 1989 Farmer was transferred to the United States Penitentiary in Terre Correctional Institute in Oxford Wisconsin. Initially she was housed in isolation but eventually was placed in the general male population. Within two weeks, one of her cellmates beat and raped her (*Farmer v. Brennan*).

Fortunately, Farmer had a strong enough sense of self to file suit against the warden and others responsible for placing her in physical danger. Her complaint noted that USP-Terre Haute was known as an especially violent institution, and that as a transsexual, she would likely be the victim of assault. Lower courts found in favor of the warden, arguing that because Farmer did not explain to authorities that she was at risk, they could not be held accountable for her safety; but the Supreme Court disagreed, stating that if officials knew of and disregarded an excessive risk to inmate safety, they could be held accountable for violating the Eighth Amendment.[8] So the case was remanded, sent back to be heard by the lower courts once again.

Farmer's story does not end there, for she left a legacy. *Farmer v. Brennan* has become a commonly cited case for attorneys prosecuting prison rapes and other prison assaults—as it was in the Schwenk case (below). Also important, because the case went to the Supreme Court, *Farmer v. Brennan* continues to serve as a report on the rights of incarcerated persons, especially transsexual women, as the justices published detailed opinions regarding the human rights of incarcerated persons.

The majority opinion, published by Justice Souter, held:

> The Federal Constitution does not mandate comfortable prisons, but neither does it permit inhuman ones; the treatment which prisoners receive in prison, and the conditions under which they are confined, are subject to scrutiny under the Constitution's Eight Amendment . . . the Eight Amendment places restraint on prison officials . . . and imposes duties on prison officials, who must provide humane conditions of confinement by insuring that inmates receive adequate food, clothing, shelter, and medical care, and by taking reasonable measures to guarantee the safety of inmates . . . [P]rison officials have a duty to protect prisoners from violence at the hands of other prisoners, and although prison conditions may be restrictive and even harsh, gratuitously allowing the beating or rape of one prisoner by another . . . is not part of the penalty that criminal offenders pay for their offenses against society.

The story of Crystal Schwenk is equally troubling to that of Dee Farmer because of the violence she faced. Like Farmer, Schwenk identified as female long before her incarceration. Female-identified from the age of twelve, by the time of her arrest, she was also using nonprescription hormones. In June 1993, she was incarcerated in the male Washington State Penitentiary in Walla Walla (*Schwenk v. Hartford*, et al.; Rose 2001, 512).

It was here that Schwenk's case diverged from that of Farmer. While Farmer was assaulted by another inmate, Schwenk was assaulted by a prison guard. Shortly after her arrival at Walla Walla, she was placed in Baker, a medium security unit at the prison where Robert Mitchell was a guard. Mitchell began harassing Schwenk shortly after her arrival at Baker.[9] His harassing behavior ranged from winking to imitating oral sex, to making threatening comments, to making obscene gestures while watching Schwenk in the shower (*Schwenk v. Hartford*). Mitchell asked Schwenk for sex, promising makeup and "girl stuff" in return; when she refused, he groped her. His harassing behavior escalated to a full-blown attempted assault. Mitchell threatened retribution, Schwenk held her own and filed an administrative grievance, which was denied because, at the time, inmates had only five days to file complaints after an alleged incident. She then filed a complaint in federal court; thus the larger public came to know of the assault.

And it is here that Schwenk's case provides us with critical information about police violence in the prison system, for Mitchell did not deny Schwenk's allegations of harassment and violence; instead, he denied that such actions were illegal. Schwenk claimed her Eighth Amendment rights were violated as well as her rights under the Gender Motivated Violence Act (GMVA).[10] Mitchell argued that Schwenk was not protected by the GMVA, because it protected women from violence against men, not men from violence against other men. He also argued that transsexuals are not protected by GMVA (*Schwenk v. Hartford*; Rose 2001, 523).

Like the Farmer case, the court's decision in *Schwenk v. Hartford* tells us much about the status of transsexual women in the U.S. penal system. Citing *Farmer v. Brennan*, the court held that Mitchell knowingly violated Schwenk's Eighth Amendment rights—that all incarcerated persons were to be protected from sexual violence, and that "being violently assaulted in prison is simply not 'part of the penalty that criminal offenders pay for their offenses against society' " (*Schwenk v. Harford*). In relation to the GMVA, however, they decided that while it protected all people from gender-motivated violence and that rape is always a gender-motivated offense, Mitchell might not have been aware of its applicability to his behavior and could therefore claim qualified immunity (from civil charges).

Mitchell was able to challenge charges of attempted assault because the courts continue to treat inmates and transsexuals as less valuable than other members of society and because of a critical flaw in the very way that the law is constructed in the United States. Crime under our rule of law does not consist in creating "harm" but in violating laws—laws that may address harm but, as demonstrated above, often do not. Laws are rooted in custom and enforce protestant understandings of gendered customs, many of which have nothing to do with harm (Magnani and Wray 2006, 8). Hence, Dee Farmer was sent to prison for committing a nonviolent crime, while Robert Mitchell harassed and attempted to assault another human being (to the point of forcing his penis into her buttocks), threatened the victim with retribution if she spoke out, and was allowed to claim qualified immunity.[11] If the dominant concept of crime in the United States was shifted to focus on harm, no such claim would be possible.

CANARIES

Unfortunately, the experiences of Farmer and Schwenk are not unique. Perhaps this is why Rosenblum has argued that transsexual women are the modern "miner's canary" (2000, 551). While the Farmer case created a precedent for prosecuting prison rape cases, it also created a proof standard that is often difficult to meet, holding that prison officials have to "know of and ignore 'excessive' risk to inmate health or safety" in order to be culpable for allowing/facilitating such violence (Farmer; Rose 2001). Today, when accused of facilitating violent crimes against inmates, officers can still claim ignorance. A history of systemic violence and indifference produced the Farmer and Schwenk cases, and a history of violence continues to flow from that same system.

Even the harassment of Schwenk is part of a long history of documented police violence against transsexual women. When Rosio Melgoza was arrested, officers allegedly "touched her breasts and genitals with their hands and a nightstick." She was strip-searched in front of male inmates, then placed in a cell with those same inmates where she was repeatedly sexually assaulted; Susan Marie Pollock was harassed by prison guards; Michelle Murray alleged "that a prison guard assaulted her, and that other guards propositioned and attempted to assault her" (Rosenblum 2000, 526). This violent treatment extends to transsexual immigrants who are held in INS detention centers (Rose 2001, 527).[12] It is the recent research of Dean Spade and Kendall Thomas that sheds light on our larger society's role in creating such violent spaces. If we agree with their arguments that U.S. citizenship is rooted in gender—that those who violate the "gender contract" are viewed as placing themselves outside of society and its basic protections—then the police who enforce social contracts would also view such people as noncitizens, or perhaps even nonpersons (Spade 2006, 218; Thomas, 2006, 316).

While U.S. prisons are noted for their violence, transsexual inmates are hypervulnerable to such violence because of the manner in which our laws and, in relation, our penal system are gendered. Prisons and jails are organized according to the gender binary that dominates U.S. culture. Like the colonial dress codes of yesteryear, placement in such facilities is based on genitalia. Thus, even if a transsexual woman has been living as a woman since the age of twelve, has breasts, and is visibly feminine, she is placed in a male detention center (Rosenblum 2001, 523; National Center for Lesbian Rights 2006).[13]

HETEROTOPIAS

While prisons are reflective of the values and institutions of our larger society, they are also constitutive of them. It is critical that we acknowledge this relationship, because it is only in doing so that we will be able to develop effective strategies for addressing the violence of the U.S. penal system. It is Michel Foucault who first mapped the function of heterotopias in human societies. According to Foucault, in such places, "all the other real sites that can be found within the culture, are simultaneously represented, contested, and inverted." They are specific sites, oftentimes seen as forbidden, which transform the people who enter into them. Their function in relation to the larger society is that they reflect the larger society at the same time that they play a significant role in constructing it (Foucault 1986, 24; Sánchez 1995, 50). If we map the role of prisons in U.S. society, we can see how they both construct and are reflective of the dominant gender systems of our larger society. The treatment and status of transsexual women in such institutions are reflective of their status in the larger society, but also construct and are constructed by it. Finally, the experience of incarceration, for transsexual women, influences their status in a manner that contributes to their specific status as outsiders in the dominant culture, a status that is critical to maintaining a social system rooted in gender binaries.

Heterotopias are places set apart that only certain people can enter. In the United States transsexual women, especially working-class transsexual women, comprise a portion of those bodies forced into the prison system because of the larger gender systems that structure the dominant society. Dean Spade has mapped how most public services in the United States are constructed through gender binaries: public schools, public bathrooms, and homeless shelters all require placement within a male or female category in order for a person to access resources (2006, 227). Organizations such as Human Rights Watch note that many young transsexuals are pushed out of the public school system due to threats and harassment. Without their high school diplomas, such students are at a double disadvantage for finding work (2001, 60). As adults, when transsexual women apply for jobs, even if they have survived the school system, they negotiate the application process in a society where the rule of law seldom protects transgender and transsexual people from discrimination. Even in progressive cities such as San Francisco, nearly 50 percent of transgender residents report employment discrimination (National Center for Lesbian Rights and Transgender Law Center 2003).[14] As argued by Dean Spade, "Access to participation in the U.S. economy has always been conditioned on the ability of each individual to comply with norms of gendered behavior and expression" (221). As U.S. antipoverty programs in the late twentieth century became increasingly punitive, they also became increasingly hetero-and gender-normative, effectively cutting off many transgender women from critical survival resources (Spade 2006, 224).

The gendered society in which we live, in other words, sets up transsexual women for incarceration, especially working-class women, who need public services such as public education for survival. For those women who do become caught in a web of poverty, when they are arrested for credit card fraud, possession with intent, prostitution, or a number of other nonviolent offenses that poverty stricken women sometimes turn to for survival, they are then placed within a penal system organized by sex and sent to a corrections institution based on their genitals.

The prison system, then, is constructed, in part, through the bodies and punishment of people who violate the gender contracts under which we all live. At the same time, their status outside of the prison system is both reflective of this status and constitutive of it. It is a dialogical relationship where the two construct and fuel each other. Thus an average of one transgender person is murdered every month, because they are transgender. According to the Southern Poverty Law Center, most of these, based on the "extreme brutality" of the murders, would be classified as hate crimes. In one a study of transgendered people living in Washington D.C., 17 percent of those polled reported being assaulted with a weapon because of their gender identity (Moser 2007). As of December 2007, 62 percent of the U.S. population was not covered by any kind of transgender inclusive nondiscrimination law (National Gay and Lesbian Task Force 2007). Even in a city known for its gender rights, such as San Francisco, transsexual women report job discrimination and police harassment (National Center for Lesbian Rights and Transgender Law Center 2003).[15]

Equally alarming, to those concerned with human rights, is the function that the U.S. penal system serves in transforming inmates—including transsexual inmates—into legally marked and surplus people. While transsexual women are discriminated against by the dominant society before incarceration, after incarceration they are exconvicts. They are placed in a nationwide database known as the Criminal Offender Record Information system (CORI). Such records are never expunged and affect not only an individual's relationship to police but also their access to housing and employment in professions such as child and elder care. People arrested for prostitution who plea down to charges of "lewd and lascivious behavior" must register as sex offenders, further alienating them from civil and community resources (Magnani and Wray 2006, 83).[16]

So we return to our gendered society and our gendered rule of law. Gender is policed through our rule of law. Those who transgress gender are pushed out of public institutions such as bathrooms and schools and discriminated against in the workplace. When such economic violence results in incarceration, transgender women are placed in men's institutions where they are faced with sexual, emotional, and physical violence. Inmates who are released do not become full citizens; they retain their status as people who violate gender norms, and they are marked by the CORI system; they and their families become part of an exploitable labor force, available to work the least desirable jobs for minimal wages. In addition, if they were charged or pled to felony charges, they cannot receive many kinds of federal aid. The violence of the prison system, then, is not an aberration but instead flows from the violent policing of gender that is an intricate part of U.S. society. If we are ever to challenge the violence of our prison system, we will have to work for structural change.

BEYOND SOLITARY CONFINEMENT: A PROPOSAL FOR RESTORATIVE JUSTICE NOW

The move to reform prisons is as old as the prison system itself (Davis 2003, 45). Yet the primary means for protecting transsexual women within the U.S. penal system remains solitary confinement (Rosenblum 2000, 530). Developed as a prison reform in the early nineteenth century, isolation and solitary confinement were soon criticized as cruel. Today, organizations such as Human Rights Watch categorize isolation as torture. In the United States the practice has a long history. The shorter version goes like this: Quakers and other progressives fought to introduce isolation in the early U.S. penal system as a reform, to allow inmates to reflect on their crimes and reform themselves; soon visitors to the United States from Dickens to de Tocqueville were criticizing the system as abusive, noting that it led some inmates to insanity; in the late nineteenth century solitary confinement units were shut down; in the second half of the twentieth century, they were revived, with a vengeance, as a means of dealing with problem inmates; reports of mental breakdown, hallucinations, self-mutilation, and suicide attempts by inmates placed in isolation continue (Talvi 2007, 124; Davis 2003, 50; Magnani and Wray 2006, 23). Yet, in male correctional institutions, solitary confinement remains the dominant means for protecting transsexual women from violence on the part of other inmates. In the state of New York, the penitentiary has begun to house gay and transgender inmates in a separate housing unit. While this is a dramatic step above solitary confinement, it still fails to address the larger systematic problems that construct prisons as violent spaces, especially for transsexual and transgender people. Because prisons function as heterotopias, and thus dialogically relate to the larger society, an effective reform to the penal system will have to address the way in which the system relates to the larger society.

What follows is one vision of an alternative system, based on the work of Magnani and Wray and the American Friends Service Committee. Like other calls for restorative justice, it calls for a reevaluation of how we understand crime and concrete steps toward changing the larger system. At the heart of restorative justice is the belief that retributive justice produces harm. At the heart of restorative justice is also a holistic understanding of society, that we are all connected; thus "mutual accountability—the collective responsibility of [people] to care about and take care of one another" is key (Wachtel and McCold 2001, 114).

This is not science fiction. In addition to justice workers such as those found on the Friends Service Committee, a growing number of scholars have begun to map the manner in which the meaning of crime has changed over time (Gilmore, 2007, 5). So I have modified the model developed by Magnani and Wray to account for the role of gender binaries in constructing the violent system in which we live and to focus on the everyday steps that each of us can take as we work for change. Magnani and Wray identified twelve areas where we can work toward change. I present to you eight—that all of us, whether transgender, male, or female, mujerista, feminist, or humanist—can work toward.

1. Fight for laws that address harm rather than violation of social norms. In California, the three strikes law has placed nonviolent offenders in prison, for life, because the legislation that voters approved did not stipulate that the "three strikes" needed to be violent or harmful offenses (Magnani Wray 2006, 67; Vitiello 1997, 402). Likewise, because harm and freedom from harm to-date is not at the heart of our rule of law, officer Mitchell was able to claim qualified immunity after harassing and then attempting to rape an inmate. Using harm as a base for writing and approving our laws will both reduce the number of people sentenced to prison because they do not conform to dominant gender roles and help to protect all people, including incarcerated people, from harm. The 2006

decision of the Federal Bureau of Prisons to make sexual contact between guards and inmates a felony is a step in this direction, though we have yet to see how effective this will be given that inmates still fear retribution for reporting infractions (Talvi 2007, 56).

2. As long as the penal system exists, fight for community citizen review boards of all police and independent ombudsmen in all correctional institutions. Human Rights Watch has identified lack of oversight as one of the primary causes of police violence, yet in most towns, citizen review boards do not exist. In those where they do such boards do not have the power to discipline abusive behavior (1998, 34); the reality of ombudsmen in jails and prisons has yet to be realized. A lack of accountability on the part of police means that the abuse of and discrimination against transsexual women outside of prisons will continue, and the lack of ombudsmen means that sexual violence against all inmates continues to be a threat.

3. Volunteer. Volunteer as a visitor, literacy teacher, creative workshop organizer, wherever your skills lie (Magnani and Wray 2006, 178). While we work for all of these changes, we need volunteers in our correctional institutions to increase the oversight under which employees work and also to disrupt the function of the prison as a heterotopia set apart. We need people inside the system who are neither employees nor inmates—who can speak to both—who can relay information from the institution to the larger society on a regular basis.

4. Strengthen our social safety net with programming for the poor: universal health care, residential and out-treatment care for the mentally ill, education for incarcerated persons, accessible low-income housing, a living wage, the list goes on. Until we have tangible resources for low-income people to survive and improve their lot in life, poor and low-income people will continue to be pushed from the margins of society to the penal system (Magnani and Wray 2006, 176; Davis 2003, 106).

5. Educate ourselves about international law and strategize on ways it can be utilized to protect human rights (Magnani and Wray 2006, 182). In 1992 the United States signed the International Covenant of Civil and Political Rights (ICCPR). Article 10 of the agreement states that persons "deprived of their liberty should be treated with humanity and with respect for the inherent dignity of the human person." Yet the U.S. failed to comply with this agreement (Human Rights Watch 1998, 111). International law holds untapped possibilities for the protection of incarcerated persons.

6. Eliminate the death penalty. As long as anyone in our society can be labeled as surplus, or unworthy of life, people who violate social norms will be at risk for receiving such a label. Delecia Hammock, an inmate at the Tennessee Prison for Women in Nashville, said this most eloquently when she wrote, "[T]here are no disposable people. A society which practices that [will] eventually implode" (quoted in Talvi 2007, 1).

7. Move away from our retributive model of justice. If we ever want to be whole, as a society, we need to slow down and think about what makes a society healthy. When people violate rules necessary to the well-being of society, when they harm others, our focus should be on how to heal that harm. How do we reintegrate offenders into society? How do we heal people who have been harmed by violence? South Africa became noted for engaging such a system postapartheid. Several first people nations in Canada now insist on justice models that are restorative and rooted in their own histories and culture (Magnani and Wray 2006, 164). In a number of counties in the United States, misdemeanants are now tried in courts that focus on restorative justice—where those who break the law face sentences that heal the harm they have created and are provided with access to resources that will reintegrate them into society. Hartford Connecticut's Community Court is known for following this model (Johnstone 2001, 124).[17]

8. Dismantle the use of gender binaries throughout society. Small steps can be taken. In those places where we work we can change applications so that male and female are not the only gender boxes to check. We can study those municipalities that have passed nondiscrimination clauses and follow their examples. We can insist on gender-neutral toilets, especially in places of employment and in public schools. Increasingly, international airports (and some urban malls) have male, female, and family restrooms. If airports can do this, so can other sites.

At the heart of this proposal lies the firm belief that the well-being of our society is dependent upon radical prison reform—reform that reaches beyond prisons and into our larger society. Because our society stands in a dialogical relationship to its prisons, the current ills of our society will continue to be reproduced as long as prisons exist in their current form; likewise the hyper-violence suffered by transsexual women and other women within prisons will continue as long as the larger society treats some people as surplus and as long as violation of social customs, gendered social customs, can mark a person as surplus. The function of gender binaries in constructing our current society and penal system is as old as the system itself. Thomas/ine was brought into court long before the penitentiary system existed in the United States. Because these systems are so entrenched, it will take small steps, by all of us, to shift them; focusing on freedom from harm, placing healing and wholeness at the center of our legal system, and mapping and dismantling today's gender contract is one path toward creating this shift. If transsexual women are the canaries in the mine shaft, challenging gender systems in our strategies for justice is critical to the well-being of all of us.

NOTES

1. This chapter benefitted immensely from my discussions with Lori Saffin as she completed her larger project.

2. Both Talvi and DeCrow argue that working-class and poor women are exposed to and subjected to more violence than more economically advantaged women.

3. Baumler notes that, as the U.S. prison system moved west, "gender prejudice" was an integral part of the system.

4. Rafter notes that even reformatories were populated with working-class people. Working-class and poor men and women of color were sent to penitentiaries or leased out as laborers, working-class and poor white women were sent to reformatories, and middle-class white women advocated for reformatories to house and reform the working class.

5. In British colonial society, all children wore gowns. Gendered clothing played a significant role in constructing adult identities.

6. Ohio laws stipulated that people could wear the clothing of their choice as long as they were not attempting to pass as the other sex. Clearly then, this was a case of the law being used to police gender representation. Once Milburn constructed a metal plate reading, "Randolph Milburn. I am a man" to wear with his dresses, he was permitted to wear them without arrest (Hirschfield, 277).

7. Goldberg has documented that while 85 percent of the U.S. general population have high school diplomas, only 33 percent of state prison inmates do. Similarly, as of 2000, more than half of all prison and jail inmates had reported incomes of less than ten thousand dollars.

8. It is the Eight Amendment that banned "cruel and unusual punishment."

9. Here I am drawing from Mitchell's case where he challenged the charges against him. As discussed below, he did not claim innocence of any of the alleged behavior. Instead he requested qualified immunity based on technicalities.

10. The GMVA was passed as part of the Violence against Women Act of 1994. Much of the Violence against Women Act has since been dismantled by the courts (Rose 2001).

11. According to Schwenk, Mitchell threatened to have her moved from medium security into a high-security unit where sexual assault would likely result.

12. Rose cites the case of an immigrant woman who was raped at the Krome detention center in Florida. The victim, Christina Madrazo, was raped twice, once *after* she reported the crime.

13. The exception to this rule is New York, where there are now housing units for gay, transgender, and transsexual inmates.

14. The San Francisco Department of Health completed a similar survey in 1999 with similar findings.

15. For San Francisco, "more than 1 in 4 respondents [had] been harassed or abused by a police officer" (3).

16. Magnani and Wray point out that under the popular "Megan's Law," all sex offenders must register their names, place of employment, and address with local police and that this information is not confidential. Unfortunately, most databases do not distinguish predatory behavior from nonpredatory behavior.

17. Hartford's Community Court has been in existence since 1998; whether or not it can weather our current economic downturn and increased demonization of marginalized people remains to be seen.

REFERENCES

Baumler, Ellen. Summer 2008. "Justice [as an Afterthought]: Women and the Montana Prison System." *Montana Magazine of Western History*,: 41–59.

Braithwaite, John. 2003. "The Practice of Restorative Justice: Holism, Justice, and Atonement." *Utah Law Review*: 389–412. Lexis Nexis Database.

Davis, Angela. 2003. *Are Prisons Obsolete?* New York: Seven Stories.

DeCrow, Karen. 1975. *Sexist Justice: How Legal Sexism Affects You.* New York: Vintage. U.S. Department of Justice, Federal Bureau of Prisons. "Program Statement: Patient Care." U.S. Department of Justice, 2005. http://www.bop.gov/policy/progstat/6031_001.pdf.

Foucault, Michel. 1986. "Of Other Spaces." *Diacritics* 16 (1): 21–27.

Gilmore, Ruth Wilson. 2007. *Golden Gulag: Prisons, Surplus, Crisis, and Opposition in Globalizing California.* Berkeley: University of California Press.

Goldberg, David Theo. 2000. "Surplus Value: The Political Economy of Prisons and Policing." In *States of Confinement: Policing, Detention, and Prisons*, ed. Joy James, 205–21. New York: St. Martin's.

Human Rights Watch. 2001. Hatred in the Hallways: Violence and Discrimination against Lesbian, Gay, Bisexual, and Transgender Students in U.S. Schools. New York: Human Rights Watch.

———. 1998. Shielded from Justice: Police Brutality and Accountability in the United States. New York: Human Rights Watch.

Johnstone, Quintin. 2001. "The Hartford Community Court: An Experiment That Has Succeeded." *Connecticut Law Review* 34: 123–56.

Juang, Richard. 2006. "Transgendering the Politics of Recognition." In *Transgender Rights*, ed. Paisley Currah, Richard M. Juang, and Shannon Price Minter, 242–61. Minneapolis: University of Minnesota.

Little, Ann M. 2001. " 'Shoot That Rogue, for He Hath an Englishman's Coat On!': Cultural Cross-Dressing on the New England Frontier, 1620–1760." *The New England Quarterly* 72 (2):238–73.

Magnani, Laura, and Harmon Wray. 2006. *Beyond Prisons: A New Interfaith Paradigm for Our Failed Prison System.* Minneapolis: American Friends Service Committee.

Minter, Shannon, and Christopher Daley. 2003. *Trans Realities: A Legal Needs Assessment of San Francisco's Transgender Communities.* San Francisco: National Center for Lesbian and Transgender Law Center. http://www.transgenderlaw.org/resources/transrealities.pdf.

Moser, Bob. 2003. "Disposable People: A Wave of Violence Engulfs the Transgendered, Whose Murder Rate May Outpace That of All Other Hate Killings." *Southern Poverty Law Center Intelligence Report,* http://www.splcenter.org/intel/intelreport/article.jsp?=149&printable=1.

National Center for Lesbian Rights. 2006. *Rights of Transgender Persons.* http://www.nclrights.org.

National Gay and Lesbian Task Force. 2007. "Jurisdictions with Explicitly Transgender Inclusive Nondiscrimination Laws," www.thetaskforce.org.

Rafter, Nicole Hahn. 1985. *Partial Justice: Women in State Prisons, 1800–1935.* Boston: Northeastern University Press.

Rosenblum, Darren. 2000. " 'Trapped' in Sing Sing: Transgendered Prisoners Caught in the Gender Binarism." *Michigan Journal of Law and Gender* 6:499–571. Lexis Nexis Database.

Saffin, Lori. 2008. "Bodies That (Don't) Matter: Systems of Gender Regulation and Institutions of Violence against Transgender Persons: A Queer/Critical Race Feminist Critique." PhD diss., Washington State University.

Sánchez, Rosaura. 1995. *Telling Identities: The California Testimonios.* Minneapolis: University of Minnesota.

Spade, Dean. 2006. "Compliance Is Gendered: Struggling for Gender Self-Determination in a Hostile Economy." In *Transgender Rights,* ed. Paisley Currah, Richard M. Juang, and Shannon Price Minter, 217–41. Minneapolis: University of Minnesota.

Talvi, Silja J.A. 2007. *Women behind Bars: The Crisis of Women in the U.S. Prison System.* Emeryville: Seal.

Thomas, Kendall. 2006. "Are Transgender Rights Inhuman Rights?" In *Transgender Rights,* ed. Paisley Currah, Richard M. Juang, and Shannon Price Minter, 310–26. Minneapolis: University of Minnesota.

Truss, James Martin. 1995. "The Subjection of Women . . . Still: Unfulfilled Promises of Protection for Women Victims of Domestic Violence." *St. Mary's Law Journal* 26: 1149–1204. Lexis Nexis Database.

Valdes, Francisco. 1995. "Queers, Sissies, Dykes, and Tomboys: Deconstructing the Conflation of 'Sex,' 'Gender,' and 'Sexual Orientation' in Euro-American Law and Society." *California Law Review* 83 : 3–128. Lexis Nexis Database.

———. 2005. " 'We Are Now of the View': Backlash Activism, Cultural Cleansing, the Kultur Kampf to Resurrect the Old Deal." *Seton Hall Law Review* 35: 1407–63. Lexis Nexis Database.

Vaughan, Alden T. 1978. "The Sad Case of Thomas(ine) Hall." *Virginia Magazine of History and Biography.* 86 (2): 146–48.

Vitiello, Michael. "Three Strikes: Can We Return to Rationality?" *Journal of Criminal Law and Criminology* 77 (2): 395–481.

Wachtel, Ted, and Paul McCold. 2001. "Restorative Justice in Everyday Life." In *Restorative Justice and Civil Society*, ed. Heather Strang and John Braithwaite, 114–29. New York: Cambridge University Press.

CHAPTER THIRTEEN

Prison Rape

Johanna Hudnall

Just Detention International is the only organization in the United States that works exclusively to end sexual abuse behind bars. My contact with them began in the late 1990s after I had been raped by a staff member in a California State Prison. Just Detention International recognizes that sexual violence is a global problem, and it will be expanding its international program. Prisoner rape is a problem that affects large numbers of men, women, and youth.

In 1997, while incarcerated at the Central California Women's Facility in Chowchilla, I was raped by a staff member of the California Department of Corrections and Rehabilitation. I was placed in a cage for approximately eight hours while inmates and staff continuously badgered and threatened me. Eventually, I was escorted to an interview room and questioned while being smirked at and mocked by the investigating sergeant who was initiating the questioning. He continuously tried to coerce me into saying that another inmate had assaulted me. After several hours, I was placed into segregation. While in segregation, I came across a legal service, Legal Services for Prisoners with Children (LSPC), and I contacted it for assistance. One of the attorneys, Cassie Pierson, employed with LSPC received my letter and then sent me information regarding Just Detention International, which at that time was called "Stop Prisoner Rape." I truly feel its members saved my life. My mental health was in jeopardy, and I had absolutely no assistance from the facility. Although I was in need of medical care, all the prison officials were concerned about was a pregnancy test. In 2003, I began serving on the board of advisors for Just Detention International, and today I remain devoted to this nonprofit advocacy organization, an organization committed to ending the widespread problem of sexual violence behind bars.

Prisoner rape is a violation of the international human rights law that meets the definition of torture: the intentional infliction of severe physical or mental pain or suffering for an illicit purpose and committed, consented, or acquiesced to by public officials. The rape of persons in detention has been classified as torture by several international bodies. The United States has ratified treaties that prohibit torture, slavery, and cruel, inhumane, or degrading treatment or punishment. The U.S. Supreme Court has held that prisoner rape is a violation of the prohibition of cruel and unusual punishment in the Eighth Amendment to the U.S. Constitution. All fifty states and the District of Columbia criminalize rape and sexual assault, and all but two states have statutes addressing the sexual abuse of inmates by prison staff.

A study in four Midwestern states found that approximately one in five male inmates reported a pressured or forced sex incident while incarcerated. About one in ten male inmates reported that they had been raped. Rates for women, who are most likely to be abused by male staff members, vary greatly among institutions. In one facility, 27 percent of women reported a pressured or forced sex incident, while in another facility, 7 percent of women reported sexual abuse. Youth in detention are also extremely vulnerable to abuse. Research shows that juveniles incarcerated with adults are five times more likely to report being victims of sexual assault than youth in juvenile facilities, and the suicide rate of juveniles in adult facilities is 7.7 times higher than that of those in juvenile detention centers. The United States also holds more than two hundred thousand people per year in immigration detention. Of those detained every year, five thousand are unaccompanied children. These individuals, many of whom have not been charged with a crime, are vulnerable to sexual abuse from detention officers and fellow detainees.

Prisoner rape affects everyone. It costs taxpayers dearly in the forms of higher rates of recidivism and reincarceration, increased violence, higher rates of substance abuse, lawsuits brought by victims, mental health services, and medical care, including HIV and other sexually transmitted infections. During my rape, I contracted hepatitis C. The facility where I am currently housed refuses to treat the disease. As I remain incarcerated, I have to wonder if anyone outside of the victims, Just Detention International, and those involved with this organization realizes that prisoner rape shatters the lives of thousands of people every year. It's a perversion of justice and an affront to our society's values.

The daily trauma of being behind bars makes the stress of the rape even more difficult. I'm living in a constant reminder of how and where I suffered.

Although I have been transferred to another state, that, too, comes with its own set of difficulties. Prior to this incident I was in the process of mending a fragile relationship with my family due to the circumstances of my being incarcerated, but because of threats against my family by the man who raped me, I felt forced to silently sever those ties out of fear for their safety. Now, some fourteen years later, I have started to reach out to a family who had all but given up on me. I cannot imagine the reach and impact this situation has had on them. It isn't easy to seek first to understand and then to be understood.

When I reflect—and I often do—I think about the guilt I carry. Not only does it encompass my family and my friends from long ago but also the women I left behind who suffered along with me in the Security Housing Unit (SHU) in Chowchilla, California. Although it is unclear to me why some of them were there, I'll never forget all that we shared, silence and screams, and I never doubted that they, too, suffered just like me—all alone. We all had an unforgivable thing in common; we were left troubled from violence brought by the hand of another.

Survivors of rape experience the assault and healing process in a very personal way. Rape is a highly personal crime in which you are treated like you do not matter. It's deeply dehumanizing. Being raped while incarcerated takes away your right to explore your options and does not allow you to reject any that do not feel right or safe.

By far, I feel the most damaging long-term effects come from the secrets that I must keep pertaining to those months that I spent housed in SHU in a live-alone, walk-alone circumstance. It made me vulnerable prey for the many staff who came to work with hunters' souls. I have not yet been in safe enough circumstances to express the terror I experienced during that time, as I am still incarcerated. However, I feel certain that my day will come when I can finally be relieved of such a heavy burden.

We are mothers, fathers, daughters, sons, sisters, and brothers who have family and/or loved ones who await our safe return. Please be a part of helping to end sexual violence behind bars.

CHAPTER FOURTEEN

From Women Prisoners to People in Women's Prisons: Challenging the Gender Binary in Antiprison Work

Julia Sudbury

In October 2007, more than 250 Lesbian Gay Bisexual Transgender Intersex Queer and Questioning LGBTIQQ former prisoners, activists, attorneys, and community members came together at City College in San Francisco to generate a national conversation on transgender imprisonment. The conference, Transforming Justice, highlighted the experiences of transgender former prisoners through personal testimonies, written narratives, and photo-diaries. As the transgender former prisoners' lives unfolded on the screen and through personal testimonies, it became clear that the conference was raising important questions for scholars and activists committed to defending the rights of incarcerated women and to ending women's imprisonment.

In this chapter, I first explore some limitations in existing research and activism on "women in prison." I argue that most of this work—and I include my own body of scholarship here—has been complicit with the repression of the gender fluidity and complexity that exist in both men's and women's prisons, jails, and juvenile halls. By examining the experiences of transgender and gender nonconforming prisoners, I demonstrate the violence involved in the production and maintenance of the gender binary in penal regimes. Finally, I aim to develop a new theoretical framework for research and activism on "women in prison," which makes visible and counters the state's power to define and police gender categories. This *antiracist genderqueer framework* necessarily pays attention to the complex intersections among race, class, gender identity, and sexual orientation that structure the experiences of people in conflict with the law. This approach poses significant challenges to the "business as usual" of feminist research and antiprison activism. I invite readers to consider how their own praxis might need to change in order to engage with the challenges posed by transgender and gender nonconforming prisoners and activists.

My research methodology draws from the insights of feminist action research and participatory action research. This essay is grounded in ten years of activist ethnography in the antiprison movement in the U.S. and Canada.[1] In addition, I have quoted from the testimonies by transgender former prisoners gathered for the Transforming Justice conference. Finally, I interviewed four black transgender antiprison activists. These activists had worked as volunteers and paid staff with the following organizations: Prisoners HIV/AIDS Support Action Network, the Prisoners' Justice Action Committee and the Prisoners' Justice Day Committee in Canada; Critical Resistance, California Coalition for Women Prisoners, Audre Lorde Project, Prison Moratorium Project, the Trans/Gender Variant in Prison Committee of California Prison Focus, Legal Services for Prisoners with Children, and All of Us or None in the U.S. By incorporating extracts from testimonies and qualitative interviews, I intend to ground my analysis in the subordinated knowledge produced by marginalized and resisting communities. As Patricia Hill Collins observes, this subordinated knowledge has the potential to reveal new insights that are not available to those who occupy a position of privilege in relation to interlocking systems of oppression (Collins 1990). Those of us—myself included—who conform to societal expectations for gender coherence (between the name, genitalia, self-identity and external presentation for example) may be blind to the violence of gender dualism, even if we ourselves have experienced sexism and homophobia. In order to produce scholarly knowledge that moves beyond the binary gender system, it is essential to start from the lived experience and everyday theorizing of those whose existence it disallows.

RESEARCH ON "WOMEN IN PRISON": TWO ASSUMPTIONS

Gender Diversity in Women's Prisons

In this section, I unpack two assumptions that underpin most research (and much activism) on "women in prison." These assumptions form the basis of this work's complicity with the gender binary system. The first is that *all people incarcerated in women's prisons and jails are women.* In the past few years, organizations such as the California Coalition for Women Prisoners (CCWP), Critical Resistance and Justice Now, a nonprofit that provides legal advocacy for people in women's prisons, have shifted the language they use to describe their constituencies. For example, while Justice Now's mission statement refers to ending "violence against women and stop[ping] their imprisonment," materials produced by the organization more recently demonstrate a shift in thinking. In an invitation to a strategy session on gender and prison expansion, "violence against women" was rewritten to read "harm against female-bodied and women-identified people" (Justice Now 2008). This shift represents a deliberate process of moving from a "women only"-oriented feminist analysis to a broader "gender justice" platform that recognizes a range of experiences of gender oppression. Similarly, these organizations have adopted new language to describe those held in women's prisons. For example,

CCWP, which was founded in 1995, now uniformly uses the language "people in women's prisons" rather than "women prisoners," used when it was established.

The new language adopted by these organizations is the outcome of struggle and advocacy by transgender and gender nonconforming activists over the past decade. But the shift is far more than a merely linguistic one. By insisting on using "people in women's prisons," these activists challenge an assumption that has been central to the development of feminist prison studies, feminist criminology, and "women in prison" activism during the past three decades. Previous work by scholars and activists alike assumed that all those labeled by the state as "women" (or female inmates) and thus housed in women's prisons and jails were indeed women. In the context of the women's liberation movement which shaped the formative years of this work, making "women's imprisonment" visible was a radical move that challenged the androcentrism of both criminological research and antiprison activism.

Yet, there were two problems with this approach. First, it ignored the reality of gender fluidity and complexity that actually existed within women's prisons. Second, it legitimated and bolstered the state's power to determine and police the gender identification of those it imprisons, thus stripping transgender and gender nonconforming people in women's prisons of their fundamental right to gender self-determination.

It is interesting to note that researchers have long been aware of and grappled with the diversity of gender identity and sexual orientation that they encountered on entering women's prisons (Hensley and Tewksbury 2002). Some of the earliest and best-known research in this area included extensive attempts to document and understand same-sex relationships inside (Ward and Kassebaum 1965; Giallombardo 1966). From the 1930s onward, researchers met and interviewed prisoners who were in committed relationships inside and referred to their partners as "my man," "my woman," or "my husband" (Selling 1931). Viewed through the lens of heteronormativity and an unquestioned adherence to ascribed gender categories, early researchers viewed these relationships as "pseudofamilies" and argued that they were adaptations to life within an unnatural "society of women." Transgender and gender nonconforming prisoners were seen as mimicking the husband in a heterosexual marriage because they were deprived of male contact. These studies were deeply compromised by their classist, heterosexist, and racist bias (Otis 1913).[2] However, they are evidence that from its inception, research on women's prisons has been confronted with the question of how to theorize the presence of prisoners who do not conform to gender norms. Despite the empirical evidence of gender diversity, researchers have failed to ask gender nonconforming prisoners how they self-identify and have continued to assume a uniformity of gender identity within women's prisons to the present day.

In the past decade, groundbreaking scholars in the field of queer and transgender studies have transformed the way we think about gender. First, they have shown the commonsense notion that there are only two genders to be the outcome of a violent and coercive process of gender policing. That is, the gender binary is not a *given* but a social construction deeply steeped in patriarchal, heteronormative, and racist violence. Second, these scholars have documented the multiplicity of gender identities and the richness of the cultural forms that they have engendered. The work of Judith Halberstam and Bobby Noble in particular has documented a continuum of female and transgendered masculinity encompassing a range of gender identities, from Ags (Aggressives), Studs, and butches to transmen, bois, and FtMs (Halberstam 1998; Noble 1998). While most of this work has focused on cultural production, particularly literature and performance arts, as the cutting edge of gender expression and resistance, the same diversity of gender expression can be documented inside women's prisons. Indeed, despite their invisibility, gender nonconforming people in prisons and jails are on the frontline of the battle for gender self-determination in the face of state power and coercion. Rejecting state-imposed gender categorization and acknowledging the gender self-identification of all those in prisons, jails, and juvenile detention is the first step in supporting this struggle.

Women Prisoners in Men's Prisons

The second erroneous assumption underpinning much prison research and activism is that *all women prisoners are in women's prisons*. To early feminist criminologists committed to making visible and ending the unequal treatment of women prisoners, it seemed obvious that their research site would be the women's prison. Yet this apparently self-evident correlation relies upon the erasure of people in men's prison who identify and live as "women" (or "girls") but were categorized at birth as male.

   Feminists have had negative and sometimes heated reactions to the suggestion that feminist spaces—and by extension feminist research agendas—should incorporate transwomen. The case of Kimberly Nixon, a transsexual woman who sued Vancouver Rape Relief and Women's Shelter (VRR) when she was denied access to its volunteer program, is exemplary of the polarized and sometimes hostile debate around calls for "trans inclusion" (Chambers 2007). Many feminists were outraged that Nixon inflicted an expensive and protracted court case on a small nonprofit providing support to survivors of rape and domestic violence. In contrast, lawyer and trans advocate Barbara Findlay named Nixon the "Rosa Parks of transwomen," suggesting that the case was only the beginning of a movement for full access to women's spaces by transwomen (Rupp 2007).

   The reaction to Nixon should be viewed in the context of the history of the shelter movement and more broadly the women's liberation movement. Feminists can look back three decades to an era when feminist bookstores, women's shelters, and women's studies programs were won only by dedicated struggle. The call for trans inclusion comes at a time when women-only spaces are threatened by neoliberal cutbacks to social welfare, as well as the "postfeminist" generation's lack of commitment to these spaces, leading to closures and mergers of women's bookstores, women's colleges, and women's centers. As women-only spaces disappear, some feminists view demands for inclusion by trans activists as colluding with a wider backlash against feminist autonomous organizing. As such, they often revert to the defensive stance that was necessary in the 1970s when such spaces were under attack by antifeminist men who saw women-only policies as unnecessary and exclusionary. While it is important to contextualize the feminist reaction against trans inclusion, and to honor the difficult choices made by volunteers and community organizers working on the frontline of the feminist movement, we also need to be vigilant about the convergence of arguments in defense of women's spaces and the transphobic defense of "womanhood" against nonnormative femininities.

Feminists who seek to oppose trans inclusion make three main arguments. First, they argue that "born" women have common experiences of surviving sex discrimination and patriarchal violence that are not shared by transwomen, leading to a need for separate and different programs and organizations. Second, and relatedly, they argue that although transwomen may experience gender discrimination, they are relative newcomers to that experience, having been raised with male privilege. In the Nixon case, for example, the Rape Relief collective argued that Nixon could not be an effective helpline volunteer because she "did not share the same life experiences as women born and raised as girls and into womenhood" having been "brought up through a boyhood and lived as a man achieving success as an airline pilot." This argument ultimately prevailed in the Supreme Court, which in 2003 ruled that VRR did not discriminate and that the organization did indeed have the right to organize "as women only" (Vancouver Rape Relief Society Website). Third, they argue that the presence of "male-bodied" persons in organizations serving vulnerable women may retraumatize women seeking support.

At the Michigan Women's Festival, this argument was actually embraced by transsexual feminists who pushed the landmark women's music and arts festival to relinquish their "Womyn-born-womyn" only admission policy in favor of one that would allow postoperative transsexuals but deny preop and other transwomen. The distinction was important, they claimed because "male genitals can be so emblematic of male power and sexual dominance that their presence at the festival . . . is inappropriate." By privileging transsexuals who had the resources for surgery, the proposed policy discriminated against low-income transsexuals and transsexuals of color, as well as those who prefer to inhabit a more interstitial gender identity (Koyama 2008).

Whether for or against trans inclusion, those involved in the debate have seldom engaged with the lived experiences of the transgender people who are most likely to encounter state and interpersonal gender violence: low-income transpeople of color (Koyama 2008; Incite! 2008).[3] These experiences make visible the assumptions and misconceptions present in the three arguments outlined above. Testimonies by imprisoned transgender activists at the Transforming Justice Conference demonstrate that transwomen, like "born" women, are subjected to extreme forms of domestic and sexual violence.[4] However, the former's lack of recognition as "women" exacerbates experiences of violence by placing means of redress and support out of reach. The pathway to prison of Yolanda Gonzalez, a prisoner at the California Medical Facility in Vacaville, was similar to that of many women serving life sentences for defending themselves: "I was convicted of second degree murder for killing my abusive boyfriend in self-defense." However, her treatment by the criminal justice system was even more punitive: "Although I fit the profile of a 'battered wife' and had been living as a woman for several years, I was not allowed to use this defense because the court system viewed me as male" (Transforming Justice 2007).

Once in prison, the women survived horrifying incidences of rape, violence, and coercion. Nikkas Alamillo-Luchese shared one such experience. Coerced into a sexual relationship with a violent cellmate, she was attacked by him one day: "I woke up bleeding anally . . . It became obvious to me that R. and one of his friends had raped me and stolen my belongings while I was unconscious. The door had been locked, but R. had staff open it to get to me; it was a privilege as a 'pet' of the wing" (Transforming Justice 2007). Nikkas' testimony reminds us that having male genitalia is no determinant of whether one becomes a victim or a perpetrator of sexual violence. After reporting the abuse to a guard who refused to believe her, Nikkas continued to be subjected to sexual assault and physical violence and intimidation. These experiences of gender violence do not necessarily follow an earlier life lived with male privilege, as Kimberly McBride, also at CMF shares: "Since the age of 6 I felt different and knew I was a little girl." Similarly Yolanda Gonzalez states: "I have always been Transgender and considered myself a woman from my earliest childhood" (Transforming Justice 2007).

These testimonies reveal that transwomen, especially transwomen of color, experience gender violence and domination in ways that are similar but not identical to born-women. However, they do so without any of the protections that may be associated with gender incoherence. In the context of sex-segregated prisons, this lack of protection means that a prison term may be a sentence to repeated sexual assault and verbal abuse. This suggests that feminist researchers, who have long been dedicated to challenging the unequal treatment and abuse of women in prison, should have a particular incentive to expend their research beyond the born-women-only model. In order to do so, however, we would need to jettison two implicit foundations of feminist criminal justice research. First, that all humans can be divided into two genders, neatly demarcated by differences in genitalia and proven by what is on our birth certificates or government ID. Second, that only women who are assigned to the female gender at birth experience sexual violence and gender oppression. In so doing, we would make visible the complicity between feminist research and the *gender enforcement* activities of the state. The next section examines how the criminal justice system creates and polices the gender binary out of the messy and complex reality of gender fluidity.

POLICING THE BINARY

When scholars enter the prison to carry out research, we enter a site that is overdetermined by the race- and gender-enforcing activities of the state. Yet those activities are most often overlooked, rendered invisible by hegemonic racial and gender ideologies that naturalize what we are presented with: an apparently sex-segregated population of predominantly people of color. Feminists of color have pointed to the socially constructed and performative nature of racialized gender identities. Rather than "being" a Chicana, they argue, we "perform Chicana" through an ongoing series of choices, identifications, and behaviors (Segura 1992). These choices and identifications may be loosely aligned with the gender and racial assignations of our families, communities, and the state, or they may be in direct conflict with them. The criminal justice system is intolerant of such unruly self-determination. Presented with a "motley crew" of racially and culturally syncretic, diversely gendered defendants—Ags and FtMs, top femmes and soft butches, bois and Andros, MtFs, trannies, and genderQueers—the state sets about allocating this transgressive polymorphism into predefined categories (Sharma and Wright 2009).[5] Ags, butches, bois, and FtMs become "female offenders" and are housed in "women's correctional facilities." MtFs and trans-sexuals become "male offenders" and are sent to "men's" facilities. Mexicanas of Miztec ancestry become white/ Hispanic. Black Puerto Rican Tainos become African American. As feminist researchers, we often replicate the violence of this misidentification by adopting the official categorization and ignoring the testimonies of those who challenge the state's power to define and police their racial and gender identification.

Policing the gender binary begins at home where children are pressured to engage in culturally appropriate gendered behavior and play and to wear gender appropriate clothing. For many gender nonconforming young people, the teenage years are when conflicts with parental and school authorities over gender identification become most fraught, as behaviors that were seen as a childhood phase continue into adolescence (Mallon and DeCrescenzo 1985; Human Rights Watch 2001). Conflict in the home over gender identification or sexual orientation often precipitates greater involvement in street life, and in some cases homelessness (Cochran et al. 2002).[6] This in turn leads to involve-ment in criminalized survival strategies, from sex work to petty theft, as well as drug and alcohol use as coping strategies (Cochran et al. 2002). Transgender and gender-variant young people who leave home because of transphobic violence or verbal abuse are also criminalized through "status offenses," which prohibit running away, truancy, alcohol consumption, or "incorrigibility" (disobeying parents). The construction of these behaviors as offenses puts young people who have been abused or abandoned by parental figures in conflict with the law, often beginning a cycle of policing, appearances in the courts, and institutionalization (Steinhardt 1996). The criminalization of gender nonconforming young people, as with all young people, is racialized. Young people of color are more likely to be stopped by the police and to be sent to criminal court and spend more time in detention (Feld 1999; Office of Juvenile Justice 2002). Thus gender variance in adolescence is most likely to lead to criminalization and institutionalization for young people of color.

While transgender young people face the challenge of age-related poverty, transgender and gender nonconforming adults continue to face poverty due to labor discrimination (San Francisco Bay Guardian 2006).[7] Pushed out of the labor market, many transwomen work in the sex industry as a means of survival and also in order to experience the community and support of other transwomen. Transwomen and men also face insecure housing or homelessness as a result of unstable or underemployment and discrimination by landlords (*San Francisco Bay Guardian* 2006). The intersection of racial and transgender discrimination in the labor and housing markets creates a highly vulnerable positionality, which is exacerbated by the role of law enforcement.

The dangers of gender variance are most visible in police mistreatment of transgender people of color. An investigation of police abuse and misconduct against LGBT people by Amnesty International documented widespread identity-based abuse related to sexual orientation, gender identity, race, age, and economic status. The report concluded: "Law enforcement officers profile LGBT individuals, in particular gender variant individuals and LGBT individuals of color, as criminal in a number of different contexts, and selectively enforce laws relating to 'morals regulations,' bars and social gatherings, demonstrations and 'quality of life' " (Amnesty International 2005; Incite! 2008). This criminalization of nonnormative gender identity, in a context of intersecting systems of oppression, leads to extremely high rates of incarceration for transpeople of color. While national statistics are not available, a survey of 515 transgender people in San Francisco found that 64 percent of the MtF respondents and 29 percent of FtM respondents had been incarcerated (SF Department of Public Health 1999; Minter and Daley 2003).[8] The cumulative effects of parental and school intolerance and abuse, housing and labor discrimination, criminalization and law enforcement-targeting produce the *racialized (trans)gender entrapment* of transgender and gender nonconforming people of color (Richie 1995).[9] This process channels transgender and gender nonconforming youth and adults into juvenile halls, jails, and prisons where gender policing is experienced at a heightened level.

Gender Enforcement behind the Walls

Those of us who fit relatively comfortably within the normative limits of the binary gender system often fail to understand the coercive force that is necessary for its continuation. Feminists have long noted that, far from a biologically given identity determined at birth, *gender*, like *race*, is a "very demanding verb" (Trent 1997; Butler 1990). Criminologists have demonstrated the ways in which prison regimes are gendered, often seeking to induce particularly gendered behaviors as a means of reforming "unruly women" (Dobash et al. 1986; Howe 1994; Faith 1993). Yet this insight has infrequently led to interrogations of role of the prison in (re)producing the binary gender system itself. The neat division of prison populations into two genders is achieved at the expense of transgender and gender nonconforming prisoners who are policed and punished because of the threat they pose to the gendered order of the penal system.

The violence of gender policing is psychological, emotional, physical, and sexual. Transgender and gender nonconforming people are assigned to a juvenile hall, prison, or jail based on their "legal" gender identity as given on their birth certificate. As such, their self-definitions and lived experiences of gender are ignored in favor of a classification based on their genitalia. In an interview, antiprison activist Bakari called attention to the mismatch between the penal system and the lived experience of living outside the binary: "You have male and female prisons. I ain't male or female, so which one do I get to go to? And you're housed according to your genitalia, which to me does not connote gender."

On entering California Institute for Women, Bakari was forced to give up street attire of boxers, baggy jeans, and a long shirt and to put on "feminine" clothing. Bakari saw this as an attempt by prison authorities to assert their power by policing gender expression: "How they control you and mandate you to this gender binary is if you're in a women's facility you must wear whatever society says is for women . . . At CIW when I first got there, I had on boxers; they took them, said they were contraband . . . Then they make you wear panties and a mumu, an old lady housedress." Some guards use the misalignment between a transgender prisoner's self-identity and appearance and his or her government classification as a basis for psychological abuse, for example by calling transwomen "he" or "Sir." Another interviewee, Nathaniel, explained the psychological impact of this type of discrimination:

> [F]or trans people, depression and suicide, you can have really high risk factors for that when you're consistently being denied for who you are. When people take away your opportunity to have self-determination which happens in many ways in prison, but can be so detrimental when you're a trans woman and you're put in a men's prison, and you're denied your hormones and you're denied being called the name that you chose and you're being called "he" all the time.

Assignation by genitalia rather than self-identity is particularly devastating for transsexual prisoners. Since many transsexuals do not chose or cannot afford gender reassignment surgery, prisoners who may have had hormone treatment and "top surgery" (to remove breasts) will be assigned to an institution according to a gender assignation based on one part of their body, which does not match the rest of their physical and emotional experience. This means that a prisoner who lives and works as a woman, and is known by friends and family as a woman, will be placed in a men's prison. Yolanda Gonzalez shared this experience:

> Being a Transgender woman with fully-developed breasts upon enter-
> ing prison, proved to be a nightmare for me. While I was still in the
> orientation, I had a Facility Captain . . . tell me that I was not going
> to be allowed onto the general population mainline due to my having
> breasts. And that due to feminine appearance, I would be in extreme
> danger of sexual attack, and/or being raped by other prisoners. Just
> my presence in the general population would jeopardize the safety and
> security of the prison. (Transforming Justice 2007)

Studies of rape in men's prisons indicate that the creation of an environment of
hypermasculine control and dominance contributes to the high rates of sexual
assault against feminine, young, and new prisoners (Sabo, Kupers, and London
2001). Rape and sexual exploitation are sometimes encouraged by guards, who
provide access and impunity as a means of controlling social hierarchies and
maintaining order (Lee 2008).

   In addition to the initial victimization of physical or sexual assault, transgender
prisoners experience secondary victimization when they report abuses that are
ignored or disbelieved. When Nikkas reported multiple violent sexual assaults:
"The officer went and told R. that I had reported him. R. assaulted and raped
me the next day . . . I didn't report the incidents again because a correctional staff
member told me that if I filed a formal report, I would be send to Administrative
Segregation (the "hole") automatically and there would have to be an investigation
for making 'false allegations.' " (Transforming Justice 2007) In the context of a
penal system that is based on a rigid and definitive gender division, transgender
prisoners are most frequently viewed as a threat to the "security" and "order" of
the prison. Their victimization or potential victimization is therefore seen as an
indication of disorder rooted in the presence of the transgender person, rather
than a human rights violation rooted in the violence of the gender binary system
and devaluing of those who do not conform to it. Having identified transgender
prisoners as a problem to the smooth functioning of the prison, administrators
see removal of the prisoner from general population as the solution. As a result,
transgender prisoners are often placed in "protective" housing. This may be a
cell block or pod reserved for those considered vulnerable to abuse, or it may be
administrative segregation (National Center for Lesbian Rights). Also known as
the "hole," administrative segregation is where prisoners viewed as disruptive or
violent are sent for punishment and "correction." Transgender prisoners locked
in administrative segregation are denied many of the privileges available to other
prisoners, including access to work, recreation, education, and association with
others. Segregation is therefore experienced by transgender prisoners as another
form of punishment for gender nonconformity.

TOWARD AN ANTIRACIST, GENDERQUEER ANTIPRISON AGENDA

What would it take to develop an agenda for feminist research that is in soli-
darity with transgender and gender nonconforming people in both men's and

women's prisons? This final section seeks to develop a new theoretical framework for feminist antiprison activist research that makes visible and counters the state's power to define and police gender categories. I outline five principles that might be applied to a wide range of research projects. First, while feminist researchers, in particular women of color, have demonstrated the importance of applying an intersectional lens to research on prisons, actively engaging the complex articulations of race, class, gender, and sexuality (Richie 1995; Díaz-Cotto 2006; Sudbury 2006; Ross 1998), we need to expand our understanding of intersectionality to include the impact of gender identity (Demmons 2007). This does not simply mean adding gender identity to the "shopping list" of oppressions. Rather, it means a rigorous theoretical interrogation of the ways that gender policing and the punishment of gender nonconformity structure racialized and class-based experiences of imprisonment.

Second, our research practice needs to recognize the gender complexity and fluidity of human beings warehoused in prisons. Rather than adopting an unquestioning stance toward state-generated gender categorizations, we should adopt a gender self-determination model. This would require us to question how people in prison self-identify, rather than assuming that we can read the person's gender from the prison in which he or she is incarcerated. This also means recognizing the ways in which gender expression and identity are racially and culturally specific. Researchers would therefore need to familiarize ourselves with common gender terminology and identities adopted within different racialized communities.

Third, and relatedly, we need to acknowledge the existence of female masculinity and gender nonconformity in women's prisons. Shifting our language from "women in prison" to "people in women's prisons" is a starting point, but it is certainly not enough. Future research could examine and challenge the psychological and physical abuse of gender nonconforming prisoners in women's prisons, including prison policies that mandate inappropriate clothing or further criminalize prisoners seen as "masculine" or "aggressive." Or it might explore the role of transgender and gender nonconforming people in and released from women's prisons in building a movement to abolish prisons. Our work can also rectify the history of research by women that exoticizes and stigmatizes nonnormative gender and sexual identities in women's prisons.

Fourth, we need to adopt a more expansive conceptualization of womanhood. If, as demonstrated in the testimonies in this chapter, femininity does not depend on genitalia at birth or in the present moment, then our solidarities with women prisoners would need to reach beyond the women's prison. By including the experiences of transwomen in our analyses of women in prison, we expand our understanding of the role of the criminal justice system in policing gender roles for all women. The lives of transwomen make the social construction of gender visible and force us to examine the ways in which gender is policed by the state. As such, their lives can serve as an entryway for feminist interrogations of gendered state violence. Our research can also serve to promote alliances and heal the wounds between feminist and transgender movements, by demonstrating that imprisoned trans- and born women share an interest in and commitments to gender justice and antiviolence work.

Finally, our research agenda should be informed by the subordinated knowledges of transgender and gender nonconforming communities and antiprison activists. This means learning from and working with antiprison organizations that have shifted toward a transgender solidarity model, as well as transgender and LGBT organizations that are taking up questions of transgender criminalization and human rights abuses in prison. By rooting future research in the priorities that emerge from antiprison and transgender activism, we make amends for the history of complicity between feminist research and violent gender policing by the state. We also create more nuanced and complex work that addresses the concerns of those working for change at the grassroots. I call this approach an "antiracist genderqueer antiprison framework" to signal a feminist praxis that actively challenges the state's power to define and police gender while simultaneously challenging the racialized build-up of the prison-industrial complex. As we explore ways to apply this framework to our research and activism, we can draw on the wisdom and experience of transgender and gender nonconforming activists and prisoners of color. Their refusal to be silenced is the starting point for what may become a paradigm shift in feminist antiprison work.

NOTES

1. I was a founding member of Critical Resistance, a national organization dedicated to dismantling the prison-industrial complex, and have worked with and alongside Incite! Women of Color against Violence, the Prison Activist Resource Center, Justice Now, Legal Services for Prisoners with Children, National Network for Women in Prison, California Coalition for Women Prisoners, Arizona Prison Moratorium Coalition, the Prisoner Justice Day Committee, and the Prisoner Justice Action Committee, Toronto. For an in-depth discussion of antiprison scholar-activist methodology, see Julia Sudbury, "Challenging Penal Dependency: Activist Scholarship and the Antiprison Movement."

2. For example, the earliest documented research on same-sex relationships behind bars focused on the "unnatural relationship" between black and white young women in reform schools and was clearly driven by a segregationist agenda.

3. An important exception is the work of Incite! Women of Color against Violence, who have thoughtfully engaged with questions of trans inclusion though dialogues with trans activists of color. Incite!'s national project on law enforcement violence makes visible gendered state violence against women of color and transgender people of color.

4. See also Lee 2004.

5. I borrow the term "motley crew" from Nandita Sharma and Cynthia Wright, who use it to invoke transgressively border-crossing alliances among revolutionary subjects.

6. A study of 375 homeless adolescents found that LGBT youth were more likely to leave home than their heterosexual counterparts, due to physical abuse, alcohol use in the home, and conflicts over sexual orientation.

7. For example, a survey of 194 transgender people living or working in San Francisco found that nearly 60 percent were living in poverty, 40 percent did not have

a bank account, only 25 percent were working full time, and 9 percent had no source of income. While discrimination in housing and employment against transgender people is outlawed in thirteen states and the District of Columbia, low-income and marginalized-housed transgender people have little access to such legal protections. Despite passage of the California Gender Non-Discrimination Act 0f 2003, 57 percent of those surveyed reported experiencing employment discrimination, and only just over 12 percent had filed a complaint.

8. Of transgender people surveyed, 10 percent self-identified as homeless, and another 31 percent were living in unstable situations. Nearly 27 percent reported experiencing housing discrimination.

9. I am refining a concept coined by Beth Richie.

REFERENCES

Amnesty International USA. 2005. *Stonewalled: Police Abuse and Misconduct Against Lesbian, Gay and Transgender People in the U.S.* Amnesty International USA, 4. http://www.amnesty.org/en/library/asset/AMR51/122/2005/en/dom AMR511222005en.pdf (accessed October 30, 2008).

Butler, Judith. 1990. *Gender Trouble: Feminism and the Subversion of Identity.* New York: Routledge.

Chambers, Lori. 2007. "Unprincipled Exlusions: Feminist Theory, Transgender Jurisprudence and Kimberly Nixon," *Canadian Journal of Women and the Law* 19 (2): 305–34.

Cochran, Bryan N., et al. 2002. "Challenges Faced by Homeless Sexual Minorities: Comparison of Gay, Lesbian, Bisexual and Transgender Homeless Adolescents with Their Heterosexual Counterparts." *American Journal of Public Health* 92 (5):773–77.

Collins, Patricia Hill. 1990. *Black Feminist Thought: Knowledge, Consciousness, and the Politics of Empowerment.* Boston: Unwin Hyman.

Demmons, Shawnna. Spring/Summer 2007. "Race, Class and Transgender." *The Fire Inside* 35.

Díaz-Cotto, Juanita. 2006. *Chicana Lives and Criminal Justice.* Austin: University of Texas Press.

Dobash, R. Emerson, Russell P. Dobash, and Sue Gutteridge. 1986. *The Imprisonment of Women.* New York: Routledge.

Faith, Karlene. 1993. *Unruly Women: The Politics of Confinement and Resistance.* Vancouver: Press Gang.

Feld, Barry C. 1999. *Bad Kids: Race and the Transformation of the Juvenile Court.* New York: Oxford University Press.

Giallombardo, Rose. 1966. *Society of Women: A Study of a Women's Prison.* New. York: John Wiley.

Halberstam, Judith. 1998. *Female Masculinity.* Durham, NC: Duke University Press.

Hensley, Christopher, and Richard Tewksbury, "Inmate-to-Inmate Prison Sexuality: A Review of Empirical Studies." *Trauma Violence and Abuse* 3 (2002): 226–43.

Howe, Adrian. 1994. *Punish and Critique: Towards a Feminist Analysis of Penality.* London: Routledge.

Human Rights Watch. 2001. *Hatred in the Hallways: Violence and Discrimination against Lesbian, Gay, Bisexual, and Transgender Students in U.S. Schools, 2001.* http://www.hrw.org/reports/2001/uslgbt/toc.htm (accessed October 31, 2008.)

Incite! Women of Color against Violence. 2008. *Law Enforcement Violence against Women of Color and Trans People of Color: A Critical Intersection of Gender Violence and State Violence.* Redmond, WA: Incite! Women of Color against Violence.

Justice Now. 3 March 2008. Personal email communication.

Koyama, Emi. "Whose Feminism Is It Anyway? The Unspoken Racism of the Trans Inclusion Debate." http://eminism.org/readings/pdf-rdg/whose-feminism.pdf (accessed October 28, 2008).

Lee, Alexander L. Summer 2004. "Gendered Crime and Punishment: Strategies to Protect Transgender, Gender Variant, and Intersex People in America's Prisons." *GIC TIP Journal.* 4–16.

———. 2008. "Prickly Coalitions: Moving Prison Abolition Forward." Ed. CR10 Publications Collective. *Abolition Now! Ten Years of Struggle and Strategy against the Prison Industrial Complex.* Oakland: AK.

Mallon, Gerald P., and Teresa DeCrescenzo. 1985. "Transgender Children and Youth: A Child Welfare Practice Perspective." *Child Welfare* 2: 215–41.

Minter, Shannon, and Christopher Daley. 2003. *Trans Realities: A Legal Needs Assessment of San Francisco's Transgender Communities.* San Francisco: National Center for Lesbian Rights and Transgender Law Center. 26–27. http://www.transgenderlawcenter.org/tranny/pdfs/Trans%20Realities%20Final%20Final.pdf (accessed October 31, 2008).

National Center for Lesbian Rights. Undated. Rights of Transgender Prisoners. http://www.nclrights.org/site/DocServer/tgprisoners.pdf?docID=1285 (accessed October 31, 2008).

Noble, Bobby J. 1998. *Masculinities without Men.* Vancouver: University of British Columbia Press.

Office of Juvenile Justice and Delinquency Prevention. 2002. *Disproportionate Minority Confinement, 2002 Update.* Washington, DC: US Department of Justice. http://www.ncjrs.gov/pdffiles1/ojjdp/201240.pdf (accessed October 30, 2008).

Otis, M. 1913. "A Perversion Not Commonly Noted." *Journal of Abnormal Psychology* 8: 113–16.

Richie, Beth. 1995. *Compelled to Crime: The Gender Entrapment of Battered Black Women.* New York: Routledge.

Ross, Luanna. 1998. *Inventing the Savage: The Social Construction of Native American Criminality.* Austin: University of Texas Press.

Rupp, Shannon. 3 February 2007. "Transsexual Loses Battle with Women's Shelter." *The Tyee.* http://thetyee.ca/News/2007/02/03/Nixon/ (accessed October 31, 2008).

Sabo, Don, Terry Kupers and Willie London. 2001. *Prison Masculinities.* Philadelphia: Temple University Press.

San Francisco Bay Guardian and Transgender Law Center. 2006. *Good Jobs Now! A Snapshot of the Economic Health of San Francisco's Transgender Communities, 2006.*

http://www.transgenderlawcenter.org/pdf/Good%20Jobs%20NOW%20report.pdf (accessed October 31, 2008).

San Francisco Department of Public Health. 1999. *The Transgender Community Health Project*, 1999. http://hivinsite.ucsf.edu/InSite?page=cftg-02-02#S5.1X (accessed November 6, 2008).

Segura, Denise. 1992. "Chicanas in White Collar Jobs: 'You have to prove yourself more.' " *Sociological Perspectives* 35:163–82.

Selling, L. 1931. "The Pseudo-family." *American Journal of Sociology* 37: 247–53.

Sharma, Nandita, and Cynthia Wright. 2009. "Organizing the Motley Crew and Challenging the Security of National States." In *Activist Scholarship: Antiracism, Feminism and Social Change*, ed. Julia Sudbury and Margo Okazawa-Rey. Boulder, CO: Paradigm.

Steinhart, David J. Winter 1996. "Status Offenses." *The Future of Children, the Juvenile Court*. 6 (3): 86–99.

Sudbury, Julia. 2009. "Challenging Penal Dependency: Activist Scholarship and the Anti-Prison Movement." In *Activist Scholarship: Antiracism, Feminism and Social Change*, in Julia Sudbury and Margo Okazawa-Rey. Boulder: Paradigm.

———. 2006. *Global Lockdown: Race, Gender and the Prison-Industrial Complex*. New York: Routledge.

Transforming Justice. 2007. "Letters from Trans and Gender Non-Conforming Activists in Prison." *Transforming Justice Program Book*. 8. Available online: http://www. transformingjustice.org/100907.tjprogrambook.pdf (accessed October 31, 2008).

Trent, Judy Scales. 1997. "Notes of a White Black Woman." In *Critical White Studies: Looking Behind the Mirror*. ed. Richard Delgado and Jean Stafancic. Philadelphia: Temple University Press.

Vancouver Rape Relief Society. "Chronology of Events in Kimberly Nixon vs. Vancouver Rape Relief Society." http://www.rapereliefshelter.bc.ca/issues/knixon_chronology. html (accessed October 28, 2008).

Ward, D., and G. Kassebaum. 1965. *Women's Prisons: Sex and Social Structure*. New York: Aldine.

3x Denied

Dawna (Lessie) Brown

Ruth Snyder
Malaquias Montoya

Missing

Ricky A. Taylor

Bound

Joanie Estes-Rodgers

Connie Convicta and Vato Emiliano Comics

Ana Lucia Gelabert

G-5

Exhibition View 1 (above)

Photo by Rosemarie Chiarlone

Exhibition View 2 (above right)

Photo by Rosemarie Chiarlone

Panty Series #11 (right)

Photo by Rosemarie Chiarlone

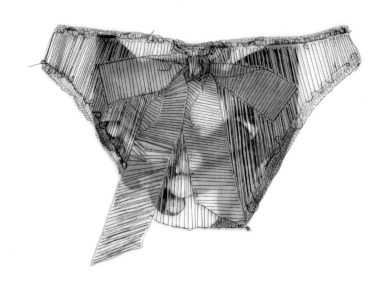

Exhibition View 3
Photo by Crystal Molinary

Subruler of the Element X

Photo by Isabel Moros-Rigau

CHAPTER FIFTEEN

Giving the Voiceless a Voice

Renita Phifer

My name is Renita Phifer, and I'm currently serving time at Bedford Hills Correctional Facility located in Westchester County; it is the only maximum-security prison for women in New York State. During the course of my eleven years of incarceration at Bedford, a total of ten officers have been prosecuted for sexual assault. There were also two children born to female prisoners as a result of forbidden relationships, and there were several abortions performed as a result of impregnation that derived from forced intercourse. As a prisoner, a woman cannot consent to any sexual act; pursuant to section 130.05 of the Penal Law, this removes any legal ability on the part of the inmate to consent to sexual conduct.

Female prisoners are particularly vulnerable to sexual abuses by correctional personnel because of the power dynamic between prisoners and guards. There are specific methods in which certain guards use their authority to abuse women under the guise of security. This also includes the usage of verbal abuse to chip away at a female prisoner's self-esteem to the point that she is willing to do anything to elevate her status with her abuser. That method of abuse is employed at Bedford Hills Correctional Facility on a consistent basis through verbal harassment; almost every woman at Bedford identified the use of disrespectful or threatening language by certain officers. Although the superintendent reiterates a "zero tolerance policy," she basically trivializes complaints against her staff, which is a major source of concern of the Correctional Association of New York and is reflected in its annual report regarding abuses at Bedford and can be obtained through its website at www.correctionalassociation.org.

Another method for violating women involves abusive pat frisks that consist of nonroutine pat downs combined with sexual comments and propositions that cause fear and frustration, as the victim is often hesitant to file a complaint due to fear of reprisals. That changed to a certain degree due to a civil suit under *Stacy Hamilton v. Glenn Goord* (98 Civ. 8022) resulting in courts' acknowledgment that those type of pat frisks violated Eighth Amendment protections against cruel and unusual treatment of female prisoners and would only be justified in emergency situations when no female guard is present.

The most troubling concern among the women at Bedford Hills Correctional Facility at this time is the few male officers who are carrying batons. This issue was addressed recently at a meeting with the superintendent, where the women from general population wanted to know why there has been a sudden presence of male officers carrying batons, when there are many women at Bedford who have suffered domestic violence and abuse by men and are traumatized. In the past, physical force with a baton by a male guard was not needed to restrain a female prisoner. Must women be subjected to witnessing men beating women with batons? The administration's response: "We are monitoring the situation closely." Those types of responses are typical and basically mean that until someone is beaten to a bloody pulp, we aren't liable. The overall ineffective self-monitoring of Bedford's administration carries over to its purported zero tolerance policy against staff-on-inmate sexual abuses. This issue is also listed as a principal concern in the December/January 2008 Women, Girls, and Criminal Justice (www.civicresearchinstitute.com).

Because of the administration's position, there is an increasingly tense overall atmosphere where the negative effect of a more punitive, as well as hostile, environment reverberates throughout the facility. It was difficult to witness the emotional and moral subjugation of my peers. I couldn't stand by and not try to do something to stop the abuses, so I distributed a survey that gave my peers an opportunity to name their abusers. I've obtained over two hundred responses to that survey, which I managed to get out of the prison, and had them delivered to the Women in Prison Association. Although they lack the power to effectuate change, they are the only regulatory agency that is monitoring Bedford Hills Correctional Facility. My purpose for providing the Women in Prison Association with the surveys was to establish that it is crucial that the superintendent comply with the Prison Rape Elimination mandates of chapter 147§15601 through §15609 provision for open forums to address abuses.

Due to my lack of faith in that ever happening, I've taken steps to ensure that my peers who have suffered abuse aren't isolated and silenced. The mechanism for this that was available to my peers initially was through writing poetry; several women, including myself, submitted our work to Juila Taylor, who was at that time the program manager at A Thousand Kites, which is an organization in Kentucky that sponsors a radio program for prisoners and that posts prisoners' poetry and short stories on their website (www.thousandkites.org).

I've also sent copies of the surveys to the organization Just Detention International (JDI), which was very interested in contacting the victims of abuse at Bedford. The women were sent a JDI input questionnaire by Ms. Rothstein.

This was a major victory because JDI not only pushes for policies that ensure institutional change; it also publishes a widely distributed newsletter, *Action Update*, which is devoted to ending the widespread problem of sexual violence behind bars. JDI lobbies to effectuate measures to prevent sexual abuse. It also publishes federal reports regarding annual hearings on prison rape, which focus on facilities found to have the highest and lowest incidents of sexual abuse. This ensures institutional accountability for sexual abuse, changes society's attitude toward prison rape, and promotes access to resources for survivors of sexual assault behind bars. Those preventive mechanisms compel institutions to adhere to mandates of the Prison Rape Elimination Act, as failure by state officials to certify compliance with these standards will cause them to lose 5 percent of their corrections-related federal funding. Although I'm in prison, I'm a human being and, as such, refuse to be dehumanized or to stand by while it happens to others. Nor could I accept being told to mind my own business when some of the male staff's actions would be a crime in mainstream society. I couldn't ignore what was happening because to do so would be a silent acceptance of it. The reason that I possess a desire to advocate for my peers stems from a very basic aspect of humanity within me, and that is love. We are all that we have in here, and being labeled a convict, prisoner, or societal outcast hasn't removed it from our core. I have found it extremely ironic that those deputized to promote societal norms flout the very laws of prison governance codified within correction law and the standard minimum rule for the treatment of prisoners. Am I unique? No, women in prison fight to maintain their dignity on different levels every day—all of these fights are important to our survival.

Because of my efforts to obtain assistance for my peers, I was locked in an isolation segregation building, not for creating a disturbance, but for listing names of known batterers. I was told by administration that by listing the names of male officers, I was harassing them! After my release from isolation confinement, there still wasn't anything in writing prohibiting surveys, and it took the superintendent fourteen months to put a rule prohibiting surveys in writing, which was a violation of my rights mandated by article 6 Management of Facilities pursuant to Correction Law 137. Due to my knowledge of that legislative mandate, I've filed five grievances where I challenged the superintendent's ability to issue a penalty without the existence of a written rule. The fact that I won each one was significant because the grievance panel is comprised of two inmates who are voted for by population to represent them and a sergeant who represents security. The governance of the Inmate Grievance Committee derives from Department of Corrections Directive 4040, which was implemented after the Attica riot. The purpose of the IGRC is to give prisoners a forum to challenge violations of standard policies defined within the directives, correction law, and facility rules. Interestingly, each of the five sergeants was designated by the facilities watch commander, who is of a higher rank that a lieutenant. Yet the superintendent expected me to have knowledge about unwritten rules that her own supervisory security staff did not know existed.

Last, the culmination of the issues of abuses of power begins and ends with the inconsistent enforcement of rules and policies within the hierarchy of administration at Bedford. Unfortunately, that means that the superintendent's draconian policies are the determining factor of what, if any, action will be taken against the batterers at Bedford. What the superintendent will do without a second thought is to silence victims of abuse through intimidation to ensure that Bedford's secrets remain hidden. One of the tactics utilized by administration is to have the deputy of security escort members of the Women in Prison Association around the facility and stand there during their interviews with women in population, as opposed to having a civilian staff member escort them. Obviously, no inmate is going to feel at liberty to say too much about what she knows, due to her fear of reprisals. Those types of violations contributed to my desire to give a voice to the voiceless.

section III

Education, Writing, and the Arts

Caught up on the Whirlwind
Valencia C.

This piece reflects in a way the twists and turns in which human beings (women in this particular case) are going through society and the judicial system. It shows how women became numbers as opposed to human beings as soon as they got caught up in this whirlwind of society. It reveals how they are virtually tossed around like a twig or a leaf in the wind. From the court system to the so-called correctional system and back to free society, women will be rejected again and again for having made a mistake, and they will end up back in hands that toss them from one bad situation to the next and the next and the next. Unfortunately, the contrast of social classes will determine their fate. As we see continually, rich and poor are unequal. As for those who are already a number, they have experienced this iniquity firsthand. For those who are not, beware of getting caught in this ruthless whirlwind.

This work is based on testimonies, biographies, and memoirs of women's experiences as numbers—statistics that show little of the vast and long tentacles of the problem. These sad facts inspire me, but at the same time I do not begin to understand completely the cruelty we show toward one another as humans, without any regard or compassion. It is literally as if something has broken my heart every time I come across one of these stories, of circumstances that go beyond imagination, of how senseless we can be to each other in this society and this world.

As a twig or a leaf is tossed when it gets caught in the spiral of this whirlwind, so are women when they get sucked up in this system. Anywhere you look, only the elite seem to have the right for another opportunity or help, a privilege not available to most of us.

Historical Contextualization

Ashley E. Lucas

Prisons are seldom imagined as hotbeds of education, literacy, creativity, or the arts. The cramped, loud, restrictive nature of incarcerated life poses significant challenges for those who wish to study, write, or make art, as do the dearth of books, writing materials, art supplies, and work space. The level of access that outside educators, artists, and community volunteers have to prison populations differs widely from state to state and prison to prison and is largely determined by wardens, who have the right to arbitrarily allow or cut off such programs without warning or explanation. As a result, prisoners' formal opportunities for higher learning or creative expression rarely remain stable throughout an individual's time served. Despite all that, educational and artistic programs are a widespread phenomenon in U.S. prisons, and their work is supplemented by the informal, improvised training, given by prisoners to their peers, in basic literacy, creative writing, visual art, and other areas of study, such as cultural history, ethics, and parenting. As with all archival and historical documentation of the history of prisoners in the United States, we know more about the experiences of incarcerated men in this area than about women, frequently ignored in the scholarly, journalistic, and creative literature dealing with these issues.

Women who have the opportunity to take college classes during their incarceration are four times less likely to return to prison than women who do not (Talvi 2007). However, overall educational programming in prisons remains dismally underfunded and often relies on the generosity and goodwill of outside volunteers. Some of the most consistent and successful college-level educational programs in prisons have thus emerged from partnerships between faculty members at universities and prison administrators. The Inside-Out Prison Exchange Program has become the most widespread and well-known model for college-prison educational collaboration. First developed as a program in 1997, this pedagogical model involves university faculty members teaching classes to undergraduates and incarcerated people who all meet together inside the prison once a week for a semester. The national headquarters of Inside-Out at Temple University offers week-long training institutes for faculty members and in this manner has effectively propagated this pedagogical model across the United States (Inside-Out Center Website). In her chapter in this book, Simone Weil Davis analyzes her experiences as an Inside-Out teacher and reflects on the nature and function of this form of educational instruction.

As for arts programs in women's prisons, it is difficult, if not impossible, to document with any precision how many such programs have existed, where they happened, how long they lasted, and what sorts of creative work they produced. Because arts programming in prisons, like most prison-related activism, is usually done by one or a small handful of people in each locale, records are seldom kept of the creative workshops' activities. Usually these outside volunteers are so busy with the immense labor of creating, maintaining, and (all too frequently) defending these programs that they have little energy and few resources remaining to document the creative work itself. Some such workshops end up producing art exhibits or performances in or outside the prison, but because photography and videography are often not allowed in prisons, the audiences of such events are limited to those who can attend them in person.

At times groups of creative writers have self-published chapbooks or collections of creative writing or founded small presses to print limited runs of a prison group's writing. Occasionally larger presses have published short fiction, essays, and poetry by incarcerated women as part of edited collections of writings by and about prisoners. Novelist Wally Lamb and the women of York Correctional Institute have put together the best known such collections in the United States: *Couldn't Keep It to Myself* (2003) and *I'll Fly Away* (2007). Both collections were published by HarperCollins and received significant popular attention, much of it inspired by the lawsuit filed against the writers at York Correctional by the State of Connecticut a week before *Couldn't Keep It to Myself* was slated for publication, demanding that the women use the proceeds from the sale of their book to pay the state for the cost of their incarceration at the rate of $117 a day. After Lamb launched a full-scale media and legal campaign to stand up for the writers, the state backed down and settled the lawsuit out of court. Though the success of the women of York Correctional was a great stride toward making average citizens recognize the value of prisoners' creative work, incarcerated writers still struggle to make their voices heard.

Despite the lengthy and substantial tradition of prison journalism in the United States, little scholarly attention has been paid to the genre as a whole, and women's contributions are only mentioned in passing. Of the two major books on the subject, Russell Baird's *Penal Press* (1967) does not discuss women's writings at all but does include publications from women and girls' facilities in his index of "Correctional Institution Publications." The more recent *Jailhouse Journalism* (2002) by James McGrath Morris devotes only a few scattered paragraphs to incarcerated women. Eleanor Novek's chapter in this section of *Razor Wire Women* provides a rare analysis of journalism from within a women's prison.

After creative writing, prisoners' visual art has had the largest audience outside prison walls. In 1979 the Delaware Department of Corrections began its still extant Prison Arts Program when a volunteer artist started holding workshops at a women's prison (State of Delaware Website). As chapters in this section will describe, the Prison Creative Arts Project (PCAP) in Michigan and Women on the Rise! in Florida both hold widely attended exhibitions of prisoner artwork in galleries. The *Interrupted Life* exhibit of art by incarcerated mothers, curated by Rickie Solinger, has toured college campuses and galleries throughout the United States. The Prisons Foundation in Washington, D.C., has a permanent prison art gallery, and it sells many products online emblazoned with prisoners' artwork (Prisons Foundation Website), as do the Seattle-based PrisonArt.org, Texas-based BigHouseArt.com, and a host of other websites. This commercialization of prisoner art is controversial in some prison activist circles, especially when the people selling the artwork profit monetarily from sales and the incarcerated artists do not. Though most of the prisoner artwork online appears on sites that sell the artwork, some activist websites, such as WomenAndPrison.org, display prisoner art without selling it. At least one book-length study of prisoner art has been published; Phyllis Kornfeld's *Cell Block Visions* (1997) provides a brief overview of the global history of prison art and then analyzes artwork seen by Kornfeld in workshops she led. Though the book provides an invaluable look at prisoner art generally, only two women have their work featured in the text. A book-length examination of women prisoners' artwork has yet to emerge.

Because their work exists in a material form, women writing or creating visual art in prison document themselves in ways that performing artists do not. The vast majority of what has been written about music in prisons focuses on famous performers, Johnny Cash chief among them, who held concerts in prisons. On rare occasion, a prisoner musician such as Leadbelly has risen to fame, and folklorists and musicologists have recorded a number of albums of prisoners singing work songs or the blues—almost always men. Very few accounts of music programs in women's prisons exist, but in 2008 radio journalists in the United States reported brief news stories on orchestras in women's prisons in Venezuela (Kinkel 2008) and Alaska (Shurtleff 2008). It is highly likely that religious choirs and other musical groups have formed organically or been directed by volunteers or prison officials in women's prisons, but records of these musicians and their performances may or may not exist.

Documentation of dance groups in prisons remains spotty as well, but a few extant groups have made information about their activities available on the internet. Interestingly, other than the Philippine prisoners who rose to YouTube fame dancing to the Michael Jackson song "Thriller," most information available about prison dance programs deals with incarcerated women. In 1994, choreographer Leslie Neal and her dance company began teaching workshops with incarcerated women through a Florida-based program known as ArtSpring

(ArtSpring Website). The Pat Graney Company of Seattle, with its *Keeping the Faith—The Prison Project*, has conducted workshops in women's prisons since the turn of the millennium, and it also holds training sessions for other dance companies interested in doing prison work (Pat Graney Company Website). Since 2004, the Avodah Dance Ensemble has worked with incarcerated women, at risk girls, and women returning home after incarceration in Connecticut and Delaware (Avodah Dance Website). Though these dance companies are doing extensive work in women's prisons, comparatively little has been written about them.

Finally, theater programs in prisons, though still understudied, have received far more attention than other performing arts programs in prisons. In his 2007 book, *The Proscenium Cage: Critical Case Studies in U.S. Prison Theatre Programs*, Lawrence Tocci asserts that forms of theater have been staged in U.S. prisons since at least the 1890s, when women prisoners were staging their own Christmas pageants. Tocci also notes that since the early 1980s, many of the community groups doing prison theater are made up of feminists working in women's prisons. More theater programs have taken place in U.S. women's prisons than could possibly be described here; we can only sample the scope of the work these groups are doing. Rhodessa Jones and the women of the San Francisco County Jail use the Medea myth as a starting point for self-discovery and creativity in performance, as is discussed in further detail in Sara Warner's chapter on the Medea Project in this volume. From 1988 to 1998, Jean Trounstine staged plays with women at the Framingham prison in Massachusetts and in 1991 published a book entitled *Shakespeare behind Bars: One Teacher's Story of the Power of Drama in a Women's Prison.* Playwright Eve Ensler conducted a writing workshop at the Bedford Hills Correctional Facility in New York and then fashioned a script out of the women's writing. Ensler brought a cast of famous actresses, including Rosie Pérez, Felicia Rashad, and Glenn Close, into the prison to do a reading of the play *What I Want My Words to Do to You*, and in 2003 PBS broadcast a documentary by the same title, which included footage from the writing workshop as well as the performance. University of Michigan professor Buzz Alexander started teaching a theater class for just two women prisoners in 1990. That class led to the founding of both the Prison Creative Arts Project (PCAP) and a still-active theater troupe, the Sisters Within, which now resides at the Huron Valley Women's Prison.

When read together, the following chapters and pieces of artwork provide a sense of the ways that education and art can intellectually and emotionally sustain communities of incarcerated women and the volunteers and teachers engaged with them. The imprisoned women described here display remarkable innovation, integrity, and craft. Their abilities could better serve our society if we sought out alternatives to incarceration that would cultivate these types of skills and talents. Focusing on women in these terms becomes particularly important in a society where wage gaps between the sexes, gendered notions of labor and power, and high rates of domestic violence continue to disproportionately deny women equal opportunities for growth and advancement. If we deem the 2.3 million incarcerated people among us to be expendable and unworthy of full civil and human rights, then those who are released are forever marked as pathologically criminal, regardless of the nature of their initial conviction or their present behavior, and their talents are then more often than not lost to society forever. Section 3 of this book argues for decarceration by emphasizing not just the humanity of the incarcerated but also the ways in which education, writing, and the arts can transform the lives of people who have been systematically discouraged from identifying themselves as intellectual and creative beings.

REFERENCES

ArtSpring.Org. 2009. http://www.artspring.org/ (retrieved on January 30, 2009).

Avodah Dance Ensemble. 2009. "Women's Correctional Facilities and Youth Detention Centers." http://www.avodahdance.org/inspire.html (retrieved on January 30, 2009).

Baird, Russell N. 1967. *The Penal Press*. Evanston: Northwestern University Press.

Inside-Out Center Website. http://www.insideoutcenter.org/ (retrieved on January 25, 2010).

Kinkel, Randy. 29 June 2008. "This Week in Classical Music." KBAQ 98.5 FM. http://www.kbaq.org/music/thisweek/20080629 (retrieved on January 30, 2009).

Kornfeld, Phyllis. 1997. *Cellblock Visions: Prison Art in America*. Princeton: Princeton University Press.

Lamb, Wally, and the Women of York Correctional Institution. 2003. *Couldn't Keep It to Myself: Testimonies from Our Imprisoned Sisters*. New York: Reagan Books.

———. 2007. I'll Fly Away: Further Testimonies from the Women of York Prison. New York: HarperCollins.

Morris, James McGrath. 2002. *Jailhouse Journalism: The Fourth Estate behind Bars*. New Brunswick: Transaction.

Pat Graney Company. "Keeping the Faith: The Prison Project." http://www.patgraney.org/faith.html (retrieved on January 30, 2009).

"Prison Arts." State of Delaware Website. http://doc.delaware.gov/information/PrisonArts.shtml (retrieved on January 25, 2010).

Prisons Foundation Website. http://prisonsfoundation.org/ (retrieved on January 25, 2010).

Shurtleff, David. 14 July 2008. "Women's Prison Takes on Mozart." NPR Music. http://www.npr.org/templates/story/story.php?storyId=92520296&ft=1&f=1012 (retrieved on January 30, 2009).

Talvi, Silja. 2007. *Women behind Bars: The Crisis of Women in the U.S. Prison System*. California: Seal.

"Thriller Prison Dance." YouTube Website. http://www.youtube.com/watch?v= hMnk7l-h9M3o (retrieved on January 25, 2010).

Tocci, Lawrence. 2007. *The Proscenium Cage: Critical Case Studies in U.S. Prison Theatre Programs*. Youngstown, NY: Cambria.

Trounstine, Jean. 2001. *Shakespeare behind Bars: The Power of Drama in a Women's Prison*. New York: St. Martin's.

Women and Prison: A Site for Resistance. 2009. http://womenandprison.org/ (retrieved on January 30, 2009).

Episodes 1 and 4 of the Connie Convicta and Vato Emiliano Comics

Ana Lucia Gelabert

ARTIST'S STATEMENT

The goal of the Connie and Vato cartoons—sixteen episodes so far, download-able at www.realcostofprisons.org/comix/gelabert—is to raise citizens' awareness and expose the farce that the gargantuan American prison industrial complex has become. This impacts not only the 2.3 million American prisoners and their families but many other Americans as well. For instance, in Texas, state college students must incur tens of thousands of dollars in debt to afford $7,000 a year for tuition—tuition costs that in 1995, when Governor George W. Bush began his massive prisons buildup only cost $120 a semester. The general citizenry pays for the prison buildup and later on suffers the results of millions of human beings being brutalized beyond endurance, suddenly being set free on society without proper means to remake their lives. It's time to be smart on crime, not merely tough on crime.

CONNIE Convicta & VATO Emiliano
by Ana Lucia Gelabert (rev. May. MMVII)

1

CONNIE, VATO and their 3 children — Victor (5½), Millie (4) and Jason (2) — enjoy a modest but happy life at their Houston apartment.

(Their dog LOPINTÁN)

When **DOWNSIZING** costs Vato his job. Then in the sudden economic downturn Connie's part-time also VANISHES...

DOW-JONES

The meager TWC unemployment checks won't cover even a third of the family's expenses and their savings run out quickly.

Weeks and MONTHS of anxious job searching on want ads... inquiries... phone calls... drop ins... walk ons... YOU NAME IT!... to prospective employers... all fail miserably.

WANT ADS

In desperation, Vato tries the "hire-by-day" leeches: not only the pay ain't enough... but the TWC finds out and CANCELS the meager unemployment checks!

HIRE BY-THE-DAY
½ MINIMUM SALARY
N
BEN
NO
SAFE

SI VALETIS BENE EST. VALEO.

p.1-1

The very last straw: their landlord serves them a "pay or be evicted" ultimatum. Connie and Vato seem to have reached the end of the line...

PAY OR ELSE!

But they still have EACH OTHER.

After watching on PBS a documentary on successful capitalist entrepreneurs like... JOHN D. ROCKEFELLER, HENRY FORD, E.I. DuPONT, Wm. R. HEARST... and brief public library research, CONNIE and VATO decide to become capitalist entrepreneurs!

First they buy some equipment...

St. Dimas PAWN SHOP
CHEAP S.N.S.A. ON SALE
CHEAP GUNS!

Then go visit their first client...

LIQUO

Unfortunately for them —their dismal lack of experience— they get caught few blocks away from their very first "business venture."
ARRESTED...
BOOKED...
JAILED... and
SEPARATED!

p.1-2

CONNIE Convicta & VATO Emiliano

by Ana Lucia Gelabert   Feb. 10, MMV (rev. 5/4) †

⁴ (CONTINUED FROM No. 3)

Enter offender TERESA WASHINGTON, from TDCJ-CID* Mountain View unit:

Around 1980, while testifying in Houston on the Ruiz v. Estelle federal court case, then TDC* director ESTELLE said under oath that at least 70 PER CENT of TDC's 20,000 prisoners could be released AT ONCE without any danger to Texas society.

Texas had then 14 million people...

(†) stats for 2003-5

---

⁹In the 1980's it was TEXAS DEPARTMENT of CORRUPTION (TDC). Name changed (to foil prisoners calling it so) to TAXPAYERS DUPED on CUSHY JOBS—for INCOMPETENT DEPENDENTS (TDCJ-ID). Of late re-renamed as TDCJ-CID: add CRASS before Incompetent Dependents. Same old...

Texas now has 21 million people: a 50% increase over 1980. But the overall TDCJ** has swelled to 210,000 prisoners: a tenfold increase!

Of whom at least 150,000 could be released NOW with no danger to society (based on 1980 Estelle's criteria).

Leaving an overall TDCJ population of 60,000 prisoners: still three times the number in 1980 and SIX TIMES HIGHER than justified by Texas population increase 1980 - 2003.

SI VALETIS BENE EST. VALEO.

p.4-1

Adding up the reduced TDCJ expense and the state's take on those "extra 150,000 captives" then holding GAINFUL & PRODUCTIVE JOBS, the State of Texas would take additional revenues of over

$8 BILLION

each and every year.

WHICH WOULD ENABLE TEXAS TO:

1. Cancel plans to toll any new (or even ancient) roads;
2. Lower tuition at state colleges to about ONE-THIRD of today's;
3. Raise salaries of TDCJ guards by at least 25% (="more professionalism");
4. Create about 140,000 scholarships at vocational, technical & community colleges;

and sure, why not, at least while OIL remains at $50 a barrel:

5. A TAX CUT! Lower state's sales tax from 8.25% now, to perhaps as low as... 6.25%?   YOU DO THE MATH!

(**)As shown by Homer Brown in a 1990's paper published by Austin-ABC, Texas operates SIX (6) separate state prison systems; besides TDCJ-CID: TDCJ-SJ (state jails); transfer units; therapeutic units; "mix & match" bundle of industrial, pre-release, pre-revocation units; besides 10,000 in county jails for lack of TDCJ beds. However, the PUBLISHED figures are only true for TDCJ-CID.

OH, SHISH... SHORE IT CAN BE DONE!

BUT IF AND ONLY IF

Y'ALL DA PEOPLE

DEMAND THAT IT BE DONE!   VALE.

p. 4-2

201

CHAPTER SIXTEEN

Inside-Out: The Reaches and Limits of a Prison Program

Simone Weil Davis

Prison bars are meant to keep people in; they also keep people out. In tandem with the other powerful social forces that keep people divided, especially those that cluster around race, class, and gender, the tall walls and razor wire fences of U.S. prisons and jails ensure that our internalized maps of what we consider home are skewed, pitted with lacunae. These blanks, blind spots, and alienations don't just impoverish us; they make it possible for things as they are to continue—including this country's unprecedentedly high rate of incarceration. With our sense of connection, community, place, and identity distorted, our ability to function as political agents on behalf of change is severely limited. In the present chapter, I consider one program that seeks to chip away at the *conceptual* walls, at least, that our carceral system throws up.

Both in terms of rate and sheer number, the United States is the world's most zealous jailer. More than 2.2 million Americans are incarcerated. A 2008 Pew Center on the States Report explains that "for the first time, more than one in every 100 adults is now confined in an American jail or prison" (Warren et al. 2008). The number of American women confined in jails and prisons is growing at an especially dizzying rate, up eightfold since 1980 (Vicini 2006; Women's Prison Association; Sentencing Project 2007). Women of color, their families, and their communities are far harder hit by the current rush to incarcerate than are whites. The Sentencing Project tells us that "in 2005, black women were more than three times as likely as white women to be incarcerated in prison or jail, and Hispanic women 69% more likely" (Sentencing Project). The already-cited Pew Center on the States report points out that the shameful one in one hunderd ratio applies, too, to black women between the ages of thirty-five and thirty-nine, even though women in general are almost ten times less likely than are men to be incarcerated (3). Statistics can dizzy the reader and unavoidably dull our sense of connection to individual exigency. So, in a story that is shaped by racism, the pressing needs of vast numbers of people, each one of whom is fully implicated in the heat, struggle, and passion of his or her life, hold me to account as I write these words.

The Inside-Out Prison Exchange Program is a national pedagogical project offering semester-long, college-level classes behind bars to groups of students, half of whom are incarcerated and half of whom are college students from "outside." One function of Inside-Out is simply to provide a means whereby college work can be reintroduced to those who are incarcerated. Since 1994, when Pell grants for individuals in prison were repealed, educational programming behind bars has been severely curtailed. Perhaps an even more fundamental goal of these courses is to form a working community among members who might otherwise never meet: lines of class, race, and social abjection are crossed as students work together over time on a common pursuit. Course themes most often focus on the study of some aspect of our society's approach to crime and punishment. Geographically proximate, only a van ride apart, participants in an Inside-Out class acknowledge something usually rendered opaque; our fates are inextricable, and we are already living together but emphatically not in community.

In this challenge and temporary dissolution of some of the structural barriers that keep the status quo up and running, Inside-Out classes are catalysts for social change. Normally, as people keep to their separate demographic camps, potential allegiances and alternative analyses lie dormant, and the urgent pull of shared humanity goes unfelt. In student feedback from dozens of Inside-Out courses conducted around the country, again and again, both inside and outside participants use the word *transformational*. Here, I want to consider the nature of that transformation and ask questions about its relevance and limits. To make the walls permeable between inside and out is to defy an initial premise of imprisonment, namely, the stigma and segregation of those deemed "criminal." Is this course model an instance of "prison reform," a palliative improvement that only makes a fundamentally flawed system seem more tolerable and thus sustainable? Or is it closer to a revolutionary gesture, helping to affect a paradigm shift that our society needs to make in order to move beyond the prison industrial complex?

The Inside-Out Prison Exchange Program was founded in 1997 by Lori Pompa, a social worker who teaches in Temple University's Criminal Justice Department (Inside-Out Website). As she tells the story, the idea for such a semester-long engagement was hatched in the midnineties by a chance comment from a man serving a life sentence; he was part of a panel discussion during a prison tour on which she had brought her class. Each term, she would hold these tours, always including a conversation between her students and a group of incarcerated men or women, a chance for them to share ideas and perceptions about the criminal justice system. As one such far-ranging exchange drew to a close, the entire group felt keenly aware that their conversation simply was not over. Paul, a gentleman on the panel at the prison, approached her and urged that she offer a semester-long shared class. Lori took his idea as a challenge, a directive. Within two years the Inside-Out Prison Exchange Program had begun.

Working first with the Philadelphia jails and then with Graterford Prison, Pompa eventually joined by one or two colleagues, began to regularly conduct semester-long courses on different aspects of the criminal justice system. The student population would be 50 percent Temple students and 50 percent incarcerated students, and the classes were conducted at the correctional facility. This brought higher education behind bars, while for the outside students, merely entering a prison or jail led to understanding something about the architecture of power that cannot be fully conceived secondhand. Pompa writes of the program's trajectory that, after several years of running Inside-Out courses on her own, "as a 2003 [George] Soros Justice Senior Fellow, [I] collaborated with others on both sides of the prison walls to develop Inside-Out into a national model of transformative pedagogy. To date, more than 130 instructors from 90 colleges and universities in 33 states and abroad have taken part in the Inside-Out training, with dozens of Inside-Out classes offered throughout the country each semester."[1]

Though Pompa and colleagues created the Inside-Out model in the context of teaching criminal justice majors, since the Inside-Out Instructor Training Institutes began, courses have been offered across many disciplines, with participating schools ranging from community colleges to institutions such as Amherst College and Vassar. Equally wide-ranging are the sorts of correctional facilities where classes have been conducted, from day reporting centers at county jails to maximum security state prisons, both men's and women's facilities. Using a variety of approaches, some participating colleges have figured out ways to offer credit to inside participants.[2] What remains constant is that semi-anonymity and confidentiality are programmatic: only first names are used; contact is limited to class time; and inside students are not expected to share information with classmates about the circumstances that led to their incarceration. In a sense the height of artifice, these carefully set parameters and guidelines allow something very real to unfold in the classroom, precisely because the "normal" way people interact in our society—not natural at all, but extremely socially determined—can be very insidious, compelling, and damaging. A protocol that demarcates a safe space is a meaningful show of respect for the *might* of what's being defied: that is, classism, racism, social divisions. Breaking patterns of mistrust, blind privilege, and presumption, inside and outside students sit in a circle and work together as equals over the course of many weeks. They learn from one another; they collaborate.

The Inside-Out classes that I have conducted in a Northeastern state are creative writing and literature classes that bring students from the small, all-female liberal arts college where I teach together with women incarcerated in our county. (A sampling of the assigned readings is offered in an appendix at the end of this chapter.) My cofacilitator, Lysette Navarro, herself formerly incarcerated, is a creative writing teacher with a local nonprofit that offers creative writing workshops to incarcerated and formerly incarcerated women (Sheehan 2005).[3] Teaching these classes has deepened my questions not only about the way we "do" crime and punishment in the United States but also about the way we conceive and practice another of our central institutional projects, education. Whether critiqued as "cultural capital" or lauded as "money in the bank," education is often described as the key to individual social mobility, something that one acquires and then possesses as an individual, a currency that can buy one benefits. As a result of my engagement with Inside-Out, I join Paulo Freire, Myles Horton, and others, to endorse not only far greater access to education but also its radical reconceptualization: a redefinition that emphasizes community creation and collective purpose rather than individual self-"betterment" and "upward" mobility, one that turns literacy from a noun to a verb, from a possession one acquires and owns into a practice between people (Horton and Freire 1991).

Here, I also challenge the assumption that when women reveal themselves through writing, their story must necessarily follow the conventions of either the confession or recovery narrative. Even with therapeutic writing designed to confront trauma, these tales of the individual are not all that's told, when women sit in a circle and write. In my own Inside-Out courses, our work did indeed lead to reflections on gratitude, guilt, and personal healing; importantly, it led just as organically to analysis of social inequity and calls for political change. I use accounts and documents from the Inside-Out classroom to propose that it is only via heavy-handed shaping and funneling of the therapeutic discourse that questions about systemic institutional and political violations *can* be bracketed off and disregarded, in favor of the "merely" personal. How can an unorthodox seminar or an impassioned poem or story change anything? That is my focus here.

THE REACH AND LIMITS

Maybe my own Inside-Out education began in earnest on the day the first paper was due. It is February 17. I plan on collecting the papers at the end of class. On the agenda for class time is a discussion of the assigned reading, and I am struck by how slowly comments seem to be coming, in stark contrast to our last class session. "What's the problem?" I wonder, grumpily. Finally, one inside student, Joanie, raises her hand and says, "I don't know about anyone else, but I wrote my paper all night last night, and I worked hard on it. I wanted to read it out loud and get feedback."[4] So we change tack and devote much of the rest of class time that day to student volunteers reading their entire papers aloud and sharing our responses. This marked a shift, as women in the circle claimed ownership over the process we were inventing together. The assignment had been to write about "jailface" (like pokerface squared, this is author Patricia McConnel's term) and to respond to this related passage about "*corázon*" from Jimmy Santiago Baca's memoir, *A Place to Stand* (McConnel 1995; Baca 2001). In Arizona's notorious Florence State Prison, Jimmy's friend Macaron tells him:

All you got here is heart *corázon*. Only *corázon*. And if you don't have it, every day will be a hell you've never imagined. When the mind says, I am human, the heart growls, I am an animal. When you wish to scream, the heart says, Be silent. When you feel hurt, you numb yourself. When you're lonely, you push it aside. Strip yourself of every trace of the streets, because it will hurt you here. Here you have no feelings, no soul; only your heart will help you survive. Forget everything except survival. Don't ask why—there are no reasons. You didn't exist before coming here; your life before here never happened. The only thought that drives you on is to be alive at the end of the day, and to be a man, or die fighting proving you are a man. That's the code of the warrior. (Baca 2001)

Joanie responded, in part:

"The jail face," as terminology puts it, is having to say nothing, do nothing, but you act as if anyone who dares to cross your imaginary line becomes the bait. You are like a magnet; others, for some reason, see the walls and run to you for a "sense of belonging." They take orders like soldiers readying for battle; nothing is too hard for them to accomplish. Like you, they probably came in "jail-faced," but found out quickly that it takes more than a look, you need heart. Perseverance, the relentless effort to get back up no matter what, that which surpasses any logic given to the natural mind of handling situations, your ability to carry on even after the soul breaks, the eyes blind, the spirit dies.

How strong are you, really? [. . .] This is anger, so angry that the vessel that allows it all to happen, to pump life into their veins, has become the sole carrier of all the pain, disappointment, strife and resentments of everything they have ever known. Macaron's outlook on things caused him to be able to feel the only way he knew how. He tried to explain sanity with insanity, and his soul never had the chance to seek beyond Macaron's way. Relying only on our own strength, it is impossible to reach beyond a break. I had never seen the good in me. For as long as I could remember, everything I'd loved had left me. I had done too much to go back and too much to go forward. I couldn't change, but my heart that lives inside me wanted desperately to see what all the suffering was for, why I had to resort to imprisonment, and why I was running.

With nuance and probity, Joanie's insights in the above passage detail the depth of experience that looms behind the silent mask, a threatening veneer of invulnerable cool. So her essay read aloud to inside and outside students breaches not only education's "ivory" barriers but also the protective scaffolding of "jailface," as well. A sheltered outside student, in other circumstances and without a class like this one, would likely "read" the text of that mask's surface and skitter off, uncomprehending.

One could understand and appreciate Inside-Out solely as an innovative way to help get educational programming to an underserved population, but in instances like this, its participants make it rather more. What we mean by education is itself mutated when Joanie insists on turning her paper from evaluative fodder into a communicative beam. From that day on, students voluntarily read course papers aloud to one another and then provided feedback. The point of writing for class changed: not hoop-jumping for evaluation, but the creation of community through expression and careful listening. Just as the specific use value of an object can flatten out and fade away behind the glare of its exchange value once it has become a commodity, so too does the *content* of a student paper become almost moot, once it has been dubbed with a letter grade. In this classroom, by contrast, it seemed on the face of it perverse for writing to be generated and then not shared.

A noticeable portion of the writing we did, whether in dialogue with assigned reading or in reaction to a creative writing prompt, was grippingly personal. To share such work in the circle, then, is already itself a charged *entrusting* of the group that had its own memorable impact. This "confessional" mode is not central to all Inside-Out courses, not by a long shot, but it is consistently part of my own, which leads me to the following reflections about the very gendered practice of writing that is dubbed "therapeutic." Questions about the scope and potential of this kind of writing in my own course converge with my broader investigation here of the reach and the limit of Inside-Out's transformative possibilities more generally.

Confession: this narrative project drove Saint Augustine, of course, and, more than a thousand years later, Jean-Jacques Rousseau (Augustine 2001; Rousseau 1995). The need to come clean about one's sins—or to justify them—and to shape a plot around crisis and conversion, is one central motor driving the genre of autobiography and even the emergence of the novel (Riley 2004). Of great currency today and often conflated with confession is *therapeutic* writing, seen as one path to liberation from the effects of endured trauma through. When we suffer a traumatic experience, perhaps its worst affront is the sense that jurisdiction over our lives and experience has been forcibly ripped away; when a survivor of trauma writes about the experience, he or she gets to grab the narrative reins back and reshape the story over which someone or something else had wrested control. If he or she shares the work, both writer and audience benefit. The fact of mutual gain in a safe space makes overwhelming ghosts dwindle, somehow, to a manageable size. This converging of literature, medicine, pedagogy, self-help, and feminist praxis has resulted in some very powerful writing, along with a regular cottage industry of publications about writing's use in healing (Anderson and MacCurdy 2000; *Writing and Healing* 2000; McKenzie-Mavinga 2002; Jones 2006; Oennebaker and Stone 2003).

To call a piece of writing "confessional"—in spite of all this or, perversely, because of it—is to level a feminizing slight. (Reading *True Confessions Magazine* was the quintessence of guilty pleasure, for this writer coming up.) In a piece entitled "Confessional and (Finally) Proud of It," Sue William Silverman quotes book reviewer Michael Skube, who has described women's memoirs that treat incest as "awfully tiresome," "nonliterary and faddish." He shudders, "[P]eople are spilling their guts out, confessing the unimaginable and sometimes the purely imaginary" (Silverman). So, when people think about women writing, especially on avowedly "personal" topics, ideas about the cathartic, healing powers of writing on trauma get thickly braided, interwoven, with profound literary disdain for gut-spilling; gendered disdain for "womanish whining"; encrusted ideas about sinfulness and redemption; pop-Freudian notions about confessional discharge; and voyeuristic yearning for the tell-all we are now trained to slather for. How do women negotiate with all this, when they pick up their pens? Canadian scholar Irene Gammel insists on

> the experimental and creative energy with which women have negotiated their positions within the larger realms of confessional politics. Many 'real-life' stories encode an awareness of the confessional reality principle, of possible appropriation and recolonization of their life stories; suspicion and skepticism mark their self-representation, signaling that theirs is not the unmediated cry from the female heart. Women encode boundaries and warnings, signaling their desire to create their own safe space in which to articulate their personal and sexual lives, while defying confessional entrapments. (Gammel 1999)

Perhaps the theme of "entrapment" is somewhat overdetermined in an Inside-Out classroom. To write as an incarcerated woman is to write into the implicit assumption of predetermined guilt and an oft-reiterated obligation to rehabilitate on paper. The work of emerging from crisis becomes dangerously blurred with the *mea culpa,* and both are stage managed, as much as can be possible, by the correctional context.

Often fending off their more punitively minded colleagues, well-meaning rehabilitators working within corrections consider it a key piece of their mission to offer incarcerated women access to programming that will highlight, address, and heal the lasting trauma of sexual abuse and domestic violence. They note, rightly, that the great majority of women behind bars are there for nonviolent drug-related offenses, that a very significant majority of women who wind up incarcerated struggle with addiction and depression and have been the victims of sexual and domestic violence (Sentencing Project 2007; Greenfield and Snell 2000; Harlow; Shaw 1995; DeCou and Van Wright 2002).[5] So they very appropriately seek woman-centered treatment and programming solutions, including arts programming, that will address these social and psychological ills.

This emphasis on a complex of personal dysfunctions and psychologi-
cal vulnerabilities, however, can overshadow *another* set of demographic facts
about the women who go to jail and prison; overwhelmingly, the incarcerated
are women of color, poor, under- or unemployed, lacking adequate access to
education or health care, and increasingly, facing homelessness (Women's Prison
Association 2003). As a reminder, if we look at the set of women who *break*
drug laws versus those who *are sentenced* for it, that demographic breakdown is
entirely different and in fact cleaves closely to the ethnic and class ratios in our
society at large (Beatty et al. 2007).[6] Across the board, for these women social
services may have proved inadequate, absent, or even an active aggravation of
their difficulties. The violence they have survived may well be not domestic, or
not solely domestic, but state-sponsored.

Perhaps the United States is criminalizing poverty, giving corporate criminals
carte blanche while tracking poor people of color toward a prison-industrial
complex that has ballooned into a juggernaut, unmatched around the world.
Perhaps as a society, we are normalizing tyranny, what Fyodor Dostoevsky called
the "habit" that will "coarsen and stupefy the very best of men to the level of
brutes," and growing inured to it when we tune in shows such as *Prison Break*
and *Inside San Quentin* (Dostoevsky 1985). Perhaps white celebrity convicts (Mar-
tha Stewart, Robert Downey, Jr., Paris Hilton, and maybe even Scott Peterson)
function as the entertaining exceptions that mask the entrenched inequalities of
the carceral system. In recent years, celebrity mug shots have become an almost
iconic new index of notoriety.[7] If all these processes are under way, what ends
are they serving? And how can they be interrupted?

These questions do bob up. They persist and nag. They are not necessarily
welcomed by rehabilitators, who genuinely seek empowerment for "their clients"
but face a double bind: the unspoken imperative remains that the elicited agency
must be limited to personal healing and recovery. Reflection on structural, insti-
tutional injustice—reflection that might lead to queries about the very system in
which rehabilitators work—is dubbed whining, a shirking from the accountability
that makes personal transformation possible.

This stance is unsurprising and emerges from a long, gendered history of
rehabilitative corrections. From their inception in the nineteenth century, gender-
specific rehabilitation and reform philosophies have urged that harsh punishment
be replaced by *a training in norms*. Thereby, the successfully retooled woman
would embrace self-regulation, a submissive femininity, and a vigorous gratitude,
ready to sign on unquestioningly to an American Dream that may well have
no place for her beyond permanent subjugation (Freedman 1984; Britton 2003;
Johnson 2004; Chesney-Lind and Pasko 2004).

The common contemporary therapeutic emphasis in criminal justice theory
on low self-esteem, addiction, and the coercive boyfriend seems to keep its focus
squarely upon the female "offender" (and a dangerous partner) and thereby to
lift scrutiny away from state practices and social conditions that may have had a

sweeping impact on a woman's choices (Richie 1996). Perhaps all the psycholo-
gizing is simply a stand-in for political analysis, a distraction, a way to discredit
and dissipate a well-earned rage that should not be "healed" but turned toward
activism. What is needed, surely, is not purging, but protest, not rehabilitation,
but radical change.

One could argue that, as practiced, "therapeutic" writing of the sort often
generated in my Inside-Out courses is at heart about releasing steam and rec-
reating acceptable confession narratives that presume guilt and emphasize only
gratitude. One might hearken back to a warning issued thirty years ago by Michel
Foucault to those who rushed to celebrate all "voice" as liberation (Foucault
1990). Looking around today, we can see what is valid in his warning: from the
judge to the priest to the oral examiner to the therapist to the talk show host,
the person who shapes the discourse often has more social power than she who
gushes forth, on cue, with a volley of words. Yes, not every talker gains from
her outpouring—think of the ridiculed guests on Jerry Springer or the rejected
contenders on reality TV, their lowbrow expressivity instigating guffaws. And
by contrast, think of the power held by the wizard of Oz, omnipotent only so
long as he is tucked silently away in his curtained box, unmarked as he pulls
the levers and orchestrates the showy hegemony out front. He is potent precisely
because he keeps his voice unheard.

As an object lesson in this regard, we might reflect on the wonderfully
titled video, *What I Want My Words to Do to You* (Gavin et al. 2003). (The
title quotes a creative writing prompt that inspires several great poems featured
in the film.) This 2003 documentary introduces playwright and monologist Eve
Ensler's longstanding creative writing workshop for women incarcerated in upstate
New York at Bedford Hills. This valuable project is marred somewhat, I would
argue, by its structural commitment to eliciting the penitence tale and by Ensler's
unquestioning claim of the right to act as confessor. In classroom sequences,
she pushes workshop participants to come to terms with their crimes as if that
were the only story they by rights had to tell; she appears consistently to funnel
the writers' speech into the confessional mode. Again and again the participants
gently, insistently deepen the conversation and carve out more room for nuance
than her initial stance allowed. (It must be noted, of course, that Ensler *includes*
these exchanges in her film and that she helped to sustain an atmosphere where
such free exchange could take place.) At one point, Ensler remarks that a mother's
neglect "is *the* core deprivation," and continues, "I would venture to say that
no one in this group had a core." Having overshot her role as facilitator, she is
corrected immediately in her presumption by women around the circle, one of
whom references the loving foundation offered by her grandmother, another of
whom suggests that with a circle of, say, executives on the outside, you would
be likely to hear the same yearning for parental attention. I am not convinced
that we understand the mass incarceration of women most deeply by seeking its
cause within the individual psyche. In 1970, George Jackson wrote from Soledad,

> For a real understanding of the failure of prison policies, it is senseless
> to continue to study the criminal. All of those who can afford to be
> honest know that the real victim, that poor, uneducated, disorganized
> man who finds himself a convicted criminal, is simply the end result
> of a long chain of corruption and mismanagement that starts with
> people like [then-governor Ronald] Reagan and his political appointees
> in Sacramento . . . All other lines of inquiry would be like walking
> backward. You'll never see where you're going . . . Men are brutalized
> by their environment—not the reverse. (Jackson 1994)

Must these women's writing process be above all about coming to terms with
their own guilt? What is lost when that storyline is made to predominate above
all others? As former Weather Underground member Judith Clark recites in
Ensler's documentary, "I want my words to leave you thirsty for complexity and
the deep discomfort of ambiguity . . . I want to make you wonder about your
own prisons. I want you to ask why." *What I Want My Words to Do to You* shows
both the (partly voyeuristic) impulse to demand confession from incarcerated
women and the "complexity" that is possible when the familiar narrative arc of
transgression and repentance is superseded.

Exactly this uncomfortable, fruitful complexity manifests itself in one of the
books on our reading list, Patricia McConnel's 1995 novel *Sing Soft, Sing Loud*
(McConnel 1995). McConnel's book is one of a very few full-length literary
works about incarceration by a woman familiar with the experience, particularly
rare because she was not incarcerated as a political activist. This novel shifts many
expectations. It shakes itself loose from a rigid, encapsulating assumption that
the incarcerated or formerly incarcerated woman who manages to pick up a pen
will surely confine herself to an account of her "self." Though McConnel does
emphasize in an afterword that much of what we read is based directly on true
life, this is not the author's *Bildungsroman;* this is not a confessional narrative
that concludes with salvation.

First, there are *two* narrators in *Sing Soft, Sing Loud.* Iva and Toni are distinct
from one another but not so tightly enmeshed as to be diametrical; they are
neighbors in the jailhouse community, and they speak and perceive differently.
Throughout the novel, women are sustained by singing, songs heard and shared
often beyond sight lines and across bars, through air vents and open windows.
This becomes a trope for solidarity and the power of unity across difference.
We listen to Toni and Iva describing the feel of their lives and the choices they
make and have made. They are not passive victims but active agents in their
own lives, though very real forces fiercely constrict the field of choices open to
them. The conclusion of McConnel's novel is remarkably hard to read and very
surprising. It is only through Toni's invocation of Herman Hesse's *Siddhartha* that
the reader finds the tools to understand what is, in essence a Gnostic/Buddhist
encounter with the annihilation of the self. This emerges out of crisis, a very
gendered moment of coerced sex work and a concomitant experience of profound

debasement and alienation. "The thread is broken," "a phone has been left off the hook." As the final chapter's narrative concludes, a new, almost dreamlike clarity sounds, as Toni picks up the reins but in search of a kind of renunciation of identity that crosses over into a deeply eerie liberation. The move, especially as a denouement, is utterly distinct from the expected endpoint of a Christian-inflected redemption and recovery narrative. Our culture's predominant stories about "rehabilitation" demand only a grateful echo from incarcerated women who write. McConnel's novel offers something far stranger and far more rich.

It looks to me, from within another workshop circle, that reading and writing in barrier-bending communities can lead precisely to the fruits and the "deep discomfort[s] of ambiguity" that typify McConnel's novel and that Judith Clark called for in Ensler's documentary. In so doing, this work may lead to other manifestations of change. And in this process, the personal cannot be disentangled from the political, except via a carefully manipulated tunneling of the conceptual field. If second wave feminism has left us with one lesson supposedly learned, it would be that (Women's Studies Listserv 2008). In our classes it seemed always obvious that "low self-esteem," domestic violence, sexual abuse, and all the tragic corollaries that spring from them do not occur in a vacuum. They occur across the full span of society, in every regional, cultural and economic niche. In fact, one telling and very gendered bond between us, in the Inside-Out circle, was how many of us, as women, knew firsthand about this kind of harm.

None of the authors we read limited themselves to either the personal or the political; all talked about both domestic and institutional violations and the crucial interplay between them. Jarvis Jay Masters, a Buddhist on death row at San Quentin, writes about the scars from childhood beatings marking his own body and those of his friends on the yard; he also reports the groans and astute commentary on his floor the day Thurgood Marshall resigned from the Supreme Court (Masters 1997). In her nineteenth-century abolitionist memoir, *Incidents in the Life of a Slave Girl,* Harriet Jacobs details the sexual harassment she endured from her owner, and with equally visceral disgust she lambastes the 1850 Fugitive Slave Law that turned Northerners into willing bounty hunters (Jacobs 2000). When we discussed Dorothy Allison's *Bastard Out of Carolina,* our conversation turned to the fact that all abuse unfolds in a larger context and is shaped by that context (Allison 2005). Tyrannical husband Number One, for instance, may also be a tyrannical boss who carries his sense of prerogative from arena to arena. But at-home Tyrant Number Two, by contrast, may be an exploited employee and a humiliated son, who vents his frustration on his family, like Bone's step-father in *Bastard.* In his role as domestic despot, the second man may actually be working in concert with the very social forces he resents the rest of the time, by compounding the struggles of the people he tyrannizes at home.

Further, the impacts of at-home violence are either treated or aggravated by conditions beyond the private sphere. Access to health care, housing, employment, even transportation and education opportunities, all so contingent upon economic means, are all relevant here. In class, students pointed out that many

of the women in Allison's novel are forced by poverty to persist in violent mar-
riages; these energetic women are not hogtied victims by any means, but because
of class inequities, they negotiate among an array of bad choices. (During one
term, this led to one of the most multifaceted and charged debates about pros-
titution I have ever witnessed in a classroom setting.)

Thanks in part to the careful circumscriptions provided by Lori Pompa's
pedagogic model, our reading and writing circle was a well-bounded safe space;
in this class, our intellectual and creative work often did emphasize healing, in
a way utterly foreign to standard procedure in a college classroom. Consistently,
the scope of our conversation widened from personal healing to broader social
and political issues about class disparities, racial tension, and the often-triggering
dehumanizations of the criminal justice system itself. Maxine, an inside student
in our class, argued that complaining about society or the government can be a
way for an individual—especially an individual addict—to evade the hard work
of thinking about his or her own accountability. But must it be? All told, our
conversations suggested that someone ready to embrace responsibility for her
own actions is *also* ready to function as an active agent in the civic sphere, and
that includes the demand for justice. A person cannot be an effective agent of
change, or of much else, if the wounds from violation go unaddressed.

Once we have begun to think in deep ways about the times we have caused,
witnessed, or survived harm, we will soon turn to the systems and contexts that
necessitate and produce injustice. Shoshana Pollack, fruitfully critiquing the typi-
cal deployments of "self-esteem discourse" among criminologists, remarks that
"*political agency*, the opportunity for effecting change in women's lives, provides
the context in which *subjective agency* evolves" (Pollack 2000). I would argue
that some version of the reverse is also true: subjective agency, once arrived at,
will—if given free reign and not corralled by the discursive pressure to self-
pathologize—lead inexorably toward political agency, or the hunger to seize it.

And that might be how a poem could be said to change anything. George
Oppen, a poet and political activist who felt that poetry and activism should
not be conflated, insisted that we recognize poetry's limits: "We must cease
to believe in secret names and unexpected phrases which will burst upon the
world" and through their sheer lucidity wreak political change (Oppen 2007). To
address this lingering challenge, I turn to the preface of a chapbook of writing
by women at Riker's Island (cited in Judith A. Scheffler's anthology of women's
prison literature, *Wall Tappings*). The chapbook preface declares:

> [T]his anthology is a crime. A crime of conspiracy, an informed,
> fully-consenting adult decision to commit poetry, an invention of the
> imagination that will never tear down the bars or break the system's
> back, but has ripped off some room for people to "breathe together"
> (another definition of "conspiracy") and pulled off a heist of institu-
> tional supermind, liberated the space as a continuum. This anthology
> is about possibilities. (Muske and Rosenblum 2002)

The chapbook itself is provocatively entitled *Songs from a Free Space,* and that is what creative collaboration can do; it may not "break the system's back" all at once, but it can claim a liberated space, between women or maybe just between the ears. One inside student writes:

> So here I must stay in / those rooms in my head.
> Take my rights, take my pride, / But this soul it is mine.

And that leads to "possibilities."

In profound ways, those possibilities are expanded upon, when the working circle brings together incarcerated and nonincarcerated students, as with Inside-Out. If power exists and asserts and replicates itself *via* a web of relations, concretized in institutional spaces and naturalized through repetition, then a shift in "empowerment" can itself only truly manifest *via* changing relations. Inside-Out's careful commitment to a dehierarchized pedagogy, to education as nexus rather than capital, and to the work of collaborative inquiry can set the stage for and even set in motion what Iris Marion Young calls "participatory democracy, critical self-reflection and collective action" (Young 1994).

Our responses to Jarvis Jay Masters (the Buddhist living on San Quentin's death row) we sent directly to the author, and each time we received from him a vivid, lengthy reply. One incarcerated student wrote to him, in part:

> When you talked about your scars, Oh my God, my tears were running down, because I've got painful scars, too. [. . .] Sometimes I think I am chasing death, that death is following me. [. . .] You made me realize that life is very important and not to give up. Jarvis, keep your head up. Keep up your good work with your books. [. . .] Just writing to you, I am crying like a baby, because I hate feeling that pain. Well Jarvis, take care and again, God bless you. I will keep you in my prayers. You are my new friend. (Esperanza)

This student had engaged effectively and bravely with Masters' book, and her to-the-bone responses to *Finding Freedom* educated all her classmates in what it means to read deeply. But encountering the same book means something different for readers who have never themselves been thrown into solitary confinement or heard violence break out in the middle of the night, never been strip searched or had their visiting privileges revoked on a whim.

One approach to this experiential gap came through the writing that inside students generated and shared with classmates. Nan's poem "Confinement" proved a lesson to the outside women in her class, while sounding the music that the inside women in the group all knew too well and felt moved to hear articulated:

> It is not being put in a physical space and made to stay that is
>   the prison.

It is the sound of the sally-port as it "CLANGS" into place
     behind you, the
"CLICK CLICK" of the cell door latch locking in.
The air pressure's "HISSSSS" of the cell door settling permanently
     into place.

The sound of the loud speaker, "Lock in, lock in for count."
The sound of the correctional officer's well-shined shoes, "clack,
     clack, clack,
clack,"
Pause "Clack, clack, clack, clack," as he tallies his prisoners.

The sound of seventy plus women in a cement and metal room
     all talking of the
lives they had, a roar of laughter, regrets, and threats of doing it
     again.

The sounds of voices building relationships through a ventilation
     shaft, "Hello,
who's that? Your baby's daddy?" Or a rap song drifting up from
     the hole. [. . .]

It's the sound of someone waiting in anguish, shedding soft silent
     tears, that
secures the soul and confines the mind.

To survive the sound of confinement one must remember the
     sweet sounds of
freedom, your daughter's voice, the purr of your cat, the wind in
     the treetops . . .

Nan's careful building of a soundscape here lets her readers hear how carceral power can ring along the senses; crucially, its clangs and hisses cannot drown out the contained but vibrant agency of the confined women Nan conjures in her poem. In a prose piece about the onset of confinement structured around descriptions of her own changing face, inside student Beth (real name) addresses her readers directly, with a challenge: "I am then led [from the courtroom] to a waiting area with holding cells. My face takes on another appearance at this point. 'O.K.—this is really happening.' *Imagine that look*" (emphasis mine). So, in instances of expressivity like Joanie's paper, Nan's poem, or Beth's prose, we see "empowerment" linked not to the power of positive thinking but to the work of communication. The writer's expressivity must be matched in kind by the reader's understanding ("imagine that look"), with the purpose of changing social relations by fostering a new comprehension across the deep divisions of stigmatization, class, and race.

This work took more than one form. Inside-Out classes have made me accept that parallels of which I have always been suspicious—and in fact that remain suspect—have an import and impact that cannot be overlooked, in the unfolding. It seems vulgar for people who have never been incarcerated to say that they know about what it feels like to be in jail because they have felt confined in a loveless marriage or by restrictive parents or even by the internal constrictions of their own neurosis. False equations dangerously elide important distinctions between people, differences that demand an alert, sober respect. But exactly such linkages were made in class, and these parallels mattered to all the participants *because they entailed an empathic negotiation in real time*—something happening in the room there and then through the act of exchanging stories for the purpose of understanding; in fact, most all the participants took heart from the fact that *everyone* in the class had suffered losses, injustices, that everyone in the class had had harm done to them and had themselves been the cause of harm. So when outside women expressed empathy about incarceration or life on the street or something else they might not have experienced directly (in part due to the dumb luck of racial or class privilege), and were able to locate that empathy by referencing struggles of their own, no matter how different, this did not alienate the incarcerated women in the circle, as I would have guessed it would. The multidirectional empathy and the courage that it took to share a story mattered more than the divisions between us.

That leads to a final point: the force of generosity in the class. Class time was studded with moments of kindness between students, when individuals took an assignment or in-class exercise as an unbidden opportunity to help another classmate. This generosity flowed in all directions and never bore the one-way strain of philanthropy. Students gave voice to each other's concerns, stepped in with words of encouragement when another student's spirits flagged, never dismissed one another for a failure to understand, and looked beyond and beneath classed (and raced) stereotypes about "college girls" and "convicts" to address the intellect and personality beyond. Examples included inside students supporting outside students who had loved ones facing incarceration . . . and who had never mentioned that fact in a school setting before. Then there was Maxine.

Maxine apparently did not do well after class ended; she was absent when we held an admissions event for inside participants at end of term. She had wrapped (concluded her sentence) a couple of days earlier, and according to staff, just fifteen minutes after she had landed at the voluntary rehab program and halfway house for which she had signed up, "she was seen on the streets, walking rapidly away, smoking a cigarette." Maxine was one hub of our classroom community, a beautiful woman who looked far too young to have a nineteen-year-old daughter; who had been incarcerated for drug-related offenses seven times; who talked in our class for maybe the first time ever about having been raped repeatedly by her father; who showed her love and generosity to the rest of us every class. The day author Dorothy Allison came to our class to talk with us about *Bastard Out of Carolina,* Allison talked about the lovable men in her family who could nonetheless "casually be monsters."[8] And Maxine had started to cry, hard enough that she headed out to the hall. A facilitator and a fellow student both jumped up to join her. When she came back, Maxine talked clearly and often all the rest of the morning. She had been strong enough to open up to a traumatic memory and thanks to the generosity of her fellows, strong enough to talk about it. The difficulties that loomed in her life so soon after our graduation in no way undermine the contributions she made as a student; they certainly do put the brakes on a too-utopian sunniness about Inside-Out's project of social transformation. A complex set of forces worked together to prompt Maxine's return to the streets. Staring directly at the limits of Inside-Out and other "change agents" in the face of such magnetic, cumulative, tragic force, one is left with a deep hope—that these agents are in fact working the way a powerful undertow works in the ocean (to use an image of Pompa's) to elicit a profound upheaval, a paradigmatic shift, even against the force of such tides.

The first year I taught the class, one student's final paper took up the topic of generosity. Hanna Wason (real name) begins with a catalogue of the many restrictions placed on any Inside-Out class, including, "No smoking allowed, and gift exchanges are unacceptable under any circumstances. Respect confidentiality; no full names. No point of contact after the class." She soon points out that, contraband regulations notwithstanding,

> gift exchanges became the focal point of our classroom. In fact, we all exchanged massive gifts that we may not have known we had . . . How did we get by the metal detectors and uniformed officers without being caught in the act? How could they not have noticed? While we were being monitored for our clothing and the items we brought into the classroom, our large gifts were invisible to anyone who was not a part of our precious circle. Our secret presents flooded our classroom, expanding across the room, bringing each person closer together . . . While we weren't allowed to tell one another our last names, I learned more about the women in my class than I know about my close friends . . . Through this class, I've learned that words make the best presents. They can be written down or verbally said; either way they are full of meaning. The best words are the ones that are spoken honestly and trustingly.

So perhaps we can benefit from thinking of education as part of a gift economy, rather than as cultural capital; we can go further and think of it as *contraband,* remembering the Riker's Island chapbook previously cited: "[T]his anthology is a crime of conspiracy [. . .] to 'breathe together' (another definition of conspiracy)." My cofacilitator Lysette Navarro remarks, "Inside-Out shows you that your mind and soul still belong to you. And then when that happens, there's a revolution in the room. You contribute something and speak out yourself, and then all of a sudden, everyone wants to give something, throw something in, you can feel the room shift, the automatic clicking as connections are made."[9] People typically talk about education as opening doors, and I will, too. Those doors open, however, not just to provide a point of entry to hopeful individuals eager to buy into society's predetermined avenues for upward mobility. No, these doors allow not just entry, but *egress*. And they leave us with a new map of where we live, new means to traverse social distance, and a new capacity to act collectively.

NOTES

Thank you to Lois Brown, Melissa Crabbe, Kerry Dunn, Holland Hendrix, Ashley Lucas, Lysette Navarro, Don O'Shea, Lori Pompa, and Don Weber.

1. Lori Pompa, e-mail message to author, October 1, 2007.

2. Some schools offer credit outright free of charge; some promise to extend retroactive credit should the student wind up enrolling later; some offer continuing education credits; some collaborate with a local community college or extend their staff education program to include inside students. Inside students who do not receive credit for these courses do at least emerge with certificates of completion, the professor's letters of recommendation, possible "good time" earned, and enhanced familiarity with college-level work. Admissions events organized by Inside-Out professors help illuminate the often-obscured path to higher education.

3. Voices from Inside, co-founded by Sara Weinberger and Carolyn Benson, is a nonprofit that offers creative writing workshops to incarcerated and formerly incarcerated women. Self-expression without self-determination, though, is a limited gain, so Voices from Inside also trains interested participants to lead such workshops themselves. A crucial further component of their mission is to provide venues to bring these voices *outside* so that personal growth is conjoined always with social growth. See also www.voicesfrominside.org.

4. Unless otherwise indicated, all student names listed here are pseudonyms.

5. The Sentencing Project tells us, for instance, that 73.1 percent of women in state prison in 2005 were identified as mentally ill (compared to 55 percent of men held in state prison). The Department of Justice's Bureau of Statistics reported in 1999 that almost 60 percent of women in state prisons had experienced physical or sexual abuse prior to their incarceration the figure for women in jails was 48 percent. More than 33 percent of women in U.S. prisons and jails the same year reported childhood sexual or physical abuse, while the prevalence for same among women in the general population is estimated at between 12 and 17 percent (Sentencing Project).

6. "Survey research shows that whites and African Americans report illicit drug use and illicit drug sales at similar rates. However, at the local level, African Americans are admitted to prison for drug offenses at much higher rates than whites. In 2002, African Americans were admitted to prison for drug offenses at 10 times the rate of whites in the 198 largest population counties in the country." And "as of 2003, twice as many African Americans as whites were incarcerated for drug offenses in state prisons." See Beatty, Petteruti and Ziedenberg 2–3.

7. For examples, see http://www.thesmokinggun.com or http://www.mugshots.com. There is much to admire in Ensler's documentary, but the high profile cases and high percentage of women in for murder in her workshop mean that *representativeness* is not among its virtues. In state prisons, 66 percent of the women incarcerated are there for nonviolent offenses. In the county system where I teach, 85 percent of the women are there for nonviolent offenses. Women who have killed have voices that matter; they do not, however, help us comprehend the reasons for the huge swell in the ranks of incarcerated women.

8. In-class remark, Dorothy Allison, April 20, 2007.

9. In conversation with author, March 2007.

APPENDIX: SELECTED READINGS,
INSIDE-OUT AT—COUNTY, 2006–2008

Agah, Azadeh, Shadi Parsi, and Sousan Mehr. 2007. *We Lived to Tell: Political Prison Memoirs of Iranian Women.* Toronto, ON: McGilligan Books.

Allison, Dorothy. 2005. *Bastard Out of Carolina.* New York: Plume.

———. 2007. "Stealing in College." Eds. Fiftal Alarid and Paul Cromwell. *In Her Own Words: Women Offenders' Views on Crime and Victimization, An Anthology.* New York: Oxford USA.

Baca, Jimmy Santiago. 2001. *A Place to Stand: The Making of a Poet.* New York: Grove.

Castillo, Ana. 2000. *I Ask the Impossible.* New York: Anchor.

Chevigny, Bell Gale, ed. 1999. *Doing Time: 25 Years of Prison Writing.* New York: Arcade.

Justice Works, Editorial Board. 1999. *Breaking Silence: Voices of Mothers in Prison.* New York: Justice Works.

Frank, Anne. 1993. *Anne Frank: The Diary of a Young Girl.* New York: Bantam.

Jacobs, Harriet A. 2000. *Incidents in the Life of a Slave Girl, Written by Herself.* New York: Penguin Classics.

Johnson, Paula. 2004. *Inner Lives: Voices from African American Women in Prison.* New York: New York University Press.

Lamb, Wally and the Women of York Correctional Institution. 2003. *Couldn't Keep It To Myself: Testimonies from Our Imprisoned Sisters.* New York: Regan/HarperCollins.

Masters, Jarvis Jay. 1997. *Finding Freedom: Writings from Death Row.* Junction City, CA: Padma.

McConnel, Patricia. 1995. *Sing Soft, Sing Loud.* Flagstaff, AZ, Logoria.

Scheffler, Judith A., ed. 2002. *Wall Tappings: An International Anthology of Women's Prison Writings, 200 to the Present.* New York: Feminist Press/CUNY.

Wilde, Oscar. 1996. "De Profundis" and "Ballad of Reading Gaol" (1898). In *De Profundis, Ballad of Reading Gaol and Other Writings.* Ware, Hertfordshire, UK: Wordsworth Editions, 1999.

Zehr, Howard. Portraits and Interviews. *Doing Life: Reflections of Men and Women Serving Life Sentences.* Intercourse PA: Good Books.

———. 2001. *Transcending: Reflections of Crime Victims.* Intercourse, PA: Good Books.

BIBLIOGRAPHY

Allison, Dorothy. 2005. *Bastard Out of Carolina.* New York: Plume.

Anderson, Charles M., ed. Spring 2000. Special issue of *Literature and Medicine* on the topic of "Writing and Healing." 19:1.

———, and Marian M. MacCurdy. 2000. Introduction. *Writing and Healing: Toward an Informed Practice.* Urbana, IL: National Council of Teachers of English.

Augustine of Hippo. 2001. *The Confessions of St. Augustine.* Trans. Rex Warner. New York: Signet.

Baca, Jimmy Santiago. 2001. *A Place to Stand: The Making of a Poet.* New York: Grove.

Britton, Dana. 2003. *At Work in the Iron Cage: The Prison as Gendered Organization.* New York: New York University Press.

Chesney-Lind, Meda, and Lisa Pasko. 2004. *The Female Offender: Girls, Women, and Crime.* Thousand Oaks, CA: Sage.

DeCou, Kate, and Sally Van Wright. 2002. "A Gender-Specific Intervention Model for Incarcerated Women: Women's V.O.I.C.E.S. (Validation Opportunity Inspiration Communication Empowerment Safety)." In *Serving Mentally Ill Offenders: Challenges and Opportunities for Mental Health Professionals,* ed. Gerald Landsberg, et. al. New York: Springer, 172–89.

Dostoevsky, Fyodor. 1985. *The House of the Dead.* Trans. David MacDuff. New York: Penguin,

Gavin, Madeleine, Judith Katz, and Gary Sunshine. 2003. *What I Want My Words to Do to You.* New York: American Documentary/POV.

Foucault, Michel. 1990. *The History of Sexuality: An Introduction, Vol. I.* New York: Vintage Reissue.

Freedman, Estelle B. 1984. *Their Sisters' Keepers: Women's Prison Reform in America, 1830–1930.* Ann Arbor: University of Michigan Press.

Gammel, Irene. 1999. Introduction. In *Confessional Politics: Women's Sexual Self-Representations in Life Writing and Popular Media,* ed. Irene Gammel. Carbondale: Southern Illinois University Press.

Greenfeld, Lawrence A., and Tracy L. Snell. December 1999. "Women Offenders." In U.S. Department of Justice, Bureau of Statistics. http://www.ojp.usdoj.gov/bjs/pub/pdf/wo.pdf (accessed January 2, 2008).

Harlow, Caroline Wolf. "Prior Abuse Reported by Inmates and Probationers." In U.S. Department of Justice, Bureau of Statistics. December 1999. http://bjs.ojp.usdoj.gov/content/pub/pdf/parip.pdf (accessed January 2, 2008).

Horton, Myles, and Paulo Freire. 1991. *We Make the Road by Walking: Conversations on Education and Social Change.* Philadelphia: Temple University Press.Inside Out. 2010. "The Inside-Out Center." http://www.insideoutcenter.org (accessed February 27, 2010).

Jackson, George. 1994. *Soledad Brother: The Prison Letters of George Jackson.* Chicago: Lawrence Hill Books.

Jacobs, Harriet A. 2000. *Incidents in the Life of a Slave Girl, Written By Herself.* New York: Penguin Classics.

Johnson, Paula. 2004. *Inner Lives: Voices from African American Women in Prison.* New York: New York University Press.

Jones, Ann Hudson. December 2006. "Writing and Healing." *The Lancet* 368: S3–S4.

Masters, Jarvis Jay. 1997. *Finding Freedom: Writings from Death Row.* Junction City, CA: Padma.

McConnel, Patricia. 1995. *Sing Soft, Sing Loud.* Flagstaff, AZ: Logoria.

McKenzie-Mavinga, Isha. 2002. "Creative Writing as Healing in Black Women's Groups." In *Working Inter-Culturally in Counselling Settings,* ed. Aisha DuPont-Joshua. New York: Routledge, 14–38.

Muske, Carol, and Gail Rosenblum, eds. n.d. *Songs from a Free Space: Writings by Women in Prison.* New York: New York City Correctional Institution for Women/ Free Space Writing Program.

Oennebaker, James W., and Lori D. Stone. 2003. "Translating Traumatic Experiences into Language: Implications for Child Abuse and Long Term Health." In *From Child Sexual Abuse to Adult Sexual Risk: Trauma, Revictimization and Intervention,* ed. Linda J. Koenig et. al. Washington, DC: American Psychological Association.

Oppen, George. 2007. *Selected Prose, Daybooks and Papers.* Ed. Stephen Cope. Berkeley: University of California Press.

Pollack, Shoshana. (2000). "Reconceptualizing Women' Agency and Empowerment: Challenges to Self-Esteem Discourse and Women's Lawbreaking." *Women and Criminal Justice* 12(1):75–89.

Richie, Beth E. 1996. *Compelled to Crime: The Gender Entrapment of Battered Black Women.* New York: Routledge.

Riley, Patrick. 2004. *Character and Conversion in Autobiography: Augustine, Montaigne, Descartes, Rousseau and Sartre.* Charlottesville: University of Virginia Press.

Rousseau, Jean-Jacques. 1995. *The Confessions; and Correspondence.* Ed. Christopher Kelly, Roger D. Masters, and Peter D. Stillman. Trans. Christopher Kelly. Hanover, NH: University Press of New England for Dartmouth.

Sentencing Project. 2007. "Women in the Criminal Justice System: An Overview." http://www.sentencingproject.org/doc/File/Women%20in%20CJ/women_cjs_overview(1).pdf (accessed February 27, 2007).

Sentencing Project. May 2007. *Women and the Criminal Justice System: Briefing Sheets.* http://www.sentencingproject.org/doc/publications/womenincj_total.pdf (accessed February 27, 2007).

Scheffler, Judith, ed., 2002. *Wall Tappings: An International Anthology of Women's Prison Writing, 200 to the Present.* New York: Feminist Press at CUNY.

Shaw, Margaret. 1995. "Conceptualizing Violence by Women." In *Gender and Crime,* ed. E. Dobash, R. P. Dobash, and L. Noaks. Cardiff: University of Wales.

Sheehan, Jacqueline. 2005. *Women Writing in Prison: An Anthology.* Chicopee, MA: Voices from Inside.

Silverman, Sue William. 2008. "Confessional and (Finally) Proud of It: For Women Only." http://www.suewilliamsilverman.com/work4.htm (accessed May 29, 2008).

Vicini, James. December 9, 2006. "U.S. Has the Most Prisoners in the World." Reuters. http://www.infoshop.org/inews/article.php?story=20061209152432728 (accessed February 27, 2010).

Warren, Jenifer, et. al. 2008. "One in 100: Behind Bars in America 2008." Pew Center on the States/Pew Charitable Trust. http://www.pewcenteronthestates.org/uploaded Files/8015PCTS_Prison08_FINAL_2-11_FORWEB.pdf (accessed February 27, 2010).

Women's Prison Association. May 2006. "The Punitiveness Report-HARD HIT: The Growth in Imprisonment of Women, 1977–2004." Women's Prison Association. http://www.wpaonline.org/institute/hardhit/index.htm (accessed February 27, 2007).

Women's Prison Association. December 2003. "WPA Focus on Women and Justice: A Portrait of Women in Prison." Women's Prison Association. http://www.wpaonline.org/pdf/Focus_December2003.pdf (accessed February 27, 2010).

Women's Studies Listserv. 2008. "Archived Discussion of Phrase 'The Personal is Political.' " http://userpages.umbc.edu/~korenman/wmst/pisp.html (accessed February 3, 2008).

Young, Iris Marion. (1994), "Punishment, Treatment, Empowerment: Three Approaches to Policy for Pregnant Addicts," *Feminist Studies* 20(1):50.

CHAPTER SEVENTEEN

Desiree

Leslie Levitas

Desiree had an air of confidence as she sauntered down the street. From her cockiness, you wouldn't know that she was on the run: running from an abusive husband in another state, running from the police in another county, most of all, running from herself. She'd finally stopped running when she landed on the bunk across from me in B-tank on the sixth floor of the county jail.

I'd been there for twelve days of a thirty-day sentence and knew the routine: endless repetition, day after day. The fluorescent lights went on at 5:00 a.m., and trustees started moving up and down the line, passing out watered down chicory from a brown urn. Then came the clatter of the thick plastic breakfast trays with cut out square sections for powdered eggs, soggy cream of wheat, and four slices of bread that tasted like cardboard. Four more slices came in the bag lunch and four more on the dinner tray. Meals could be predicted by the days of the week: hot dogs on Tuesday, chicken on Sunday, beans at least three times a week.

Then came pill call three times a day, mail call, phone lists to sign up for, inspection on Wednesday, laundry exchange twice a week. Each activity a rerun of a rerun, all punctuated by a constant droning over the loudspeaker by the guards: "Martinez, attorney visit. Baxter, roll it up."

An endless cycling of people streamed in and out of the clanging metal doors: inmates, social workers, chaplains, and so on. The guards changed with the clock at 7:00, 3:00, and 11:00. You knew what kind of night it was going to be because it was Friday, and Fisher was working the swing shift. If not for the orange sweatshirts and green jumpsuits that identified them, and perhaps a twist of fate, the guards and their charges might have been interchangeable: all doing time, in one way or another.

Gina

Desiree

How was it possible that so many women were being arrested in San Francisco? So many being warehoused in concrete and steel structures, designed to protect themselves or others? Many of these women I knew from the streets. Those I didn't all seemed to know each other. "Hey, cuz," said one to another, slapping five as if it were a family reunion. "How's your folks?" They'd probably never laid eyes on each other, but this was a way of establishing solidarity and letting people like me know what it was like to be in the minority for the first time in my life.

So when Desiree rolled in, I was a little relieved to see a familiar face from the Mission. A home girl, you might say. Even though we didn't really know each other, I'd seen her plenty of times moving up Sixteenth Street, smoking her camels, in and out of hotels, disappearing around corners, coming back an hour later with her Thunderbird, a bag from McDonald's, and money in her pocket. She seemed to know everyone: the dealers, the runners, even the cops.

We nodded to acknowledge each other, and I said, "What's up?" more as a statement than a question.

"I got caught in a sweep," she said. "Fucking Moran's trying to make Sergeant. Thinks he's slick."

"What do you mean?" I asked.

"He thinks I'm going down, but he's got a surprise coming," she said throwing her bedroll on the bunk.

Sweeps happened on a regular basis throughout the city. Mondays and Wednesdays for parolees. Tuesday and Thursdays for vice. It was all timed to coincide with court calendars and bus runs to state prison. This way, enough people could be moved through the system by Friday afternoon to make room for the ones who would come in over the weekend.

Desiree had made her bed and settled on her bunk and now pulled out a crumpled pack of cigarettes from who knew where. She had gotten them past the guards who'd strip searched her on the way in and knew she could get at least three dollars apiece for them here.

"Who's got some fire?" she asked, cavalierly. Another woman in the cell stared up blankly and rolled back over, sleeping her time away.

"Crystal's a trustee," said Lupe, a young Latina on the bunk below me. "She'll hook you up."

Desiree seemed to take being here in stride, with the same bravado that usually served her so well on the streets. Word was that she had at least three felony warrants but never seemed to do any real time. Some said she had dirt on a judge; others called her a snitch. Knowing she was wanted, she was usually careful, but this time she'd been in the wrong place at the wrong time. Despite her connections, she'd probably be here for a while, at the very least until a court appearance on Monday.

Some time later, I drifted off to sleep, thinking that at least someone relatively safe would be next to me for a few nights. My eyes opened early the next morning, following dreams of escape from jail, from reality, from the mess

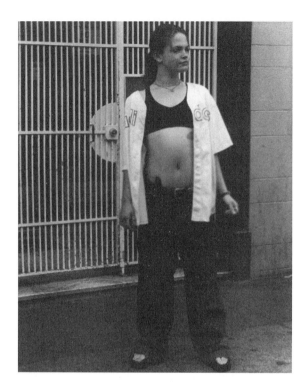

Meredith

I'd gotten myself into. Like every day, I mentally made note of my remaining time: seventeen days and a wake up. Coming fully awake, I glanced across and was startled to see that Desiree's bunk was empty. I leaned over the side of my bed and looked down at Lupe with dismay.

"Your homie bailed out about 3:00 a.m., mija," she said before I had a chance to ask.

How had that happened? I wondered. Sure, I was glad for her, but it seemed impossible that she even had a bail. Even if her current charges had been dropped, San Mateo County would surely have picked her up to face her charges there.

I laid back and stared at the ceiling, thinking about Desiree. She could get herself out of jail, but could she get it together to change her life? Odds were she'd probably already committed another crime of some sort by now.

And what about all the other women here with me? Was this just another system set up to fail us? Many had gotten through the education system without ever learning to read. The foster system left others neglected and abused. The health system labeled us and gave out legal drugs to alter our moods and behaviors. A hundred opportunities could come our way, but we might never recognize them, much less be able to embrace them.

Sure, Desiree had gotten out for now, but what was next for her? And for every Desiree who did, by some miracle, make it out of a self-imposed prison, there were a hundred others who wouldn't. Where would it end for them?

CHAPTER EIGHTEEN

Restorytive Justice: Theater as a
Redressive Mechanism for Incarcerated Women

Sara Warner

There are many different stories I could tell you about incarcerated women. The most obvious, and perhaps the most overwhelming, is statistical. The statistical story goes something like this: 1 out of every 100 citizens of the United States is currently behind bars. With more than 2.3 million people locked up, the United States has the highest incarceration rate in the entire world (Warren et al. 2008, 3).[1] While men are roughly thirteen times more likely to be jailed than women, females are the fastest-growing sector of America's prison population. Their numbers have increased at double the rate of males since the mid-1980s. One out of 265 women aged twenty-nine to thirty-five is currently serving time. If we break this number down by race, we see a marked (but not unexpected) disparity: 1 out of 355 white women; 1 out of 297 Hispanic women; and 1 out of 100 African American women are serving time (Warren et al. 2008, 6). The current incarceration rate for African American women exceeds that of white men as recently as the 1980s. If these patterns continue, and there is every indication they will, by 2010 there will be more female inmates in this country than there were people behind bars of both sexes just thirty years ago (Currie 1998, 14). Ironically, feminism and demands for parity have contributed to the escalation in incarceration rates and to increasingly repressive measures inside women's correctional facilities.

What is perhaps more alarming than the sheer volume of people currently behind bars is that crime has steadily declined in this country since the mid-1990s. From 1990 to 1998, murder rates fell by almost 50 percent, but during this same time period crime stories in the news quadrupled. While crime rates today are comparable to the 1970s, the incarceration rate is four times higher than it was then. In other words, it's not crime that has increased; it's punishment. A host of new facilities have been erected to house our surging inmate population. More than 3,300 new prisons were built in the United States during the 1990s, at a cost of $27 billion. In California alone, twenty-one new prisons have been constructed since the 1980s. The Golden State is home to thirty-three prisons that house more than 170,000 inmates, almost double the number they were designed to safely and humanely detain. California is also home to the largest jail on earth. The Twin Towers Correctional Facility, in the heart of Los Angeles, processes more than 6,000 arrests per day (Beiser 2001).

These staggering figures have inspired one journalist to crown our generation "The Age of Incarceration" (Gonnerman 2008). Statistical abstraction paints an alarming picture, but as an amalgamation of facts without a narrative structure, it does not explain why or how so many people in this country are incarcerated. As Angela Davis cautions, "unmediated use of statistical evidence . . . can discourage the very critical thinking that ought to be elicited," by these figures as "[i]t is precisely the abstraction of numbers that plays such a central role in criminalizing those who experience the misfortune of imprisonment. There are many different kinds of men and women in the prisons, jails, and INS and military detention centers," Davis reminds us, "whose lives are erased by" statistical abstraction (Davis 2003, 92).

To put these figures in perspective, I could, as Davis and others do, tell you the story of the rise of the prison industrial complex, which is best described as "a set of symbiotic relationships among correctional communities, transnational corporations, media conglomerates, guards' unions, and legislative and court agendas" whose interest is not in rehabilitating offenders but in making profit from their labor (Davis 2003, 107).[2] The prison industrial complex has roots in the convict leasing system, which provided inexpensive labor after slavery was abolished.[3] Corrections is one the country's top growth industries, with an increasing number of companies, state-owned prison industries, military contractors, and privately owned correctional facilities seeking to cash in on lucrative contracts.[4] Businesses such as Starbucks, Victoria's Secret, and Microsoft have become increasingly dependent upon the minimal operating costs of prison factories and cheap labor (for whom they pay no benefits such as healthcare or retirement to a workforce who cannot unionize). The proliferating prison industrial complex requires not merely a sustainable population of inmates but an expanding one.

Prison population has been bolstered by a slate of state and federal policies enacted in the past several decades. Bills such as California's "three-strikes" law (affirmed by the U.S. Supreme Court in 2003) and New York's Rockefeller laws (revised in 2009) impose longer terms and sentence offenders to mandatory jail time for nonviolent and first-time offenses. Tougher sentences for repeat offenders and stricter penalties for parole violations help ensure that more than half of inmates who are released are back inside within three years, so there is no shortage of laboring bodies (Davis 2003, 4). Mandatory drug-sentencing laws have had the biggest impact on incarceration rates, especially when it comes to women.

The number of women sentenced to prison for drug crimes rose 888 percent between 1986 and 1996. 58 percent of women in federal prison are serving time for drugs, compared with 48 percent of men (Lapidus et al. 2005, 3). The war on drugs has resulted in (yet another) war on women, and it has been particularly taxing on women of color, who are more likely to serve time and to serve longer sentences for similar offenses than whites. African Americans comprise 56 percent of all drug sentences but account for only 12.4 percent of users (Mauer and King 2007, 19). Black women are ten times more likely to be reported for substance abuse during pregnancy than women of other races (Lapidus et al. 2005, 30). In the prison industrial complex, minority women are subject to what Angela Davis calls "surplus punishment," disproportionate time behind bars layered on top of a "pandemic of private punishment," including institutionalized racism, sexism, and poverty (Davis 1998, 112).

Davis is a leading voice in the prison reform movement calling for restorative justice. Restorative justice is a broad term encompassing a variety of redressive measures promoting peaceful approaches to violations of legal and human rights. Proponents range from religious conservatives who advocate for faith-based initiatives inside correctional facilities to radical leftists such as Davis who call for decarceration and whose "ultimate aim" is "removing the prison from the social and ideological landscapes of our society" (Davis 2003, 107). Restorative justice is based on reparation and reconciliation rather than retribution and vengeance. Generally speaking, it conceives of crime as a violation of people and relationships, rather than a transgression of abstract law, and it promotes healing in addition to or in lieu of punishment.

Restorative justice is not a formula, but a foundational philosophy, one that is adapted to meet the needs of specific incidents, people, and sociocultural contexts. Many countries around the world have turned to restorative justice to combat a variety of social ills, including South Africa's much celebrated Truth and Reconciliation Commission (TRC), which employed these principles to address the injustices of apartheid and effect a remarkably peaceful transition to a nonracial democracy.[5] Many public officials in the United States are wary of restorative justice techniques because they are afraid they will appear soft on crime, thus alienating voters. Many nongovernmental agencies, however, have embraced this philosophy and have been working in conjunction with the legal system for decades and with a great deal of success.

In its most utopian incarnation, restorative justice serves as a counternarrative to the punitive discourse that categorizes our criminogenic legal system. More than simply an alternative way of telling the story of the prison industrial complex, restorative justice makes it possible to imagine a different ending, one in which so many people do not end up behind bars, or at least that is its promise. While there is much to admire about this holistic approach to transgression, restorative justice is not without its limitations. In this chapter, I explore some of the conceptual problems of a restorative justice approach when dealing with female offenders. I offer a hybrid model, what I call "restorytive" justice, as a corrective. Restorytive justice understands transgression as what Victor Turner calls a "breach in the social drama," and it utilizes ritual, specifically storytelling theater, as a redressive mechanism. This chapter concludes with an examination of the Medea Project's Theater for Incarcerated Women, which serves as a paradigmatic example of restorytive justice.

RESTORATIVE JUSTICE

The primary aim of restorative justice, as the name suggests, is to restore or make whole those who have been violated. Viewed through this lens, crime "creates obligations to make things right," says Howard Zehr. "Justice involves the victim, the offender, and the community in a search for solutions which promote repair, reconciliation, and reassurance" (Zehr 1990, 181). All three parties (called "stakeholders") are understood to suffer harm in varying degrees. Rather than perpetrators owing a "debt to society," which she pays by completing some form of state-imposed punishment (serving time, paying a fine, etc.), offenders owe a specific debt to the victim, a debt that can be repaid only by healing the damage caused. Instead of measuring how much punishment has been inflicted, restorative justice measures how much harm has been repaired or prevented. The goal is a balanced and cooperative approach that attends to the needs of everyone involved. This stands in sharp contrast to our current juridical system, which is focused almost exclusively on perpetrators. More time and money are invested in catching and punishing rapists, for example, than on counseling services and other social programs for victims, who are denied an officially recognized juridical interest in the justice system. In fact, the role of the victim typically ends when the crime is reported. Offenders are the center of a criminal trial, and victims may not even appear. Even if the victim does take the stand, her testimony may or may not be central to the proceedings. In other words, the one(s) most directly affected by crime are typically the least involved of all parties.

In restorative approaches to justice, stakeholders are encouraged to play an active role in the process rather than leaving resolution and restitution to agents of the state. The tripartite focus to heal injury, hold offenders accountable, and build peace and order within communities represents a more collaborative relationship among individuals, societies, and governments in responding to crime than the current penal system does. The four cornerstones of restorative justice are as follows: *encounter*, the identification of the damage caused by the crime; *amends*, the development of means to remediate the damage; *reintegration*, mobilization of community resources for the benefit and betterment of victims and offenders; and *inclusion*, incorporation of the victim(s) input into any formal criminal proceedings when necessary and/or appropriate (Van Ness and Strong 2006). Depending upon particular circumstances, one or more of the cornerstones may hold more weight. The degree of the victim's inclusion, for example, may differ depending upon the severity of the infraction, the risk participation holds for her, and/or the sincerity of the perpetrator.

There are many cases of successful restorative justice programs. There are also countless examples of failed interventions. There are many potential pitfalls, and even experiments conceived with the best intentions can go awry. It is very difficult to balance the multiple and conflicting needs of the stakeholders and to reach a conclusion that satisfies all parties. Lack of resources, improper training of mediators, inadequate oversight, and insufficient stakeholder preparedness can lead to disastrous results. There is no guaranteed that offenders will experience remorse and transform their behavior. They may simply go through the motions, performing gestures of repentance in order to escape punishment and, in some cases, offend again. Finally, there are some cases in which face-to-face encounters between stakeholders may intensify the harm, resulting in further victimization.

There are conceptual problems with the model as well, especially when dealing with female offenders. These include restorative justice's inability to effectively deal with (1) situations in which individuals are both the victim and the agent of crime, which women often are; (2) the fact that reintegrating offenders into the communities from which they came unwittingly reifies dysfunctional social structures that contributed to the harm in the first place; and (3) the overreliance on personal testimony, which often fails to take into consideration the ways in which rhetorical structures of confessing and witnessing reflect and reinforce society's racial, class, and gender biases.

Restorative justice operates on the assumption that criminal behavior is primarily a violation of one individual by another. Dependent as it is upon discrete stakeholder positions, restorative justice is not adequate to address partial or complex notions of guilt, innocence, and responsibility, as in cases where the agent of a crime is also a victim. This is particularly important when dealing with female offenders. Sixty percent of women behind bars report being physically and/or sexually abused, and many believe the number to be much higher (Greenfeld and Snell 1999). This abuse often goes unnoticed and unpunished, which greatly complicates the issue of the female offender's culpability.

If a woman kills her abusive husband in an act of self-defense, a link between victimization and criminal activity is easy to establish. Often, however, a connection is neither obvious nor direct, as in the case of sexual abuse. In a situation in which a mother turns a blind eye to the fact that a husband or lover is molesting her daughter and that child acts out by shoplifting, doing drugs, or engaging in prostitution, how can we expect any meaningful resolution to emerge by positioning this young woman as an offender when she is clearly both an agent and an object of crime? How can we expect a person in this situation to feel remorse for her actions and change her behavior when the more heinous crimes committed against her are likely to go unacknowledged and unaccounted for?[6]

Restorative justice casts the third stakeholder, society, as an injured party that is made whole by the reintegration of both victim(s) and offender(s) into its fold. All too often, however, the social is guilty of conspiring in the victimization, as in the molestation scenario I just outlined. In such cases the community engenders or sanctions the offense in question. How does restoring a victim of sexual abuse to a family and/or community that condones violence against women achieve anything close to justice?[7] As Dennis Sullivan and Larry Tifft note, the harm caused by misogynist, racist, and classist social structures is much more pervasive and damaging than any single crime (2001). Rather than fleshing out the complex ways in which harm affects people's abilities to lead safe and healthy lives—which in this case might involve drawing attention to childhood sexual abuse as a systemic defect of the heteronormative nuclear family structure—restorative justice focuses its efforts on reintegrating victims and offenders back into the diseased communal fabric. For restorative justice to really work, it must insist upon societal transformation.

Some scholars and practitioners have suggested that restorative justice represents a feminist response to crime because it focuses on care instead of punishment. Eschewing reliance upon state power to exact a resolution, it encourages forgiveness, love, and mercy. Others have ventured that restorative justice reflects a precolonial, non-Western approach to transgression and a return to premodern and/or indigenous approaches to justice.[8] According to Kathleen Daly, this type of logic relies upon false binaries and power inversions in which subordinated and marginal groups are aligned with more superior justice forms (Daly 2002). It homogenizes racial, cultural, and gender differences; romanticizes alterity; and may result in unjust resolutions that reinforce oppressive social hierarchies.

A prime example of the ways in which deeply entrenched asymmetrical forms of social relations can uncritically play themselves out in restorative justice programs involves the rhetorical structures of confession and witnessing. Whereas courts of law and juridical proceedings aspire to a dispassionate quest for the truth, restorative justice facilitates a passionate pursuit of reconciliation. Proceedings rely heavily upon testimony in which stakeholders recount not only the "facts" of the case but also their feelings about the offense. In a typical encounter, parties meet (face-to-face or through a mediator) to give their side of the story, describing in detail what happened and its affects. In an ideal situation, these subjective accounts facilitate empathy among the parties, which is thought to be necessary for reconciliation. Confessions and pleas for forgiveness remind us of the relational wounds caused by crime. While such encounters can be healing for both victims and offenders, this model fails to take into consideration the fact that modes of confessing and witnessing tend to conform to predictable narrative modes of address and expectations for comportment that inflect and inscribe a homogenous set of discursive and political effects. These structures are laden with socioculture biases. Parties who follow the established and expected scripts of repentance are rewarded, while those who do not can be penalized.

Taking the issue of harm seriously requires an approach that does more than reify a flawed system or bolster misogynist and racist ideologies. Attending to the complexities of social deviance, criminality, and victimization requires adapting and revising traditional restorative practices. Julie Stubbs suggests that this may be best accomplished by the development of hybrid models that draw from a variety of structures, including the criminal justice system (Stubbs 2007). What I call "restorytive justice" is one such model. It opens up possibilities for telling new stories about crime because it focuses on storytelling itself as a redressive measure. The inspiration for this concept is the Medea Project: Theater for Incarcerated Women, a San Francisco–based community arts organization.

RESTORYTIVE JUSTICE

Restorytive justice is a redressive mechanism designed to remediate crimes in such a way that the victim, offender, and social are all potentially transformed by the experience. A crime is one example of what anthropologist Victor Turner calls a "breach" in the social order. A breach constitutes the first act in a *social drama*, "a sequence of social interactions of a conflictive, competitive, or agonistic type" (Turner 1988, 33). If serious, it produces a *crisis*, which is resolved through the deployment of *redressive machinery*. Redressive machinery can take various forms, such as codified legal proceedings, religious injunctions, or informal arbitration hearings. If successful, the social drama concludes in *reconciliation*, and if not in a *schism*, in the parties agreeing to differ and/or to continue the conflict. The purpose of the redressive phase of the social drama, according to Turner, is not only to ameliorate crisis but to "attempt to ascribe meaning to 'social dramatic' events" (Turner 1982, 12). This phase entails, in other words, creating a story we tell ourselves about ourselves, about how we came to crisis, how we will repair the breach—or not—and what effect the reconciliation or schism will have on our lives and in the world.

Redressive machinery involves some sort of ritualized and/or aestheticized cultural performance. While this is typically deployed in and through a court of law (or one of its surrogate venues), it can be staged in other sites, including the theater. Turner sees "in theatre something of the investigative, judgmental, and even punitive character of law-in-action, and something of the sacred, mythic, numinous, even 'supernatural' character of religious action—sometimes to the point of sacrifice." Greek tragedy in particular serves as "a hypertrophy, an exaggeration of juridical and ritual processes" (Turner 1982, 12). It enacts social dramas, depicting individuals and communities in crises striving for resolution. The protagonists struggle to remediate breaches they themselves precipitated, sometimes knowingly and sometimes in ignorance.

The primary difference between these two modes of redressive machinery, the law and theater, according to Turner, is that the former operates in the *indicative* mode, on the level of facts and actual outcomes, and latter in the *subjective* mode, on the level of fiction and hypothetical possibilities. The law tells us what is, while theater shows us "all that may be, might be, could be, perhaps even should be" (Turner 1982, 77). The law is conservative—by which I mean it seeks to conserve the status quo, to protect it from harm or change. Theater, on the other hand, may serve as a conservator of extant practices and ideology, but it can also function as a source of new images and new ideas.

While the law seeks to restore balance after a breach, theater, I want to suggest, enables us to "restory" or "rescript" the social order.

Prison theater can serve as a powerful weapon in understanding and healing breaches in social dramas in ways that do not simply reinforce the very social structures that gave rise to the crisis in the first place. Its efficacy stems, in part, from the fact that it is an embodied and participatory form of learning. Theater promotes literacy, involves physical exercise, encourages community building, and helps keep the inmates engaged. I do not mean to suggest that perpetrators should be sentenced to acting class instead of jail or that people should perform plays instead of completing community service. As a form of restorytive justice, prison theater is most efficacious when it works in conjunction with the courts and the criminal justice system. As paradoxical as it might sound, imprisonment can be liberating for some inmates, especially for women. The razor wire separates female offenders from (at least some of) the people and forces that led them to criminal activity. The theater workshop occupies what Turner calls a "liminal" space, a space betwixt and between the *indicative*—the real world where individuals are reduced to their prison ID numbers or criminal labels such as "drug addict," "whore," and "thief"—and the *subjunctive*—where individuals can not only "be themselves" but rehearse new identities and new ways of being in the world.

THE MEDEA PROJECT'S THEATER FOR INCARCERATED WOMEN

Of the hundreds of progressive, arts-based programs inside America's correctional facilities, the Medea Project: Theater for Incarcerated Women provides the most provocative model of restorytive justice. For more than twenty-five years, Rhodessa Jones, the founder and artistic director, has led a volunteer team of artists, activists, social workers, and formerly incarcerated women in the creation of original theatrical performances with inmates at San Francisco County Jail. In the late 1980s, Jones, a performance artist and activist, was hired by the jail as an aerobics instructor. Though this was her first job working with inmates, she was hardly a stranger to "the life." The eighth of twelve surviving children born to migrant laborers, Jones has had her share of narrow escapes with violence, drugs, poverty, and domestic abuse. An unwed mother at sixteen, she worked as an exotic dancer to support herself and her child. Her own story could have come to a tragic end were it not for theater, which she credits with saving her life.

During aerobics the inmates would talk, sharing stories about their lives. These conversations led Jones to create a one-woman show based upon four women in the class. *Big Butt Girls, Hard Headed Women* played to packed houses across the country and garnered numerous awards, inspiring Jones to create a company with inmates who would not only write and produce their own material but stage it at professional theaters for public audiences. Jones' dream was possible because she lives in San Francisco, a city that is invested in utopian idealism, supportive of radical social experimentation, and positioned at the vanguard of the penal reform movement.⁹ The sheriff at that time was Michael Hennessey. He sent shockwaves through the system when he hired Michael Marcum, a civilian and a convicted murderer, as his assistant sheriff (Benner 2000). Marcum, who at age eighteen shot and killed his abusive father, served seven years in a maximum security prison. He saw more violence and brutality behind bars than he ever did at home. When he was released, he had no job skills and no prospects. The only thing prison prepared him for was a life of crime.

Marcum vowed to make a difference for battered women and abused children and to advocate for more effective rehabilitation programs in correctional facilities. He became a counselor who impressed Hennessey to such an extent that the sheriff promoted the excon to a top position over the objections of his staff and in opposition to public protests. Before he retired, Marcum worked at San Francisco County Jails 7 (the men's unit) and 8 (the women's unit), which he called "program facilities," where he oversaw the implementation of innovative rehabilitation efforts for inmates, whom he called "clients," including yoga, Buddhist meditation, and classes such as Gay Life Skills. When Jones approached Marcum about a theater program for female inmates, he endorsed it and forwarded it to Hennessey, who gave the green light for a pilot program.¹⁰ The Medea Project made its debut to a sold-out audience at San Francisco's Theatre Artaud in 1992.¹¹

Hennessey, Marcum, and Jones agreed on the following conditions for the theater program: participants must be approved by the Sheriff's Department and must consent to all security protocols. Inmates must be in good standing to enroll in the workshop. During the show's run at the public theater, inmates must be escorted and monitored at all times by uniformed, armed guards. Participants are allowed to change out of their jail-issued orange jumpsuits to don costumes for the show, but they must wear their identification bracelets, and they must be on stage and visible at all times. Uniformed, armed guards must be positioned at all entrances and exists to the theater and stationed in the front row of the audience, creating a hypervisible "fourth wall" between the actors and spectators. This is to prevent prisoners from fleeing the scene, to ensure the safety of patrons, and to protect the inmates, who may have an enemy, accomplice, or pimp with malicious intentions in the crowd.

The theater program group took its name from the subject of their first production, an adaptation of the ancient Greek tragedy *Medea* by Euripides. A woman in the workshop, Deborah, was arrested on charges of infanticide and was awaiting trial. She had committed what many consider to be one of the most horrifying acts imaginable. A chemist with a degree from UC Berkeley and a promising career, Deborah did not fit the stereotypical profile of a criminal. Her problems began when she started dating a drug user who introduced her to cocaine. Deborah soon became addicted both to crack and to this man. Caught in a downward spiral, she sacrificed everything: career, self-respect, even her child. When Deborah's lover left her for another woman, she, high on drugs, smothered their baby.

Child killers, like pedophiles, don't fare well behind bars. The other inmates ostracized and taunted Deborah mercilessly. This situation reminded Jones of *Medea*, a play about a queen who relinquishes her throne, her country, and her family for a man who leaves her for another woman when she is no longer useful. In retaliation, Medea kills their two sons. Jones told the inmates this story and asked them to explore the myth in relationship to their own lives. She gave them a series of questions as guidelines: Why do women love so much? Why are women willing to sacrifice everything, including their children, for a man? and Is being in jail and losing custody of your children any more or less of a sacrifice than the one Medea made? In response to Jones' questions, the participants wrote essays, poems, raps, and monologues about their experiences.

Medea struck a chord with the inmates. In fact, the Greek myth seemed almost tame in comparison to the stories the inmates told, which included traumatic episodes, extreme violence, and near-death experiences. "Storytelling," as Rena Fraden has observed, "can be a con game, a trick used against one's foes. It can also be the beginning of a different drama—a way to imagine, if not live out, a new life" (Fraden 2001, 48). Some of the stories the women told in response to the myth of Medea were true, but most of them blended fact with fiction. Many were outright lies. Participants do not always tell the truth in Medea Project workshops, especially not in the beginning. For many women, the truth is simply unbearable. For others it is buried too deep to excavate. Some fear the repercussions of divulging a secret they were told never to tell. Some choose not to make themselves vulnerable to people whom they will encounter again on the street, a hostile world where their stories could be used as ammunition against them. Some simply see no reason to trust a room full of strangers.

Whether or not a woman speaks the truth, she benefits from the opportunity to tell her story. Each participant decides which story she wants to tell and how she wants to tell it. Regardless of its veracity, the participant tells the story to the group *as if* it were true. The embellishment of fact with fiction is an important part of the theatrical process. It is also, as we shall see, an integral part of the healing process. Most of the participants' stories take place in the realm of what political philosopher and playwright Drucilla Cornell calls "the imaginary domain," which she describes as "the moral and psychic space to dream and to make sense of one's own person," the space "to reimagine and express the person whom we seek to be" (Cornell 2002, xx). The imaginary domain "gives to the individual, and to her only, the right to claim who she is through her own representation. Such a right "necessarily makes her the morally and legally recognized source of narratives and resymbolization" (Cornell 1998, 10). Cornell argues that a claim must be made in the imaginary domain before principles of distributive justice can be defended or enacted in the real world.

Restorytive justice operates in the imaginary domain, in the realm of the subjunctive. It expresses possibilities, dreams, and wishes, blurring fact with fiction and fantasy with reality. This differentiates it from most modes of redressive machinery, including our judicial system. The law, like theater, is rooted in ritualized forms of storytelling, but the genres it employs—confession, testimony, witnessing, and so on—are all discourses of truth, at least in theory anyway. The pursuit of truth is, in essence, the path to justice. Juridical discourse is dependent upon the idea that an impartial and objective truth exists. Failure to establish "the truth and nothing but the truth" fundamentally detracts, theoretically speaking, from the legitimacy of the enterprise. Unlike the law, restorytive justice does not seek to deduce the truth. On the contrary, it is grounded in the notion that truth (with a capital "T") is not only impossible to achieve in most cases but it is often an unnecessary, perhaps even undesirable, element of the story.

The Medea Project's process highlights the difference between the limited efficacy of juridical models of truth and the unlimited potential of theater's indeterminacy. It works against the notion that there is a singular and definitive account that could encapsulate the accumulation of forces and events that lead women to criminal behavior. In lieu of a verdict, Jones works toward the production of a multiplicity of truths, not all of which can (or even should) be reconciled into a grand narrative. Rather than conceiving of justice as something that is served by ascertaining the truth, the Medea Project asks us to think of justice as a story without an end, as a story that never ends.

Of course, theatrical productions must have an end. They often have a beginning and a middle as part of their narrative arc as well. Jones achieves this by selecting stories told by the inmates and stitching them together into a production. In that inaugural workshop, she and a key member of her troupe, actress and director Edris Cooper-Anifowoshe, created a loose adaptation of the Greek tragedy based upon the inmates' stories, which they titled *Reality Is Just outside the Window: The Tragedy of Medea Jackson*.

The myth of Medea has an unexpected and, for many people, unsettling ending. After murdering her children and refusing their father's request to bury them, Medea escapes in a winged chariot sent by her grandfather, Helios, god of the sun. She is never brought to trial, and her crimes go unpunished. In rehearsals, the inmates balked at the idea that the protagonist would get away with murder. They felt it was important to hold Medea accountable for her crimes and insisted that she be arrested. Jones said she would craft the script according to their wishes, but she encouraged the women to think beyond Medea's incarceration, to imagine what Medea's life will be like once she has served her time and is released from prison. Jones also asked the participants to consider what might have happened to Medea had she made different choices. Would she have been able to avert crisis?

What the inmates came to understand through the rehearsal process is that the issue of Medea's guilt is quite complicated. The only innocents in the story are the children. Everyone else is culpable of some offense: Medea, her husband, her husband's mistress (the princess), the mistress's father (the king), and the chorus. The king, motivated by self-interest—he wants his daughter to marry Medea's husband—rather than his duty to protect the citizenry, adds insult to injury by banishing Medea, exacerbating her murderous rage. The chorus is guilty because it knows something foul is afoot, but it does nothing to intervene. In Greek tragedy the chorus represents the community. By failing to act, the chorus enables Medea's heinous crimes to take place. All parties in the play are, to some extent, both victims and agents of crime, so why should Medea be the only one who is punished?

The murder of the children is a breach so deep that reconciliation and a restoration of the social order are not possible. Medea's departure from Corinth signals the disintegration of her family and the dissolution of the political structure. There is no hope of saving her marriage and no attempt to rescue the city from the brink of destruction, and there is never any suggestion that Medea could or should be reintegrated into the communal fold. The myth, in other words, forecloses the possibility of restorative justice. Nothing much survives the devastation, except, of course, the protagonist. One might go so far as to say that Medea's survival depends upon Corinth's destruction, or at least her extraction from it. The myth ends with the queen en route to a new home in a new land. There is no indication that this place will be better than where she came from, but it does represent change and the possibility of a different life. The fact that the myth ends on such an ambiguous note prompts the participants in Jones' workshop to interpret Medea's future for themselves, and the possibilities are limited only by their imagination.

It was an act of serendipity that Jones gravitated toward Medea during that first workshop, but she knew a winning formula when she stumbled upon it. The myth of Medea served as a productive point of departure for the troupe because it touched upon many of the most pressing issues in the participants' lives. Since the theater program's inception in 1992, Jones has used a mythic narrative as the foundation for every one of the group's productions. Each myth offers a unique set of possibilities and challenges for the troupe and presents a different set of questions and quandaries for the participants to explore. An early production used Demeter and Persephone to deal with kinship issues, mother/daughter bonds, and sexual abuse (as Persephone is abducted and assaulted by Hades in the story). Another group riffed on Sisyphus to investigate cycles of violence, addiction, and recidivism. Yet another began with Inanna, a myth about a Sumerian queen who journeys to the underworld and back, which served as a gateway to discuss the descent into criminal behavior and the obstacles facing recovery.

Myths refuse what Megan Sweeney calls " 'know-it-all' criticisms, common sense scripts, and . . . narrow . . . notions of reasonableness," while simultaneously allowing the inmates to tell "the kinds of stories that make perfect sense to women who end up behind bars" (Sweeney 2004, 469). Myths transport us from the quotidian time into messianic time, dissolving the restrictive confines of the real. They operate outside the logic of simple cause and effect, eschewing the binary logic of true/false. Mythic narratives work well for Jones because these stories are subjunctive, pure potential. Even if a story starts out as "the truth and nothing but the truth," it moves from the indicative to the subjunctive as it is crafted for inclusion in the theatrical performance.

Myths do not depict easy solutions to complex problems, nor do they reassure us with happy endings, such as those found in contemporary fairy tales. They do, however provide a productive way for thinking about social breaches and their solutions and about crime and its consequences. Myths provide no answers, only questions. As Walter Benjamin has observed, the most powerful stories are the ones that are "free from explanation" (Benjamin 1986, 89). In myths, "the most extraordinary things, marvelous things, are related with the greatest accuracy, but the psychological connection of the events is not forced upon the reader. It is left up to him to interpret things the way he understands them" (Benjamin 1986, 89). Interpretations of myths may become fixed, but the stories themselves remain fluid and open to endless rereadings. The rereading and retelling of life stories constitutes the work of the Medea Project.

With all this talk of myth, the Medea Project might sound to some like child's play. While Jones encourages the women to have fun—which helps them feel safe, open up, and deal more effectively with the root of their troubles—her theater workshop is serious business (and it should not be emulated without carefully considering the risks involved). It is incredibly difficult for participants to share their stories and even more painful to rehearse them over and over again. In acting out these stories, the inmates physically and psychically reinhabit old wounds, relive dangerous situations, and revisit some of their most difficult memories. The stories are shared with the group, by which I mean they are retold and reenacted by many members of the workshop. The goal is to generate as many different ways of rendering the story as possible and to show inmates how their behaviors and actions are interpreted by others. This helps participants assess an event, to gauge what happened and why, to think about how things might have had unfolded differently, and finally, to strategize new ways of reacting to a similar situation should it arise in the future.

Jones grants the women a great deal of autonomy in deciding how to stage their stories. In the workshop and public performance, for example, Deborah must decide how she wants to tell her tale. Where does she begin? What does she make the central focus: the man, the drugs, or the crime? Does she paint herself as a victim? Does she cast herself as an agent? Does she include mitigating circumstances, such a family history of substance abuse or violence? What about the infanticide? How does she narrate this? In the storytelling workshop, Deborah can rehearse a variety of possibilities. She can play the protagonist as the woman she was, the woman she became, as well as the woman she never was (and perhaps never will be) but wishes to become. The responses from the workshop participants affect the way Deborah tells her story and, more important, how she revises and reshapes it for performance. Changes in Deborah's delivery can impact the way the other women see and treat her, which, in turn, influences how she feels about herself and acts toward others.[12]

This rescripting of "social dramatic events" is a key component of restorytive justice. It takes place in the jail during the workshop process and later, on a larger scale, at the theater during the public performance. During rehearsals, women have the opportunity to address the harm they have done to themselves and to other women. The public event provides a forum in which they can make amends for wrongs they have committed against members of their family, their associates, as well as the community at large. They can speak out against those who have harmed them and against those who stood by while the abuse was inflicted. The audiences at Medea Project performances do more than see a show; they bear witness to the lives of the inmates and to their role—as members of society—in both the breach and its redress. Spectators are implicated in these women's stories, implicated in the social drama of prison reform.

Storytelling is an inherently communal experience. Though ephemeral, stories make an impression on both the teller and the listener. As Benjamin has observed, "[t]races of the storyteller cling to the story the way the handprints of the potter cling to the clay vessel" (Benjamin 1986, 92). By revisiting a Medea Project performance in their heads once the show is over or by recounting the experience to family, friends, or coworkers, an audience member is transformed into a storyteller, into a participant in the Medea Project. Like the inmates, these storytellers will have to decide what tales to tell, how to tell them, to whom, and under what circumstances. In this way, Medea Project performances position audience members as cocreators of meaning in the act of restorying the social.

In contrast to commercial theater, the Medea Project does not end when the final curtain falls. In many ways, the drama is just beginning. While Jones and her troupe would like the inmates' stories to have happy endings, the truth is that most of them will not. There are a number of Medea Project graduates, remarkable women like Felicia Scaggs and Angela Wilson, who stop using drugs, get jobs, regain custody of their children, and lead productive lives after they leave the program. Most participants, however, serve their time and return straight to "the life" they have always known. The majority of them will find themselves back in jail. Some women will take part in Medea Project workshops multiple times, with little or no lasting impact. Jones is under no delusion that her theater experiment is a panacea that is going to radically transform the lives of most participants. Incarcerated women face incredible obstacles on the road to recovery. The Medea Project is a struggling nonprofit organization that works with inmates for a very short time period. It is not a rehabilitation facility, and there is limited contact with participants once the show is over.

With such a negligible success rate, what is the efficacy of the Medea Project? Why should taxpayers support restorytive justice projects like this? To put it simply, the only way we are going to intervene into the social drama of incarceration in this country is to think outside the box. In order to tell ourselves different stories about crime and punishment, rehabilitation and recidivism, we must support radical efforts at reform. In order to do that, we have to challenge the largest group of stakeholders, the community, which is where the Medea Project has its greatest impact. Thousands upon thousands of people have attended Medea Project performances. A typical audience includes friends and family members of the incarcerated women, members of the Sheriff's Department, government officials, social workers, political activists, artists, and average theater-going citizens. Over the years, people have been so moved by a production that they have come forward with offers of financial support, job opportunities, scholarships, and a host of other services. Jones routinely receives applications to join her troupe and requests for help in starting similar programs in other facilities. These donations of time and money are essential to the continued functioning of the Medea Project and related organizations.

The Medea Project challenges us to imagine a time and a place where women no longer have such stories to tell, and it inspires me to work toward making that time a reality. I attended my first Medea Project performance in 1996, while a graduate student at San Francisco State University. When I moved to New Jersey to complete my PhD at Rutgers, I invited Jones and her troupe to campus to perform and to share their process with the local community. It was the first time formerly incarcerated women had traveled with the group outside of the Bay Area. The university production was much less dramatic than a typical Medea Project show, by which I mean there were no paddy wagons escorting the participants to and from the theater, no armed guards occupying the exits and entrances, and no orange wrist bands distinguishing the incarcerated women from the volunteer members of the troupe. If the audience response was any indication, the show was no less powerful. This event convinced me that anyone who sees or reads about a Medea Project production becomes implicated in the process of restorytive justice. By recounting this history, I now implicate you. I'm optimistic that some of you will become storytellers, passing on the tales of these resilient women. Each retelling is a rehearsal of a more just society.

NOTES

1. This number rises considerably if we factor in people on probation or parole.

2. "Prison industrial complex" was coined by Mike Davis. See "Hell Factories in the Field: A Prison Industrial Complex," *The Nation* 260 (7) (February 20, 1995): 229–34.

3. After the abolition of slavery, the South developed laws to restrict the freedom of newly emancipated blacks. These Black Codes were rearticulations of Slave Codes, and they racialized crime and punishment. Within relatively short periods of time, blacks outnumbered whites in jails and prisons across not only the South but the entire United States, and the penal system assimilated various forms of punishment associated with slavery. See Davis, *Are Prisons Obsolete?* especially chapter 2.

4. More inmates mean more budget dollars go to corrections, which leaves less money for things like education, health care, transportation, infrastructure, and sustainability research. It costs states on average twenty-five thousand dollars per annum to maintain an inmate, whom we cannot expect to pay child support, restitution, or taxes while incarcerated. In the past twenty years, the amount of money the government spends on corrections has quadrupled, to a whopping $49 billion per annum. One out of every fifteen dollars in a state's budget is earmarked for corrections, or about 6.8 percent of the average operating costs (Warren et al. 11–16). If we combine these figures with the billions we have spent on Bush's "War on Terror," it is no wonder we find ourselves in the midst of a recession.

5. In the case of South Africa, the TRC was seen as a way to restore justice but also as a way to transition to a new form of government. This process is also known as "transitional justice," a way of moving to a democratic form of government. See Priscilla Hayner, *Unspeakable Truths: Confronting State Terror and Atrocity* (New York: Routledge, 2001). The establishment of the TRC and the choice to employ restorative justice techniques instead of holding a war crimes tribunal in the wake of apartheid is not without its critics. See Kader Asmal et al. *Reconciliation through Truth: A Reckoning of Apartheid's Criminal Governance* (New York: St. Martin's, 1998); Alex Boraine, *Country Unmasked: South Africa's Truth and Reconciliation Commission* (Oxford: Oxford University Press, 2001); and Kenneth Christie, *The South African Truth Commission* (New York: St. Martin's, 2001). For perspectives on postapartheid policies a decade after the transition, see Grant Farred and Rita Barnard, eds., *After the Thrill Is Gone: A Decade of Post-Apartheid South Africa* (Durham: Duke University Press, 2004).

6. Childhood sexual abuse offers many challenges to the foundational assumptions of restorative justice. See Ann-Marie McAlinden, "Are There Limits to Restorative Justice? The Case of Child Sexual Abuse," in *Handbook of Restorative Justice: A Global Perspective,* ed. Dennis Sullivan and Larry Tifft (New York: Routledge, 2006), 299–307.

7. This matter may be especially complicated in immigrant communities. See Rashmi Goel, "Sita's Trousseau: Restorative Justice, Domestic Violence, and South Asian Culture." *Violence Against Women* 11(5) (2005): 639–65.

8. See John Braithwaite, "Restorative Justice: Assessing Optimistic and Pessimistic Accounts," in *Crime and Justice: A Review of Research,* vol. 25, ed. M. Tonry (Chicago: University of Chicago Press, 1999), 1–127; Jim Consedine, *Restorative Justice: Healing the Effects of Crime* (Lyttelton, New Zealand: Ploughshares, 1995); Elmar Weitekamp, "The History of Restorative Justice," in *Restorative Juvenile Justice: Repairing the Harm of Youth Crime,* ed. Brazemore and Walgrave (Monsey, NY: Criminal Justice, 1999), 75–102.

9. San Francisco has a history of pioneering penal arts experiments, including Herb Blau's famed production of Beckett's *Waiting for Godot* in San Quentin in 1957. The production was staged with professional actors for inmate audiences, but it has inspired generations of artists to work directly with incarcerated populations.

10. Marcum and Hennessey are both retired now, and though the jail continues to offer innovative programming, the new directors are not as progressive or daring as their predecessors.

11. Subsequent productions have been staged at Lorraine Hansberry, Yerba Buena Center for the Arts and other locales around the Bay Area.

12. For a more detailed account of the workshop process, see my earlier essays: "The Medea Project: Mythic Theater For Incarcerated Women," *Feminist Studies* 30 (2) (Summer 2004): 483–509, and " 'Do You Know What Bitch Is Backwards?' Mythic Revision and Ritual Reversal in the Medea Project: Theater for Incarcerated Women," *Dialectical Anthropology* 26 (2) (2001): 159–79.

REFERENCES

Benjamin, Walter. 1968. "The Storyteller, Reflections on the Works of Nikolai Leskov." *Illuminations*. Trans. Harry Zohn. Ed. Hannah Arendt. 83–107. New York: Schocken Books.

Beiser, Vince. 2001. "How We Got to Two Million: How Did the Land of the Free become the World's Leading Jailer?" *Mother Jones*. July 10. http://www.vincebeiser. com/debt-to-society/prisons_download/overview.html.

Benner, Jeffrey. March 16, 2000. "Politically Correct Punishment." *Mother Jones*.

Cornell, Drucilla. 1998. *At the Heart of Freedom*. Princeton: Princeton University Press.

———. 2002. *Between Women and Generations: Legacies of Dignity*. New York: Palgrave.

Currie, Elliot. 1998. *Crime and Punishment in America*. New York: Holt.

Daly, Kathleen. 2002. "Restorative Justice: The Real Story." *Punishment and Society* 4: 55–79.

Davis, Angela, 2003. *Are Prisons Obsolete?* New York: Seven Stories.

———. 1998. "Public Imprisonment and Private Violence: Reflections on the Hidden Punishment of Women." *New England Journal on Criminal and Civic Confinement* 24: 344–50.

Fraden, Rena. 2001. *Imagining Medea: Rhodessa Jones and Theater for Incarcerated Women*. Chapel Hill: University of North Carolina Press.

Gonnerman, Jennifer. July/August. 2008. "Slammed: The Age of Incarceration." *Mother Jones*. http://motherjones.com/politics/2008/07/slammed-welcome-age-incarceration.

Greenfeld, Lawrence A., and Tracy L. Snell. 1999. "Special Report: Women Offenders." The Bureau of Justice Statistics (December). http://www.ojp.usdoj.gov/bjs/pub/pdf/wo.pdf.

Human Rights Watch. May 2000. "Punishment and Prejudice: Racial Disparities in the War on Drugs." 12(2). http://www.hrw.org/legacy/reports/2000/usa/.

Lapidus, Lenora, et al. March 15 2005. "Caught in the Net: The Impact of Drug Policies on Women and Families." American Civil Liberties Union. http://www.aclu.org/drugpolicy/gen/23513pub20050315.html.

Mauer, Marc, and Ryan S. King. 2007. "A 25-Year Quagmire: The War on Drugs and its Impact on American Society."Washington, D.C.: The Sentencing Project. http://www.sentencingproject.org/Admin/Documents/publications/dp_25yearquagmire.pdf.

Sullivan, Dennis, and Larry Tifft. 2001. *Restorative Justice: Healing the Foundations of Our Everyday Lives*. Monsey, New York: Willow Tree.

Stubbs, Julie. 2007. "Beyond Apology? Domestic Violence and Critical Questions for Restorative Justice." *Criminology and Criminal Justice* 7 (2): 169–87.

Sweeney, Megan. 2004. "Prison Narratives, Narrative Prisons: Incarcerated Women Reading Gayl Jones's 'Eva's Man.' " *Feminist Studies* 30 (2): 456–82.

Turner, Victor. 1988. *The Anthropology of Performance*. New York: PAJ.

———. 1982. *From Ritual to Theatre: The Seriousness of Human Play*. New York: PAJ.

Van Ness, Daniel and Karen Heetderks Strong. 2006. *Restoring Justice: An Introduction to Restorative Justice*. Cincinnati: Anderson.

Warren, Jennifer, et al. 2008. "One in 100: Behind Bars in America." Washington, DC: Pew Center on the States. http://www.pewcenteronthestates.org.

Zehr, Howard. 1990. *Changing Lenses: A New Focus for Crime and Justice*. Scottsdale.

CHAPTER NINETEEN

On Visual Politics and Poetics: Incarcerated Girls and Women Artists

Jillian Hernandez

A grainy drawing depicts two young girls whose names are not given. "Girl One" wears a white smock with a frilly lace collar. "Girl Two" dons a striped dress and a ribbon in her hair that fails to smooth back the unruly bangs that jut out beneath it. Girl Two protectively clutches Girl One's shoulder. Girl One looks out to the viewer with suspicion, as if knowing she is being read. It is explained that the physical "anomalies" of the five-year-old girls depicted, such as facial asymmetry, are biological indications of their innate delinquency.

This illustration is found in *Criminal Woman, the Prostitute, and the Normal Woman*, a text published by criminal anthropologist Cesare Lombroso in 1893. Lombroso applied a positivist, scientific approach to investigating the phenomena of female deviance. Drawing from social Darwinist methodologies, he framed delinquency in the context of degeneration in a hierarchical evolutionary scale and located criminality in the body through cranial and genital anomalies revealed through visual examination and anthropometry, the then popular practice of measuring human subjects.

Lombroso argued that European female criminals are throwbacks to early stages of human evolutionary development, and he often compared them to "savages" such as Africans and Native Americans. He attempted to support these colonialist, racist, and sexist claims by references to visual materials such as drawings and photographs of incarcerated women and girls such as the one described above, illustrations of indigenous women,[1] and reproductions of criminal women's tattoos. These images served to evidence criminal women's unbridled sexuality, the atavistic nature of their physiology, and virile or masculine appearance. *Criminal Woman, the Prostitute, and the Normal Woman* (previously known as *The Female*

Offender) has been significantly influential in scholarship concerning "delinquent" women in the West. Historian and Lombroso scholar Mary Gibson describes how it was the only work of its kind for decades, as female criminals were not a subject widely investigated in criminology, and how it "continued to influence interpretations of female crime until the 1970s; it became the classic text in its field" (Lombroso 2004, 4).[2]

The reading and representation of the body have persistently affected the treatment of women and girls in the penal system. In "Appearance and Delinquency: A Research Note," criminologists Jill Leslie Rosenbaum and Meda Chesney-Lind point to how conventional notions of physical attractiveness inform the way girls' cases are processed in the juvenile justice system. In examining the files of intake personnel at the California Youth Authority from the 1960s, Chesney-Lind and Rosenbaum found that 71 percent of male case workers made references to the physical appearance of girls in their evaluations. They state, "From the descriptions of the girls' appearance [by male staff], four general categories emerged: attractive, unattractive, plain/wholesome, and "well-built." Of the wards whose appearance was mentioned, 26 percent (19) were described as attractive (e.g., 'the ward is an attractive, physically mature 13-year old')" (Chesney-Lind and Rosenbaum 1994, 256).

Although they have found that references to the attractiveness of court-involved girls in intake evaluations has declined in recent decades, the authors link the effects of such biased visual readings to the persistent use of *status offenses* to target girls for state interventions. These are noncriminal offenses such as running away, curfew violations, and "incorrigible" behavior, actions with which legal adults could not be charged. Sexuality has implicated girls in the justice system since the establishment of early-twentieth-century reform institutions such as the State Industrial School for Delinquent Girls (Geneva, Illinois) and the Home of the Good Shepard (Memphis, Tennessee) through the labeling of their sexual activity as "immoral" and "incorrigible" (Knupfer 2000; Shelden 1981).

Despite the passage of the 2002 Juvenile Justice and Delinquency Prevention Act, which prohibits the placement of youth charged with status offenses in secure facilities, a report published by the U.S. Department of Justice Office of Juvenile Justice and Delinquency Prevention finds that females continue to be more likely to be held for status offenses (i.e. "technical violations") than males (2004, 14). Once involved in juvenile courts, girls are often in the problematic position of contending with staff who perceive them as "more difficult to work with" than boys. As the authors of "Girls' Delinquency and the Justice Implications of Intake Workers' Perspectives" note, "The major themes of the negative attitudes about girls [by juvenile probation and parole officers] were girls' attitudes and the perception that girls are manipulative and uncooperative" (Maupin, Maupin, and Leisenring 2002, 65–66). The view of girls summarized by the authors is widely held by staff in U.S. juvenile justice departments.

In this chapter I will demonstrate the potential of visual politics to work *progressively* as an awareness-raising tool and vehicle for incarcerated girls to express their agency and subjectivity while involved in a punitive juvenile justice system through interactions and collaborations with women artists. My observations are based on the work created by the women and girls involved in the Women on the Rise! program run by the Museum of Contemporary Art (MOCA) in Miami, Florida, at the Miami-Dade County Juvenile Detention Center (JDC) through a partnership with the Girls' Advocacy Project, a Florida initiative that serves girls while they await adjudication. I will particularly focus on *MOD 11: Discourses with Incarcerated Girls*, an exhibition of works artists produced in response to their experiences teaching at the detention center I curated at the Bas/Fisher Invitational art space in Miami. The exhibition, for which the title was derived from the name of one of the girls-only cellblocks at the center, was on view from October 13 through November 11, 2007.[3]

Prior to the recent surge of interest in the 1970s feminist art movement spurred by the establishment of the Feminist Art Project, the Feminist Future Symposia held at the Museum of Modern Art (New York), inauguration of the Elizabeth A. Sackler Center for Feminist Art at the Brooklyn Museum, and the WACK! Art and the Feminist Revolution exhibition organized by MOCA, Los Angeles, the relationship between artistic practice and social activism has been generally underaddressed in women's studies. Feminist artists such as Carol Jacobsen have been making interventions into women's correction institutions for many years. Jacobsen has utilized film, installation, and photography to draw attention to the realities women face in prison. Her film *Segregation Unit* (2000) was a response to the media ban imposed by Michigan's governor on state correction facilities due to human rights investigations conducted in its women's prisons. The film is based on documentary footage of a female inmate at Scott Prison being forcibly restrained by correction staff.

The works Jacobsen has shown in museums and galleries serve as "public education" tools for the Michigan Battered Women's Clemency Project, which files petitions and appeals for court-involved women. In "Creative Politics and Women's Criminalization in the United States," Jacobsen writes: "As an artist, making issues of women's criminalization, past and present, visible in emotionally arresting ways to ever-widening audiences is a necessary antidote to my howling rage at such persistent injustice" (2008, 468–69). *MOD 11: Discourses with Incarcerated Girls* is akin in "creative politics" to the work Carol Jacobsen has done with the Clemency Project.

The exhibition was a free, citywide event drawing on cultural, law, social justice, and philanthropic constituencies through the support of the Women's Fund of Miami-Dade County and Miami-Dade County Department of Cultural Affairs. In addition to the exhibition, I moderated a panel discussion that served as the public awareness, discourse-generating component of the project. The panel included the artists and Vicki Lopez Lukis, statewide expansion director for the Girls Advocacy Project.[4] Lukis, a formerly incarcerated woman and exoffender activist, discussed the abuse, poverty, and violence that most incarcerated girls suffer and the real reasons why they become involved in the juvenile justice system such as the reclassification of status offenses (Chesney-Lind and Belknap 2004). She also contextualized the violent crimes committed by the girls within the larger framework of the community violence and trauma they have experienced (Schaffner 2004).

A standing-room-only audience attended the panel, and hundreds of visitors viewed the work on display. The issue of incarcerated girls was raised through the lens of art making and advocacy work. Support from an organization such as the Women's Fund, which conducts activism and provides financial support to essential gender-based social justice programs in Miami demonstrates the promise of arts and community coalition building. Although the JDC girls could not visit the exhibition because they are not allowed to attend field trips, they continue to work with most of the artists and girls outside of the detention center served by Women on the Rise! viewed the show, and met with several of the artists.

MOD 11: MAKING MIAMI'S INCARCERATED GIRLS VISIBLE

"Aggressive," "mean," and "delinquent" girls are visible in contemporary culture through films such as *Mean Girls* (2004), TV talk shows such as Maury Pouvich, and news stories on the violent behavior girls display on YouTube videos. The MTV (Music Television) reality show *Juvies* focuses on the experiences of male and female youth detained at Lake County, Indiana's, Juvenile Justice Center. The show portrays the day-to-day routines of incarcerated girls and provides some context regarding their family and community life, yet the dramatized reenactments of their "crimes" and focus on Judge Mary Beth Bonaventura recalls sensationalized "real life" programs such as *Judge Judy* and cable station MSNBC's *Lock Up* series. The realities of poverty, physical/sexual abuse, and community violence experienced by thousands of girls implicated in the juvenile justice system are rarely represented in these media. As researcher Leslie Acoca describes, "The persistent invisibility of girl offenders is particularly remarkable given that they currently represent the fastest growing segment of the juvenile justice system" (2004, 78).

Though in line with national trends of rising numbers of girls entering the system, the "rates of arrest and incarceration for girls in Florida—that is the number of arrests and incarcerations as a percentage of the total population of girls—are considerably higher than elsewhere." In the 2008 Florida Department of Juvenile Justice Blueprint Commission report "Getting Smart about Juvenile Justice in Florida," researcher Angela Wolf found that in that state, girls "appear to be treated more harshly for less serious offenses than are boys. In the last five years for example, about 75 percent of girls referred to the Department of Justice had *not* committed a felony; where about 55 percent of boys referred had not committed a felony" (Florida Department of Juvenile Justice 2008, 29). Most female inmates at the Miami-Dade County Juvenile Detention center are girls of color, reflecting the overwhelming racial disparity in U.S. correctional facilities.

This is the troubling context in which Women on the Rise! workshops at the detention center take place. I launched the program in 2004 in response to the lack of arts instruction for girls enrolled in alternative schools and social service institutions, and it is conducted on-site in the facilities of organizations that serve girls throughout Miami-Dade County. Women on the Rise! (WOTR) is a series of workshops in art and art history based on the work of contemporary women artists such as Ana Mendieta, Carrie Mae Weems, and Shirin Neshat, among others. Art history lessons focus on the issues of identity addressed in their work, and the images are used to engage students in critical thinking. Workshops also include experimental hands-on projects based on the practices of the artists featured.

In addition to the workshops conducted at each partnering institution, Women on the Rise! organizes field trips for students to view exhibitions of work by women artists at MOCA and other cultural venues in the community. As girls incarcerated at the Miami-Dade County Juvenile Detention Center cannot attend field trips, I invited women artists from the community to run workshops there as visiting teachers.[5] Artists presented images of their work to the girls and led them in hands-on art projects.[6]

The majority of girls served by the program annually are those residing at the detention center. Women on the Rise! workshops there are conducted in an undersized space with up to thirty students, one small table, and no screen for projecting images. Classes are led in the center of the cellblock (also called a "mod"), which is the focal point of the space. Doors to the girls' individual cells ring the perimeter of the structure, and windows that face the outdoors are slathered with opaque black paint. The mod poses consistent challenges to the goal of helping the girls to think beyond it. The space persistently reminds them of their status as detainees through the uniforms and relentless buzzing of correction officer walkie-talkies.

As sociologist Laurie Schaffner accurately describes in her book *Girls in Trouble with the Law*, "Juvenile detention centers can be tense hotbeds where conditions are volatile, and the youth brought in from the streets or from other facilities are typically unsure of what is going to happen to them next" (2006, 17). Conducting WOTR classes in the mod can sometimes be a harrowing and emotionally taxing effort as girls desperately seek information from staff about their court dates or are on painful calls home during workshops. At times correction officers are unhelpful, especially when they feel the girls have "acted up" and are undeserving of a fun "special class."

The disaffecting, austere, and panoptic quality of the mod does not undo its temporal status as an artroom and its attendant fostering of *deviance*, as educators Martin Rosenberg and Francis Thurber have noted, "The artroom is one of the few classroom settings where students can be frequently and genuinely rewarded for divergent and individual thought" (Rosenberg and Thurber 2007, 23). The implementation of an art class in the mod is a process fraught with practical limitations, occasional failures, and remarkable creative successes. In addition to the challenges posed by the physical aspects of the institution, projects executed at the detention center are limited by regulations concerning contraband items. Materials such as scissors and cameras cannot be used with the students due to security and confidentiality concerns. These materials, cameras especially, are essential elements of standard Women on the Rise! lessons. Detention center policies have presented considerable challenges to the program, yet they have served to push the instructors to creatively problem solve. The artists who have worked with me at the detention center are Rosemarie Chiarlone, Susan Lee Chun, Nereida Garcia Ferraz, Naomi Fisher, the GisMo collective (Jessica Gispert and Crystal Molinary), Isabel Moros-Rigau, Ali Prosch, and Kathleen Staples.

I curated *MOD 11: Discourses with Incarcerated Girls* as a result of the profound and creatively fruitful collaborations between the girls and artists.[7] The works in *MOD 11* vary in both content and media, as the artists manifested impressions of working with the girls in varied, unpredictable ways. The disparate works share a concern with subjectivity and agency in both their quotidian and philosophical contexts. Agency is articulated in these projects as the ability to control your actions—meet with a friend or choose a perfect weekend outfit—activities to which the girls have temporary, yet painful restriction to. The artists also engage with larger questions of agency as it relates to the girls' sexual lives and the constricted ability to express subjectivity they suffer as inmates. In some pieces the artists express deeply personal reactions to their experiences at the detention center. In what follows I thematically describe, interpret, and

Installation shot of pieces by Nereida Garcia Ferraz, Ali Prosch, and Rosemarie Chiarlone. Photo: Rosemarie Chiarlone.

contextualize the works in the exhibition. I conclude the chapter by providing pedagogical strategies, some drawn from suggestions by the girls and JDC staff, for visiting practitioners working in detention settings.

I would not suggest that the works discussed in this chapter faithfully represent all of the more than seventy girls who participated in workshops led by WOTR artists in the spring and summer of 2007. The inability to document the workshops through video/photography and the role of the artists and myself as teachers (not researchers) prompts the utilization of personal experience, visual analysis, and references to feminist scholarship as methodologies in this chapter.[8] These resources work to illustrate issues of prevalence in the girls' lives and how the girls and artists affected each other. The reproduction of artworks in this volume will likely elicit a multiplicity of readings beyond those outlined here.

UNDOING THE DOCILE BODY

The juvenile justice system purports to serve a protective, welfare function for the youth in its charge. The explicit aim of processing these youth as detainees in a "child-friendly" miniprison is to keep them safe from the outside world and each other. Philosopher Michel Foucault has shown how punishment is the most oblique aspect of the modern penal process (1977, 9) as discourses of security, correction, and education obscure the punitive and disciplinary functions of the prison. Artist Nereida Garcia Ferraz read Foucault's *Discipline and Punish: The Birth of the Prison* while conducting her work at the detention center.

In her lesson the artist provided the girls with pages from *The New York Times* that she spray-painted black while allowing fragments of text and image to remain visible. Students were instructed to respond to and embellish the pages using white, red and gold charcoals and pastels. Garcia Ferraz utilized this technique in the drawings she created for the exhibition. The artist's works in *MOD 11* were sparked by thoughts that came to her as she read the book and considered her students. For example, the drawing *El Arbol Torcido* (The Twisted Tree, 2007) is her reinterpretation of an illustration found in *Discipline and Punish*. The original image, titled *Orthopedics or the art of preventing and correcting deformities of the body in children* (1749) by N. Andry depicts a bent tree being constrained and reshaped. *Orthopedics* demonstrates how notions of degeneration and deviance were linked to the body in modernity, recalling Lombroso. The illustration exemplifies the notion that "wayward" children are to be "corrected" through the constriction of their bodies. Garcia Ferraz's appropriation of the image points to the persistence of penal practices that work to make the bodies of young girls docile.

The semiotics of the "deviant" body are the focus of the artist's painting *El Apartado* (The One Who Is Separated, 2007). The title points to the outsider status of the incarcerated girl represented in the work, whose stigmatization is symbolized by a uniform and a dunce cap. The vivid orange hue of the painting that references the color of JDC uniforms washes out the identifying features of the subject's body. A thick orange line encloses the figure and severs her connection to the lush South Florida landscape in the background. The girls are in a homogenized (and homogenizing) group situation in the mod; in response to this, Garcia Ferraz has attempted to connect to them as "individual young women with friends, lovers, mothers, daughters, husbands, and neighbors, ending up away from the streets for a period of time in a gray area of society."[9]

Susan Lee Chun's work in *MOD 11,* titled *Peace, Love, Harmony* (2007), also referenced the girls' uniforms. Uniforms appeared in Chun's work prior to her engagement with the JDC girls. Upon her relocation from Chicago to Miami in 2004, which has a small population of Asian Americans, the artist experienced more overt forms of racism than she ever had before. Chun responded to these experiences through works such as *Camouflage No. 5* (2005), where she utilized signifiers of whiteness, such as a plaid uniform and blonde wig, to function as a disguise. The artist utilized the uniform to immerse her body into a room where the walls and floor were covered in plaid fabric. In describing the work Chun has stated, "The installation's primary function is to act as a stage or platform that I perform within, depicting the process of assimilation and the stark contrast between my ability and inability to conceal my identity."[10]

Chun was struck by rules regarding dress and style that were posted in the mod that had gendered and racial overtones such as, "No weaves, extensions, artificial nails, etc." allowed. The regulation seemed to further homogenize the girls beyond the uniform. The artist read *Uniforms Exposed: From Conformity to Transgression* by Jennifer Craik in the period she was visiting JDC. Craik echoes Foucault's articulation of how welfare institutions function as sites where disciplining pedagogies are implemented in her description of the emergence of uniforms in the United Kingdom.

> The introduction of compulsory school uniforms was entirely in keeping with the role of schools as disciplining institutions to shape young boys into citizens. The first of the English charity (or "Bluecoat") schools to adopt a uniform was Christ's Hospital founded in London in 1552—and other charitable foundations soon followed. Generally, there was little attention to the children in charity care—"welfare" was meant to contain a perceived social decay (abandoned or orphaned children) with the visible sign of the problem being institutionalized and "hidden away." (Craik 2005, 58)

The centuries-old phenomenon Craik describes reverberates in many contemporary juvenile justice facilities that are inaccessible to the public, where there is tension between the protective role of the institution and its constrictive, normalizing regulations.

Like Garcia Ferraz, Chun aimed to underscore the subjectivity of the girls she worked collaboratively with to create *Peace, Love, Harmony.* In her JDC project the artist provided girls with swatches of fabric upon which they generated designs for a garment they would potentially wear. The students created lively patterns using bright colors, text, and shapes such as rainbows and hearts. Among the works was a piece in which the words *LOVE/PEACE/HARMONY* were emblazoned in blue and green. For Chun, the hope and promise articulated in the girls' works, executed under circumstances of considerable duress, attested to their resilience. In describing her workshop the artist stated,

> In the time I had the opportunity to spend with these young girls, I became aware of how their vibrant and resilient personalities consistently revealed themselves although their current situation was not the ideal. What turned out to be encouraging and moving for me where these unexpected moments, smiles, and laughter from their personal narratives regarding what they wish they had inside the facility or what they missed, such as favorite foods (flaming hot Cheetos, wings, home cooked meals), family, familiar spaces (home, bedrooms, pillows). It was the energy and content of their dialogue that became the highlight and inspiration for the garments.[11]

In her *MOD 11* piece Chun created hooded sweatshirts in the orange hue of the girls' uniforms.

Peace, Love, Harmony recalls artist David Hammons' sculpture *In the Hood* (1993), which references the stereotype of the deviant black male "hooded" figure

Installation shot of pieces by Susan Lee Chun, Kathleen Staples, Ali Prosch, and Naomi Fisher. Photo: Rosemarie Chiarlone.

and the ghetto in which he is situated. In Chun's piece, the austere sweatshirts that hung in the exhibition space were activated by the girls' vivid, light-hearted designs that lined the interior of the hoods. The artist's infusion of the girls' creativity and hope into the garments destabilized the normalizing function of their state-issued uniforms.

GIRLHOOD EROTICS

In addition to dress and style, agency and subjectivity are also expressed with the body through sex. The work of artists Rosemarie Chiarlone and Ali Prosch touch upon the problems and poetics of girls' sexuality. Chiarlone's *Panty Series* (2006) suite of photo-collages were inspired by her initial workshop at JDC. In the work, the intricately sewn undergarments created by the artist frame photographic fragments of male and female bodies. The representation of male figures in the work signals their role in constructing notions of "feminine" sexuality. Although men hold the dominant position of power, they do not escape the entrapment of gender norms. This double bind is articulated in *Panty Series #11*, where the vertical stripes that pattern a woman's underwear cage a man's hands.

In her project with the girls Chiarlone provided them with a wide array of garments from secondhand stores that they were instructed to embellish with poetry, lyrics, and designs using markers. The artist presented students with images from her residency project at the Atlantic County Women's Center *Journey to Healing: Surviving Domestic Violence and/or Sexual Assault* that was on view at the Noyes Museum of Art in Oceanville, New Jersey, from February 4 to May 7, 2006. The subject matter of Chiarlone's work struck a chord with the girls, and the workshop became a space in which they expressed the anger, hurt, pride, and pleasure they associated with their sexual experiences. The artist states, "The works of two girls really stand out in my mind. One expressed being sexually assaulted at a young age on a small garment . . . Another created a powerful drawing on a large garment conveying her homosexuality. Each seemed very self-motivated to share her experience."[12]

The girl Chiarlone refers to first created a moving work using a pink, long-sleeved blouse onto which she inscribed, "Why did you rape me motherfucker! I was only 11!" in large, bold letters. The other applied an intricate, corset-like design onto a plain t-shirt using the colors of the LGBT pride flag. The student's decision to express her sexual identity in this context was also courageous, given the challenges lesbian, bisexual, and transgender inmates face in detention. Schaffner notes, "Sleeping, showering, and dressing become harrowing locations of harassment for gender-explorative youth and for their frightened and ill-prepared fellow detainees . . . One young woman testified that when she was locked in detention, she was never given a roommate because she was a lesbian and that special showering arrangements were made to prevent her from showering with other girls" (2006, 139–40). Chiarlone felt that the workshop "facilitated a form of healing. As a result, I completed a series entitled *Panties* that addresses

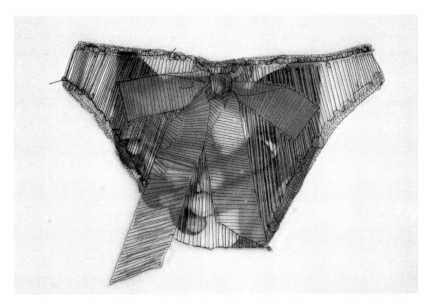

Panty Series #11 (2006), Rosemarie Chiarlone, silver gelatin print, cotton thread on Dura Lar: 21" x 23.

connection and disconnection in the context of humans as sexual being."[13] In a subsequent workshop at JDC, the artist provided students with pillowcases upon which they represented their dreams with text and images. In describing the workshop Chiarlone wrote, "Most of the girls conveyed her existence, identity, and future linked directly to a [male] lover. One girl decorated her pillowcase with the words *Property of . . .* and the boy's name . . . First, she is the property of her parents, now of the Miami-Dade County Juvenile Detention Center, and her dream is of being the property of her 'rescuer.' "[14] What most concerns WOTR instructors about expressions such as the one described is that some girls end up in detention for taking the rap for their boyfriends. However, we do not judge the girls' choice of topic or approach to making their pieces. We instead encourage them to think of other dreams/thoughts to depict in addition to thoughts about their partners. Perhaps daydreams about reuniting with romantic partners keep the girls optimistic while they are in detention.

The problem of court-involved girls' sexual agency is decidedly opaque. Schaffner notes how boyfriends, who are usually older, are often the only source of support for many incarcerated girls who have empty families due to incarceration, death, and/or caregivers who must work more than one job to make ends meet. "Dealing with an older boyfriend could be injurious, but considering the alternative of putting up with ongoing abuse, hunger, or homelessness, dealing with an older man might seem less bad. As a least-harmful compromise strategy, girls' tactics of getting involved with older boys and men in order to meet ordinary needs is neither legal nor healthy, but it might save girls' lives and get them through adolescence. (Ibid. 112) In response to this workshop, Chiarlone created *Cinderella's Days and Dreams*, a pillow onto which the words *Property Of* are embroidered with hair" (2007).

Unlike Chiarlone's male-defined Cinderella, in Ali Prosch's work, the girls themselves are the desired subjects of their fantasies. The arguments in psychologist Sharon Lamb's book *The Secret Life of Girls: What Good Girls Really Do—Sex Play, Aggression, and Their Guilt* resonate with Prosch's *MOD 11* project. The book centers on stories of women's sexual experiences during childhood. Lamb discusses male identification, coercion, and abuse; however, *The Secret Life of Girls* is primarily concerned with addressing the guilt and shame girls feel about the pleasure and power they experience during childhood sexual play. In her effort to advance a new perspective within the victim-oriented discourse of girls' sexuality, Lamb describes how girls are not mindless receivers of mass media images and how they are often the subjects of their own desires (2001, 39).

> They are their own best audiences and use mirrors to watch themselves be transformed into sexy grown-ups. In these mirrors they sense the power of the sexual. That's why these games are private and usually halt when a parent or other adult enters the room . . . Their gaze can't be reduced to a male's gaze. To say that they look at themselves as they imagine a man would suggests that a woman can't look at herself as a sexual being without pretending to be a heterosexual man. It makes her sexuality only a gift derived from male attention. (2001, 43–44)

The girls depicted in Prosch's drawings for *MOD 11* are situated in a whimsical world where they are subtly engrossed in their own sensuality. The drawings *Girl on Chair I, Girl on Chair II,* and *Castle* (2007) have a still, private feel to them, due in part to their intimate size and the immediacy of the graphite marks upon the pages, which look as if they have been torn from a diary. The young women occupy solitary domestic spaces and don Victorian-era clothing. One girl is depicted straddling the arm of a chair with her back to the viewer. The other, dressed in an outfit reminiscent of Lewis Carrolls's Alice, reclines on an ornately decorated couch with her legs spread, seeming lost in a daydream while her hands rest on her pelvis.

The students appreciated Prosch's frank and humorous approach to sexuality in her workshop at JDC, in which she presented them with images from her photographic series *On Top* (2003). In the photographs a verdant South Florida landscape is littered with women riding atop the backs of men on all fours as if playing "horsy." Prosch's staging of the bodies in the photographs destabilizes the art historical convention of the reclined female nude set against a pastoral backdrop. The stoic, defiant gazes of the women in the photos signal the feminist undertone of the work, communicating the seriousness of this "game" to the viewer. When Prosch asked the students to identify an issue the *On Top* series was concerned with, a girl shot her hand up and assertively offered, "It's about power."

The artist's drawings in *MOD 11* were inspired by a project in which she provided the girls with images of flowers and Victorian-era designs to create small-scale collages. Although the girls often exhibit a very a-romantic, nitty-gritty attitude toward sexuality and pleasure, the project elicited expressions of whimsy in the girls, whose status as children is often undermined by a penal system that makes consistent efforts at trying them as adults through practices such as *direct filing*.[15] In addition to reminding us that incarcerated girls are children, capable of conjuring beautiful works in the face of institutionalization, Prosch's works should also remind us that the possibility of a pleasurable and healthy sexual life for these girls is not foreclosed.

The GisMo collective's (Jessica Gispert and Crystal Molinary) *MOD 11* project provides an innovative vantage point for engaging discourses of girls' sexual representations in visual culture. The artists were born and raised in the ethnic South Florida enclave of Hialeah-Miami Lakes, a largely working-class Cuban exile community. In their satirical depictions of Latina stereotypes, Cuban conceptions of bourgeois femininity collide with the raunchy sexuality of main-stream hip hop. GisMo's work is inspired by the musical genre known as Miami bass or "booty" music, exemplified by the controversial hip hop group 2 Live Crew. When presenting their work to the girls at JDC, the piece that generated the most responses from students, uncontrollable laughter among them, was the video *Booty Sandwich with Bass* (2005). The work humorously depicts the artists dancing energetically to a song by 2 Live Crew with their friends. The girls not only related to the artists because of their taste in music, but in their positive, in-your-face attitude regarding their "overweight" bodies. Several girls in the cellblock shouted "Big girls—that's right!" as the video played.

GisMo frames their adoption of booty music as an oppositional stance to mainstream Euro-American beauty standards and norms of bourgeois, "demure" feminine comportment, a view that diverges from scholarship that describes representations of women in hip hop as damaging to girls (Schaffner 2006; Sharpley-Whiting 2007; Stephens and Few 2007; Stephens and Phillips 2003; Weekes 2004). The artists found that the dancers featured in Luke's[16] videos looked more like them than any other women they had seen on television growing up. Engaging with GisMo provided the students with a feminist model of hip hop–inspired sexuality that disarmed the male-identified nature of booty representations by infusing them with their own meaning, a strategy many of the girls already practice. As Lamb posits in *The Secret Lives of Girls*, "Girls play an active role in taking in these [popular culture] images, rearrang-ing them somewhat, and creating new expectations for themselves. But while they obey the images and re-create them, they also undermine them" (Lamb 2001, 47). The liminal space between pop culture appropriation and subversion is where contemporary feminist art thrives. This "disidentificatory" approach, to use performance theorist José E. Muñoz's term, facilitated the connection the girls made to GisMo's work. Muñoz's description of the term is as follows, "Disidentification is the third mode of dealing with dominant ideology, one that neither opts to assimilate within such a structure nor strictly opposes it; rather, disidentification is a strategy that works on and against dominant ideology" (Muñoz 1999, 11).

GisMo recalled their adolescent lives in the project *Miss, You Look Like a Bratz Doll* (2007). The title was inspired by a humorous exchange between a student and me, in which she compared me to a Bratz doll. Referencing the toy, which is unpopular among feminists who believe they are hypersexualized, fit the artists' project as it centers on the girls' urban aesthetics (Hernandez 2009). Bratz dolls provide girls of color with one of the few alternatives to Barbies and what are generally held as more positive, asexual images of white girls playing soccer with swinging, golden blonde ponytails. The artists provided JDC girls with paper-doll type images of themselves that the students transformed into fictional characters with accompanying narratives. The girls used markers and colored pencils to design hairstyles, clothing, and accessories on the figures and envisioned everyday scenarios for their characters such as going on a date or hanging out with friends.

The artists then created a series of photographs drawing from the girls' designs and stories. The photographs were later arranged into an album by JDC students and displayed in the exhibition as if they were situated in the bedroom of a Miami teen. The artists state,

> Growing up our bureaus were our altars, the place where we kept the relics of those we held close to our hearts. This almost insignificant space served as a sanctuary for day dreaming, reminiscing, and recollecting our thoughts. Where our bureaus were our altars—our slambooks were our bibles. In them we kept records of our friends, styles, and the minutia of everyday adolescent life. The girls at the detention center don't get to have a bureau full of picture frames or photo albums housing their adolescent memories. In *Miss, You Look Like a Bratz Doll* we have collaborated with the girls to create a collective album of fictional Miami characters.[17]

The girls framed their works in the context of friendship. In compiling and embellishing the album the girls celebrated images of the artists looking bored at school, going to family parties, and modeling.

Schaffner has described the frequency and severity of *girl hating* among female inmates in juvenile justice settings, which she frames in the context of internalized misogyny (2006). Women on the Rise! staff have also witnessed instances of girl hating; however, on the whole, the students tend to bond, particularly by braiding each other's hair, as they do not have products or mirrors with which they

Installation view of *Miss, You Look Like a Bratz Doll* (2007), GisMo (Jessica Gispert and Crystal Molinary) multimedia installation, dimensions variable. Photo: Crystal Molinary.

can style their own. Although they do form cliques at times, the mood among students is generally one of solidarity vis-à-vis their status as "locked up," especially when they feel the staff has treated someone unfairly. Some could argue that the positive woman-to-woman relationships the girls depicted in *Miss* are undermined by the conformity of the scantily dressed characters they crafted to hypersexual, mainstream, male-identified standards of attractiveness. However, I find that unlike the typological women often represented in pop culture, the characters created by the girls in GisMo's work are subjects who have relationships and are connected to place, thus making them more difficult to exoticize (Hernandez 2009).

COLLABORATION

Like GisMo, Isabel Moros-Rigau's works in *MOD 11* titled *Subruler of the Element X* (2007) were created in collaboration with the JDC girls. The artist presented her nonnarrative films to the students that feature animated biomorphic fabric sculptures. As needles and scissors are not allowed in the facility, the artist taught the girls to use tying, knotting, and braiding to execute their works. The girls created a host of abstract, human, and animal forms from t-shirt fragments, yarn, and swatches of cloth. Dresses, hair, bodies, and wings were skillfully crafted by the students using only their hands and the materials available. These were grouped together in the exhibition space to create a sculptural form upon the wall. Inspired by the girls' ingenuity, Moros-Rigau decided to take the project further in her subsequent workshop.

The artist created a four-foot fabric doll of a female body the girls worked collaboratively to dress using a wide array of fabrics. The primal, totemic qual-

Installation view of *Subruler of the Element X* (2007), JDC girls and Isabel Moros-Rigau, mixed-media, dimensions variable. Photo: Isabel Moros-Rigau.

ity of the resulting sculpture recalls the fabric work of French, New York–based artist Louise Bourgeois, who has been featured in Women on the Rise! lessons at the mod. Bourgeois is a pivotal figure in contemporary art, who, despite the fact that she is more than ninety years old, continues to produce innovative multimedia work.

The girls relate to Bourgeois despite her difference in age and cultural background due to the highly personal content of her work. One of the first contemporary artists to openly engage with personal experiences in their practice, Bourgeois is known for her singular ability to infuse abstract forms with emotion. She has returned to her childhood practice of sewing in recent sculptures, recalling her work in the family tapestry repair business (Morris 2003). Bourgeois' childhood is the consistent subject of her work. The artist's anger at her father, who openly and regularly expressed his disappointment with her having been born female (and thus gave her his name) and engaged in an extramarital affair with her nanny, remains the predominant force of her practice.

The girls connect to Bourgeois' dramatic work as it melds figuration and abstraction. For example, students often express a connection to the fabric work *Spiral Woman* (2003), in which Bourgeois expresses violent rage via the contorted, twisted neck of a hanging figure. Pain and righteous anger are given voice and form in Bourgeois' work, which draws the girls in and presents them with a possible artistic strategy for expressing their feelings. Although the works they created with Moros-Rigau do not overtly speak to their lives, they are charged with emotive power.

FINDING RELEASE IN PAINTING

The emotionally and psychologically freighted experience of visiting the detention center informs Naomi Fisher's untitled painting (2007) in the exhibition. The work reflects a dream she had the night before what was her third workshop with the girls at JDC. Fisher was reading texts in Jungian psychology at the time, keeping a dream journal, and learning about the tarot. These new interests prompted her to present something different to the girls, as the previous drawing workshops she conducted were based on her provocative photographs and paintings of women in nature. In her most recent session at JDC, Fisher provided students with copies of images from the feminist Motherpeace and Barbara G. Walker tarots. Her aim was to provide them with imagery of archetypal female characters that possess both positive and potentially negative attributes, as the girls sometimes internalize the stigma of being incarcerated.

Fisher's goal was to present them with a complex view of anger, strength, power, and peace, themes she has explored in previous workshops in which the notion of making "mistakes" is problematized. In describing her approach to a drawing workshop at JDC, an activity the girls are usually hesitant about as they feel they do not have the skills to participate, the artist recalls, "I would show them my artwork and say that to make my series of fictional portraits I would first draw the eyes and then let the face freely form around them. For their project, I would try to get them to start drawing in a similar way, starting with the eyes and letting the face form, embracing and incorporating their mistakes."[18] The girls culled symbols from the tarot characters they related to most and created hybridized images they affixed onto poster board to create their own cards. The most popular among the students were variations of the Priestess of Swords, Daughter of Wands, and Priestess of Wands.

Whereas Fisher's painting was created the night prior to her lesson, Kathleen Staples' *MOD 11* pieces were executed an evening following her workshop at JDC. In her project with the girls, the artist instructed them to liberally pour paint over large sheets of paper with no effort to create recognizable images. They then utilized blow dryers to move the paint along the surface of the page to generate patterns and facilitate drying. After the paint dried, the girls were prompted to highlight marks and shapes that interested them in the patterns using charcoal.

The artist's free form approach to painting is echoed in *Arisen* and *Frith* (2007), in which she applied layers of paint over the canvas to create a thick and luminous texture upon the surface. The works are caked with the candy-colored tones of pink and aqua that are conventionally associated with girlhood. The color in the works arose from her thoughts about the girls that night. Staples states, "They are so powerless over their space and their actions. So many freedoms are taken from them that they are left only with what they can keep inside themselves—the freedom of thinking and feeling . . . For me, freedom is intrinsic to the act of painting . . . The nature of the art allows me to paint any way I want, and even to let the paint do what it wants, to give paint its own freedom."[19]

THE POLITICS OF VISUAL POETICS

The *MOD 11* exhibition and panel discussion provided a forum for presenting complex views of detention center inmates that move beyond the troubled history of "deviant" girls and the visual to raise awareness of their needs and shift uninformed and biased perceptions of them as uneducated, viciously violent, and sex obsessed "bad girls." The contrasting works, which were connected by their explorations of agency and subjectivity, vacillated between the political and the poetic. Expressions of pain mingled with images of whimsy, hope, and sensuality. Where Nereida Garcia Ferraz reminded us of the threat incarceration poses to the girls' sense of self, Chun's work showed how they work creatively to maintain it. Ali Prosch's capricious drawings were grounded by Rosemarie Chiarlone's focus on girls' male identification. GisMo's work became a platform through which the girls asserted their aesthetic sensibilities and celebrated bonds of female friendship. The sculptures Isabel Moros-Rigau created with students revealed their fearlessness in taking on new forms of art making—creating imaginative works with meager resources. Paintings by Kathleen Staples and Naomi Fisher attested to the emotive weight of working in the mod and underscored the importance of working through mistakes and attaining freedom.

The staff members of partnering organizations provide MOCA with their assessment of the Women on the Rise! program and descriptions of how it impacts the girls in their care on an annual basis. In the partner evaluation for the 2006–2007 year in which the MOD 11 project was conducted Girls Advocacy Project (GAP) staff noted the following:

> WOTR has had an overall positive effect on the behavior of the girls detained at JDC (Juvenile Detention Center). In addition to the educational, cultural, and inspiration effects, GAP personnel have observed that verbal and physical altercations have decreased during/after the WOTR workshops and that the girls' engagement in the presentations has increased. Such effects promote a safe and learning-conducive environment vital to the success of any programming in a detention facility.
> A few of the girls have expressed interest in focusing on careers in art and strengthening their artist talents.
> WOTR offers an educational and cultural opportunity for enrichment which is often absent in these youths' lives.
> WOTR meaningfully explores female gender issues, which encourages self-awareness, bolsters potential for improvement, and perfectly compliments GAP's own gender-specific programming.

GAP's feedback attests to the potential of visual art and engagement with women artists to make a meaningful mark on the lives of court-involved girls. Such workshops should be implemented in juvenile justice facilities throughout the nation in order to provide youth with opportunities for self-expression, critical reflection, and awareness of social issues that impact their lives.

In closing I will briefly offer some pedagogical strategies for visiting practitioners working with girls in detention settings.

> *Involve correction officers and other staff in your program:* The work we conduct at the detention center often adds a workload to the staff, as we introduce outside materials into the space that they must insure are safely removed from the facility (i.e. beads, paint brushes, strings of yarn). They also amend their routines to accommodate the time slot of our lessons. Involving staff as *participants* in your program helps build rapport and support a positive workshop environment.
> *Avoid sensitive content if you do not have counseling staff on hand*: We did not anticipate the emotional response a student had to Rosemarie Chiarlone's presentation as her work had no images of violence or victimization. A GAP counselor we work in tandem with helped us respond to the situation, and the girl expressed she felt better

after participating in the workshop. Many court-involved girls have experienced a range of traumatic events, and it is difficult to gauge what may trigger a response. Be sure to have a qualified staff member on hand if a project covers sensitive issues.

Be flexible: When girls see our art materials, such as paper and pencils, they immediately want to use them to write letters to friends, partners, and family. We allow the girls time to do so within the workshop period. This helps build rapport with and participation from the girls.

Be sensitive to the mood of the group: A host of factors contribute to the mood of a cellblock on a particular day. You may want to approach your lesson differently (focus on the most "fun" aspect or abbreviate it) if the girls seem sullen or anxious. Plowing ahead as planned usually results in an awkward workshop atmosphere. When some girls do not want to participate we do not take it personally or pressure them to work. We have found that often they often come around and begin working when they feel ready.

NOTES

The author thanks the girls and artists whose moving work inspired this chapter in addition to the staff and supporters of the Museum of Contemporary Art, Miami, Girls Advocacy Project, Miami, and Women's Fund of Miami-Dade County. This chapter benefited from insightful feedback from the reviewers and editors.

1. This includes vaginal diagrams.

2. Quotes from Gibson are found in the introduction to Lombroso's *Criminal Woman, the Prostitute, and the Normal Woman.*

3. I had previously organized exhibitions of work by *Women on the Rise!* students at the Roxy O' Neal Bolton Women's History Gallery (on view May–June 2007) and the Miami International Airport (September–December 2007), which provided them with a platform through which to present their work to the public.

4. Save for Susan Lee Chun (who had a previously scheduled performance that night) and Ali Prosch.

5. I relocated from Florida to New Jersey in August 2007 to pursue a PhD in women's and gender studies at Rutgers University. The program is now administered by artist Isabel Moros-Rigau and continues to reach hundreds of girls on an annual basis.

6. This chapter is focusing on workshops related specifically to the *MOD 11* exhibition; the artists, with the exception of Ali Prosch, who relocated to California in summer 2007 to attend CalArts, are continuing their work with Women on the Rise!

7. Rosemarie Chiarlone had already created work inspired by JDC students (*Panty Series,* 2006), prior to the conception of the *MOD 11* show.

8. Unless otherwise noted, artist's quotes are derived from *artist statements* submitted to the author via e-mail (most, but not all, artists in *MOD 11* composed artist statements).

Artist statements are unpublished documents in which artists articulate the concepts that inform their work. These documents are provided to curators to aide them in the process of generating essays and other didactic materials related to exhibitions.

9. E-mail correspondence with author September 24, 2007.

10. E-mail correspondence with author May 11, 2007.

11. E-mail correspondence with author October 2, 2007.

12. E-mail correspondence with author August 9, 2007.

13. Ibid.

14. Ibid.

15. A procedure that gives prosecutors the discretion to try minors in criminal court.

16. 2 Live Crew front man.

17. E-mail correspondence with author September 17, 2007.

18. E-mail correspondence with author October 10, 2007.

19. E-mail correspondence with author September 9, 2007.

REFERENCES

Acoca, Leslie. 2004. "Outside/Inside: The Violation of American Girls at Home, on the Streets, and in the Juvenile Justice System." In *Girls, Women and Crime: Selected Readings*, eds. Meda Chesney-Lind and Lisa Pasko. Thousand Oaks, CA: Sage.

Chesney-Lind, Meda, and Joanne Belknap. 2004. "Trends in Delinquent Girls' Aggression and Violent Behavior: A Review of the Evidence." In *Aggression, Antisocial Behavior, and Violence among Girls,* eds. Martha Putallaz and Karen L. Bierman. New York and London: Guilford.

———, and Jill Rosenbaum. 1994. "Appearance and Delinquency: A Research Note." *Crime and Delinquency* 40 (2): 250–261.

Craik, Jennifer. 2005. *Uniforms Exposed: From Conformity to Transgression.* Oxford and New York: Berg.

Florida Department of Juvenile Justice. 2008. Getting Smart about Juvenile Justice in Florida: The Report of the Blueprint Commission.

Foucault, Michel. 1977. *Discipline and Punish: The Birth of the Prison.* New York: Vintage Books.

Gibson, Mary S. 1982. "The 'Female Offender' and the Italian School of Criminal Anthropology." *Journal of European Studies* 12 (3): 155–65.

Hernandez, Jillian. 2009. " 'Miss, You Look Like a Bratz Doll': On Chonga Girls and Sexual-Aesthetic Excess." *National Women's Studies Association Journal* 21 (3): 63–91.

hooks, bell. 2003. *Rock My Soul: Black People and Self-Esteem.* New York: Atria Books.

Jacobsen, Carol. 2008. "Creative Politics and Women's Criminalization in the United States." *Signs: Journal of Women in Culture and Society* 33 (2): 462–70.

Knupfer, Anne Meis. 2000. " 'To Become Good, Self-Supporting Women': The State Industrial School for Delinquent Girls at Geneva, Illinois, 1900–1935." *Journal of the History of Sexuality* 9 (4): 420–46.

Lamb, Sharon, Ed. D. 2001. *The Secret Lives of Girls: What Good Girls Really Do—Sex Play, Aggression, and Their Guilt.* New York: Free.

————, and Lyn Mikel Brown, EdD. 2006. *Packaging Girlhood: Rescuing Our Daughters from Marketer's Schemes.* New York: St. Martin's.

Lombroso, Cesare, and Guglielmo Ferrero. 2004. *Criminal Woman, the Prostitute, and the Normal Woman.* Durham and London: Duke University Press.

Morris, Frances. 2003. *Louise Bourgeois: Stitches in Time.* exh. cat. Dublin: Irish Museum of Modern Art.

Muñoz, Jose Esteban. 1999. *Disidentifications: Queers of Color and the Performance of Politics.* Minneapolis and London: University of Minnesota Press.

Riley, Sirena J. 2002. "The Black Beauty Myth" In *Colonize This! Young Women of Color on Today's Feminism,* ed. Daisy Hernandez and Bushra Rehman. Emeryville, CA: Seal.

Rosenberg, Martin, and Frances Thurber. 2007. *Gender Matters in Art Education.* Worcester: Davis.

Ross Leadbeater, Bonnie J., and Niobe Way. 2007. *Urban Girls Revisited.* New York and London: New York University Press.

Schaffner, Laurie. 2004. "Capturing Girls' Experiences of 'Community Violence' in the United States." In *Girls' Violence: Myths and Realities,* ed. Christine Alder and Anne Worrall. Albany: State University of New York Press.

————. 2006. *Girls in Trouble with the Law.* New Brunswick and London: Rutgers University Press.

Sill, Robert. 1994. *David Hammons in the Hood.* exh. cat. Springfield: Illinois State Museum.

Sharpley-Whiting, T. Denean. 2007. *Pimps Up, Ho's Down: Hip Hop's Hold on Young Black Women.* New York and London: New York University Press.

Shelden, Randall G. 1981. "Sex Discrimination in the Juvenile Justice System: Memphis,Tennessee, 1900–1917." In *Comparing Female and Male Offenders,* ed. Marguerite Q. Warren. London: Sage.

Stephens, Dionne P., and Layli D. Phillips. 2003. "Freaks, Gold Diggers, Divas, and Dykes: The Sociohistorical Development of Adolescent African American Women's Sexual Scripts." *Sexuality and Culture* 7 (1): 3–47.

Stephens, Dionne P., and April L. Few. 2007. "The Effects of Images of African American Women in Hip Hop on Early Adolescents' Attitudes Toward Physical Attractiveness and Interpersonal Relationships." *Sex Roles* 56: 251–64.

Weekes, Debbie. 2004. "Where My Girls At? Black Girls and the Construction of the Sexual." In *All About the Girl: Culture, Power, and Identity,* ed. Anita Harris. New York: Routledge.

U.S. Department of Justice: Office of Justice Programs—Office of Juvenile Justice and Delinquency Prevention. 2004. *Juvenile Offenders and Victims: National Report Series Bulletin.* Report prepared by Melissa Sickmund.

CHAPTER TWENTY

Hope in a Box: Sanity Sold Separately

Sisters of Unique Lyrics (SOUL)

The Sisters of Unique Lyrics (SOUL) is a poetry workshop that meets weekly at Scott Correctional Facility, a maximum-security women's prison in Plymouth, Michigan. SOUL was established as a poetry workshop in 2004 through the Prison Creative Arts Project (PCAP), an organization housed in the English Language and Literature Department of the University of Michigan, Ann Arbor. PCAP's mission is to strengthen the community through creative expression. Since SOUL began, more than thirty women have participated, and it is one of the longest running poetry workshops offered by PCAP. At the time that this collection was written, SOUL was comprised of eight women, including the two facilitators who provided a loose structure for the workshop but who were fully active participants in the poetic process.

Each week SOUL comes together to share poetry written from assignments or prompts inspired by lines from our writings, relevant topics in our lives, or as a part of a planned series. Inside of the workshop, poetry is read by its author, as she stands in the front of the room. After reading and listening to the piece, generally more than once, the other sisters reflect on, comment on, and question the author's work. Using creative criticism, SOUL guides and challenges each member with critical minds and loving eyes.

Twenty-week cycles of SOUL culminate with a vibrant reading at Scott, where guests come to celebrate our individual and collective poetry. This experience showcases our talent and growth while providing us an opportunity to be heard. Attendance has grown exponentially, thanks to PCAP's ongoing relationship with Scott's administration. The initial three outside guests granted to SOUL's first poetry reading has grown to more than thirteen in addition to least a dozen women from the inside. Our readings always include a group poem that is theatrically delivered. Traditionally, we also ask the audience members to create their own poetry during intermission—integrating their work into our performance. As our cycle comes to a close, we compile our best or most important pieces and self-publish them in an anthology of our work. To date, SOUL has produced six anthologies.

SOUL is a unique workshop because there is not a one-dimensional vision, rather a mosaic of voices. We are activists of the mind, feeding our mission to strengthen ourselves and our lives with each other's brilliance. Poetry transforms us by creating and replenishing our arsenal of reasons to keep pushing forward. We are encouraged by bunkies and friends, anticipated by prison guards and college students, and read voraciously by would-be SOUL sisters and academics alike. It is the act of continuous love and support given to each other that provides the sustenance of survival: hope.

We invite you to read this collection, "Hope in a Box: Sanity Sold Separately," as not simply a body of poetry, but as a representation of our own discovery into the depths of the lives of women and prison.

Morgan Willis and Alycia Welch facilitated SOUL at the time this collection was written. Both were long-standing members of PCAP, as well as graduates of the University of Michigan in Ann Arbor. Collectively, they facilitated more than five arts workshops in Michigan. They facilitated SOUL together for over two years. As is customary, the faces of SOUL have since changed. Scott Correctional Facility closed in 2009, and its residents moved to Huron Valley Complex in Ypsilanti, Michigan. Two of its members were released from Michigan Department of Corrections custody, and new members have joined the workshop along with two new facilitators. SOUL continues to be a living, breathing body, its members connected through our shared experience.

THE SISTERS

SOUL is a group of astounding women. We come from all over the world, with razor-tipped minds and tongues bearing deep wisdom. We each are bound by our own struggles. Our poetry is not seeking to undo an injustice, but to fuel our visions of self as more powerful, more open, and more honest than we were before our pens hit the page. This is the plane on which we converge; equally footed authors of inspiration. SOUL is the politics of being branded a million weakening names and turning them into empowering verse.

Inside the room we live real lives. Our Tuesday nights are full of emotion as we try to balance our experiences with visions of our better selves. We lament lost opportunities, missed connections, a day without mail, or an irate exchange. Women write eulogies for cut down trees, release the ghosts of dying parents, ease the need to suffer imbalance, and create personal reminders to maintain faith. Life pushes hard against closed walls. Inside of SOUL, crafting poetry is the way we push back.

It is a likely assumption that coming into a women's prison to create art is done with the hope of bringing some form of liberation into a stifled space. Liberation, after all, is the collective realization of small freedoms, and poetry is an artistic means of realization. While this notion is true, the experience of SOUL is a journey that travels far beyond the idea of freedom. It is an experience that fuses empowerment and expression. Poetry within SOUL brings words strength beyond their ordinary meaning.

Writing with women who are passionate about their lines, their messages, and how they pertain to each other is an incredible breeding ground for hope. Storytelling becomes an act of courage. Word play becomes the power of eloquence. Criticism evolves into innovation, and we become better suited to address our own needs and desires.

Even with the privilege of "not residing on grounds," as it was tactfully stated in our most recent workshop, I cannot imagine my weeks and months without SOUL. It has quickly become a support beam in my life. I have been humbled by the privilege to even know these women who have been my school, church, therapy, job, checkpoint . . . and I theirs. Though I am embarrassed that these are among the people most have branded as weak and voiceless, I am grateful that the women of SOUL do not give up. We feed on fire and ink, on the spirit of hope and on the unique lyrics that give us poetry, our artistic means of self-realization. —Morgan Willis, SOUL Sister/Facilitator

POETRY, WOMEN, AND PRISON

There is a glow fixed in the memory of a writer, a reminder of the first time our pen touched paper, and we felt at ease with the design. While it is difficult to predict the luster of this glow, it is certain to accompany each writer's career, adding further burnish to the crease of every line. For many of its members, SOUL is the source of this glow.

It may seem incongruous, then, that SOUL meets at a women's prison. Prison is deemed a place devoid of opportunity and overflowing with downtrodden individuals lacking a will for expression, a place extinguished of hope and covered by shadows. Women residing in prison are considered a particularly gloomy nuance, so often classified as prostitutes, victims of abuse, drug addicts, and desperate mothers whose futures have been dimmed by tragedy.

However, it is a willful defiance, a refusal of these imposing constraints that pushes SOUL's pen past walls and raises it in deviation from a world that fears what it cannot see and disguises what it cannot confront. What began as an assignment to simply write words on paper has invoked a challenge to confront shadows, our collection of secrets stored behind walls of our own psychological construction, that are as visible as a pregnant bump. It is the steady, casual intimacy with this collection of unlocked fears and untold desires that glows from the lines of our poetry. Eventually, each woman's discoveries beget a distinctive voice and dance in an artwork of her own design. In this way, members of SOUL become impregnated with possibilities.

As a facilitator of SOUL, I have faced my own shadows, my own box of secrets. I have been challenged with fortitude by my sisters to cultivate a keen understanding of the complex world in which we are engulfed. Though I never wanted to be a poet, cultivating a true poetic identity always seemed a rare yet stunning occurrence, a source of great envy. I longed for the unique and inherent trait that true writers seemed to carry on their personality pallets, moving words with refreshing splendor.

It wasn't until I was invited into SOUL that I learned poetry instead requires cultivating an intrinsic insight into the depths of human life. My sisters have pushed me past dark places to give rise to fine ink strokes, connecting beauty with unspoken secrets. I have been given the opportunity to cultivate my ability and forced to surrender to the deepest of human emotions. As a result, I have learned the brilliant design of poetry from simple lessons on the power of mistakes, the impossible limits of time, and the heart of forgiveness, without which I could not have begun a journey into writing. Minute, by stone steady minute, the creative depths of a moving pen have been infused into every aspect of my life.

SOUL is a flame that burns beneath a caldron of silence and brews poetry, uniting to discover writers breathing behind walls. The experience is so profound we cannot help but indulge others: past members connect with current members and extend inspiration to future ones. Poetry, the art of word design, is a means to foster leadership and ultimately changes lives. While prison walls are thought to strip its residents of opportunity and handicap their desires, the women of SOUL have adapted a unique ability to respond to desperate times and unite, as sisters, to clothe each other even in the bleakest conditions. In this way, the women of SOUL are activists of their own lives.

SOUL is a glow fixed in the memory of so many of its members, and while it is difficult to predict the luster of this glow, it is surely one that will never extinguish. —Alycia Welch, SOUL Sister/Facilitator

"DREAMING FREE | FREE DREAMING"

The title of this collection, "Hope in a Box: Sanity Sold Separately" is a combination of prompts that inspired our group piece, "Dreaming Free | Free Dreaming." The act of fusing poetic voices and words to shape a single poem is no easy task. Created in parts, each woman began her contribution as a freewrite (an unfiltered exercise of expression that asks the writer to just keep writing, without stopping, on a particular subject). "Hope in a Box" and "Sanity Sold Separately" became two prompts—assigned one at a time, asking each woman to create poems that fed on her freewrite. After several weeks, the body of the poem began to take form, as we mixed and matched words, emotions, lines, and sounds. The poetry that emerged characterizes the poetry of SOUL: beautiful order from individual exploration—with a message of raw, honest hope.

Dreaming free | Free dreaming

My hope is layed away
in a dusty box waiting.

Yesterday was a letter—
tomorrow not a letter . . .

Can't sit right here to
waste my time
even when time I only got.

Free dreaming, burned by fire.
Hope in a box
wrapped with barbed wire.

Hope was born, the day I lost my cross-legged dreams
waiting to stretch reality.
Swingin' and shinin'
burnin' bright like life is diamond . . .
they found me there

womanhood caved in irony
half-eaten by the molasses sky.

Hope lived in the clouds,
her boxed remains
not carrying much but her life and the ink in her pen,
stories spread open on lily pads, pregnant
frog hop the hope they breathe.

Taunt smoke to solidify
a price that is very
high, maybe too high

(it don't come cheap in here)
like everything else.

Pissed off at the world
and I don't know why.

It's got to be somewhere.
Trapped inside.

Sometimes in life things aren't what they seem to be.

Dreaming free.
Free dreaming.

Beauty gets distorted,
leaks through the plot-holes,
her boxed remains
not carrying much but her life and wishes for
tomorrow's greatness

and I don't know why.

I was missing the day I lost my freedom.

Screamed tear-showers
and breathed loud.

Told the truth—

lost my breath—

in between tight fingertips it won't let me go.

Can't sit right here to
waste my time
even when time I only got.

SOUL, 2007

"SO YOU'RE LISTENING THROUGH THE WALL"

"So You're Listening through the Wall," is a prompt inspired by a request for poems from a class at the University of Michigan. Initially, the aim was to explore the general needs of people in prison. Inside of SOUL, the exploration of people's needs in prison begged several questions: Do fundamental needs really change? If so, is viewing the opinions of a group women who are incarcerated as the representative voice of "prisoner need" an act of isolation or stereotyping beyond that which already exists in and about prison? These ideas were debated heavily inside the workshop, and the work that emerged was a powerful collection of poetry that speaks to the experience of women, of prison, and of the desire to be heard as an individual—not a prisoner or a victim.

Protection

When I listen,
I can hear you through the walls that I built,
Walls high so I don't get hurt.
Next to where your love is lying and panting,
Exhausted and slowly expiring
By the wall it cannot scale.

If you are listening through this wall I built,
I want you to know one thing,
This wall is for my protection.
I want to love you,
But for that to happen,
You have to tear this wall down,
Then I will be exposed and open for you to hurt me.
I want to love you,
But it's too risky.
I hate these walls I've built,
But it's for my protection.

L. Faulk

Busy World Reject My Soul

Here I am
In the dark morning
Sitting down
No where to go
No car to drive
No job to work
Only a book of Algebra
I need to practice.
But not today
Is not my day
I'm feeling sick
I'm sick feeling
Beyond these walls
There is a busy world
I know because
You don't write
To let me know

Your death or life
Sometimes
I am lost in
The middle of
My mind
Can't fix my life
What made you think
I can fix yours?
I am working on
My future
Living good
My present
Laughing of myself
Dreaming free
Free dreaming
Happy!
You know I am
Angry,
Not anymore
You choose to
Forget about me?
Yes, go ahead
Is what I pray
Because I'm tired
I'm tired of your fears
I'm tired of your shit
A man is a man
When you know how
To become one.
I'm not the perfect
One for you
I know, and never will
Not when you can't
Be there for me
Yesterday was a letter
Tomorrow not a letter
Can't sit right here
To waste my time
Even when time
I only got.

Carmen Huerta Martínez
Aka La Reina Del Occidente

Prick Poison

So . . .
you're listening through the wall
listen carefully
I am speaking directly to you
and if you need visual
of what I look like
I look like you
may be shade lighter or darker
   a gender on left or right
with culture from north or west
   south or east
but I look like you
laugh, sob, breathe, grow like you
you see, I am human, too
society labels me 'criminal'
if you too keep seeing me distantly
then this wall will grow

    tall and fat

So you're listening through the wall
listen carefully
my life clogged when January snowed in 2000
I froze. I killed. I died.
I slowly melt to live.
and if you were me
a young legal immigrant
fresh from plane, not speaking fluent English
not knowing 911 or U.S. laws
   or whom and how to ask for help
and made atrocious mistake
not as choice or last resolution
but out of utter confusion, helplessness
   depression and desperation

In fiery moments
You won't get bail with foreigner label
your interpreter will sleep
   while court proceeds
your rights will be stolen from you
   empty pockets will bring losses
your American dreams will
crumble to deportable trash

wall will suck you in deep
  dark wild forest

humiliation will strip your identity
   label you with number
give you a cube to sleep in
same routine to slowly wither and fade into

You will cry, write letters asking for help
but society will exhale you like carbon-die-oxide
leaving you alone with bundles of battles

So you're listening through the wall
listen carefully
I made my mistakes, ate my guilt
repented, learned, and matured
completed given recommendations and extras
but bureaucracy is still chewing me
not just me
hundreds and hundreds like me
   I won't tell you about
grade less food and drugs
harassments and rapes
or how women cry for their children at night
   die because of healthcare neglect
or what happens to children that come in
or elders that need aid to move around
because that will fill a book
and may bore you
   or prick your conscience
   I won't drain you with details
but I want to ask
   if it matters to you
that Pluto is not considered
a planet anymore
because scientist changed the definition of planet?
   The same thing happened to
Michigan's Parolable Lifers
who have served much more than
   their judge imposed
but are still caged hostage passed their outdates
because parole board changed the definition of Life?

Does it matter to you?
   Would it if we were your
     mother, sister, daughter, wife, or lover?
Does it matter to you
if scientist tomorrow may
decide that Homo sapiens are
monkeys not human beings?
   Would it?
WHY ARE You listening through the wall?

My life is clogged
   your flows on
would is full of creepy politics and wicked wars
   warnings and warmings
at local, community, country, and global level
you hear it, see it, live it

The question drools
will you keep flowing
   in your comfort zones?
or will you plunge into
what matters to you as human beings
and do something?

Kinnari Jivani

Drooling Yolk

It was my words.

I carried them,
here
where clocks tick once a minute
hands can't turn back.

It was my words.

If I could scramble them
drooling yolk
I'd spend my days with a whisk
making brownies out of sour dough
impossible to hear again.

If time
were as dusty as chalk
I'd erase the minute
the one clock tick it took.

If my words
could carry us to Africa
where clocks tick directionless
as fish swim the ocean,
maybe my words
would evaporate in dry heat
off the curl of my lips,
and maybe the hot sun
would melt your frozen icicles.

It was my words.

A carrier of guilt
I walk with the rest of time's travelers
who can't undo mistakes
can't swim like fish in a directionless ocean
can't use hands to turn back,

but I'll try
to rewrite
revise
try the impossible,

but if you're listening,
I can't say it won't happen again,
can't say yolks won't drool sour dough
I was never that good of an artist.

All I can do is move forward
with the rest of time's travelers,
write these profresh
lines of regret
beneath my hands
and hope you listen
when I say
I'm sorry.

Alycia Welch

"ME GO TRIPPIN' "

"Me Go Trippin' " was a prompt inspired by Nikki Giovanni's well-known poem "Ego Trippin' (There May Be a Reason Why)." Each woman received a copy of the famous work, and we read it aloud inside the workshop. We were all deeply inspired by the example we had of poetry providing the space to be shameless in our definition of self-love and pride. As Giovanni took the reader through time and space, decorating herself as the hand of creation—the women of SOUL left modesty at the door and created poetry that defied limitations. Our egos were allowed to swell, as knowledge evolved into wisdom and our beauty became timeless. Without apology or tip-toeing discomfort, we rocketed past the ways in which the world defines us. This process of reshaping ourselves with the brace of unshakeable confidence is the essence of redefinition and empowerment. This prompt is frequently mentioned inside our workshop, and whenever a sister shares a piece that has the spirit of unapologetic i-really-am-friggin-awesomeness, we immediately go to "me go."

Twisted Elegance

Flapping wings screaming to the desert sun.
This is the way she strides.
Legs stretching to thunder pools, and moons hidden behind
  dull stars.

Lions roar and snakes crawl in the amazon which lies in her
  heart.
She is a soldier.
A hero of past wars.

A delicate new life living in lightening flashes.
She breathes fire creating light to guide the child just born.

Wind singing future hopes as mountains glide into rivers
  deep.
She is the idol carved in stone.
Beauty masked, smile suppressed, tripping over worlds too far
  away.

She doesn't understand why lightening only flashes when it
  rains;
or why an eclipse can take away your eye sight.

But she continues to live in brilliance,
but only in her dreams.

She is the world of fear.
A mother of rebirth for a nation of hurt.
She is a soldier.
A hero of past wars.

And this is her life.

D. McDade

Chaos Creater

Took hell for summer
home to ride blaze
of fire.
Told satan so long
demons be gone
it's all me.
Society's reject
never should have been born
I break up families
and happy homes for fun.
Suicide bombers
hatemongers try to impress—
want to do like I do.
Chaos creater be so bad
bigotry and poverty were
my good ideas.
I carry weapons of mass
destruction in my back pocket
put a twist in my hips
dare foolish ones to touch.
My exhale brings pain
inhale dirty, dirty
not worth a damn
too major for a cold cell
If I die
better bury me under the jail.

Tara Moore

Morganville (Megotrippin')

I will smooth it.
Coo you into daydreams,
pry the candy out of your hands—
thank you baby,

You didn't even know you were singing my song.

By 16, I spoke sixteen languages,

Hood love thug dork dyke dirty jam juvenile old soul dj sister
    sistah example warning smooth . . . the shit . . .
I pimped.
(Spoke the world in tongues.)
Me? I? I am brilliant.
Midwife for the rebirth of cool,
Jumped the tracks back
When the revolution was meeting in my basement.

I don't own televisions or speakers
The Plan knocks on my window every morning and guides
    me into step.
Blur lines so hazy, that crazy was thought to be right.
But that night, was actually day.
It was me.
I was standing in the sun's way.

Shine, shiiiiinnnnne
Like the gloss on dimes, convinced, its not all women . . .
just Me.
Write home, baby. This is the best of—
Made up kid gloves
to touch my dome without streaks.

I speak,
and the concrete hardens . . . minds broaden—
So true
God gave me a piece of myself and told Me to walk free.
I don't own shoes.
I make news.
By inhaling.

                                            mw

CHAPTER TWENTY-ONE

The Life Inside: Incarcerated Women Represent Themselves through Journalism

Eleanor Novek

INTRODUCTION: WHY THE CAGED WOMAN WRITES

According to a report by the Sentencing Project (2007), more than 1 million women are currently under the supervision of the criminal justice system in the United States, and more than two hundred thousand of these women are confined in state and federal prisons or local jails. The number of women in prison has increased at nearly double the rate of men since 1985, and women now account for 7 percent of the total population in state and federal prisons. As Beth Richie (2004) observes, women's correctional facilities are concentrated pits of misery populated by women whose lives are characterized by brutal economic disadvantage, racism, and victimization. In a women's prison, she observes, "behind the razor wire fences, concrete barricades, steel doors, metal bars, and thick plexiglass windows, nearly all the manifestations of gender domination that feminist scholars and activists have traditionally concerned themselves with—exploited labor, inadequate healthcare, dangerous living conditions, physical violence, and sexual assault—are revealed at once" (Richie 2004, 438).

Under these conditions, essential human connections are stifled in a thousand painful ways, and a woman in prison experiences a kind of social death. Under the rigid rules of a correctional facility, every human contact is treated as an occasion for criminal behavior. Thus, many forms of interaction with other people inside and outside of the institution are forbidden, while those that are allowed are closely watched and tightly controlled. At the women's prison I observed, if an inmate is fortunate enough to have a family visit, it takes place under heavy surveillance. Guests are screened through metal detectors and subject to drug-sniffing dogs, waiting in long lines, crowded visitation areas, and no privacy or touching. When visits end, inmates are strip-searched for contraband. In a typical institution, prisoners who live in one residential wing may not freely associate with those in another wing, and if they seem too close to a cellmate, they may be transferred to different cells. Women in minimum security areas may not speak with those in maximum security. And to prevent guards and inmates from getting too friendly, inmates are transferred to new job assignments every six months.

Mediated communication is also heavily scrutinized. Guards may open and inspect incoming and outgoing mail—letters, publications, and packages—and confiscate anything deemed inappropriate. Prisoners have no internet access and may not be allowed to own computers or word processors. They can make phone calls, limited to five, ten, or fifteen minutes, but only to a narrow list of approved numbers; calls can be monitored and are very expensive. Television is ubiquitous, but inmates' access to newspapers, magazines, and books is rationed. Library hours are brief, and library collections are minuscule, with the most popular law volumes likely to disappear or have pages torn out.

Under these conditions, writing is a strategy that lets women resist the social death of incarceration and define at least some of the terms that shape their experiences. Prison writing can be seen a form of defiance and a "testament to surviving the dislocations of prison life" (Gaucher 2002, 12). For incarcerated women, "Words come together to knit broken narratives, break through silence, and create new worlds, new visions. Within the dehumanizing social practices of the jail, writing becomes an act of resistance, sometimes obvious, sometimes masked" (Stanford 2004, 277). Scheffler (2002) argues that prison writing allows women to exert some influence over their lives; "In an environment where women are too often treated like children, the incarcerated woman writer can maintain some control over her world by ordering reality according to her own perceptions and organizing principles" (Scheffler 2002, xxxv).

Prison writers are also driven by a deep desire to affirm their value as human beings. This is especially important for female inmates, Scheffler (2002) says, who have been "relegated to one of society's most degraded institutions" (xxxiii). Through their prose, Ross says, incarcerated women express how they begin and sustain relationships, envision an audience, maintain authority, make judgments and claims, and build community (Ross 1996, 87).

The form of prison writing described in this chapter falls under the broad category of prison journalism. The first known prison newspaper in the United States appeared in the nineteenth century, according to historian James McGrath Morris. As tools of prison reformers, these early publications reached a varied readership; at some institutions, inmates were encouraged to read them for moral development, while at others, only citizens outside the walls were considered a fitting audience. At times, Morris (2002) notes, prison newspapers have functioned variously as tools for vocational training, vehicles for moral instruction and reform, expressions of prison culture, and activist strategies for prisoners' rights.

The prison newspapers that survive today (apparently an ever-diminishing number) are part of the tradition of outsider journalism. Like the press created by other oppressed groups outside the commercial mainstream—including early feminists (Steiner 1992), gay and lesbian activists (Streitmatter 1995), homeless people (Howley 2003), migrant workers (Hamilton 1993), dissident soldiers (Lewes 2001), and people with AIDS (Long 2000)—newspapers created by prisoners are acts of resistance that spring from a context of repression (Novek, 2005a). Even inside the most threatening structures of domination, "people in myriad and creative ways carve out space for resisting, contesting, subverting authority, and refurbishing their own identity and dignity" (Conquergood 1995, 85).

The performance of outsider journalism establishes a semipublic sphere of resistance that offers writers the opportunity to challenge the forces that oppress them. In prison newspapers, I have written elsewhere (Novek 2005b), incarcerated people capture the day-to-day atmosphere of the penitentiary as they live and understand it. The public forum they construct is valuable to the writers and to their audiences as well, as attested to by the genre of prison literature that has flourished in the United States and other countries, especially since the 1960s (Gaucher 2002). This discursive space is especially precious to imprisoned women who, through writing, witness against the institutions that seek to "destroy their humanity in the name of justice" (Scheffler 2002, xvii). These writers experience "an exercise of power in a place that attempts to deny power to those who are imprisoned there" (Stanford 2004, 278).

This chapter offers a media ethnography that describes the ways incarcerated women at one correctional facility represent themselves in journalistic writing. Ethnography is a research method that focuses on the stories people tell about their own social worlds. "Truth and facts are socially constructed, and people build stories around the meanings of facts. Ethnographers collect and tell these multiple versions of the 'truth' " (Denzin and Lincoln 1995, 4). In this case, multiple versions of the "truth" about prison life have been written by women incarcerated at a minimum-to-maximum security correctional facility for women located in the mid-Atlantic region of the United States. The chapter offers an interpretive analysis of articles from fifty issues of a prison newspaper the prisoners published between 2001 and 2008.

Because the correctional world is closed off from external scrutiny and socially isolated, the stories most people hear about life in prison come from overheated political rhetoric and mass media. Exploiting clichés of the penal institution for drama and titillation, shows such as *Prison Break*, the HBO series *Oz*, and countless Hollywood films create an image in the public mind of prison as a wilderness where all the inmates are vicious and must be restrained in thrillingly violent ways. Ethnographic thick descriptions of prison life can help counteract the distortions spread by exaggerated, entertainment-driven mass media images of prison.

Such systematic examinations can also reduce "errors of romanticization" (Katz 1997, 394) by which people who are seen as possessing deviant social reputations are viewed through a middle-class "veil of mystery" that is sustained, rather than dispelled, by the glimpses of them provided in the news and routine police reports. Ethnography offers scholars the opportunity "to document local meaning, that is, the meaning of subjects' actions to the subjects" (Katz 1997, 395) and to direct a more clear-headed level of attention to people so categorized. If we truly want to understand the lives of the people warehoused in the U.S. corrections system, it makes sense for us to learn about their experience through their own words and meanings.

BIRTH AND DEATH OF A PRISON NEWSPAPER

In 2001, a colleague and I began volunteer-teaching journalism classes at the state prison described above. We hoped to empower the participants in the classes to use journalism in claiming a voice by writing and publishing their own newspaper. In prison, women do not learn economic survival skills to use when they leave the institution; on the contrary, they are likely to lose or exhaust whatever social and emotional resources they have. In bringing a journalism class to the prison, I wanted to offer participants opportunities for self-expression, social support, enhanced self-efficacy, and a chance to build proficiencies in skills that might some day enhance their employment options.

The twice-monthly classes began in September 2001. Lessons covered news judgment, developing story ideas, writing in news style, interviewing, opinion writing, editing, grammar, spelling and punctuation, page design, and the use of word processing and layout software. Students wrote news articles, features, and poems that focused on the facts of their daily lives and experiences; they also collected writings from women who did not take part in the class. The members of the class began to study layout and editing and published their first edition of the newspaper in February 2002.

Eventually the inmates were able to produce one issue of their newspaper a month, and they did so for several years, using the institution's computers and a tiny office space that was also used for other purposes. Over this period of time, more than one hundred women attended journalism classes and served as the newspaper staff, editing and composing the newspaper each month. Numerous articles, poems, and other writings also poured in from prisoners who were not taking part in the class; for several years, the newspaper staff received so many submissions of poems that the entire August issue was devoted to poetry. Although the inmates had a hard time keeping track of all the submissions and occasionally lost an article, almost every piece of writing submitted was printed.

Most issues of the paper contained a mix of news and feature articles, opinion columns, personal essays, poetry, recipes, puzzles and cartoons. During the first three years, about a third of the articles came from the journalism class and followed at least some journalistic norms; they were fact-based stories built on written reports, interviews, or eyewitness observation of events. Another third were opinion essays, giving voice to the authors' personal beliefs. The remaining articles came from outside the class and represented the most diverse formats, including recipes, puzzles, cartoons and other contributions.

Stapled at one edge and decorated with clip-art or pencil sketches, the publication resembled the home-made newsletters and outsider journalism of earlier decades. Occasionally, colored ink highlighted the front pages, which were adorned with large clip-art illustrations. Cameras are generally forbidden at prisons, so photographs were rare; but occasionally the institution took photos at special programs or visitor speeches, and these ran inside the newspaper, along with inmates' drawings, cartoons, creative fonts, and clip-art. The women wanted the publication to be printed commercially on newsprint, so it would "look like a real newspaper," but neither permission nor funding could be arranged for this, so instead it was printed at a men's prison on 8 1/2 by 11-inch office paper.

The class met on a biweekly basis for three and a half years, from September 2001 until March 2005. In early 2005, prison officials said they had observed several incidents of computer misappropriation in the office and attributed them to the newspaper's inmate staff. They began objecting to the degree of computer access enjoyed by the prisoners, saying that inmates' computer use should be supervised by state employees, not by civilian volunteers. My colleague and I felt pressured to end the class and our involvement with the newspaper.

After the class had ended, the women were still permitted to publish the newspaper but under greatly curtailed circumstances. Groups of women were no longer allowed to meet and plan the paper or hold lengthy discussions of the topics they would write about. Any inmates using computers for newspaper editing or layout had to be supervised by a state employee. Without the journalism class as inspiration, the number of articles submitted for publication declined sharply. Between 2005 and 2008, the newspaper's frequency of the production dropped from monthly to quarterly and then even less frequently.

A prisoner who had been one of the most active and thoughtful writers took over the editorship of the newspaper at some point in 2005. (Though no longer teaching at the facility, I was corresponding with her on a regular basis.) In the Spring 2007 issue of the paper, almost half of the articles were written by this woman, who published this plea to her fellow inmates: "Without your submissions, this paper cannot continue. I have diligently done the best I can to keep this paper alive, but due to the limited amount of submissions, I see this paper coming to the end of the road. You matter! Your voice is important!" After shepherding a few more issues without much participation from other inmates, the woman quit in frustration in mid-2008.

In describing prison life through the journalistic writings of inmates between 2001 and 2008, this chapter portrays "the life inside," the social world of the prison, through the written voices of its occupants. It focuses on four dominant themes—loneliness, redemption, survival, and critique—that reflect the voices with which the women chose to represent themselves to the outside and inside worlds. To protect the privacy of the participants, this chapter does not disclose the name or location of the institution, the title of the publication, or the identities of any prisoners whose writings are quoted in this study. At the time of this writing, the newspaper is no longer publishing, but a number of the authors who wrote for it are still incarcerated.

THEME 1: PRISON IS A LONELY PLACE

Women writing in prison often express a deep, abiding isolation. The sudden separation from family members and other loved ones following arrest and conviction is wrenching and highly traumatic, with an aftermath of confusion, sadness, and fear. In perhaps the most common recurrent theme expressed in inmate journalism, the authors present themselves as caring, feeling women who have been uprooted from relationships as mothers, daughters, sisters, wives and lovers. Many are tormented by the loss of daily connection to their children, like the woman who writes, "I am a mother, yet I am not there . . . I have missed holidays, birthdays, and doctor appointments. I have missed their tears of joy and disappointment. I have missed their daydreams and nightmares. I have missed grooming their nails and doing their hair. I have missed walks in the park and playing on swings. I cannot count all that I've missed . . . there's just so many things" (September 2005).

Surveying their new social world, the newly incarcerated woman recognizes its harshness. "Prison life is a very lonely life," an author writes. "You're taken from comfort and consistency and tossed into loneliness and pain. First comes shock, eventually acceptance, and finally utter loneliness. Nothing is familiar, everyone is a stranger. You're apart from your family, and you have no friends" (February 2002). Getting to know people in this strange environment is intimidating; though convicted of crimes themselves, many women find their fellow inmates obnoxious and untrustworthy at first glance. As one inmate describes it, "I have spent many lonesome hours here amidst the masses of those who struggle to find themselves or to be 'somebody' in prison while still glorifying their own lack of judgment and moral debasement in the places we all come from" (January 2006).

As time passes, the women do develop friendships, but prison relationships are unstable and unpredictable. "For me, it's been like living surrounded by eggshells; you never know when something is going to crack," one writer observes. "The person that eats with you at mealtime today can become someone that won't even speak to you tomorrow" (Spring 2008). Women try to reach out to one another, but they suffer consequences; sometimes they are taken advantage of and pressured for snacks or cigarettes, physically abused, or abandoned by their new cronies. An author notes, "In life, certain people will impersonate understanding. They will smile at you. They will assure you that everything is just fine . . . They may even say, 'Yes! I understand!' Yet when the moment comes for a demonstration of understanding, what you will get is misinterpretation, misrepresentation, miscommunication, and you will get blamed for the misunderstanding" (July 2005). Another contends, "Anyone can say they love you or that they are your friend, but it's only for the moment . . . Why do we need friends when they're only there for when they can use you?" (January 2007).

The close scrutiny of other inmates and corrections officers may add another layer to the emotional mine field. In a wry look at the prison rumor mill, a poet observes that "prison gossip could be bad for your health." She describes how "everybody does it, there's no need to lie, you hear the faint whispers as you walk by. These women think they know you—but they really have no clue. They should mind their own business and worry about what they do" (Summer 2007).

Under these conditions, vulnerability and affection are dangerous, for they can expose a woman to exploitation, betrayal, and abuse. Thus, a woman warns her readers, "I would advise people to be cautious when trusting someone in this kind of environment . . . It is very difficult to make friends in a place like this. There are a lot of miserable people here who want everyone around them to be miserable, too. They try to steal your joy away or put you down when you're feeling good" (January 2005). Another advises, "It's best to have friends supporting you from home so that you don't need a friend here. My reason for saying so is because you really don't know the person for who they truly are when you meet them here . . . The person they portray themselves to be here can be completely different from who they are at home" (December 2006).

For those brave enough to strive to connect with others, genuine friendship does sometimes blossom; but when one woman's sentence comes to an end, the cold touch of the prison intervenes again. "People leave. It's the way it's supposed to be," writes one woman. "We bid farewell good luck and shed our tears of joy and sorrow, for the brief encounter that, if we're lucky, touched our hearts to last for a lifetime in our memories" (June 2005). Sometimes inmates die while in prison; the subtle poems of mourning that appear in some issues of the newspaper only hint at the depths of feeling the authors must suppress, lest they be isolated or drugged against their will by the custodial staff, as some women report.

The price is too high for many women, and they revert to self-imposed separation, avoiding close friendships and group affiliation for their own emotional protection. "Keeping to myself" is widely recognized as a strategy for avoiding disciplinary problems and betrayal. Moving from the prison's maximum security wing to its minimum security area, one woman expresses pride in her new reputation for good behavior. "I try to stay to myself and away from the cliques because I don't want to be a part of that mix," she writes (Summer 2007). In a poem, another writer advises her readers, "Misery loves company—be a loner" (Spring 2008).

THEME 2: REDEMPTION FOUND HERE

Despite the social isolation, many writers see the prison as a beneficial kind of "boot camp" experience that rescues them from their weaker selves and sets them on a path to a better life. Coming from backgrounds of abuse and addiction, the writers portray themselves as victims wandering in a daze of desperation and violence until prison forces them to take stock of their lives. These writers see incarceration as offering an opportunity for personal development, temporary relief from vulnerability on the street, and the possibility of spiritual enlightenment. Many writings contain references to a higher power, God, Jesus, or Allah, as an intervening force; they describe encounters with faith that have helped the authors survive the suffering of incarceration. Others see the modest learning opportunities offered by the institution as an avenue for self-discovery.

One woman writes: "Was I arrested or rescued? Being on the streets, hanging out in places where danger constantly lurked, using drugs, and doing things that were not good for me, was leading me to an early grave. Prison has given me a new understanding of what freedom means. I was rescued from self-destruction" (September 2003). Another author explains, "I am thankful for this chance to sit back and sort out what went wrong and how I can make it better, not only for myself, but for the people I love the most. This 'chance,' as I call it, is my opportunity to find myself, because somewhere I lost me" (December 2006).

Some writers take a reproving tone, admonishing themselves for foolishly throwing away the freedom they once possessed. One woman writes, "When we make mistakes, we should have the guts to stand up and take the consequences . . . I am not happy about the lack of filet mignon on the commissary list either, but I invited myself to this party, so I just better file my complaints in the recycling bin" (June 2005). Another confesses, "This is my fourth time here, and it is nothing to brag about. I thank God that I'm here and not six feet under, because a lot of people who was here on my first bust are not even existing today" (March 2003).

With their criminal behavior interrupted, some women are grateful to discover learning resources in prison, even though these are quite sparse. State funding for education only addresses the GED needs of younger inmates; inmates with resources may pay out of their own pockets for a few college-level courses, but these are offered sporadically and have long waiting lists. Other learning programs offer training in low-paid occupations (cosmetology, horticulture, office skills, starting a small business, and so on) or volunteer-led discussion groups in philosophy or other topics. Still, the writers who get involved in these pursuits see themselves as proactive learners who can look to the prison's classes and programs as a means of self-betterment. They eagerly profess their commitment to lifelong learning and encourage other inmates to pursue it as well.

One author, excited about the opportunity to earn a high school equivalency certificate, calls herself "a child left behind." She writes, "Give me a classroom instead of a piece of crack! Give me a teacher instead of a drug dealer! Give me a book instead of a beer! Give me hope instead of hate! Give me an ink pen instead of a gun!" (December 2004). Another writer expresses gratitude for Project Storybook, a volunteer program that allows inmates to record children's stories on tape for their family members. "It feels heartwarming, knowing that our children, grandchildren, nieces, and nephews, get to hear our voice reading to them, as if we were there at home, reading stories to them at bedtime" (August 2006). Other women enthusiastically describe their involvement in work readiness, music enrichment, life skills, and other programs held at the prison, including the newspaper: "It is about enlightening other women, helping them to motivate themselves, and giving them a push in a positive direction" (March 2003).

A widely repeated institutional cliché is to "do your time, don't let your time do you." For many prisoners, even the modest opportunities described here represent a new way of seeing themselves and doing their time. Atoning for the past and insecure about the future, the authors of these articles present themselves as newly aware of the possibilities of life. Whether they profess a new faith in God or claim to have developed a new appreciation for learning, these writers are eager to leave their old identities behind and put on bright new faces.

THEME 3: SURVIVING IN PRISON TAKES KNOWLEDGE— PASS IT ON

Many of the writers enjoy seeing themselves as authorities, keepers of wisdom who are willing to share hard-won insights about prison existence for the benefit of other women in similar straits. Such writings take the form of how-to articles and personal essays about life experience. In either case, the authors make the rhetorical claim that they are experts with specialized knowledge that may help other women improve their lives. The tone of such essays is usually earnest, matter-of-fact, and insistent.

Since medical care in many of the nation's prisons is hard to come by at best and incompetent at worst, health is a genuine worry for these incarcerated women. Of particular concern are life-threatening diseases that are common and easily spread in prison, such as HIV and hepatitis C. Using magazines and newspapers as sources, many women write to inform their fellow inmates of the symptoms, treatments, and effects of these illnesses. They also discuss a variety of other conditions, such as breast cancer, fibroids, osteoporosis, Lyme disease, diabetes, depression, menopause, migraines, and mental illness. Other writings inform inmates of the dangers inherent in tattoos and body piercing or caution them against irresponsible sexual behavior or staph infections. Some essays recommend good nutrition, exercise for stress reduction, yoga, and other healthy behaviors.

A few of the writers specialize in legal information. Imprisoned people are often engrossed in the status of their own cases, appeals, and motions, and they find related information about recent state and Supreme Court rulings highly significant. A number of writings focus on specific court decisions, such as changes in the state's mandatory minimum sentencing regulations for drug possession and sale, or on legal processes, such as how to understand a sentence or file an appeal. "Litigating a case in court is not easy and certainly not a rapid process," one writer cautions. "But if you have a valid claim and are willing to persevere, you may chalk up a victory" (December 2004).

Humor is a survival strategy in a penitentiary, and some of the writers soften the advice they give about prison life with playfulness. For example, inmates have no kitchens in their cells, but some wings have a microwave oven for communal use; a popular form of writing is microwave recipes. One woman asks, "Have you ever looked at a container of plain vanilla pudding on your tray, and just shake your head and think, 'Bland old-lady food?' Now look at it and think of all the great treats that start with it" (January 2007). Recipes for pies and cakes, casseroles, vegetable soup, fried rice, candy, and other goodies are offered, in prose that mimics the helpful tone of *Family Circle* or other popular magazines. Some recipe writers even parody themselves; an inmate offers dozens of ways of sprucing up a packet of ramen noodles, with syrup for "breakfast ramen," ketchup for "French fries ramen," and parmesan cheese for "fettuccini Alfredo ramen" (April 2004).

As the bland high-carbohydrate prison diet leads many women to gain weight, some writers offer advice on physical fitness. Observing that some inmates need their privacy, one author describes workout routines that can be performed in one's cell, using canned vegetables as hand weights: "For those of you looking to tone and tighten your muscles, there are a number of exercises you can do as you sit on your bunks or stand in your cube" (March 2004). And because the incarcerated women miss the mass-market bath and beauty products they once used, recipes for homemade cosmetics made with lemon juice, mayonnaise, and vegetable oil are also a part of this genre.

Other forms of knowledge also get passed along. They may be lighthearted, such as listings of AM and FM radio stations that can be heard within the prison's reception range, or recommended thrillers and romance novels from the prison library. Or they may be weighty, as when one inmate explains the institutional procedures required for seeking permission to attend the funeral of a family member. Another urges inmates to write to their children persistently. "You may have no way of knowing whether or not your child is receiving your correspondence, but if there is any chance that your child is receiving your letters, you must continue to write on a regular basis, even if they never respond," she writes. "Our children need to know that our devotion to them is unwavering and that our love for them is unconditional" (October 2003).

Some authors offer their fellow inmates tough love, urging them to use their prison time to prepare for their release. One observes, "Being in prison can be used as a time of reflection on the changes you want to make for yourself and give you an opportunity to implement them before you get out. Time here can be used to develop skills that will help you be able to keep a job or learn how to apply for a job" (March 2003). Another author demands personal responsibility from her peers. "Playing cards and chaos is no longer the thing to do. If you can remember the words to your favorite rap, then you can remember to stimulate your brain through education. In return, it will help you to a marketable skill that will help you to prosper in life outside prison" (June 2003).

Taken together, these essays of advice and ingenuity offer the reader strategies for feeling competent during her prison term. Their value to a writer is the claim of authority they allow her to make.

THEME 4: PRISONS DESERVE CRITIQUE

Even under ideal circumstances, incarceration may be highly traumatic, and a torrent of distress and complaint underlies the women's writings. Although prison administrators reviewed the newspaper prior to printing and usually censored disparaging articles, essays that criticized the facility occasionally slipped through. Writers point out a leaking roof, disapprove of a new payment card system on snack machines in visiting areas, or complain about cooked chicken with the feathers left on. In making these assessments about the shortcomings of prison management, the women turn the tables on the system that continually evaluates them and finds them flawed. Now they are the judges, and the prison itself is the offender who comes up short.

The tone of these writings is direct and displeased, with occasional flashes of humor. One woman asks why a prison knitting program is canceled: "Was it stopped to stop the creativity of women here? Was it stopped so that now there are no rewarding activities to help deserving women pass their time? Was it stopped to punish the few that are using it in inappropriate ways?" (July 2002). Another questions why prison grounds crews are set to planting flowers instead of vegetables. "I don't understand the logic in all these newly planted flowers," she writes. "I can't seem to see, taste, feel, smell, or eat any fresh vegetables, except a few pieces of lettuce occasionally! I feel there is a greater need here for better nutrition for health purposes" (April 2003).

Writing in both English and Spanish, a woman notes that Hispanic inmates' difficulties in understanding English keep them from taking part in educational and social programs at the prison. "How does the Department of Corrections expect the Hispanic women to be rehabilitated and ready for society when the programs that they provide are of no use to them?" she writes (July 2002). Another writer encourages fellow inmates to submit grievance forms because the commissary does not stock wide-toothed combs for African American hair, saying, "It is important for the women's emotional well-being to be able to look our best, or at least be presentable" (September 2004).

Some authors use humor and vivid description to satirize their living conditions. In a poem describing her experiences on "grounds detail," a work unit responsible for everything from picking up trash to mowing the grass outside the prison buildings, an inmate writes: "We rake up leaves and shovel snow, We're covered with dirt from head to toe . . . We pick up sticks, get bit by ticks, We cut down trees and get stung by bees" (December 2006). Another woman luridly describes the putrid smell of garbage faced by inmates on sanitation duty in the maximum security wing: "The scent is so foul and pungent it can be likened to regurgitated baby milk that has been left to turn sour" (April 2004).

Some writers use their pens to disparage their peers. One author observes firsthand the high rate of recidivism at the institution. "I went to the dining hall, and what did I see—nearly fifteen women that had gone to halfway houses had returned . . . How can someone say that they have their self together, when they keep coming back to prison?" (March 2005). Another writer is dismayed that few inmates cared enough about their own health to attend a no-cost screening for breast cancer at the prison: "Many women chose to decline the free services due largely to the fact that they did not wish to wait" (October 2004). In another essay, a woman chided her fellow inmates for failing to clean up their living quarters. "It makes no sense for adult women to be as nasty as I have witnessed in the units where I've lived. I mean, not flushing the toilets, hair and toothpaste all over the sinks, water spilled on the floor, blood on the toilet seats . . . I don't want to become sick or infected with some type of fungus because another prisoner failed to clean up behind themselves" (February 2004).

Other writers look at the larger picture, passing judgment on the nation's corrections practices. To them the prison system is less a personal tragedy than a national disgrace, and their outrage is for others as well as themselves. One author argues that there are better responses to drug-related crimes than imprisonment, pointing to drug treatment programs and intensive supervision for nonviolent offenders. Another woman calls for national prison reform, writing, "The present structure of U.S. prisons does not provide prisoners with life skills or the educational skills that are necessary for them to make a successful reentry or transitions to their communities and with their families" (Summer 2007). After reading a report about the special stresses that prison imposes on women, a prisoner observes, "Incarcerated women across the nation are screaming for help, but are our pleas falling on deaf ears? . . . We have very special needs. Where are the programs, education, services that we as women truly need to rehabilitate?" (April 2003).

These writers find fault with sentencing and parole policies, substandard medical care, the lack of educational opportunities, and other conditions faced by incarcerated people around the country, not just at their own facility. Such writings move the locus of the problem from the offender to the system, calling it into account instead of the other way around.

CONCLUSION: VALUING THE LIFE INSIDE

The prison newspaper described here was produced by and for incarcerated women at one particular institution, and it was never intended for the eyes of outsiders. But for the six and a half years in which it operated, the publication reached a receptive audience that included not only the inmate population but also the corrections officers, staff, and administrators at the institution, and family members outside. The women's journalistic writing allowed them to maintain a sense of personal worth in a hostile environment and created a mechanism for the development of identity and the sharing of meaning in a system that otherwise silenced its inmates. As demonstrated here, the voices of female offenders offer a complex, moving portrait of prison life as they have lived it.

An imprisoned woman may have experienced the social dislocation of prison as painful and may find it difficult to make friends and develop trust. When writing of her sadness, the author does not see herself primarily as a helpless prisoner, cut off from society, but as a woman with a profound need and desire for connection to other people. Her distress is real when she senses that this need may not be filled during the duration of her sentence, but there may be some comfort in giving voice to her pain, because it connects her to others who are experiencing the same thing.

Though the prison is a desperate and dismal place, the woman also sees it as a place of rescue and recovery. Looking back over behaviors that were self-destructive and hurtful, possibly involving drugs, prostitution, abuse, and violence, she expresses a sense of contrition and gratitude for being alive. Now her eye is on the future, and she will rely on the help of the divine, her own powerful determination for self-improvement, or a combination of both, to succeed.

Surviving a term in prison takes skills, and the writer is eager to display and share the knowledge she has earned about life behind bars. The woman considers herself an expert at navigating various aspects of the corrections system. Not only can she use her experience to improve the quality of her own life and survive incarceration as a whole person, but she is also confident in her ability to help others do the same. Applying her resourcefulness to the conditions around her, she tries to maintain mental and physical health. When possible, she likes to offer other women the benefit of her knowhow.

When she chooses to criticize the institution that confines her, the writer embodies the judgmental and critical voices that she has heard directed at herself many times. She enjoys a sense of herself as an analytical thinker whose opinions and evaluations are valuable. There is a sense of vindication as the author denounces the shortcomings of the very system that has condemned her as an outcast.

Fiske observes that the dominant institutions in a society construct the social order in their own interests by defining the meaning of self and of social relations (1993, 11). When people challenge these dominant definitions with alternative meanings, he contends, they perform important acts of defiance that legitimate their own and other oppositional views. An incarcerated woman who claims a voice and expresses her own mind and meaning challenges the system's view of herself as a deviant and redefines herself as valuable, as needed, as a person. This is "brave writing, scripted from the front lines of a battle for psychic, spiritual, and even physical survival" (Stanford 2004, 278). Though she has been isolated from society, despised, and cast out, the prison journalist envisions herself a new identity as a worthy human being, fighting for her life.

The incarcerated women journalists who speak here offer eloquent testimony about the social and personal costs of incarceration and its impact on women.

They defy the dehumanization that has been imposed on them and insist that they be seen as people with unique personalities, talents, and insights. In reaching out to one another for a shared sense of camaraderie and community, these journalists challenge society's efforts to isolate them and struggle to maintain their human identity in a soul-killing environment. Finally, in offering a persistent vision of their humanity, these women remind society that the prison-industrial complex is a wasteful, inhumane, and ultimately self-defeating way to deal with the problems of poverty, addiction, intimate violence, mental illness, racism, educational inequality, and other causes of crime.

REFERENCES

Conquergood, Dwight. 1995. "Between Rigor and Relevance: Rethinking Applied Communication." In *Applied Communication in the Twenty-first Century*, ed. Kevin Cissna, 79–96. Mahwah, NJ: Erlbaum.

Denzin, Norman, and Yvonne Lincoln. 1995. "New Ethnographies. Transforming Qualitative Research Methods—Is It a Revolution?" *Journal of Contemporary Ethnography* 24: 349–59.

Fiske, Jon. 1993. *Power Plays, Power Works*. London: Verso.

———. 1989. *Reading the Popular*. Cambridge, MA: Unwin Hyman.

Gaucher, Bob. 2002. "The Journal of Prisoners on Prisons: An Ethnography of the Prison Industrial Complex in the 1990s." In *Writing as Resistance: The Journal of Prisoners on Prisons Anthology 1988–2002,* ed. Bob Gaucher, 5–30. Toronto: Canadian Scholars.

Hamilton, Jay. 1993. "Educating Patriots, Recruiting Radicals: The Migrant Camp Newspaper at Arvin, California." *Communication* 13: 255–75.

Howley, Kevin. 2003. "A Poverty of Voices: Street Papers as Communicative Democracy." *Journalism* 4: 273–92.

Katz, Jack. 1997. "Ethnography's Warrants." *Sociological Methods and Research* 25: 391–422.

Lewes, James. 2001. "Envisioning Resistance: The GI Underground Press during the Vietnam War." *Media History* 7: 137–50.

Long, Thomas L. 2000. "Plague of Pariahs: AIDS 'Zines and the Rhetoric of Transgression." *Journal of Communication Inquiry* 24: 401–11.

Morris, James M. 2002. *Jailhouse Journalism: The Fourth Estate behind Bars*. New Brunswick, NJ: Transaction.

Novek, Eleanor. 2005a. " 'Heaven, Hell, and Here': Understanding the Impact of Incarceration through a Prison Newspaper." *Critical Studies in Media Communication* 22: 281–301.

———. 2005b. " 'The Devil's Bargain:' Censorship, Identity, and the Promise of Empowerment in a Prison Newspaper." *Journalism: Theory, Practice, and Criticism* 6: 5–23.

Richie, Beth E. 2004. "Feminist Ethnographies of Women in Prison." *Feminist Studies* 30: 438–50.

Ross, Susan. 1996. "The Writings of Women Prisoners: Voices from the Margins." In *Mainstream(s) and Margins, Cultural Politics in the '90s,* ed. Michael Morgan and Susan Leggett, 85–100. Westport, CN: Greenwood.

Scheffler, Judith A. 2002. Introduction. In *Wall Tappings. An International Anthology of Women's Prison Writings, 200 to the Present,* ed. Judith Scheffler, xxi–xliv. New York: Feminist Press at the City University of New York.

Sentencing Project, The. 2007. *Women in the Criminal Justice System. Briefing Sheets*: *1–10*. Washington, DC: The Sentencing Project.

Stanford, Anne F. 2004. "More Than Just Words: Women's Poetry and Resistance at Cook County Jail." *Feminist Studies* 30: 277–301.

Steiner, Linda. 1992. "The History and Structure of Women's Alternative Media." In *Women Making Meaning: New Feminist Directions in Communication,* ed. Lana Rakow, 121–43. New York: Routledge.

Streitmatter, R. 1995. "Creating a Venue for the 'Love That Dare Not Speak Its Name': Origins of the Gay and Lesbian Press." *Journalism and Mass Communication Quarterly* 72: 436–47.

Identifying Marks: What the Razor Wire Hides

Ashley E. Lucas

We are so familiar with the visual and descriptive indicators of female criminality as defined by mainstream U.S. media culture that we are seldom called upon to question them. If you are an incarcerated woman in this country, chances are very high that you are black, working-class, someone who did not have the opportunity to attend college, and a survivor of sexual and/or physical abuse. On television, women in prison or those in overpoliced neighborhoods are portrayed as tough, brash, and impulsive; they tend to look strung out, speak in accents, and act untrustworthily. Viewing audiences—of popular film and television, as well as the nightly news—are trained to perceive certain people as likely to be guilty of something, even if one cannot be sure of what crime that person committed. The implicit logic here is that if the courts function justly, and these are the people consistently being convicted, then perhaps indicators such as race, class, educational level, and the neighborhood where one lives actually reveal something about a person's propensity for crime. By extension, if you are the child, spouse, sibling, or even friend of someone identified as criminal, then you are likely to be guilty or dangerous as well.

This misleading and stereotypical mode for depicting incarcerated women discourages us from seeing the actual consequences of the institutional violence of prisons. Even before they become incarcerated, many working-class women and women of color are failed by the very police forces and court systems that are supposed to protect all of us. Women are frequently policed and sentenced for crimes committed by their boyfriends or husbands, and when they prove less savvy in advocating for their rights in court or in the plea bargaining process, many receive longer sentences than their male counterparts who took more active roles in the crimes in question. In impoverished neighborhoods, police forces often do little to protect women against domestic violence and neglect to enforce restraining orders against abusers, and when women defend themselves or their children against attacks, they are portrayed as calculatingly homicidal.

Sensationalized violence and dramatized arrests overshadow the lives of women facing long-term and less entertaining struggles, like seeking healthcare while incarcerated, visiting an imprisoned loved one thousands of miles from home, or lobbying against a new piece of get-tough-on-crime legislation. In highlighting the lives of the many razor wire women in this book, we seek to combat generalized suggestions of the inherent criminality of certain groups of women. We also advocate for alternatives to incarceration and policies of large-scale decarceration. In order for us to imagine and implement such a significant shift in our justice system, we must undergo a national shift in culture, away from viewing policing and incarceration as forms of desensitized entertainment and toward meaningful engagement with the health and well-being of all individuals, neighborhoods, and communities.

Despite the concerted efforts we as editors have made to evade the easy categories that frame women's incarceration, we were repeatedly reminded of the strict boundaries drawn around the very modes of thought and institutional behavior we seek to subvert. Over the course of the three years that we have been working on this book, we lost track of a few of the incarcerated women who were slated to contribute artwork or writing to this collection. A few of the women had been transferred to other prison units, and some were no longer incarcerated. Those who had been released from prison proved particularly challenging to locate, though we did manage to reach most of them.

The only woman we could not find is out on parole now, but the parole office in her county does not seem to answer the phone nor respond to messages. We used the state prison system's website to search for her whereabouts, and we discovered a list of information that revealed very little about the woman for whom we searched and a great deal about how the state perceives incarcerated women. The website provided us with a list of the charges filed against this woman, her prison number, the dates of her incarceration, her parole status, and the contact information for the unresponsive parole office. It did not indicate whether the prison system had provided her with any treatment, education, or programming that might prepare her for life after incarceration. A category labeled "Biographical Information" indicated her race, gender, date of birth, hair and eye color, weight, and height. This was, of course, not the sort of biographical information that we sought. Another box called "Marks, Scars, and Tattoos" contained a list of the regions of her body that were scarred and the added notations "Missing Right Arm" and "Missing Right Leg." What else was this woman missing? What facts about her life and identity were we and the criminal justice system missing as we struggled to perceive certain aspects of this woman's life?

Such phenotypic markers offer us a vision of a body shorn completely of narrative, of context, of—in short—anything that might actually explain who this person is, not to mention why she committed (or perhaps was simply rail-roaded for, intimidated into confessing, etc.) her putative offense. This means of describing a person elides not only her humanity but also the state's presumption of reasonable judgment. Without context or complexity in the modes in which we speak of such things as crime, convictions, and human behavior, how can we trust in the inherent justice of our system? We would not want Department of Corrections (DOC) websites to make *more* information available than they already do—prison already represents an egregious violation of the human need for privacy—but, between popular media and DOC statistics, an entire universe of knowledge and perception, of bodies and minds, of souls and stories, is going missing, and along with it—ironically—all chances of generating the kind of crime-preventing knowledge that both institutions promise in order to justify their own abuses. That gap, where it is acknowledged at all, is acknowledged foremost in the work of women artists in prison. Books like ours cannot fill that gap, but we can bring much-deserved attention to those communities, activists, and prisoners who already—in spite of every discouragement imaginable—are doing that work, bravely, brashly, joyously.

List of Contributors

Jodie Michelle Lawston is assistant professor in women's studies at California State University-San Marcos. She holds a BA in psychology and women's studies from the State University of New York at Stony Brook, an MA in sociology from the University of California, San Diego, and a PhD from the University of California, San Diego. Lawston's first book, *Sisters Outside: Radical Activists Working for Women Prisoners* (State University of New York Press, 2009), examines women's grassroots resistance efforts against the expanding carceral system. Her research interests include women's incarceration, prison labor, women's manifestations of resistance to oppression, the prison as a warehouse for the poor and people of color, prison expansion, immigrant detention, and social justice movements. Her scholarly publications include articles in the anthologies *(Re) Interpretations: The Shapes of Justice in Women's Experience*; *Milestones for American Women: Our Defining Passages*; *Gender and Society*; *Social Justice*; *Sociological Focus*; and the *National Women's Studies Association Journal*. Lawston's second book project, for which she is currently conducting research, is an examination and exploration of the ways in which the discourses that advocate detention and incarceration—as proper enforcement of immigration and criminal law—converge. She serves on the board of several nonprofit organizations that work with women in prison, and she advises students on advocating for incarcerated women. Together with Ashley Lucas, Lawston guest edited a special issue of the *National Women's Studies Association Journal*, on the topic Women and Criminal Justice: Policing, Prosecution, and Incarceration, which was published in August 2008.

Ashley E. Lucas is an assistant professor in the Department of Dramatic Art at the University of North Carolina at Chapel Hill. She holds a BA in theater studies and English from Yale University, an MA in ethnic studies from the University of California, San Diego (UCSD), and a joint PhD in ethnic studies and theater and drama from UCSD. She is working on a book manuscript, which is entitled *The Imagined Nation: Ethnographic Theatre in the Late Twentieth Century*. She was awarded a Ford Foundation Diversity Postdoctoral Fellowship for 2008–2009, which enabled her to conduct research for her second book project on the Prison Creative Arts Project. Her research and teaching interests include prison-related theater, theater for social change, Chicana/o theater, U.S. Latina/o theater, African American theater, and related topics in acting, playwriting, and comparative ethnic studies. Lucas is also the child of a prisoner and the author of an ethnographic play about the families of prisoners entitled *Doin' Time: Through the Visiting Glass*, which she has performed as a one-woman show throughout the United States as well as in Dublin and Limerick, Ireland. Her scholarly publications include articles in the anthology *Monologues: Theatre, Performance, Subjectivity* as well as the *Journal of American Drama and Theatre*; *Latin American Theater Review*; *GESTOS: Teoría y Práctica del Teatro Hispánico*; and the *Journal for the Study of Radicalism*. Together with Jodie Lawston, Lucas guest edited a special issue of the *National Women's Studies Association Journal* on the topic of Women and Criminal Justice: Policing, Prosecution, and Incarceration, which was published in August 2008.

ᜒᜒ

Brian Bilsky is a second-year master's student at the University of Hawai'i of both political science and women's studies. He has been a graduate assistant to Meda Chesney-Lind since January 2009. His interests include both the adult and juvenile justice systems and their gendered, racialized, and class-based disparities.

Barbara Bloom, PhD, is a professor in the Department of Criminology and Criminal Justice Studies at Sonoma State University. Her research and policy interests include women and girls under criminal justice supervision and gender-responsive interventions and services. Dr. Bloom is a past president of the Western Society of Criminology (WSC) and has received many awards, including the WSC Fellow Award (2003), the American Probation and Parole Association University of Cincinnati Award (2003), the American Society of Criminology Division on Women and Crime Saltzman Award (2006), and the National Council on Crime and Delinquency Donald Cressey Award (2007).

Kathy Boudin was formerly incarcerated and dedicated her time inside to the issues faced by the community of women that she engaged in programming for HIV/AIDS, parenting, and both basic literacy and higher education. Since coming home, she has continued those commitments through HIV/AIDS work, work with teens with incarcerated parents, and support for longtermers through parole reform and restorative justice work. She received her doctoral degree in education from Columbia University Teachers College in 2003. Currently she is the director of the Criminal Justice Initiative: *Supporting Children, Families, and Communities* at Columbia University School of Social Work. Writing while incarcerated was central to survival—a way to hear oneself, to communicate beyond the fences, to reflect on the life, and she wrote poetry, creative writings, and academic journal articles. Her relationship with her son during the more than two decades of incarceration was a source of life and hope.

Dawna (Lessie) Brown is fifty-seven years old. She has two children: a son, thirty-six years old, and a daughter, twenty-nine years old. She also has five granddaughters. She has been an artist for twenty-six years. She began drawing while in the county jail. She was sentenced to twenty to thirty-five years. She served twenty years, seven months, and three days. She has been off parole since September 2009 and now lives with her daughter, son-in-law, and the youngest two of her granddaughters, ages three years and eight months. While Lessie had much support from the Michigan Prisoner Reentry Program, her main source of support came from the Prison Creative Arts Project (PCAP). It was PCAP, Buzz, Janie, Mary, Sari, Amit, Ashley, and all the students of PCAP who encouraged her to enter her artwork in exhibits, and the response from the public was amazing. Because of PCAP, since her release, Lessie's artwork has been in three exhibits in New York; Manistee, Michigan; and Ypsilanti, Michigan. Lessie's most meaningful piece is *3x Denied*, and she is honored to have it displayed on the cover of *Razor Wire Women*.

Marilyn Brown, PhD, is an associate professor of sociology at the University of Hawai'i at Hilo, where she teaches courses in corrections, criminology, and deviance. Her research interests include gender and corrections, Native Hawaiian legal history, and prisoner reentry. She has published in the areas of gender and life course theory, mothers involved in the criminal justice system, colonial theory, corrections, and youth sexual orientation and aggression.

Valencia C., although not a woman, is part of this chain, since he has been another number for the past twelve years. He has been reminded every day what part of society he represents and the role he holds as a prisoner in California. He is a spiritual person who has found comfort in God while incarcerated, and in the mean time he tries to change people's views through art. If he can reach somebody's heart and offer any understanding, he has lived up to his principles. Art has become part of his joy of life when it reaches people's inmost beings, when it brings joy, happiness, and comfort, making someone's spirit up-lifted. When a person gets inspired to help, he has reached his purpose because his work has opened someone's eyes.

Meda Chesney-Lind, PhD, is professor of women's studies at the University of Hawai'i at Manoa. Nationally recognized for her work on women and crime, her books include *Girls, Delinquency, and Juvenile Justice*; *The Female Offender: Girls, Women, and Crime*; *Female Gangs in America*; *Invisible Punishment*; *Girls, Women, and Crime*; and *Beyond Bad Girls: Gender Violence and Hype*. She has just finished an edited collection on trends in girls' violence, entitled *Fighting* *for Girls: Critical Perspectives on Gender and Violence,* that will be published by the State University of New York Press.

Simone Weil Davis is now an independent scholar, living in Toronto, Canada. She has taught English, gender studies and American studies, at Mount Holyoke College, Long Island University, and New York University. She is the author of numerous articles that treat gender and culture in the United States, including one on labiaplasty, "Loose Lips Sink Ships" (*Feminist Studies* 2002), and the book *Living Up to the Ads: Gender Fictions of the 1920s* (Duke 2000). She serves on the national steering committee of the Inside-Out Prison Exchange Program and taught a series of Inside-Out courses in Springfield, Massachusetts, to a mix of incarcerated and "outside" college students. Her next book has the working title *Raising the Jailhouse Roof: Women, Writing, and Prison.* Her lifelong concern about carceral practices was instigated by her father's stint in prison in 1960 as a result of his refusal to testify before the House Un-American Activities Committee.

Jane Dorotik is a registered nurse with an advanced degree and has worked all her life as a health care professional. She worked first in the clinical arena in pediatrics at UCLA, then later with the mental healthcare organization—Telecare in Alameda, California—as the senior regional director of operations overseeing some twelve facilities/programs. She was wrongly convicted and is actively working to have her conviction overturned. She assists other women in the prison system with legal work and grievances. Jane started the "Lifers Leaving Prison Initiative" at CIW. This initiative is designed to give hope to the many lifers who have lost hope of ever being released from prison thanks to the highly political and arbitrary Board of Parole hearings. The program consists of knitting an individually chosen and unique sweater for a lifer who will "claim" her freedom. The lifer practices visualizing herself walking out of the prison gates wearing the sweater Jane has knit for her. Since the inception of the Lifers Leaving Prison Initiative eight lifers have been released back to the community proudly wearing their sweaters.

Martha Escobar is a PhD candidate in the Department of Ethnic Studies at the University of California, San Diego. Her areas of research include the politics of immigration control and incarceration. Her dissertation focuses on the experiences of migrant women, especially as they are shaped by state policies and practices of policing racialized and gendered national boundaries. She has a number of publications in abolitionist anthologies and recently guest edited with Jodie Lawston a forthcoming special edition of the journal *Social Justice,* "Policing, Detention, Deportation, and Resistance: Situating Immigrant Justice and Carcerality in the Twenty-first Century." Escobar has worked with Critical Resistance for several years and is a member of the California Coalition for Women Prisoners' Compañeras Project, organizations dedicated to ending the use of imprisonment as a response to perceived social crisis.

Joanie Estes-Rodgers is middle aged with two adult sons, who are her pride in life. She works as a bartender at the Brass Rail in Ozark, Alabama, so that she can attend college. She is a full-time student with a 4.0 GPA and is a member of the National Technical Honor Society. She graduated in 2010 from Wallace College in Dothan, Alabama. She loves to draw because it helps her to keep things from piling up in her mind—kind of a way of journaling. She is an adventurous person and believes strongly that life has a lot of wonderful experiences and adventures to offer as well as bad times, which lead to strength. She says, "Don't allow the bad things in life to blind you or hold you down. Use them to become strong."

Laura Faulk is a woman of the stars. If she could, she would spend the day splitting atoms, chemically combusting nature's smallest particles into tachyons, leptons, and gluons. She would delight in the day she could dance with photons and neutrinos, talk with quarks, and write about what they said back. She transcends the confines of prison walls, captivating readers by her uninhibited uniqueness and her connection to family and history that she plays against a backdrop of interacting elements. Her poetry is a true testament to the time she has spent in Michigan's prisons—a scientific experiment, concoctions of words fused with genius that reduce our planet to its tiniest, most infinite point until there is nothing left but infinity itself, and all she can do is float. Black holes are not a scary place for her. They are a chance for discovery.

Ana Lucia Gelabert was born in Cuba in 1938. She studied in Havana and moved to the United States "temporarily" in 1961, where she finished college. She was happily married and happily divorced and has three U.S.-born offspring and several U.S.-born grand-offspring. Ana Lucia has been incarcerated in Texas since 1984, where she is serving two concurrent "nonaggravated" life sentences. Besides *Connie and Vato* (sixteen episodes), she drew *Doña Llama* (seventy episodes, 1995–2000) in Spanish, on Latin American politics. She plays guitar, loves dancing, fast walks daily, and eats moderately.

Trangdai Glassey-Tranguyen is a PhD candidate in Ethnic Studies at UC San Diego. She is widely celebrated for her outstanding achievements, services, artistry, and scholarship. In 2004–2005, Glassey-Tranguyen received an exceptional-ranking Fulbright fellowship to carry out the Vietnamese Stockholm Project, Home in Stockholm: Vietnamese Narratives of Transnationalism and the Vietnamese Diaspora Studies Project. She received the Graduate Fellowship from Stanford University where she attained a master's in anthropology in 2006.

Shirley Haviland-Nakagawa is a second-year journalism student at Fresno City College. While reporting for the college newspaper, *The Rampage,* Haviland-Nakagawa received a first-place award from the Journalism Association of Community Colleges in California (JACC) in the News Feature Story category for an article about the struggles of the homeless. In 2008, Nakagawa shared second place in the JACC Enterprise Story/Series category with fellow students Francine Ramos and Cody Gless. In addition, Haviland-Nakagawa, Ramos, and Gless were awarded general excellence in newspaper writing.

Linda Heidenreich is associate professor and chair of the Department of Women's Studies at Washington State University where she teaches queer Chicana/o studies and critical race feminism. She is author of *This Land Was Mexican Once: Histories of Resistance from Northern California*. Her articles are published in journals such as *Aztlán*, *Chicana/Latina Studies* and the *Journal of American Ethnic History*, and her poetry in journals such as *Word Is Bond* and *Lean Seed*. She is also a former volunteer in a detention ministry program in the Inland Northwest.

Jillian Hernandez is a PhD student in women's and gender studies at Rutgers University and an independent curator. Her research interests include contemporary art, sexualities, and girls' studies. Hernandez previously worked as curatorial associate at the Museum of Contemporary Art in Miami where she created the Women on the Rise! outreach program for teenage girls.

Johanna Hudnall is a forty-three-year-old woman serving a thirty-six-year, eight-month sentence for burglary and forgery. She is a prison rape survivor and a recovering alcoholic/addict who has been clean and sober for more than five years. She is enrolled full time in college and works a full-time job. She tries to spend as much time as possible with the women in the prison's mental health unit, reading novels to them. She has learned that it is not where you live, it is how you live.

Kinnari Jivani was born in 1979 in India. The eldest of two siblings, she was raised to have a voracious soul for wisdom and knowledge by loving parents. She earned her BS in microbiology from the University in Mumbai. At twenty, she came to the States after an arranged marriage. In 2000, she was sentenced to eleven to twenty years for second-degree murder. Writing helps her exhale her emotions, clear her thoughts, and better understand the world around/within her. Through it, she discovers herself. Kinnari is fluent in Gujarati, Hindi, and English. She has taken classes in composition, sociology, African American literature, women's studies, business technology, philosophy, and yoga. She has won five awards in PCAP art exhibitions, including the Environment Service Award in 2005. The UN Environmental Program has recognized her artistic contribution to World Environment Day. Her art has traveled to Michigan, Illinois, California, and Philadelphia. She is a warrior woman with a brilliant future.

Leslie Levitas, MA, is a writer and photographer. Her oral history project entitled "Tell Me about Your Life" depicts women who have been impacted by incarceration and street life and was supported, in part, by the Peninsula Community Foundation. She produced a video and stage presentation entitled *Capp Street Talkin'*, focusing on similar themes. Since 1996 she has raised more than $9 million for the San Francisco Sheriff's Department's programs to serve all those impacted by the criminal justice system: victims, offenders, family members, and the community at large. Levitas is the author of numerous articles and has presented both nationally and internationally on related subjects.

Carmen Huerta Martínez, aka Reina del Occidente, was born in Rioverde, México, in 1979, the second child of five. After the disaster of the Gortari administration, her family moved to Monterrey. In 1995, Carmen attended preparatoria, where she studied philosophy and became politically aware of corruption. After shaving off her hair to protest the injustices of the indígenas, she ran across the border in south Texas and walked three days with her fifteen-year-old cousin without food or water in the middle of the desert. After near tragedy, Carmen decided to go back home and do something better with her life. In June 2000, she graduated and became independent. Late in 2002 Carmen was arrested in Waterford, Michigan, in the biggest cocaine bust in Oakland County history. Wisely, she let time serve *her*. She writes poetry and continues to study philosophy, ethics, English, and African American history. In 2009 she was sent home.

Tarajee Maynor was born on May 18, 1977, in Tuscaloosa, Alabama. Her family moved to Detroit before she was two and has resided there since. Tarajee was educated in the Detroit Public School system and the University of Michigan. Growing up in Detroit fostered values and resources in Tara (as she is known to her family and friends) that have proved to be life-serving. Tara had to pull on these lessons when faced with a terrible situation and went to prison in 2002. Always an avid reader, Tara has always been a lover of the written word. It was not until coming to prison that Tarajee realized her own ability to write. Writing has allowed her to learn more about herself through creative expressions. It grants a way to live free even while incarcerated. She hopes her words will reach into the heart of the reader, suspend judgment, and attach new ideas.

Dyanna McDade is one of SOUL's many beautiful women. The group's name fully explains her. She is one of a kind. She was born the third of eight and found a place to run in poetry, an escape from reality, a place where her life superseded everything. Poetry let her express her feelings about life and the cards she was dealt. Growing up in an abusive home put restrictions on her freedom of speech. She took what was dished and continued to live in her fantasy land, even when life was not worth living. All she needed was pen and paper, and she no longer existed in her world of pain. Poetry became her therapy and her oxygen mask. She lived, breathed, and bled poetry. She found her own personality and identity. A poetess, she found herself, her own true love, and embraced it. If poetry didn't exist, neither would her life.

Angela Moe is associate professor of sociology and criminal justice, with affiliation with gender and women's studies, at Western Michigan University in Kalamazoo, Michigan. She earned a Ph.D. in Justice Studies, Law and the Social Sciences from Arizona State University in 2001. Her research interests include feminist criminology, violence against women, gender and justice, sociology of the body, and gender performance/construction. Her work may be found in such journals as *Violence against Women, Criminal Justice Studies, Women and Therapy, Women's Studies Quarterly, Journal of Contemporary Ethnography, Women and Criminal Justice,* and *Journal of Interpersonal Violence.* She has served as president of the Midwest Sociologists for Women in Society; executive counselor for the American Society of Criminology, Division on Women and Crime; and founding member/deputy editor for the journal *Feminist Criminology.*

Malaquias Montoya has lectured and taught at numerous universities and colleges in the San Francisco Bay Area, including Stanford and the University of California, Berkeley. Montoya's works include acrylic paintings, murals, washes, and drawings, but he is primarily known for his silkscreen prints, which have been exhibited nationally as well as internationally. He is credited by historians as one of the founders of the "social serigraphy" movement in the San Francisco Bay Area. His visual expressions, art of protest, depict the struggle and strength of humanity and the necessity to unite behind that struggle.

Jen Myers received her BFA in modern dance from the Ohio State University in 1991. The next seven years of her life were spent performing and choreographing in Chicago. It was during this time that she met her codefendant and became involved in criminal activity. On February 28, 2006, she self-surrendered to FPC Alderson to serve a three-year prison sentence. In prison her love for writing became a vehicle for the pain and isolation she experienced. Currently she is working on developing her business as a prison consultant where she will focus on helping women with their entry into prison.

Eleanor Novek is associate professor in the Department of Communication at Monmouth University. A former newspaper reporter and editor, her research agenda is focused on communication for social justice, particularly in the contexts of prisons, outsider journalism, and service learning. She has published articles in *The Atlantic Journal of Communication; Communication Studies; Critical Studies in Media Communication; Discourse and Society; Education, Citizenship and Social Justice; The Howard Journal of Communications; Journalism; The Journal of Children and Poverty; Media, Culture and Society; NYSCA Speech Communication Annual; Peace Review; Shelterforce; and Women's Studies in Communication* and has written a number of book chapters. Since 2006 she has been a volunteer facilitator for the Alternatives to Violence Project, an organization that hosts conflict transformation workshops in prisons and other settings.

Renita Phifer is a New York prisoner who serves as an advocate for her fellow prisoners. She has been incarcerated for eleven years, during which time she has observed repeated sexual abuses of female prisoners by guards. She gathers data on the abuses and sends it to human rights groups on the outside, putting herself at personal risk because guards read all outgoing mail. She also writes poetry.

Amber Dawn Piercy graced the world with her presence on August 23, 1987, in Winnamac, Indiana. Like most people, she had the normal childhood rundown of bad memories. The great aunt who raised her since age two was the only person who stayed by Amber's side. Amber walked a crooked, broken down road that eventually led her to incarceration at the age of twenty. The nightmares in her head followed her. In prison she learned that you don't know what you have until it's gone. She never realized how much she took for granted until everything was ripped from under her. In the last two years, she has grown tremendously. Prison was not the dead end sign on her crooked road. It was something powerful that created a whole new set of roads for her to explore. She wouldn't change a single thing about herself. She was released from prison in the fall of 2008.

Je'Anna Redwood is a daughter, friend, and prisoner. Je'Anna: Sadly, life was not kind to me, nor did it wait for me to "catch up." I did, however, manage to escape the cruel grasp it had on me. I came from a dysfunctional and underprivileged home, riddled with all forms of abuse. I was the middle child of three girls, and was rescued from my poverty at age five. I went through my allotted rounds of the Child Protective Services circuit, and foster homes, before I was adopted at age seven. As faith would have it, I found the strength to forge on. Thinking I had escaped the cruel iron fist of abuse, I continually ran away, finally into the arms of a far greater evil: anger, rage, and bitterness. This eventually led me to commit murder. Now, after serving twenty-five years in prison, the discarded shards of my broken past have been miraculously fused together. What didn't kill me four and one half decades ago has made m the strong, valiant, and confident woman I have become. Still, I stand, my voice waiting to be heard.

Julia Sudbury is professor in the Department of Ethnic Studies at Mills College. Julia's research interests include African diaspora studies, women of color organizing, and race, gender, and incarceration. She has written many articles on these topics and four books, including *Other Kinds of Dreams: Black Women's Organizations and the Politics of Transformation* (1998) and *Global Lockdown: Race, Gender, and the Prison Industrial Complex* (2005). Julia does a great deal of social justice work around prison with various organizations such as Critical Resistance and the Prison Activist Resource Center, of which she is a board member.

Ricky A. Taylor was born in Arkansas in 1958. He grew up in Benton Harbor, Michigan, from the age of five. He was taught how to steal by his sixth-grade teacher, a characteristic that would lead him to his downfall. Ricky went on to finish high school, fathering one child, and joined the navy. Obtaining an honorable discharge from the navy, Ricky married and had another child. Ricky was constantly in mental turmoil, torn between the Christian upbringing of his parents and the easy money made from the skills he had learned and improved on since sixth grade. At the age of thirty-six Ricky found himself facing nineteen to forty years in prison for robbery. In prison he began to practice art, a longtime love of his that reflected his feelings and his perception of how others in his life suffered and felt because of his actions. This process of reflection produced the piece "Missing."

Patricia K. Thorn was born October 28, 1964. She had a normal childhood. She didn't go down the wrong road until she hit high school. She got into drugs, and it was downhill from there. We tried everything to help her. She was a hard worker and loved working outside. She had two sons, John and Cody. In her spare time, she would draw pictures, cards, and murals. When she was in jail, she made cards and sold them to the other inmates. She was in and out of jail most of her adult life. She could not get off those drugs. They finally got her, September 14, 2008, when she overdosed. She was a beautiful girl and loved by all of her family and friends. We miss her very much. If anyone is on drugs who's reading this, please get off them.

Sara Warner is assistant professor of theater at Cornell University and a core faculty member of the Feminist, Gender, and Sexuality Studies Program and the LGBTQ Program. Her research interests include prison theater, feminist and queer performance, dramatic literature, and affect studies. She has published widely in journals and anthologies and is working on a book entitled *Emotional States: Political Affects and Radical Lesbian Performance*. Sara has served on the board of the Center for Lesbian and Gay Studies (CLAGS), as president of the Women and Theater Program (WTP), as secretary of the Association for Theater in Higher Education (ATHE), and as the Drama Division delegate of the Modern Language Association (MLA).

Alycia Welch sprouted from the simple Michigan village of Dexter, known for its gazebo, cider mill, and Dairy Queen. Toward the end of her undergraduate career at the University of Michigan, she joined the Prison Creative Arts Project creating plays with women at Huron Valley Center, a coed prison hospital, in Ypsilanti. In 2005, she was invited to attend one of SOUL's poetry readings. She was amazed that the connection between womanhood and poetry was intimate, the depth of their words, inspiring. It was an honor to be asked to facilitate this same workshop in September of that year. SOUL is her beginning, as it is for so many women, into the exploration of writing, of sisterhood, and of celebrating self. She now lives in Houston with her husband and is employed at a transitional house for women reentering the community from incarceration. She carries her SOULbook everywhere.

Morgan Mann Willis was born and raised in the beautifully gritty Washington, D.C., where her love of words and poetry flourished. After a short stint in Boston, she moved to Ann Arbor, Michigan, to complete her BA in English Language and Literature. After joining the Prison Creative Arts Project, she participated in theater workshops in Jackson Men's Facility and Maxey School for Boys. During this time, she was given the privilege of being one of three outside guests allowed to attend SOUL's first poetry reading in 2004. The power of the collective and beautiful poetry impacted her deeply. It was with great enthusiasm that she accepted the offer to become a facilitator for the workshop in 2006. Immediately, SOUL became a creative anchor. After over two years with SOUL, she recently made a move to New York City to pursue her MFA in Creative Writing at Sarah Lawrence. She writes home often.

Index

Abram, Karen, 116, 117, 118, 122, 123, 126, 132

ACA, *see* American Correctional Association

Acoca, Leslie, 250, 267

ACLU, *see* American Civil Liberties Union

Adoption and Safe Families Act, 11, 59–61, 65, 70, 75, 78–80, 86, 88, 90

  description of, 77–78

Alexander, William (Buzz), xxiii, 4–5, 196

Allison, Dorothy, 213–214, 218, 220, 221

Altonn, H., 34, 47

Ambrose, A.M., 45, 47

American Civil Liberties Union, 43, 46, 245

American Correctional Association, 116, 118, 124, 128

Amimito, Garrett, 38, 47

Amnesty International, 54, 63, 176, 181

Anderson, Charles M., 208, 221

Anderson, Leon, 120, 130

Annie E. Casey Foundation, 34–35, 47, 48

  see also Juvenile Detention Alternatives Initiative

Antiterrorism and Effective Death Penalty Act, 76, 78

Arnold, Regina, 116, 120, 128

Arthur, Pat, 34, 47

ArtSpring, 195–196, 197

ASFA, *see* Adoption and Safe Families Act

Austin, James, 34, 47

Avodah Dance Ensemble, 196, 197

Baca, Jimmy Santiago, 206–207, 220, 221

Baird, Russell, 194, 197

Barry, Ellen, 58, 63, 117, 118, 128

Barry, Fred C., 181

Baumler, Ellen, 149, 150, 161, 162

Baunach, Phyllis Jo, 54, 64

Baxter, Sandra, 116, 118, 128

Beckerman, Adela, 58, 59, 64, 77, 89

Beiser, Vince, 230, 245

Belknap, Joanne, 115, 117, 128, 250, 267

Beltrami, John, 116, 118, 128

Benjamin, Walter, 241, 242, 244

Beyondmedia Education, 6

Bilsky, Brian, 10, 31–48, 306

Birecree, Elizabeth, 117, 118, 128

Bloom, Barbara, 10, 51–66, 77, 78, 89, 90, 116, 128, 306

Blumenthal, Karen, 53, 56, 58, 66

Bortner, Margaret, 76, 89

Bosworth, Mary, 53, 64, 89

Boudin, Kathy, xvii–xix, 4, 15, 306–307

Boyd, Belle, 4, 15

Bradley v. State, 149

Braithwaite, John, 148, 162, 164, 244

Bremner, R.H., 32, 47

Brennan, Edward, 147, 152–154

  see also *Farmer v. Brennan*

Britton, Dana, 210, 221

Brown, Dawna (Lessie), G-1, xiv–xv, 8–9, 307

Brown, Marilyn, 10, 51–66, 307
Browne, Angela, 118, 128
Browne, Irene, 131
Bureau of Justice Statistics, 16, 54, 65, 66, 90, 117, 128, 129, 130, 245
Burnham, Linda, 52, 64
Burton, Linda, 52, 66
Bush-Baskette, Stephanie, 52, 64, 117, 128
Butler, Judith, 176, 181
Buzawa, Eve, 36, 47

C., Valencia, 13, 190–191, 307
California Youth Authority, 248
Carlen, Pat, 53, 64
Chambers, Lori, 172, 181
Charmaz, Kathy, 120, 128
Chesney-Lind, Meda, 10, 23, 25, 31–48, 53, 64, 115, 116, 117, 118, 210, 221, 248, 250, 267, 307–308
Chiarlone, Rosemarie, G-6, 252, 255, 256–258, 264, 265, 266
children of incarcerated parents, xviii, 3, 6–7, 8–9, 10, 11, 15, 16, 24, 51–66, 67–74, 75–88, 107, 122, 124, 127–128, 185, 237, 238, 242, 278, 290, 292–293, 294, 301, 306
Chun, Susan Lee, 252, 254–255, 264, 266
Collins, Patricia Hill, 120, 129, 170, 181
Comack, Elizabeth, 116, 129
Conquergood, Dwight, 287, 298
Cooper-Anifowoshe, Edris, 239
CORI, see Criminal Offender Record Information system
Cornell, Drucilla, 238, 245
Covington, Stephanie, 116, 117, 128, 129
Criminal Offender Record Information system, 157
Critical Resistance, 5, 170, 180
Cummins, Eric, 5, 16, 106, 107, 108
Currie, Elliot, 229, 245

Dailard, Cynthia, 128, 132
Daly, Kathleen, 116, 129, 234, 245
Davis, Angela, 106, 117, 119, 129, 147, 149, 157, 158, 159, 162, 230–231, 243, 245

Davis, Simone Weil, 13, 194, 203–224, 308
Day, Sally, 77, 78, 89
DeCou, Kate, 209, 221
DeCrescenzo, Teresa, 175, 182
DeCrow, Karen, 148, 161, 162
deGroot, Gabrielle, 118, 129
Demmons, Shawnna, 179, 181
Department of the Attorney General, 36, 37, 47
Díaz-Cotto, Juanita, xxiii, 3, 16, 25, 88, 89, 179, 181
Ditton, Paula, 119, 129
Dodge, Mara, 4, 16, 23, 26
Dole, Robert, 79, 89
Dorotik, Jane, 11, 109–114, 308
Dostoevsky, Fyodor, 210, 221
Downey, Robert, Jr., 210
DuDeck-Biondo, Jill, 53, 54, 65

Ehrensaft, M., 58, 64
El-Bassel, Nabila, 116, 118, 129
Enos, Sandra, 53, 57, 58, 64, 76, 77, 78, 89
Ensler, Eve, 196, 211, 212, 213, 220
Escobar, Martha, 11, 75–92, 308
Esterberg, Kristin, 120, 129
Estes-Rodgers, Joanie, G-4, 11, 102–103, 309
Ex Parte Crouse, 33

Faith, Karlene, xxiii, 2, 16, 24, 26, 106, 177, 181
fallen women, 2, 23, 24, 105, 149
Farmer, Dee, 152–153, 154
     see also *Farmer v. Brennan*
Farmer v. Brennan, 147, 152–155
Faulk, Laura, 275, 309
     see also Sisters of Unique Lyrics
FBI, *see* Federal Bureau of Investigation
Federal Bureau of Investigation, 31, 47, 116, 117, 129
Federal Bureau of Prisons, 90, 152, 159, 162
Feinman, Clarice, 77, 87, 89
Feld, Barry, 176, 181
Ferraro, Kathleen, 52, 64, 116, 118, 119, 129, 131
Fineman, Martha, 51, 64

Fischer, Michael, 54, 65
Fisher, Naomi, 252, 255, 263–264
Fiske, Jon, 297, 298
Forsyth, Craig, 54, 64
Foucault, Michel, 33–34, 47, 148, 155, 162, 211, 221, 253, 254, 267
Fox, Sanford, 33, 47
Fraden, Rena, xxiii, 238, 245
Freedman, Estelle, 2, 4, 16, 23–24, 26, 105–106, 108, 210, 221
Freire, Paolo, 206, 221
Frost, Natasha, 53, 64
Fry, Elizabeth, 24
Fuatagavi, Lydia Seumanu, 37, 47
Fuller, Torrey E., 119, 129

Gabel, Katherine, 63, 76, 78, 89
Galbraith, Susan, 54, 64
Gammel, Irene, 209, 221
GAP, see Girls' Advocacy Project
Garcia Ferraz, Nereida, 252–254, 264
Gaucher, Bob, 286, 287, 298
Geiger, Brenda, 54, 65
Gelabert, Ana Lucia, G-5, 13, 15, 198–201, 309
gender
   history in prisons, 149–151
Gender Motivated Violence Act, 154, 161
Genty, Philip, 60, 65, 77, 78, 89, 90
Giallombardo, Rose, 54, 65, 171, 181
Gibson, Mary, 248, 266, 267
Gilfus, Mary, 116, 118, 120, 129
Gilmore, Ruth Wilson, 94, 99, 158, 162
Ginchild, River, 58, 63
girls, 8, 9, 10, 24, 115
   abuse, 23, 43–45, 116
   advocacy for, 24, 25
   and juvenile justice, 31–32, 36–43, 45–46, 248–250
   and the arts, 6, 14, 196, 247–266
   crimes, 23, 31–32, 38, 248, 250
   punishment, xviii, 10, 23, 25, 31–32, 33, 36–43, 45–46
   sexuality, 23, 256–261
Girls' Advocacy Project, 249, 265, 266
Girshick, Lori, 4, 16
GisMo collective, 252, 259–262, 264
   see also Jessica Gispert and Crystal Molinary

Gispert, Jessica, 252, 259, 261
   see also GisMo collective
Glassey-Tranguyen, Trangdai, 11, 93–100, 309
Glick, R.M., 53, 65
GMVA, see Gender Motivated Violence Act
Goffman, Erving, 33–34, 47
Goldberg, David Theo, 150, 161, 162
Golden, Renny, 61, 76, 89
Gonnerman, Jennifer, 230, 245
Goosby, Eric, 118, 130
Gorsuch, Nikki, 126, 129
Graham, Barbara, 2
Green, Maxine, xix
Greene, Judith, 53, 64
Greene, Susan, 52, 65
Greenaway, Antoinette, 78, 89
Greenberg, Greg, 120, 129
Greenfeld, Lawrence, 53, 65, 116, 118, 119, 129, 209, 221, 233, 245
Griffs, Nelson, 43, 48
Guba, Egon, 120, 130

Haarr, Robin, 124, 131
Halberstam, Judith, 172, 181
Hall, Thomas/ine, 151, 160, 163
Halperin, Ronnie, 59, 60, 65
Hamilton, Jay, 287, 298
Haney, Craig, 52, 65
Haney, Lynne, 61, 65
Hannah-Moffat, Kelly, 53, 65
Harding, Sandra, 120, 130
Hardon, J., 4
Harlow, Caroline Wolf, 118, 123, 130, 209, 221
Harris, Jennifer, 59, 60, 65
Harris, Mary Kay, 118, 129
Harrison Act, 105
Hartsock, Nancy, 120, 130
Haviland-Nakagawa, Shirley, 10, 67–74, 309–310
Hawes, Joseph, 32, 48
Hays, Sharon, 51, 65
Heidenreich, Linda, xxiii, 12, 107, 147–164, 310
Henriques, Zelma, 58, 65
Hensley, Christopher, 171, 181
Hernandez, Jillian, 14, 247, 260, 261, 267, 310

Hill, M., 4, 15, 16
Hilton, Paris, 201
Hirschel, David, 36, 47
Holston, Mary Ann, 54, 65
Horton, Myles, 206, 221
Howley, Kevin, 287, 298
Hudnall, Johanna, 12, 165–168, 310
Human Rights Watch, 152, 156, 157,
    159, 162, 175, 182, 245
Hurtado, Aida, 52, 65

IIRIRA, see Illegal Immigration Reform
    and Immigrant Responsibility Act
Illegal Immigration Reform and
    Immigrant Responsibility Act, 76,
    78–79, 87, 91
immigrant detention, 8, 11, 15, 75–91,
    94, 96–98, 99, 155, 161, 166, 244,
    277
incarcerated women
    abuse, 115–132, 133–143, 147–164,
        165–168, 185–188
    and motherhood, 20–21, 51–63,
        67–74, 75–91, 102–103
    demographics of, 3
    Hollywood films on, 2, 3
Incite!, 5, 173, 176, 180, 182
Ingram-Fogel, 117, 118, 130
Inside-Out Prison Exchange Program, 13,
    193–194, 197, 203–223
    description of, 204–206
Interrupted Life art exhibit, 195
Irwin, Katherine, 31, 47

Jacobs, Harriet, 213, 220, 221
Jacobsen, Carol, 249, 267
jailface, 206–207
jails, 3, 23, 24, 25, 118, 219, 225–228,
    230, 282, 285, 286
    mental health in, 11, 118–119,
        122–128
    San Francisco County Jail, 5, 13–14,
        17, 236–245
    youth jails, 10, 10–11, 31–48
James, Joy, xxiii, 3, 16, 25, 26, 162
JDAI, see Juvenile Detention Alternatives
    Initiative
    see also Annie E. Casey Foundation

Jensen, Vickie, 53, 54, 65
Jivani, Kinnari, 279, 310
    see also Sisters of Unique Lyrics
JJDPA, see Juvenile Justice and
    Delinquency Prevention Act
Johnson, Elizabeth, 58, 65, 78, 89
Johnson, Joy, 120, 130
Johnson, Kelly, 34, 47
Johnson, Paula C., xxiii, 3, 4, 17, 25, 26,
    210, 220, 221
Johnston, Denise, 62, 63, 65, 76, 78, 89
Johnstone, Quintin, 160, 162
Jones, Ann Hudson, 208, 222
Jones, Loring P., 62, 65
Jones, Rhodessa, 5, 14, 196, 236–243
    see also Medea Project
Juang, Richard, 151, 162, 163
Just Detention International, 165, 166,
    186
    see also Stop Prisoner Rape
Justice Now, 75, 170, 180, 182
Juvenile Detention Alternatives Initiative,
    34–36, 38, 43, 44, 48
    see also Annie E. Casey Foundation
juvenile incarceration, 32–34, 36–38
    and art programs, 250–266
    conditions in, 38–46
    demographics of juveniles in, 45–46
    Honolulu's Youth Detention Center,
        34–46
Juvenile Justice and Delinquency
    Prevention Act, 34, 45–46, 47, 248

Kamimura, Janis, 38, 47
Kaplan, Mark, 117, 130
Kassebaum, G., 171, 183
Katz, Jack, 287, 288, 298
Katz, Judith, 221
Kauffman, Kelsey, 56, 65
Knupfer, Anne Meis, 248, 267
Koban, L. A., 56, 57, 65
Kornfeld, Phyllis, 195, 197
Koyama, Emi, 173, 182
Kvale, Steinar, 120, 130

Lake, Elise, 116, 130
Lamb, Sharon, 258, 259, 267
Lamb, Wally, 4, 16, 194, 197, 220

Laver, Mimi, 60, 65, 78, 90
Lawston, Jodie, 1–18, 23–26, 105–108, 305, 306, 308
Lee, Alexander, 178, 180, 182
Lee, Arlene, 65, 78, 90
Lee, Doreen, 58, 60, 63
LeFlore, Larry, 54, 65
Legal Services for Prisoners with Children, 165, 170, 180
Leh, Sandra, 118, 130
Leonard, Elizabeth, 117, 130
Leukefeld, Carl, 118, 132
Levick, M., 45, 47
Levitas, Leslie, 13–14, 225–228, 310–311
Lewes, James, 287, 298
Lewis, Pamela, 55, 66
Light, Jennifer, 58, 66
Lindsley, Syd, 79, 90
Little, Ann M., 151, 162
Lofland, John, 120, 130
Lofland, Lyn, 120, 130
Logan, T.K., 118, 132
Lombroso, Cesare, 247, 248, 253, 266, 268
Lopez, Mark Huga, 78–79, 90
LSPC, see Legal Services for Prisoners with Children
Lucas, Ashley E., 7, 10, 49–50, 193–197, 219, 301–304, 305–306
Lucas, Billye, 50
Lukis, Vicki Lopez, 249–250

Macher, Abe, 118, 130
Maeve, Katherine, 117, 118, 131
Magnani, Laura, 148, 149, 150, 151, 152, 154, 157, 158, 159, 160, 162, 163
Maguin, Eugine, 118, 128
Mallon, Gerald, 175, 182
Marcus-Mendoza, Susan, 51, 66, 116, 131
Martínez, Carmen Huerta, 276, 311
    see also Sisters of Unique Lyrics
Maruschak, Laura, 54, 66
Matsuoka, Judge Carol T., 38, 43, 44, 48
Mauer, Marc, 3, 16, 25, 26, 117, 131, 231, 245
Maynor, Tarajee, 282, 311
    see also Sisters of Unique Lyrics

McClellan, Dorothy, 42, 48
McClelland, Gary, 116, 117, 118, 122, 123, 126, 132
McCold, Paul, 148, 158, 164
McConnel, Patricia, 206, 212–213, 220, 222
McDade, Dyanna, 282, 311
    see also Sisters of Unique Lyrics
McGowan, Brenda, 53, 56, 58, 66
McGuire, Dyan, 32, 48
McMahon, Martha, 51, 66
McRoy, Roth, 78, 90
Medea Project, 5, 14, 196, 232, 235–243, 244
    see also Rhodessa Jones
Miller, Brenda, 118, 128
Miller, S. L., 64
Mink, Gwendolyn, 128, 131
Minkler, Meredith, 57, 66
Mitchell, Robert, 153–154, 158, 161
    see also Schwenk v. Hartford
MOD 11: Discourses with Incarcerated Girls, 14, 247–268
Moe, Angela, 11–12, 52, 64, 115, 116, 118, 129, 131, 312
Molinary, Crystal, G-8, 252, 259, 261
    see also GisMo collective
Montoya, Malaquias, G-2, xx–xxi, 312
Morash, Merry, 124, 131
Morawetz, Nancy, 79, 90
Moros-Rigau, Isabel G-9, 252, 262, 263, 264, 266
Morris, Frances, 263, 268
Morris, James McGrath, 194, 197, 286, 298
Moser, Bob, 156, 163
Motherpeace, 263
mothers, 4, 167, 211, 236, 240, 254, 279, 282
    and war on drugs, 52
    criminalization of, 117
    in prison, xvii, xviii, xix, 3, 6–7, 8, 10, 11, 13, 15, 25, 51–66, 67–74, 75–91, 95–96, 97, 114, 119, 195, 271, 290
    crimes of, 52, 233, 237
    of prisoners, 33, 144
Mumola, Christopher, 3, 16, 53, 55, 56, 57, 58, 66

Murray, Michelle, 155
Myers, Jen, 12, 133–143, 312

National Center for Lesbian Rights,
	148, 152, 155, 156, 157, 163, 178,
	182
National Gay and Lesbian Task Force,
	157, 163
Navarro, Lysette, 205, 218, 219
Nelsen, Anne, 43, 48
Neto, V. V., 53, 65
New York House of Refuge, 32
Ngai, Mae, 94, 96, 99
Noble, Bobby, 172, 182
Novek, Eleanor, xxiii, 15, 195, 285, 287,
	298, 312

Office of Juvenile Justice, 26, 48, 176,
	182, 248, 268
Oppen, George, 214, 222
Otis, M., 171, 182
Owen, Barbara, xxiii, 3, 4, 16, 53, 54,
	62, 64, 66, 116, 128

Pasko, Lisa, 117, 129, 210, 221, 267
Pat Graney Company, 196, 197
PCAP, see Prison Creative Arts Project
Perrone, Paul, 37, 47
Personal Responsibility and Work
	Opportunity Act, see Welfare Reform
	Act
Peterson, Scott, 210
Phifer, Renita, 13, 185–188, 313
Pickett, Robert, 33, 48
Piercy, Amber Dawn, 313
	see also Sisters of Unique Lyrics
Pimlott, Sheryl, 54, 66
Pisciotta, Alexander, 33, 48
Pollack, Shoshanna, 214, 222
Pollock, Joycelyn, 3, 16, 24, 26, 16, 116,
	126, 131
Pollock, Susan Marie, 155
Pollock-Byrne, Joycelyn, see Pollock,
	Joycelyn
Pompa, Lori, 204, 205, 214, 218, 219
Potler, Cathy, 3, 16, 25, 26, 117, 131
Pranis, Kevin, 53, 64

prison
	abolition, 5, 16, 24, 26, 75, 106–107,
		147, 182, 308
	abuse, 112, 151–154, 185–188
	activism, 1
		in the arts, 194, 214, 249–250
		1970s activism, 5, 107
		contemporary, 5, 12, 13, 14, 96–97,
			107–108, 211
		see also American Civil Liberties
			Union, Amnesty International,
			Annie E. Casey Foundation,
			Human Rights Watch, Incite!, Just
			Detention International, Justice
			Now, National Center for Lesbian
			Rights, Resources for Community
			Change, Stop Prisoner Rape,
			Southern Poverty Law Center,
			Transgender Law Center, Women
			on the Rise!, Women's Prison
			Association
		men's radical prison movement, 5
		transgendered women, 169–183
		women's prison reform movement of
			nineteenth century, 2, 4–5, 23–24
	art, xix, 4, 5–6, 7, 8–9, 10, 11, 13,
		14, 20–21, 25, 42, 102–103, 144–
		145, 190–191, 193–197, 198–201,
		209, 235, 236, 243, 244, 247–268,
		269, 270, 271, 272, 280, 289, 302,
		303
		see also Prison Creative Arts Project
	dance, xix, 5, 195–196, 236, 259, 272
	healthcare, 2, 11, 15, 24, 25, 106,
		107, 113, 133–143, 230, 278, 285,
		302
	poetry, 6, 8, 12, 14, 133–143, 186,
		194, 206, 211, 214, 215, 216, 238,
		256, 269–283, 288, 291, 295
	rape, 3, 12, 112, 147, 152–158, 161,
		165–167, 174, 178, 185–188, 217,
		256, 278
	rules, 10, 41, 42, 56, 111–112, 142,
		187–188, 254, 285
	sentences, 2, 8, 10, 35, 53, 60, 70–73,
		75, 77, 81, 88, 117, 119, 126, 150,
		151, 152, 158, 160, 174, 204, 210,

217, 225, 230–231, 236, 291, 293, 297, 301
statistics, xvii, xix, 1, 3, 25, 31–32, 36–41, 43, 44, 53–58, 60, 62, 79, 106 110, 114, 117–120, 122–124, 156, 161, 166, 176, 180–181, 187, 190, 203–205, 219–220, 229–231, 233, 243, 248, 250, 285, 303
theater, 5–6, 10, 14, 49–50, 196, 229–245
see also Medea Project, Prison Creative Arts Project
writing, xviii, 5, 8–9, 13, 15, 108, 186, 187, 193–197, 205–223, 269–283, 285–299, 302
see also Baca, Jimmy Santiago; Lamb, Wally
Prison Creative Arts Project, xxiii, 6, 14, 195, 196, 269, 306, 307, 314, 315
prisoner voices
importance of, xvii–xix, 1–6, 27–29, 185–188, 203–224, 229–246, 285–300, 301–303
Prosch, Ali, 252, 255, 256, 258–259, 264, 266
Puzzanchera, Charles, 34, 48

Raeder, Myrna, 76, 90
Rafter, Nicole, 2, 4, 16, 23, 26, 53, 66, 105, 149, 150, 161, 163
Raimon, Martha, 4, 17
razor wire women
definition of, 7
Redwood, Je'Anna, 10, 27–30, 313
reformatories, 2, 4, 24, 53, 106, 150, 161
Resnik, Judith, 118, 131
Resources for Community Change, 5, 16, 106, 107, 108
restorative justice, 12, 15, 147–148, 158–161, 234, 240, 244
cornerstones of, 232
description of, 148, 231–232
drawbacks of, 233
restorytive justice, 14, 231–232, 235–236, 238–239
Reynolds, Marylee, 3, 16

Reynolds, Tina, 4, 17
Richie, Beth, 4, 16, 116, 118, 119, 120, 131, 176, 179, 181, 182, 211, 222, 285, 298
Riley, Patrick, 222
Riley, Sirena, 208, 268
Roberts, Dorothy, 51, 61, 62, 66, 78, 90
Robertson Beckley, Relda, 57, 66
Robinson, F. W., 4, 17
Roe, Kathleen, 57, 66
Romero, Mary, 120, 131
Rosaldo, Renalto, 95, 99
Rosenbaum, Jill Leslie, 248, 267
Rosenblum, Darren, 147, 148, 152, 154, 155, 157, 163
Rosenblum, Gail, 214, 222
Rosenheck, Robert, 120, 129
Ross, Luana, xxiii, 124, 131, 179, 182
Ross, Susan, 286, 299
Ross, T., 64
Ross Leadbeater, Bonnie J., 268
Roth, Campbell, 128, 131
Rousch, David W., 34, 43, 48
Rousseau, Jean-Jacques, 208, 222
Rucker, Lila, 124, 131
Ruiz, Dorothy, 53, 57, 66
Rupp, Shannon, 172, 182

Saffin, Lori, 147, 161, 163
Sánchez, Rosaura, 148, 155, 163
Sargent, Elizabeth, 116, 131
Sasser, J.E., 117, 130
Schaffner, Laurie, 250, 251, 256, 257, 259, 260, 268
Scheffler, Judith, 214, 220, 222, 286, 287, 299
Schlesinger, Traci, 3, 17
Schur, Edwin, 54, 66
Schwenk, Crystal, 153–155, 161
see also Schwenk v. Hartford
Schwenk v. Hartford, 153–155
Segura, Denise, 175, 183
Selling, L., 171, 183
Sentencing Project, 16, 26, 131, 203, 209, 219, 222, 245, 285, 299
Seymour, C. B., 60, 66

Shapiro, Lauren, 58, 66
Sharma, Nandita, 175, 180, 183
Sharp, Susan, 46, 48, 51, 66, 78, 90
Sharpley-Whiting, T. Denean, 259, 268
Shaw, Margaret, 116, 118, 126, 131, 209, 222
Shaw, Nancy, 118, 131
Sheehan, Jacqueline, 206, 222
Shelden, Randall, 31, 32, 47, 116, 129, 248, 268
Sherman, Francine, 32, 48
Siefert, Kristine, 54, 66
Sickmund, Melissa, 25, 26, 31, 48, 268
Sigurdson, Chris, 118, 119, 126, 128, 132
Silverman, Sue William, 209, 222
Simmons, Charlene Wear, 78, 90
Simpkins, S., 45, 47
Sisters of Unique Lyrics, 14, 269–283
Smith, Brenda, 128, 132
Smith, Carrie Jefferson, 77, 90
Smith, Dorothy, 120, 132
Smith, Gail T., 90
Snell, Tracy, 53, 65, 116, 118, 119, 129, 209, 221, 233, 245
Snow, David A., 120, 130
Snyder, H.N., 25, 26, 31, 48
Snyder, Ruth, G-2, xx, xxi
Solinger, Rickie, 4, 17, 195
SOUL, see Sisters of Unique Lyrics
Southern Poverty Law Center, 156, 163
Spade, Dean, 148, 155, 156, 163
Stacy Hamilton v. Glenn Goord, 186
Stack, Carol, 52, 66
Stanford, Anne F., 286, 287, 297
Staples, Kathleen, 252, 255, 264
Staton, Michele, 118, 132
Steiner, Linda, 287, 299
Steinhart, David, 55, 56, 57, 58, 64, 78, 89, 183
Stewart, Abigail, 120, 131
Stewart, Martha, 210
Stop Prisoner Rape, 12, 165
   see also Just Detention International
Streitmatter, R., 287, 299
Strong, Karen Heetderks, 232, 245
Stubbs, Julie, 234–235, 245

Sudbury, Julia, xxiii, 4, 12–13, 17, 89, 107, 169, 179, 180, 183, 313
Sullivan, Dennis, 234, 244, 245
Sutton, John, 33, 44
Sweeney, Megan, 240, 245
Sykes, G., 54, 66

Tapia, Ruby, 4, 17
Talvi, Silja, 6, 17, 25, 26, 148, 149, 150, 151, 158, 159, 160, 161, 163, 193, 197
Taylor, Julia, 186
Taylor, Ricky A., G-3, 10, 20–21, 314
Teplin, Linda, 116, 117, 118, 122, 123, 126, 132
Tewksbury, Richard, 171, 181
Thoennes, Nancy, 116, 132
Thomas, Kendall, 149, 155, 163
Thorn, Patricia K., v, 12, 144–145, 314
Thorn, Sherry, 144
Tifft, Larry, 234, 244, 245
Tjaden, Patricia, 116, 132
Tocci, Lawrence, 196, 197
Transgender Law Center, 156, 157, 163, 182
transgender prisoners, 8, 12, 36, 46, 107, 147–164, 169–183, 256
   youth, 43
transgender women, 148
   and solitary confinement, 157–158
Trent, Judy Scales, 176, 183
Turner, Victor, 232, 235–236, 245

U.S. Children's Bureau, 77, 90
U.S. General Accounting Office, 126, 132
U.S. v. Brand, 76

Van Ness, Daniel, 232, 245
Van Wright, Sally, 209, 221
Vaughan, Alden T., 151, 163
Vaughn, Michael, 117, 118, 131
Veysey, Bonita, 116, 118, 126, 132
Vicini, James, 203, 223
Vogelstein, Lynn, 58, 66
Voices from Inside, 219, 222
Volstead Act, 105

Wachtel, Ted, 148, 158, 164
Waldfogel, Jane, 58, 65, 78, 89
Walker, Barbara G., 263
war on drugs, 16, 52, 64, 88, 89, 117, 128, 231, 245
Ward, D., 171, 183
Warner, Sara, 14, 196, 229–246, 314
Way, Niobe, 268
Weekes, Debbie, 259, 268
Weitzer, R., 34, 47
Welch, Alycia, 270, 272, 280, 314–315
    see also Sisters of Unique Lyrics
Welch, Michael, 79, 91
Welfare Reform Act, 76, 78, 79, 87
White, Christina, 78, 91
White, Vonda, 1, 6
Willis, Morgan Mann, 270, 271, 315
    see also Sisters of Unique Lyrics
Wolf, Angela, 250

Wolf, Richard, 3, 16, 25, 26, 117, 130, 131
Women on the Rise!, 6, 195, 249–253, 257, 260, 263, 265, 266
Women's Prison Association, 64, 203, 210, 223
WOTR, *see* Women on the Rise!
Wray, Harmon, 148, 149, 150, 151, 152, 154, 157, 158–160, 162, 163
Wright, Cynthia, 175, 180, 183
Wright, L. E., 60, 66
writing
    and confession, 208–209
    and journalism, 285–298

Young, Diane, 77, 90, 118, 132
Young, Iris Marion, 215, 223
Yu, Chong Ho, 116, 131

Zehr, Howard, 220, 232, 245